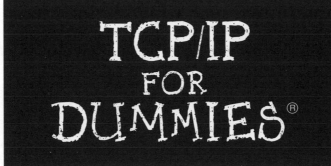

TCP/IP FOR DUMMIES®

by Marshall Wilensky
and Candace Leiden

IDG Books Worldwide, Inc.
An International Data Group Company

Foster City, CA ♦ Chicago, IL ♦ Indianapolis, IN ♦ Braintree, MA ♦ Southlake, TX

TCP/IP For Dummies®

Published by
IDG Books Worldwide, Inc.
An International Data Group Company
919 East Hillsdale Boulevard, Suite 400
Foster City, CA 94404

Library of Congress Catalog Card No.: 94-73728

ISBN: 1-56884-241-4

Printed in the United States of America

First Printing, July 1995

10 9 8 7 6 5 4 3

1E/RR/QW/ZW/IN

Distributed in the United States by IDG Books Worldwide, Inc.

Distributed by Macmillan Canada for Canada; by Contemporanea de Ediciones for Venezuela; by Distribuidora Cuspide for Argentina; by CITEC for Brazil; by Ediciones ZETA S.C.R. Ltda. for Peru; by Editorial Limusa SA for Mexico; by Transworld Publishers Limited in the United Kingdom and Europe; by Academic Bookshop for Egypt; by Levant Distributors S.A.R.L. for Lebanon; by Al Jassim for Saudi Arabia; by Simron Pty. Ltd. for South Africa; by Pustak Mahal for India; by The Computer Bookshop for India; by Toppan Company Ltd. for Japan; by Addison Wesley Publishing Company for Korea; by Longman Singapore Publishers Ltd. for Singapore, Malaysia, Thailand, and Indonesia; by Unalis Corporation for Taiwan; by WS Computer Publishing Company, Inc. for the Philippines; by WoodsLane Pty. Ltd. for Australia; by WoodsLane Enterprises Ltd. for New Zealand. Authorized Sales Agent: Anthony Rudkin Associates for the Middle East and North Africa.

For general information on IDG Books Worldwide's books in the U.S., please call our Consumer Customer Service department at 800-762-2974. For reseller information, including discounts and premium sales, please call our Reseller Customer Service department at 800-434-3422.

For information on where to purchase IDG Books Worldwide's books outside the U.S., contact IDG Books Worldwide at 415-655-3078 or fax 415-655-3295.

For information on translations, contact Marc Jeffrey Mikulich, Director, Foreign & Subsidiary Rights, at IDG Books Worldwide, 415-655-3018 or fax 415-655-3281.

For sales inquiries and special prices for bulk quantities, write to the address above or call IDG Books Worldwide at 415-655-3200.

For information on using IDG Books Worldwide's books in the classroom, or ordering examination copies, contact the Education Office at 800-434-2086 or fax 817-251-8174.

For authorization to photocopy items for corporate, personal, or educational use, please contact Copyright Clearance Center, 222 Rosewood Drive, Danvers, MA 01923, or fax 508-750-4470.

is a trademark under exclusive license
to IDG Books Worldwide, Inc.,
from International Data Group, Inc.

About the Authors

Candace Leiden is currently the Chief Technical Officer at Cardinal Consulting. Forced to learn about computers because she was afraid of slide rules, Candace has been a software developer, a system administrator, and a database designer and administrator. When she is not worrying about Emily, her six-year-old niece, knowing more about computers than she does, Candace teaches computer classes worldwide and has written courseware for several major international software companies. She is an internationally recognized speaker on client/server computing, databases, and the UNIX and Microsoft Windows NT operating systems.

Candace met Marshall Wilensky in 1981 when they both worked at the same company. She taught him everything he knows.

Marshall Wilensky has been working with computers for over 20 years (and still has fewer wrinkles than Candace). He has been a programmer, a system administrator, and has managed large multivendor and multiprotocol networks, including those at Harvard University's Graduate School of Business Administration. He is currently a Product Line Consultant for Lotus Notes at Lotus Development Corporation. He is in demand worldwide as a speaker on UNIX, networking, and Lotus Notes.

Marshall met Candace Leiden in 1981 when they both worked at the same company. He taught her everything she knows.

Welcome to the world of IDG Books Worldwide.

IDG Books Worldwide, Inc., is a subsidiary of International Data Group, the world's largest publisher of computer-related information and the leading global provider of information services on information technology. IDG was founded more than 25 years ago and now employs more than 7,700 people worldwide. IDG publishes more than 250 computer publications in 67 countries (see listing below). More than 70 million people read one or more IDG publications each month.

Launched in 1990, IDG Books Worldwide is today the #1 publisher of best-selling computer books in the United States. We are proud to have received 8 awards from the Computer Press Association in recognition of editorial excellence and three from Computer Currents' First Annual Readers' Choice Awards, and our best-selling ...For Dummies® series has more than 19 million copies in print with translations in 28 languages. IDG Books Worldwide, through a joint venture with IDG's Hi-Tech Beijing, became the first U.S. publisher to publish a computer book in the People's Republic of China. In record time, IDG Books Worldwide has become the first choice for millions of readers around the world who want to learn how to better manage their businesses.

Our mission is simple: Every one of our books is designed to bring extra value and skill-building instructions to the reader. Our books are written by experts who understand and care about our readers. The knowledge base of our editorial staff comes from years of experience in publishing, education, and journalism — experience which we use to produce books for the '90s. In short, we care about books, so we attract the best people. We devote special attention to details such as audience, interior design, use of icons, and illustrations. And because we use an efficient process of authoring, editing, and desktop publishing our books electronically, we can spend more time ensuring superior content and spend less time on the technicalities of making books.

You can count on our commitment to deliver high-quality books at competitive prices on topics you want to read about. At IDG Books Worldwide, we continue in the IDG tradition of delivering quality for more than 25 years. You'll find no better book on a subject than one from IDG Books Worldwide.

John J. Kilcullen

John Kilcullen
President and CEO
IDG Books Worldwide, Inc.

Acknowledgments

We were astounded at how many people it takes to create a book. We'd like to thank the team at IDG Books for putting up with us. Special thanks go to our editors. Ken Duncan's technical comments were always brief and so precisely on target that we think he might be clairvoyant. He actually took the time to check our binary arithmetic. Carol Henry managed to find humor in topics that made us think we would never smile again and kept an eye on the mixed metaphors. Ronnie Bucci had an infinite supply of patience when helping us with our graphics. And, finally, thanks to Anne Marie Walker, who kept us going when our energy flagged.

We would also like to thank L. Stuart Vance for his compilation of the interesting network devices in Chapter 24. We first heard of networked cola machines at his talk at the Digital Equipment Users Society, and he was kind enough to point us to other wonderful and sometimes bizarre sites on The Internet.

Publisher's Acknowledgments

We're proud of this book; please send us your comments about it by using the Reader Response Card at the back of the book or by e-mailing us at feedback/dummies@idgbooks.com. Some of the people who helped bring this book to market include the following:

Acquisitions, Development, & Editorial

Project Editor: Anne Marie Walker

Copy Editor: Carol Henry

Technical Reviewer: Ken Duncan

Editorial Managers: Kristin A. Cocks, Mary Corder

Editorial Assistants: Constance Carlisle, Chris Collins, Kevin Spencer

Production

Layout and Graphics: Ronnie K. Bucci

Proofreader: C^2 Editorial Services

Indexer: Liz Cunningham

General & Administrative

IDG Books Worldwide, Inc.: John Kilcullen, President & CEO; Steven Berkowitz, COO & Publisher

Dummies, Inc.: Milissa Koloski, Executive Vice President & Publisher

Dummies Technology Press & Dummies Editorial: Diane Graves Steele, Associate Publisher; Judith A. Taylor, Brand Manager; Myra Immell, Editorial Director

Dummies Trade Press: Kathleen A. Welton, Vice President & Publisher; Stacy S. Collins, Brand Manager

IDG Books Production for Dummies Press: Beth Jenkins, Production Director; Cindy L. Phipps, Supervisor of Project Coordination; Kathie S. Schnorr, Supervisor of Page Layout; Shelley Lea, Supervisor of Graphics and Design

Dummies Packaging & Book Design: Erin McDermitt, Packaging Coordinator; Kavish+Kavish, Cover Design

◆

The publisher would like to give special thanks to Patrick J. McGovern, without whom this book would not have been possible.

◆

Dedications

Candace would like to dedicate this book to her mother, who knows what the most important thing is in life and has proven that you can do anything if you have to. (I don't know how she ever managed.)

Marshall would like to dedicate this book to his father, who passed on the work ethic that made it possible for Marshall to finish the book nights and weekends and still keep his cool.

Contents at a Glance

Cartoons at a Glance
by Rich Tennant

Table of Contents

Foreword

· ·

If you're looking for a buzzword to capture the essence of the next great leap forward in the computerization of society, TCP/IP just doesn't seem to hack it. Few would have guessed even two years ago — even those of us who have been toiling away in the computer industry for years — that this tongue-twister acronym would come to represent what it does today. For many, TCP/IP means the dawning of the golden age of computing: universal access to the increasingly rich information resources of The Internet.

Now boasting millions of users, and more rushing to get on line every day, The Internet and the graphical World Wide Web may foretell the most significant impact on commerce and society since the development of the assembly line. Today businesses can target marketing efforts at mass groups of consumers, interactively fine-tuning the content to meet each group's own specific needs and desires. New channels of sales and product distribution that have been impossible until now, or at least astronomically expensive, can be deployed on The Internet rapidly and economically. Large corporations can create virtual organizations nimble enough to quickly take advantage of rapidly changing opportunities. Small entrepreneurs can develop virtual infrastructures to compete with the titans of industry, without having to raise huge amounts of capital.

So what's driving all this? The answer to that question is unimportant to most of the millions who will be influenced by online technology. Most consumers aren't interested in exactly how the video and sound make their way from network broadcasters into the television set; these folks only want to enjoy and learn what they watch and hear. Similarly, you don't need to know exactly how The Internet operates in order to get on line and surf the Web. But if you're the kind of person who likes to be more familiar with what's behind the screen, then *TCP/IP for Dummies* is the book for you.

This book takes you past the command lines and graphical user interfaces of Internet tools. In plain language, this volume will tell you what really happens to create the illusion of magic. It's a guide for normal people who want to know what forces are driving their lives. It's for those of you who want straightforward information, without the techno-babble that so often cloaks the wonders being created by the computer industry today.

John Landry
Chief Technology Officer and Senior Vice President
Lotus Development Corporation

Introduction

● ●

Welcome to *TCP/IP For Dummies*. If you're a traveler on the Information Superhighway (or possibly your own private network of byways), TCP/IP is the way to go. The thing about the TCP/IP communications protocol is that it's fundamentally tied in with networking and internetworking. So, we've included a bit about networks and The Internet — the mother of all networks — to show how and where TCP/IP fits in. If you're already network knowledgeable, you will probably want to skip the basic introduction to networks in Chapter 3.

The 5th Wave   By Rich Tennant

"WHAT CONCERNS ME ABOUT THE INFORMATION SUPERHIGHWAY IS THAT IT APPEARS TO BE ENTERING THROUGH BRENT'S BEDROOM."

So let's get right into it. In the paragraph above, we've already used the words *TCP, IP, The Internet,* and *protocol.* Much of Part I is devoted to explaining in detail what these and other terms mean. For now, here is a quick preview.

Term	Definition
Protocol	Rules of behavior. Network protocols such as TCP/IP are the rules of behavior and operations for transmitting data across a network.
TCP/IP	TCP and IP are two widely used network protocols. When the terms are used together, as in TCP/IP, they also represent a whole group of network protocols. Chapter 6 describes the various protocols in the TCP/IP collection.
The Internet	An international network of networks. Originally sponsored by the U.S. government, the modern Internet is controlled by the Internet Society. The Internet is useful for getting information or talking to other people about just about everything — from learning new skills, to finding recipes for dog biscuits, to advertising, to browsing online art galleries. (We'll even show you in Chapter 9 how to get that dog biscuit recipe!) The rules of operation for The Internet are the TCP/IP protocols.

This book takes an irreverent approach to TCP/IP. We've taken the mystery out of it by giving you down-to-earth explanations for all the buzzwords and technical jargon that TCP/IP loves.

This is not a formal tutorial; it's OK to skip around and use the book to learn as much or as little as you need. If you need to impress your boss and colleagues with buzzwords, you can learn just enough to toss them around intelligently at meetings and cocktail parties. On the other hand, you can go all the way and learn TCP/IP's most important features and tools, and the role TCP/IP plays in The Internet. It's all right here in your hands.

About This Book

TCP/IP is a hot topic these days, and to be well connected (networkwise, that is), sooner or later you'll have to get familiar with what it is and what it does. So if you want to understand what TCP/IP is, why you need it, and what to do with it, but you just don't know where to start, this book is for you.

TCP/IP For Dummies is really two books in one. First, the book is an introduction to the basics — it will tell you exactly what TCP/IP is and what it's for. Second, if you already understand these fundamentals, you can use the book as a reference to help you use TCP/IP applications on all kinds of computers connected to a network. You'll also learn about the many tools associated with TCP/IP.

Here are some subjects we'll cover:

- ✔ TCP/IP and The Internet
- ✔ Who owns TCP/IP and how do you get it?
- ✔ What is client/server and where does it fit in with TCP/IP?
- ✔ TCP/IP — It's not just for UNIX anymore
- ✔ Protocols and protocol suites
- ✔ Tools and applications for getting around the network
- ✔ Tools and applications for getting around The Internet
- ✔ Security — Do I need it and how do I enforce it?
- ✔ Can I program with TCP/IP?

How to Use This Book

This book is loaded with information. But don't try to read it cover to cover. You might hurt yourself. We recommend you use the book as a reference. Each topic stands alone, so you don't need a lot of prerequisite information. Look up the topic you want, in the index or table of contents, and you'll find helpful facts, instructional information, as well as some detailed techie stuff.

Most of the information you need about TCP/IP is in this book. For more information on networks, and The Internet in particular, try _Networking For Dummies_ and _The Internet For Dummies._

Conventions used in this book

In the examples, if we want you to type in a command, it will look like this:

```
COMMAND to type
```

To enter this command, you would type **COMMAND to type** exactly as you see it here, using the same upper- and lowercase letters, and press the Enter key.

When you type commands, be careful to use the same upper- and lowercase letters (some computer systems are very fussy about this). ∎

Whenever we show you something that will be displayed on the screen (such as an error message or a response to your input), it will look like this:

```
A TCP/IP message on your screen
```

Who Are You?

We have made some assumptions about you and what you're looking to get from this book:

You use some kind of computer. It doesn't matter what kind — that's part of the beauty of TCP/IP.

Your computer is already on (or would like to be on) some kind of network.

You have TCP/IP or you're considering TCP/IP as the protocol for that network.

Maybe you already know something about TCP/IP, and want to learn more.

Maybe you've heard that TCP/IP is the protocol to have for your network, but you're not sure how to get started.

Most of all, we know that *you're not really a dummy*. You're just trying something new. Pretty soon, you'll be an expert.

How This Book Is Organized

This book contains four parts. Each part contains several chapters, and the chapters are divided into smaller sections. You can thumb through the book, browsing section headings and reading just the sections you are interested in. Some of the early chapters have background information about networks that will help you understand the TCP/IP elements, if you are a beginner. Here's the layout and a quick look at what you can find in each major part:

Part I: Basics and Buzzwords — Or, How to Impress People at Meetings

This part explains why TCP/IP is such a hot topic. You'll read about the relationship between TCP/IP and The Internet, and how TCP/IP got started and where it's going. There's also some good background information about networks, in case you don't have a clue about network terminology. You'll find out about all the major buzzwords of the day, including one that should go into the next century, "where no one has gone before . . . ".

Part II: TCP/IP from Soup to Nuts to Dessert

This part contains some of the heavy-duty technical information about the protocols that make up the TCP/IP suite. You can skip over many of the topics here, depending on how deeply you want to get into theory. But don't skip this whole part! It describes, in Chapters 7 through 16, all the services TCP/IP provides for you, and discusses how the network finds you by name and address. You'll also learn about TCP/IP tools and commands and get the how-to information to make them work for you. We also examine some of the system files on your computer that support TCP/IP, and what you have to do to manage them (sometimes nothing).

Part III: For Inquiring Minds

This section covers various topics, including system security, hardware, and interfaces for programmers who are writing applications that use TCP/IP.

Now don't get all excited about the hardware topics. We know that hardware decisions are made in highly private, agonizing sessions between you and your computer salesperson. We wouldn't *dream* of interfering with that relationship, so we won't be recommending specific hardware or how to configure it. We *will* give you some general information about when a certain type of hardware is required — for instance, when you need to get a computer to function as a gateway for e-mail (Chapter 7).

As for interfaces for application programmers, we have a chapter that introduces you to the Sockets Application Programming Interface. And regardless of the name, sockets are definitely *not* hardware. Take another look at the table on page 2; the TCP/IP protocols are not tangible entities, but just rules. If this book were about etiquette, we'd tell you which fork to use, but not what silver pattern to buy.

Part IV: The Part of Tens

You may already know that every . . .*For Dummies* book has one of these Parts. Here you'll find frequently asked questions, tips, and also some very silly but true TCP/IP factoids — in sets of ten, of course. Duh . . .

Icons Used in This Book

 This icon signals you about a nerdy techno-fact that you can easily skip without hurting your TCP/IP education. But if you're a technoid, you'll probably eat this stuff up. ■

 TCP/IP is totally software, but software does run on hardware. This icon alerts you to hardware stuff related to TCP/IP software. ■

 This icon indicates a nifty shortcut or piece of information to make your life easier. ■

 This icon marks something for you to remember because it's going to come up again. ■

 This icon lets you know that there's a loaded gun pointed directly at your foot. ■

 This icon marks a section of the cookbook. It'll be beside step-by-step recipes for doing something. ■

Where to Go from Here

Check out the table of contents or the index, and decide where you want to start. If you're an Information Technology manager, you're probably interested in the buzzwords and why everyone seems to be getting on the TCP/IP bandwagon. If you're a programmer, we've got a chapter just for you (Chapter 19). If you have no idea of what a network is, you might want to start with Chapter 3, to get some background. After all, TCP/IP is communications software that lives on a network. Then go back to the table of contents to see what interests you after that.

Part I

Basics and Buzzwords — Or, How to Impress People at Meetings

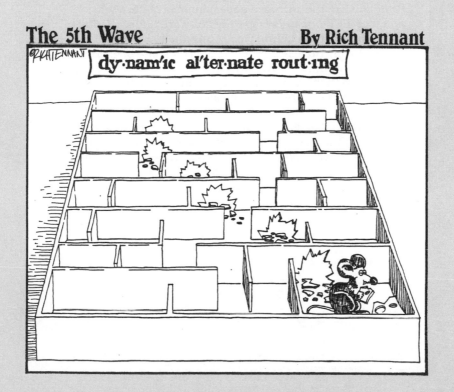

In This Part...

You can't play the game if you don't know the rules. And TCP/IP *are* the rules (protocols) of networks. Protocols are the software underpinnings of networks, and the TCP/IP protocols are the software underpinnings of The Internet. So before we get into the hairy details of the protocols themselves, we'll give you some background about The Internet, networks in general, and TCP/IP's relationship to them. You'll also learn some of the hottest buzzwords in the computer business.

Bear in mind that TCP/IP stays alive by morphing every so often, and it's almost ready to do it again. So in this Part we've also described how TCP/IP got to where it is today, and what we should all look for in the next century.

Chapter 1

TCP/IP and The Internet
(or any internet, for that matter)

· ·

In This Chapter

▶ How do you pronounce TCP/IP?

▶ What is The Internet?

▶ What does TCP/IP have to do with The Internet?

▶ What is a protocol? What is a transport?

▶ Are TCP/IP and open systems related?

· ·

You bought this book (or maybe you're just flipping through it) to learn about TCP/IP. TCP/IP stands for

Transmission Control Protocol / Internet Protocol

As you work through this book you'll learn all kinds of cool stuff about TCP/IP — including what the terms Transmission Control Protocol and Internet Protocol mean.

But let's start with something simple: how to pronounce it!

Pronunciation Guide

You wouldn't believe how some people say "TCP/IP." Pronouncing this acronym correctly is easy, however — you just say the name of each letter. Oh yeah, ignore the slash (/). Ready? Go. Say

T C P I P

Good! That didn't hurt, did it? What you said should have sounded like this:

Tee See Pee Eye Pee

Now, now, none of those off-color jokes. Just try it one more time. Don't emphasize any of the letters. Stress each letter equally, even though the *P* occurs twice, and continue to ignore the slash. Again:

Tee See Pee Eye Pee

Excellent. You're off to a great start.

Occasionally you might hear someone cut corners and say just

Tee See Pee

That's okay. The computer industry uses lots of three-letter acronyms, or TLAs. (TLA is the three-letter acronym for Three-Letter Acronym.)

You might also hear someone say simply

Eye Pee

(Here, too, you'll want to refrain from making any silly jokes, as we advised just above. *Please.*) As you'll see in later chapters, sometimes it is technically correct to say just "TCP" or just "IP," since they are the primary components of TCP/IP.

What's The Internet? And Can Penguins Use It?

The Internet is the worldwide collection of interconnected computer networks that use the TCP/IP protocol. These networks reach to every continent — even Antarctica — and nearly every country. So if your favorite penguin has an Internet address, you can invite him to your formal dinner party via electronic mail! (He'll already have a black tie.) Figure 1-1 shows how you can communicate with beings all over the world if you have TCP/IP and Internet access.

The Internet is also much more than its network connections. It's all of the individual computers connected to those individual networks, as well, plus all the users of those computers, all the information accessible to those users, and all the knowledge those people possess. The Internet is just as much about people and information as it is about computers and computer networks.

The Internet links universities, companies, governments, cities, countries, organizations, students, researchers, parents and homemakers, personal computers, supercomputers, weather stations — even candy and soda machines!

Figure 1-1:
The Internet reaches all corners of the world.

An abundance of networks exist in the United States that are part of The Internet. Many are regional networks that bring The Internet to a particular section of the country. A few of these are listed below (we apologize if we didn't name your favorite).

- NEARnet, the New England Academic and Research Network
- BARRnet, the Bay Area Research Network
- NSFnet, the National Science Foundation Network
- NYSERnet, the New York State Education and Research Network
- THEnet, the Texas Higher Education Network

Most of the other countries in the world have a single, national data-communication network. Often it is run by the government. Each of these national networks is also part of The Internet.

Traveling the Information Superhighway

The Internet is a hot topic these days, so you may hear people refer to it using some other names. Flip to Chapter 26 for a list. The term *Information Superhighway* is one of the most popular.

So if The Internet is the Information Superhighway, then *Internet For Dummies* and *More Internet For Dummies* are the road maps. The network hardware is the road surface itself. And the rules of the road are TCP/IP.

The Internet vs. An Internet

You won't find the word *internet* in most dictionaries — at least not yet — but you can look up the pieces of the word:

inter   means between, among, or within

net   is a group of communications stations
         operating under unified control

So an internet is what goes on between, among, and within communications stations on a network. Many organizations (companies, universities, and so forth) have their own internets.

An internet is also how you link one network to another — for example, to extend a local area network (LAN) so that it becomes a wide area network (WAN).

One way we distinguish "The Internet" from "an internet" is by capitalizing "The" and "Internet."

The Internet is

- ✔ The one and only international network of networks using TCP/IP. The Internet has evolved over the last 30 years.
- ✔ Public (not free, but open to everyone).
- ✔ A carrier of your electronic mail (e-mail) to other people outside your organization — even the President of the United States.
- ✔ A very convenient place to get free software.
- ✔ Where the Rolling Stones "broadcast" part of a concert in November 1994.
- ✔ Hundreds of networks, thousands of computers, millions of people, and terabytes of information.
- ✔ Where you can write to Santa Claus (at santa@northpole.net), and he'll send you a button that says "I e-mailed Santa."

An internet is

- ✔ A network of networks, normally set up for one organization. It may or may not run TCP/IP, but it must if it is linked to The Internet. It may or may not run other network protocols.

- ✔ Usually private. Only you and the other members of your organization are allowed to use it.

- ✔ A carrier of your e-mail to the other people in your organization.

- ✔ Perhaps connected to The Internet, perhaps not. If your organization has an internet that is not connected to The Internet, you cannot send e-mail to Marshall and Candace, your authors, because we do not have access to your private internet and you do not have access to The Internet, where we are. Note that "The Internet" has become a synonym for "the outside world".

Dear Emily Post: What's a Protocol?

Protocol is basically a set of rules for behavior. These rules may be unwritten, but are accepted as correct by the people using them. For example, in the 1970s, when friends met on the street they gave each other the peace sign and said "Right on!" When Siamese citizens met their King, (at least in the movie), everyone kneeled and bowed, and they spoke Siamese (but only when spoken to). When Scarlett O'Hara insisted on that off-the-shoulder green and white gown for the barbecue at Twelve Oaks, Mammy said no — "It ain't fittin'! It just ain't fittin'!"

Where do these behavior rules come from? How is it that they are so well known and understood? They aren't always written down, yet we *standardize* on certain acceptable behaviors. There are some minor differences due to circumstances and cultures, but here are some examples of situations when a certain behavior is expected, whether written down or not:

- ✔ When a youngster speaks to an adult
- ✔ When a commoner meets royalty
- ✔ When people meet and greet, as in "Right on!" or "See you later, alligator"
- ✔ In school, when you raise your hand to ask or answer a question
- ✔ On the Titanic, as in "Ladies first," or "Women and children first" (or is it "Every man for himself" nowadays?)

These are all parts of the formality of communication. Sometimes the rules are written down — the rules for driving, for example. Still, they can vary widely from country to country or region to region. The United States consists of 50 states. Each state has its own driving laws. For instance, you can turn right at a red light almost everywhere, but not in New York City. In the United States, a yellow traffic light means "Caution, prepare to stop," but in Germany, that same yellow light means "Get ready. The light is going to turn green."

Similarly, when two or more computers need to communicate, they need rules of behavior and conventions for both writing and sending their messages. ("After you." "No, after you.") Just as the people of the world speak different languages in different regions, computers may need to "speak" particular network protocols. (When in Rome . . .) If a computer is not able to speak a certain protocol, it cannot communicate with the computers that speak only that protocol.

Thus, in the world of computers, a protocol is the collection of designated practices, policies, and procedures — often unwritten but agreed upon between its users — that facilitates electronic communication between those users. So if computers linked into a network are the basis of the Information Superhighway, the TCP/IP protocols are the rules of the road.

What's a Transport?

If you need to travel from Boston to New York for a business meeting, does it really matter how you travel as long as you get there on time? You might choose to go by car, taxi, bus, plane, train, bicycle, foot, or snowmobile. Certainly there will be differences in how long the trip takes, its cost, how comfortable you are, and the exact route. But what you really want to do is get there, and for that you need *transport*.

Depending on the end point of the trip and your personal requirements, some transportation choices may be unwise, illegal, or impossible. If you needed to get to the moon, would you ride your bicycle? If you had a million dollars and a hot date in the middle of the Golden Gate Bridge in 30 days, how would you proceed? If you had one French franc and needed to get to the observation level of the Eiffel Tower in ten minutes during rush hour, could you make it?

Transporting information

How many different ways can you tell your mother you'll be home for the holidays?

- ✔ Telephone call
- ✔ Postcard or letter (if you still haven't given up on the Postal Service)
- ✔ Telegram
- ✔ Fax (if she has a fax machine)
- ✔ E-mail (if she has an account somewhere)
- ✔ Homing pigeon
- ✔ Bicycle messenger
- ✔ Tell your father and let him tell her
- ✔ Tie a note to a rock and throw it through the front window
- ✔ Just show up

Did you think of others? Does it matter which one you use as long as she gets the message?

We're used to thinking of a transport as the way we move ourselves or our things around. But computer networks just want to move *information* from one place to another. Many times we don't care exactly how the data gets where it is going, as long as it arrives

- ✔ On time
- ✔ Safely, correctly, intact, and uninjured
- ✔ Affordably

On a network, TCP/IP carries your data along and makes sure your data gets where it's going, intact, and without costing an arm and a leg. So TCP/IP is both a transport for carrying your data and a protocol with rules for how your data should move.

And there's one more piece: TCP/IP also has a set of applications, or programs, for chatting with other people on a network, for sharing files, for signing on to other computers, and more. Chapters 7 through 10 will explore these services and applications; for now, let's stick to the protocol side of TCP/IP.

The Protocol of Open Systems

TCP/IP is often called the protocol of *open systems*. Part of the reason for this is that TCP/IP is available for so many different kinds of computers and their operating systems. The history lesson in Chapter 2 explains why.

Another reason is that many network services are built on top of TCP/IP, using it as the transport. We'll cover network services in later chapters.

Does anyone know what an open system is?

The term *open systems* is one of those computer-industry buzzwords we promised you. Many of the concepts of open systems began with the UNIX operating system, and some people still believe that the terms open systems and UNIX are interchangeable. But the truth is, if you ask ten people for a definition of an open system, you'll get ten different definitions.

Here's the world's shortest definition of open systems:

Open systems provide a standards-based computing environment.

Why Do People Think UNIX Means Open (and Vice Versa)?

Remember the scene in *Jurassic Park* when Lex realizes she's looking at a UNIX system? "I know this!" she hollers, staring at the monitor and beginning to press some keys. And it's the beginning of the end for the raptors!

UNIX has been hanging around computers almost forever . . . well, for a quarter of a century, anyway. Its operating system architecture and the source code for its programs are public, but not necessarily free. Because of its published architecture, and because it is written in the C programming language, UNIX has been ported to all major hardware platforms, even the PC and the Macintosh. A PC/UNIX user can move to a mainframe and get around with moderate ease, because the basic commands are the same. UNIX is like

the MacDonald's of operating systems — wherever you are in the world, you have a good idea of what you're going to get.

When you extend this concept to network protocols, you can see why TCP/IP is the industry standard for open networking. With TCP/IP networks, users perform the Big 3 network tasks — electronic mail, file transfer, and signing on to remote computers — in the same way, regardless of connection media, Ethernet or token ring configuration (see Chapter 3), and even the computer hardware. And if your company gets you a brand-new computer system that you've never even heard of, the mail, file transfer, and remote log-on will all still work in familiar ways, compliments of TCP/IP.

These standards for open systems normally include the following:

- ✔ Application programming interfaces (APIs) such as POSIX
- ✔ Networking protocols such as TCP/IP
- ✔ Database access methods such as SQL
- ✔ Graphical user interfaces such as Motif

If your computing environment makes use of open systems, you have the freedom to mix and match those computers that let you get your work done.

The fact that TCP/IP is an internationally accepted standard for networking means that it's an excellent choice for building the network piece of open systems. However, though TCP/IP is the most widely used, it is not the only protocol that is considered a standard. In the next chapter, we'll see how TCP/IP grew into a standard, and we'll take a look at the competition.

Chapter 2

TCP/IP: Child of the Cold War

. . . .

In This Chapter

▶ How did TCP/IP become the protocols for The Internet?

▶ Does the U.S. government own TCP/IP?

▶ Why is TCP/IP so popular?

▶ Can I use TCP/IP on any kind of computer?

▶ Is TCP/IP going to be extinct someday?

▶ Who's minding the TCP/IP store?

. . . .

*T*his chapter is for you history buffs out there. It gives you some facts about the genesis and genetics of TCP/IP, as well as a peek into the future. It's also loaded with lots of the buzzwords we promised you.

What Did You Do in the War, Daddy?

In the 1960s, the United States government agency DARPA (Defense Advanced Research Projects Agency) funded research on how to connect computers in order to exchange data among them. The purpose of this research was to build command and control functions in case of a nuclear "incident."

The idea was to be able to move data across the network even if parts of the network became disrupted. For example, if a network link were taken out by enemy attack, the traffic on that link would automatically be rerouted to a different link. This reliable scheme is called *dynamic rerouting* — but your system doesn't have to be a victim of a nuclear attack for dynamic rerouting to be valuable. If a forklift cuts a cable in a warehouse, for instance, dynamic rerouting means that inventory data can still be sent across a network via a different route.

You can learn more about dynamic rerouting in Chapter 17, "The Dreaded Hardware Chapter." ∎

Bolt Beranek & Newman, Inc., a Massachusetts firm, built the first test network while additional research was being done in several California universities. This first network was called the ARPANET, and it connected academic and military research centers. By the early 1970s, the ARPANET comprised about 50 computers across the United States and Western Europe. Bolt Beranek & Newman maintained the control center for the network, called the Network Operations Center (NOC, pronounced "knock").

In the mid-1970s, the network had grown enough that DARPA began to investigate the possibility of building and connecting additional networks. The need for more network capacity drove research into technologies such as Ethernet and token ring (see Chapter 3), as well as satellite and radio communications.

Evolution, Not Revolution

As the ARPANET continued to grow, it was used for purposes quite different from the original military uses. The major users were still universities and military and government installations. But they were using the network to share all kinds of nonmilitary information, files, and documents.

The growing size and amount of its traffic made the ARPANET increasingly harder to manage, so it was split into two separate networks: MILNET for military installations, and a new ARPANET for civilian sites. Both networks still needed to be connected, so that Colonel Mustard could communicate with Professor Plum. The Internet Protocol (IP) routed traffic from one network to the other, thereby connecting the new ARPANET to MILNET. Figure 2-1 shows how the ARPANET was demilitarized.

ARPANET　　　　　　　　　　　　　　**MILNET**

Figure 2-1:
IP (Internet Protocol) connects civilians with the military.

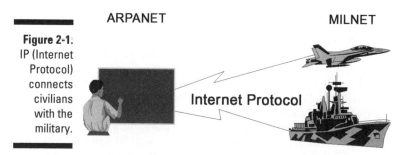

Internet Protocol

Then in 1975, the U.S. Defense Communications Agency (DCA) took over control of the ARPANET.

Birth of a protocol

DARPA funded the development of a whole set of protocols for communication on the ARPANET. This internetworking protocol suite is known by two of its parts: TCP and IP, yielding TCP/IP. The protocols were designed to support multiple connected networks. In fact, even though there were only two to start, MILNET and ARPANET, IP was from the beginning capable of connecting thousands of networks. This capability is one of the reasons TCP/IP is still so popular today.

Free Love wasn't the only thing going on in California in the 1970s. When developers of the UNIX operating system at the University of California at Berkeley added TCP/IP into their software distribution kit (BSD UNIX), TCP/IP began a rapid growth spurt, especially in academic environments. After all, this was essentially no-cost networking, at least from a software point of view. The Berkeley development group added a set of tools and utilities for using The Internet, and an application programming interface (API) called a *socket*. (See Chapter 19 for more on the sockets interface for network programming.)

In the early 1980s, the Secretary of Defense mandated that all computers connected to the ARPANET had to use TCP/IP. The following came from an electronic mail message, date and author unknown. (TCP/IP's history is studded with such anonymous contributions, the result of its development by committees of committees.) This message talks about the key reason TCP/IP has endured on all kinds of networks:

> Around 1980 the protocol was changed from NCP (Network Control Program, which did what TCP/IP does now but for only ONE network with fixed table of up to 256 hosts on the whole net) to TCP/IP (Transmission Control Protocol/Internet Protocol, which covers many networks using a common packet protocol for getting data around and between them transparently to the application processes), and that's when InterNet came into being, when ARPANet ceased to be THE NET, and InterNet instead became THE NET.

Why ARPANET Could Have Only 256 Computers

Each computer on the ARPANET had a numeric address that was 8 bits (1 byte) long. The highest-number address you can create using 8 bits is 256. So, once the 256th computer joined the ARPANET, there were no addresses left. Today's Internet, even though it has vast numbers of addresses, is facing the same problem.

A Bit about BITNET

BITNET stands for the Because It's Time Network. (Networks with cute names like this often start on college campuses.) BITNET is a large, widely used network, and a common misconception is that it's part of The Internet. Let's set this straight right now: It's not. BITNET does not use TCP/IP as its protocol. BITNET users can communicate with users on The Internet only because some BITNET *computers* also run TCP/IP. These computers, serving as connection points between BITNET and The Internet, are called *gateways*. Chapter 17 has technical information about how gateways work.

The Internet begins a network revolution

Because of a technical limitation, the ARPANET was limited to 256 computers. As use of the ARPANET mushroomed, other networks sprouted to handle the traffic. Here are a few of them:

- CSNET, the Computer Science Network
- HEPNET, the High Energy Physics Network
- NSFNET, the National Science Foundation Network
- JNET, the Japanese Computer Network (Lots of countries have their own national network, and most major corporations, including IBM, Xerox, and General Motors, have large private networks.)

Most of these networks still exist today as components of The Internet.

The ARPANET became the core for communications among all these diverse networks. DARPA coordinated meetings about this internetworked environment, and eventually created a special committee to handle internetworking evolution. In time the ARPANET itself became just one of the many networks on The Internet. All the networks were, and are today, interconnected by means of the TCP/IP protocol suite.

GOSIP, GOSIP, GOSIP: Can We Talk?

No, we haven't forgotten how to spell: It's really GOSIP, not GOSSIP. What is GOSIP, you ask? As new technologies developed, the United States became interested in a new protocol set, Open Systems Interconnect (OSI), at which we'll get another look in Chapter 5. The government techno-powers-that-be stated that government installations would be connected by OSI, instead of

TCP/IP. They named this new entity GOSIP, the Government Open System Interconnect Profile. Would you believe there is a U.K. GOSIP, as well? ■

The good news for TCP/IP is that a special United States panel has recommended that TCP/IP be recognized as a standard protocol for government communications, in addition to OSI (Figure 2-2). This is not only good for TCP/IP but for networks in general, as well, since OSI never really came to be fully functional.

Figure 2-2:
We pay
taxes for
THIS?

Who Owns TCP/IP?

As you have read, the United States government paid for the development of TCP/IP. And since the government's money actually came from you taxpayers (if you pay U.S. taxes), that means *you* paid for TCP/IP. It's okay for the U.S. government to *print* money, but not to *make* money, so the specifications for TCP/IP are in the public domain. All of the TCP/IP specifications are freely available on The Internet.

But just because you're a taxpayer doesn't mean that you can have TCP/IP for free. With the specs conveniently at hand on The Internet, however, anyone can take them and implement TCP/IP. In fact, many people have. Some of those people work at companies where it *is* okay to make money. Those people and their companies can sell their implementations if they want, or just give the products away. As a result, TCP/IP is often included with the operating systems sold with computers.

Because no one really "owns" TCP/IP, the developers of products that implement or include it do not have to pay royalties. That helps keep down the cost of the products made available to us — and keeps the profit margins fairly high, as well. So if no one owns it, who keeps house for TCP/IP? Today, TCP/IP is an international standard, watched over by The Internet Society, described later in this chapter.

The TCP/IP Declaration of Independence

When in the course of network events . . . to form a more perfect union . . .

There are many different kinds of network models and hardware technologies, ranging from circles to stars, from telephone wire to signals bounced off satellites into the ether. (If you're interested — and you don't have to be — Chapter 3 explains some of the characteristics of these technologies.) And new technologies are emerging to enhance or replace the existing ones. One of the biggest strengths of TCP/IP is that it is independent of all the available alternatives:

- ✔ It's independent of the network model. Circles or stars — TCP/IP doesn't care.

- ✔ It's independent of the transmission medium. Wire or satellite — no problem.

- ✔ It's independent of specific vendors. Take your choice.

- ✔ It's independent of the operating system and computer hardware. Pick your favorite.

TCP/IP ties networks and The Internet together, regardless of the hardware and software used to build those networks. Sometimes people think TCP/IP is only for linking computers that use the UNIX operating system, because TCP/IP has been included in UNIX for so long. Not true. These days, TCP/IP runs on and connects just about everything. You may have heard about other network protocols, such as IBM's SNA or Novell's SPX/IPX. But no protocol connects as many different hardware and software platforms as TCP/IP. This versatility is the reason TCP/IP is the world's most popular network protocol.

Dedicated to the proposition that all vendors are created equal

From the very beginning, TCP/IP was designed to link computers from different vendors, such as IBM and Digital Equipment Corporation, to name just two. Other network protocols, especially the proprietary ones that were created by computer vendors themselves, may not be this flexible. With TCP/IP, you can buy the computer you want or need, and know that it will communicate with all the others.

In addition, since all implementations of TCP/IP must work together, or "interoperate," regardless of who created them, you may have several implementations from which to choose. The various products may differ in price, number of features, performance, or in any number of other ways. Investigate your options carefully, and make the right choice for your circumstances.

Dedicated to the proposition that all platforms are created equal

We've used the word *platform* a few times now but haven't yet explained what we mean. The dictionary says a platform is (among other things) a raised horizontal surface, such as a raised floor on which a performer stands. What we mean by platform, however, is a computer on which to load an operating system. Examples of a platform are an IBM mainframe (hardware) running MVS (operating system), or a Gateway 2000 PC (hardware) running Windows NT (operating system).

A *software platform* is an operating system on which to load other system software or applications. Examples of software platforms are MS-DOS (operating system) running TCP/IP (network software), or UNIX (operating system) running AmiPro (word processing software).

Because TCP/IP is available for virtually every computer, you are free to select the computer that will best meet your needs. If you need a personal computer, buy one. If you need a supercomputer, buy several. Whatever hardware and software platforms you need or want, TCP/IP is there.

Dedicated to the proposition that all operating systems are created equal

Some computers are capable of running several operating systems. For example, a personal computer can run a combination of MS-DOS and Microsoft Windows, IBM OS/2, and others. Not to worry — you can run any or all of these and still have TCP/IP working for you. Use the operating system that best meets your needs.

In fact, though the UNIX operating system was the first to come with TCP/IP "built in," many operating systems come with it these days, including

- Microsoft Windows NT Workstation and Server
- IBM OS/2 Warp
- Macintosh System 7.5
- Windows 95 ("Chicago")

This widespread incorporation of TCP/IP is one indication of its popularity. Other vendors' TCP/IP implementations are still important, though, because they may have features that the bundled implementations don't have. For instance, Microsoft's TCP/IP for Windows for Workgroups only includes network client capabilities. If you need server capabilities, you must buy a TCP/IP product with more features. (See Chapter 4 for definitions of client and server.)

Today, there are more than 8 million PCs using TCP/IP. That doesn't include the larger computers that are not PCs. From this statistic, it's clear that, although TCP/IP is bundled on many operating systems, there is plenty of business for the other TCP/IP vendors, too.

If it's good enough for Uncle Sam, it's good enough for Cousin Bill

Question: What's another world power that is heavily into networks? Did someone say Microsoft Corporation? Bingo! Bill Gates's Microsoft Corporation built TCP/IP protocols into the Microsoft Windows NT operating system, and recommended TCP/IP as the best protocol for wide area networks (WANs).

Networks of the World, Unite

"The only thing constant is change," as the saying goes, and TCP/IP is no exception. It continues to evolve from its government beginnings. New capabilities are added almost daily. The Internet is busier than ever. Additional organizations connect every day, bringing more users on line every minute.

Here are a few important members of the team watching over this rapid growth:

InterNIC

The Internet Network Information Center, known as InterNIC (pronounced "inter nick"), maintains information about the structure and functioning of The Internet. The InterNIC assigns numeric addresses to computers and networks. Your organization must register with the InterNIC in order to connect to The Internet.

Internet Activities Board (IAB)

Created in the 1980s, The Internet Activities Board (IAB, pronounced by saying the letters *I A B*) oversees The Internet and its protocols (TCP/IP). Under the IAB, there are subcommittees that set standards and work on new solutions to Internet growth problems. These standards are developed by volunteers — people with good ideas. The IAB works together with the committees listed below to determine what direction will be set for research and development of The Internet.

Internet Engineering Task Force (IETF)

The Internet Engineering Task Force (IETF, pronounced by saying the letters *I E T F*) is responsible for keeping The Internet up and running every day. Over 70 working groups make up the IETF. Members of these groups are people with common interests who are drafting and developing Internet standards. One of these common interests is the next generation of IP protocols, IPng (discussed later in this chapter).

Are you a joiner?

IETF meetings are open to anyone willing to pay the reasonable fee. So if you want to participate in the setting of Internet and TCP/IP directions, this is the place to start.

You nonjoiners (and everybody in between) can subscribe to free monthly reports about The Internet by sending e-mail to this address:

```
imr-request@isi.edu
```

Chapter 13 describes the components of Internet addresses. ■

If you're interested in participating in discussions of cosmic importance to the IETF, send e-mail to this address:

```
ietf-request@cnri.reston.va.us
```

You will receive information about how the IETF is run, and a schedule of upcoming meetings.

RFC Alert: You can also check out RFC 1718, The TAO of the IETF — A Guide for New Attendees of the IETF. See the later section, "Democracy at Work . . . ," for details.

Internet Engineering Steering Group (IESG)

The Internet Engineering Steering Group (IESG, pronounced by saying the letters *I E S G*) is responsible for setting strategic directions and goals for The Internet. Recently, the IESG coordinated the efforts that will result in a much larger TCP/IP addressing scheme, so that The Internet will not become "full."

Internet Research Task Force (IRTF)

The Internet Research Task Force (IRTF) manages research into network protocols such as TCP/IP. (This group's name, too, is pronounced by saying the letters, *I R T F.*)

The Internet Society

The IAB, IETF, and IRTF are part of The Internet Society, which guides the future of The Internet. Figure 2-3 depicts the different groups that make up The Internet Society.

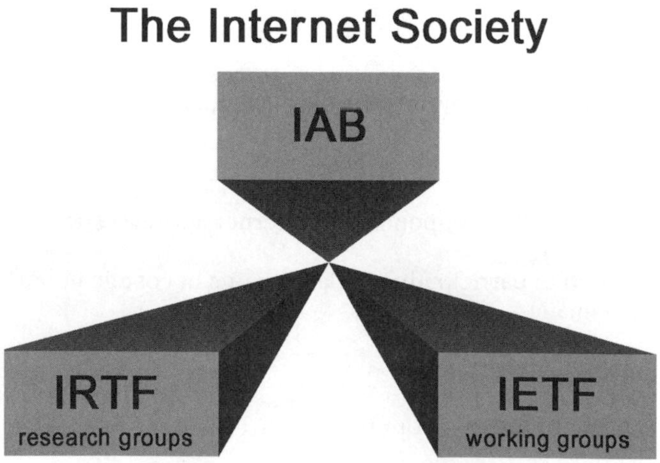

Figure 2-3: The Internet Society.

Democracy at Work: Requests for Comments (RFCs)

When someone comes up with an idea for a new or improved capability for TCP/IP, they write the proposal as a Request for Comments (RFC, pronounced *R F C*) and publish it on The Internet. There's one thing about RFCs you can depend on: As long as we have TCP/IP and The Internet, there will be new RFCs.

RFC authors are volunteers and are not compensated for their creations. Each RFC is assigned a number by which it will be known forever after. Reviewers (more volunteers) respond with comments and constructive criticism. The RFC authors then revise the feature's design and update the document. If everything goes smoothly, the RFC becomes a *draft standard*. Programmers use the draft standard as they design and build software that implements the functionality described by the RFC. Until there is real working code, the RFC is not considered documentation of an official standard.

> *RFC Alert:* We will mention RFCs throughout this book, in a paragraph like this one, when they apply to a topic. Our first RFC reference was just above, in the section on the IETF group. Appendix A tells you where to get RFCs. See also Chapters 21 and 22, "Ten Important, Useful, and Interesting RFCs."

For your information . . . (FYIs)

Some RFCs provide more general information. Though these are numbered like "ordinary" RFCs, they may also be known as FYI (For Your Information) documents or STD (Standard) documents. (You pronounce FYI by saying *F Y I*. As for STD, pronouncing the letters is harder than saying the word, so most people just say "Standard.")

IPng, the Next Generation

You have read about how the growth of the ARPANET toward its limit of 256 computers led to the creation of TCP/IP and The Internet. Nearly 25 years later, The Internet, too, is close to reaching the limits of the current address numbering system. How close is close? Well, though the estimates vary depending on the panic level of the estimator, addresses for small networks will probably run out sometime between 2000 and 2010. That's not very far away.

Back to the Future? Not!

If The Internet is close to running out of addresses, does that mean that soon it won't be able to accept new companies or individuals? Not at all. Recently, the IESG created a new task force to determine how best to enhance TCP/IP to deal with this problem. It's IPng to the rescue! (You pronounce IPng by saying the letters *I P n g.*)

IPng is the Next Generation version of IP. It will offer millions more addresses than we have now. That ought to satisfy the world for the foreseeable future. Final specs for the IPng protocol will be submitted to the IESG as a standard around December 1995. Some early implementations of the new addressing scheme will probably be in place before that date, maybe as early as July 1995. Then it's up to software vendors to develop products that understand the new addressing scheme.

The current version of IP is also known as IPv4, for version 4. IPng is also called IPv6, for version 6. We don't know what happened to version 5. ■

The next big problem

In order to offer more addresses on The Internet, the address format itself is going to change. Will all travelers on The Internet have to learn a new way to access The Internet? Will network hardware and operating systems have to change to accommodate the IPng protocol? Or will the IPng task force figure out a way for old-style IP addresses and new-style IPng addresses to coexist? Stay tuned . . . and read Chapter 13 for more information about addresses today and tomorrow.

Don't panic!

If you're worried about these future events in cyberspace, don't be. We're just trying to get you thinking about possible future directions for your network. The transition from IPv4 to IPv6 (IPng) will be slow and gradual, phased in over the next ten years at least. And you can be sure The Internet will understand both forms of IP addresses for years to come.

Chapter 3

What You Need to Know About Networks

*H*ere is the chapter we promised you about networks and TCP/IP's relationship to them. Computer networking is rapidly becoming a part of life — not just at work, but at home, too. So we think it's important to understand some basic terminology and fundamental concepts for this important technology.

TCP/IP provides *connectivity* for networked computers. (Connectivity is just a fancy way of saying *communication*.) It's hard to describe just the TCP/IP piece without introducing how the machines are organized and cabled together in the network, and this chapter discusses just that.

If you find that you need more information about networks, check out *Networks For Dummies*. ◾

What Is a Network?

A *network* is the combination of computers and other devices, plus the cabling, plus the network interface controllers that are inside the computer, and, of course, network software such as TCP/IP protocols. Figure 3-1 illustrates some of the pieces that make up a network.

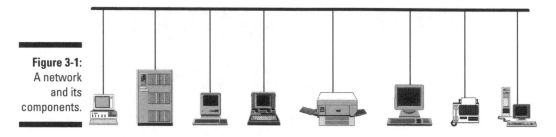

Figure 3-1:
A network
and its
components.

The protocol software governs how data moves around on the network hardware, and TCP/IP is the most widely used protocol on the largest variety of hardware.

What kinds of devices can be on a network?

Any device that sends or receives data can be part of a network. Here are some typical components:

- ✔ *Computers.* This includes PCs, workstations, computers acting as clients (that is, borrowing resources from other computers), and computers acting as servers (that is, lending resources to other computers). Chapter 4 tells you much more about clients and servers.

- ✔ *Printers.* (Most people think of printers as attached to computers, but you can put certain kinds of printers directly on the network.)

- ✔ *Cash registers and those fancy point-of-sale (POS) devices that help a store with inventory control.* The bar code scanners in modern grocery stores are good examples.

- ✔ *Connection media.* This includes cables and wires, fiber optics, microwaves, even signals beamed to or from a satellite.

- ✔ *Other hardware.* This category is quite broad, and includes repeaters, bridges, routers, gateways, terminal servers, and modems (some special modems can be attached directly to the network). There's more information about these devices in The Dreaded Hardware Chapter (Chapter 17). ▪

How does TCP/IP fit into the network?

With all these hardware possibilities for a network, you can see how important it is to have a set of rules for how data should be transmitted across the connection media among all those components. These rules are the network protocols such as TCP/IP. Some of the other network protocols available are DECnet from Digital Equipment Corporation, IPX from Novell, and NetBEUI from Microsoft.

Networks and protocols are inseparable: Without networks, there is no reason for protocols. Without protocols, a network would be a useless collection of expensive machinery. And without TCP/IP, The Internet would be an idea in search of an implementation — kind of like the wall before Humpty Dumpty decided to sit down.

The pieces of the TCP/IP protocol suite are described in terrifically techie detail in Chapter 6.

What a Network Does For You (Oooh! Ahhh! More Stuff!)

A network provides many conveniences and services to its users.

✔ You can move information and files from one computer to another.

✔ You can access shared resources, such as directories and files on other computers, without moving them. (There's a price attached to sharing resources, however; more about this in the next section.)

✔ You can share a printer attached to some other computer.

✔ You can use applications that really take advantage of the network. For example, groupware applications are applications that run across networks, letting coworkers communicate and share data. A salesperson, for instance, can create expense reports and forward them across the network to a manager for an electronic signature. The network's users may never have heard of network protocols, but it's TCP/IP that is providing the network communications part of these applications.

✔ You can send e-mail to other people who are also connected to your network. Via The Internet, you can send mail to famous people, including Santa Claus and the President of the United States, or to not-yet-famous people — including your authors! In Chapter 2, we gave you a couple of Internet addresses for sending mail to Internet committees, and you'll find others as you work through this book.

✔ You can participate in electronic discussion groups. For example, are you thinking of going to Disney World? One popular discussion group on The Internet is named rec.arts.disney. There you can get hotel and restaurant recommendations and find out about the rides and attractions in the park. If you're planning to spend your vacation learning about TCP/IP, you might prefer to check out comp.protocols.tcp-ip. For more detail on discussion groups, read about Usenet news in Chapter 7.

What a Network Does To You (Christmas This Ain't)

So you want to take advantage of shared resources? OK, but keep in mind that to share resources across the network, you must make sure you have enough resources to share. (By the way, when we say *resources*, we are talking about things on your computer that network users can share, such as hard disks, printers, and even the internal processing power of your computer.)

A network can consume your resources. For example, if you allow other users on the network to use the hard disks connected to your computer, will you still have enough room for your own files? Or if you have a printer connected to your machine, will someone else from across the network always be using it when you want to print?

If you plan to share your disk and printer resources, you should decide *who* can share with you across the network and *how much* of your resources they can share. After all, you wouldn't hand your entire paycheck over to your friendly government tax service every month, would you? Hmmm, bad example. Let's try this: You parents out there wouldn't hand over your entire paycheck to your child week after week, would you? Though it might seem that you do, most likely your child gets an allowance, which is a piece of your paycheck resource.

On the other hand, if you're thinking, "Well, I won't get into trouble if I just don't share my resources with *any* other users. I'll just use *their* disks and printers," think again. That would make you dependent on resources that are beyond your control. For example, if another computer on the network lets you store some of your files there (called *remote file-sharing*), what happens if that computer is off line for a while? Your files are incommunicado. Or if you use a printer connected to another computer, and the computer's owner turns it off and goes on vacation, how do you get your stuff printed?

Let your network be Santa, and it just might work

To make resource sharing useful and reliable, the answer is to install special computers that are dedicated wholly to sharing disks or printers with many other users. These computers are managed so that they are always available unless there is a hardware problem. They are called *file servers* or *print servers,* or simply *servers.*

For more information about using servers to share disks and printers across the network, take a look at Chapter 4 on client/server computing, as well as the section on the Network File System in Chapter 10. ◼

Figure 3-2 illustrates sharing disks and files located on a file server somewhere on the network. Depending on how the file server is set up, users may not even know that they are getting files from the network.

Watch Out for Viruses! In addition to all those files, a network can also transport a virus to your computer. Of course, floppy disks can, too. So think carefully about accessing a file server that is unfamiliar to you. We strongly recommend that you regularly and faithfully scan your computer's disks and diskettes for viruses. And *always* scan any software you copy — *before* you use it. ◼

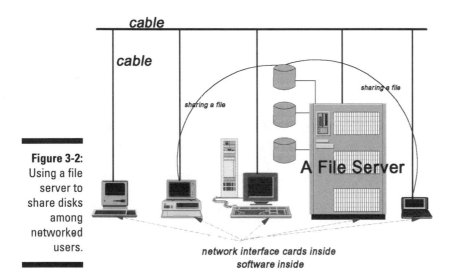

Figure 3-2:
Using a file server to share disks among networked users.

Protocols and Packets and Humpty Dumpty's Fall off the Wall

Protocols are not really tangible "things" on the network. What they do is specify how the tangible things (the network devices and computers) talk to one another. King TCP/IP tells the network devices what to do with Humpty Dumpty — your data. Each time a network device manipulates your data, it is obeying the rules set down by TCP/IP.

One of the most important rules is that your data may have to be transferred in smaller chunks — Humpty Dumpty may get pushed off his wall. TCP/IP makes sure your data doesn't get ruined in the process of getting put back together again.

All the King's horses and all the King's men . . .

The data you send and receive over the network is packaged into one or more *packets*. Each packet holds

✔ The data to transmit

✔ Control information, which tells the network what to do with the packets

The network protocol — King TCP/IP in our case — determines the format for each packet. If we hadn't told you, you might never have known that your messages are split into pieces for transmission and then reassembled, just like Mr. Humpty.

. . . Put Humpty Dumpty back together again (with the help of TCP/IP)

Once the packets are sent, they may not arrive at their destination in order. In Figure 3-3, an e-mail message is split into packets. If your data gets spread over several packets, King TCP/IP tells his horses and soldiers how to put it together again so that the message makes sense.

What Is a LAN?

LAN stands for *local area network*. (It's usually pronounced as a word, *LAN*, not as the letters *L A N*.) The computers and other devices in a LAN communicate over small geographical areas, such as

✔ One wing of one floor in a building

✔ Maybe the whole floor, if it's a small building

✔ Several buildings on a small campus

Figure 3-3:
TCP/IP
sequences
packets
correctly.

LANs can run over various network architectures. Two examples are *Ethernet* and *token ring*. These network architectures are ways for data to move across wires and cables.

How Ethernet works: Would you send me a packet of pastrami?

With Ethernet, any device on the network, from the mainframe computer at headquarters to that cash register in the local delicatessen, can send data in a packet to any other location on the network at any time. Often there are lots of machines on a network, as you know, and they'll undoubtedly be sending data at the same time. When the packets of data collide, Ethernet makes the devices stop transmitting, wait a little while, and try again. The wait time interval is random and is different every time a collision happens.

The Ethernet architecture is called CSMA/CD (Carrier Sense Multiple Access/ Collision Detection), meaning that the devices realize when a collision has occurred, and they wait and retry. With Ethernet, the data from the small dell's cash register is equal to anything the headquarters mainframe has to send. All the devices on the network are peers. Figure 3-4 illustrates an Ethernet LAN.

A Network

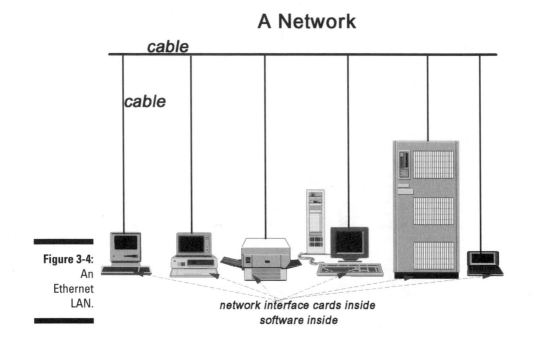

cable

cable

Figure 3-4:
An
Ethernet
LAN.

network interface cards inside
software inside

With this ring . . .

In a token ring network, the network devices are connected in a circle (ring), and a token is passed among the devices on the ring. When a device has data to send, it must first wait to get the token. Possession of the token ensures that the sending device will not be competing with any other device. If a device has nothing to send, or when it is finished sending, it passes the token. In a token ring, everyone gets an equal turn, unimpeded. Figure 3-5 shows a token-ring LAN.

Token ring versus Ethernet

First of all, whether your network runs on token ring or Ethernet technology, your data will go where it's supposed to go. The advantage of token ring is that Ethernet-style collisions do not occur, no matter how busy the network gets. On the other hand, all devices must take a turn with the token, even if they have nothing to send. So on a not-so-busy network, the devices with data to send have to wait for devices that aren't doing much besides taking the token and passing it on.

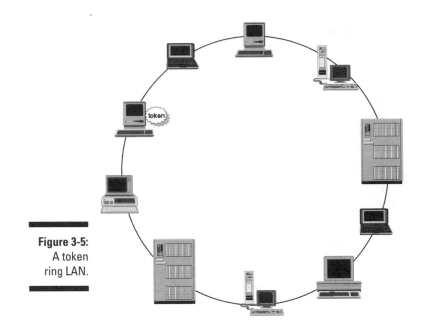

Figure 3-5:
A token
ring LAN.

So if TCP/IP isn't the issue, how *do* you pick between Ethernet and token ring?

Geez, do you really have to bother us with such a complicated question? Network design practically has its own encyclopedia, for pete's sake. OK, OK, if you insist. Listen up, now: When you're trying to pick between Ethernet and token ring, there are many factors to consider, including

✔ Total number of computers on the
   network (How big is your network?)

✔ Geographical area spanned by the
   network (How B I G is your network?)

✔ Likelihood of network failures such as
   broken cables (When an Ethernet cable
   is cut, you may still have other working
   networks in place of the original network.
   When a token ring cable is cut, you probably have one disabled token "curve.")

✔ Availability of network interface cards
   for the particular computers you're using

When all else fails, flip a coin. Or choose the technology that seems to make sense for the current problem. Who said you had to choose only one or the other? In any case, be sure to link together all of your networks!

Ethernet or token ring —
Which one for TCP/IP?

Actually, TCP/IP has nothing to do with choosing Ethernet or token ring. Remember all the good features of TCP/IP you read about in Chapter 2? Here's another one: TCP/IP runs on both of these popular network schemes. Ethernet and token ring are all about hardware. But TCP/IP is mostly about software, and it works on almost all hardware.

What Is a WAN?

What if your company has several buildings in different towns and states, or even in different countries? Does that mean that all the people who work in the company can't be on the same network because a LAN is limited by distance? Of course not. Remember The Internet? It's worldwide. You can even space out with your network by bouncing data off satellites in outer space.

A *WAN (wide area network)* spans geographical distances too large for LANs. LANs can be joined together by special-purpose hardware such as routers, bridges, and gateways, to form a WAN. See Figure 3-6.

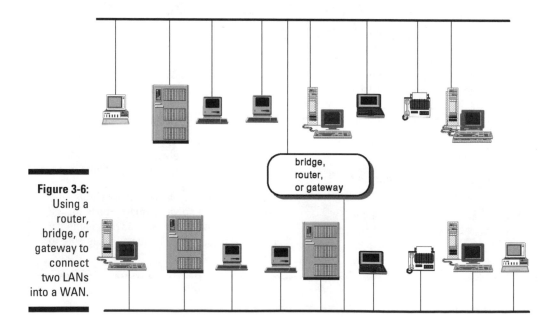

bridge,
router,
or gateway

Figure 3-6:
Using a
router,
bridge, or
gateway to
connect
two LANs
into a WAN.

Here are some other forms of WANs:

- MAN, metropolitan area network
- CAN, campus area network (but used on more than just college campuses)

LAN versus WAN — Which one for TCP/IP?

It doesn't matter. As in the question of Ethernet versus token ring, TCP/IP works for both. It can be the protocol that connects various computers on LANs as well as WANs. Your choice of network depends on the distance between the computers you want to network, not on which protocol you want to use. Remember, an internet is two or more interconnected networks, and the individual networks can be WANs, LANs, or a combination.

Mother Goose Network Services, Inc.

A *network service* is a special function available to the people on the network and their computers. You may already be familiar with some typical services, such as shared printers and e-mail.

The original design work on TCP/IP defined three categories of services, described below, which operate at specific levels of the network hierarchy. (You'll learn more about this hierarchy in Chapter 5.)

- **Connection services.** These services, operating at the lowest level of the network's hierarchy, say how data gets from one computer onto the network cable (or other connection medium), and how that data moves from the network cable to the next computer. The connection services do not guarantee that the data will arrive at the destination in the right order, or that it will even arrive at all. As strange as it seems, this unreliable communication between the computers is perfectly adequate for some applications.

- **Transport services.** These services, operating at the middle level of the network's hierarchy, augment the connection services to provide completely reliable communication between the computers. The packets are numbered to make sure the data can be placed in the right order even when the packets arrive out of sequence. The computers then perform error checking to make sure that no packets are lost or damaged.

- **Application services.** These are the functions you are probably most interested in. Application services let an application on one computer talk to a similar application on another computer, to perform tasks such as copying files. Application services, operating at the highest level of the network hierarchy, depend on connection services and transport services for reliable, efficient communication.

TCP/IP services at work

Protocols define network services. Let's use e-mail as an example. When Ms. L. BoPeep sends her message to Humpty Dumpty, TCP/IP has to tell the network devices how to do all of the following:

- Translate Mr. Humpty's name (actually, it's Humpty's computer, but let's keep this simple) to a TCP/IP format address. This is the connection service at work.

- Create the packets, and mark them "From L. BoPeep, to Humpty Dumpty." This is the transport service at work.

- Send the packets across the network. This is the connection service at work.

- Make sure the message gets to Humpty ungarbled and in one piece (well, it's not really one piece until after the packets are reassembled into the message). This is the transport service at work.

- Deliver the mail message to Mr. Humpty, himself. This is the application service at work.

Even in our elementary Mother Goose example, you can see that TCP/IP is responsible for many different network activities. That's why TCP/IP is actually a suite of many protocols, each with a specialized task to perform. You'll learn more about these tasks in Part II.

Now that you know some network essentials, we'll start to look at the advantages of TCP/IP. In the next chapter, you'll learn about clients and servers, the two most common devices on TCP/IP networks.

Chapter 4

Client/Server, Buzzword of the Century (the 20th or the 21st?)

*C*lient/server may be the computer industry buzzword of the century. Only time will tell whether it's the buzzword for the twentieth century or the twenty-first! We may not see really successful client/server solutions for a few more years, or client/server computing could turn out to be just a fad and fizzle out. So far, there is a lot of activity with a lot of promise.

As we take a look at what client/server means to a network computer user, we'll see that TCP/IP is an excellent protocol choice for client/server computing. That's because it allows so many different computers and network devices to communicate.

What Exactly Is Client/Server, Anyway?

There is no single, straightforward definition of client/server. The computer industry has wavered here, and client/server has come to mean different things to different people in different situations and at different times.

To some organizations, client/server is part of a hardware "rightsizing" plan. But does that mean downsizing from mainframe computers to smaller computers, or upsizing from personal computers to larger computers? To some other organizations, client/server is part of a software engineering plan. But is it for building applications or buying them?

Client/server computing combines traditional styles of computing into a different, distributed way of working. These traditional styles include mainframe computers and departmental minicomputers located in a central data center, non-networked PCs on people's desks, enterprise-wide databases, application programs, networking, and more.

Client/server is not defined by hardware, but by software. In the client/server game a client application on one computer requests services from a server computer. (You'll find definitions of these players later in the chapter.) There are no rules about what kind of hardware the client and server must be. You might even have a big Cray supercomputer client requesting services from a tiny little PC via some network protocol, such as TCP/IP.

So the key element in client/server computing is not hardware or even software — it's figuring out how to divide up your work and information across the network in whatever way is most appropriate for you and your organization.

What it *is*

Client/server *is*

- ✔ A style of computing. To be more specific, it's composed of various, separate technologies working together to provide a solution. These technologies include the applications, the hardware, the operating systems, and the network technologies that provide communication between the clients and the servers.

- ✔ Very popular right now. Every day, organizations are building, deploying, and evaluating client/server solutions.

- ✔ Something people think they have to have, even though they don't know what it is. That's one of the curious things about fads — the excitement is catching. (Gee, where did we put our Pet Rock? It was here a minute ago . . .)

What it *ain't*

Client/server *is not*

- ✔ The only style of computing. Mainframe computers, minicomputers, networks of personal computers, and even individual, stand-alone personal computers all still have their uses. Just because client/server is popular, it doesn't mean that these older styles are extinct.

- ✔ The best solution for everything. Sometimes people get so excited about a hot trend that they fail to determine whether the trend suits their needs. (Remember leisure suits? Back in the 1970s, most men — regardless of height, weight, or dignity — simply had to have a pastel polyester leisure suit.)

Don't Let This Happen to You

Here's a real-life example of a company that tried a client/server solution without thinking it through — and now has it stored in the back of a closet. An Information Systems manager read that client/server was the way to go, so he bought PCs to connect to his IBM mainframe that held a large database. Then he had an application developed in client/server style. Each time a user ran the client application to generate reports, the database was downloaded from the mainframe to the user's PC. The server used the mainframe only to hold the database and download it to the personal computers.

The end result was that each PC had to have enough disk space to hold the database, and all report processing was done there, on the PCs, while the mainframe sat idle. Was it really client/server? Yes, there was hardware playing the roles of server and clients. Yes, the application had a client part (the report generator) and a server part (the downloadable database).

Maybe it conformed to the letter of client/server, but it certainly did not conform to the spirit. Three factors conspired to prevent this application from being a true client/server environment:

✔ The considerable network traffic generated by all the downloads

✔ The large disk space requirements for downloading the data

✔ The lengthy report-generation time on the small PCs

The moral of this story? Just because a technology is new and popular doesn't mean that it's right for you. So stop and think before implementing new technologies. In this example, a client/server solution would have worked if the PC client was used to request a report, and if the mainframe server generated the report and sent it *(not* the whole database) back to the user at the PC.

The Server Part of Client/Server

Even though the word *client* comes first in client/server, we need to start with the definition of the *server*.

In a client/server system, a server is a computer that has a resource it can share with other computers, or a service it can perform on behalf of other computers and their users. Specifically,

A PRINT SERVER ⟶ shares ⟶ A PRINTER

A FILE SERVER ⟶ shares ⟶ DISK SPACE

A COMPUTE SERVER ⟶ shares ⟶ SPARE CPU CYCLES

Often a server is dedicated to one task only. In some very explicit configurations, the server *must* be dedicated for that purpose, either for performance or security reasons or because certain software requires it. For example, if you install Novell NetWare server software on a PC, that PC becomes a dedicated file server.

File servers: From Timbuktu to Kalamazoo

A file server shares its disk space with other computers. An advantage of having a file server, besides being able to borrow another computer's disk space, is that the shared files still look like they're on your own computer. You don't have to do anything special or different to use the files stored on a file server in your network — even if that file server is thousands of miles away in Timbuktu. Most users don't even realize they're using files that are not on their own computer.

The computers that borrow the file server's disk space are the clients. These clients may be using an operating system different from the server's and from one another's. And when you have various operating systems, you have various file formats. It's the server's job to hide those format differences from the clients.

Print servers: Closer to home

Theoretically, you could use the printer on a print server that's set up in Kalamazoo, but unless you like long commutes, it would be a pretty long walk to retrieve your printed documents. So it makes sense that print servers are most convenient if they are located geographically close to the people who use them. The print servers in a network environment make it possible for many people to share a printer, as opposed to each user's computer having its own dedicated printer.

In many offices, the printer on a print server is a fancy and powerful laser printer. The quality of personal printers, on the other hand, may range from the CEO's laser to your pathetic dot-matrix printer that jams and prints reports too faint to read even with 1,000 watts of halogen light.

File Servers and All Those Formats — How Do They Do It?

Software is what makes it all work. Say you're on a PC, where your files are in the FAT (File Allocation Table) format, and you want to use some files on a UNIX server that uses the UNIX File System. If your PC doesn't understand UNIX, how can you make any sense of the files over on the server? Easy! Software on the server translates from the server's UNIX file format to your PC's (the client) FAT format. And you never see it happen. As far as you, the client, are concerned, your file is automatically in the appropriate format for you to use. This translation is part of what is called *transparent file access* in a client/server environment.

Compute servers: Both near and far

The *idea* behind *compute servers* has actually been with us since the development of the first computers, but the term itself has only been in use a short time. A compute server is a computer that can run the program you need to run.

When computers were behemoths that filled the entire room and ran only one program at a time, you requested an appointment and physically went to the computer to run your program. Even though today's computers come in a wide variety of sizes and capabilities and most of us have one at our disposal 24 hours a day, sometimes there is still a reason to use a computer with special capabilities.

The compute server may have that expensive program you cannot afford, or that secret data that you *must not* copy, or it may simply have more disk space and power to run your program more efficiently. Traveling to the compute server is still necessary, but nowadays you can do that over the network. See Chapter 8 for more information on compute servers and "cycle stealing."

The Client Part of Client/Server

It's this simple: A *client* is a computer that borrows a resource or service from another computer.

Clients do all sorts of work, anything they want. It's not the type of work done that makes a computer a client; it's the fact that the computer is borrowing some sort of resource.

Are You Being Served?

Any computer can be

- ✔ Either a client or a server
- ✔ Both a client and a server
- ✔ Neither a client nor a server

and can change as often as necessary to provide and access any number of services.

Figure 4-1 shows an example of multiple roles: One computer provides a shared printer and is thus a print server; shares some of its disk space and files and is thus a file server; and accesses some files from another computer, thus acting as a client of another file server, as well.

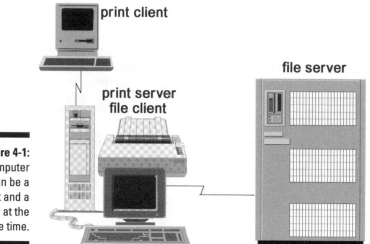

Figure 4-1:
A computer can be a client and a server at the same time.

What Does All This Have to Do with TCP/IP?

TCP/IP is one of the major enablers of client/server computing, and also one of the biggest users of it. TCP/IP's layered and modular design makes it very easy to design and implement new network services. The *peer-to-peer* nature of the computers in the client/server network means that computers can easily be servers and/or clients of these services.

In later chapters we'll look closely at the TCP/IP services that are provided by servers and consumed by clients. For now, just remember that all the members of a TCP/IP network are peers.

UNIX and TCP/IP Symbiosis

The UNIX operating system is often regarded as *the* platform for portable applications and open systems. This is because, just like TCP/IP, UNIX runs on many different types of computers.

Is Peer-to-Peer Related to Client/Server?

One of the biggest advantages of TCP/IP compared to some other network protocols is that all of the computers on the network are peers. In a peer-to-peer network, no computer is better than any other, or different from any other, at least until the system managers and users make them different. A peer-to-peer network does not *require* dedicated servers. A peer-to-peer network does *benefit* from having dedicated servers, however. Microsoft's Windows for Workgroups product is an excellent example of peer-to-peer networking. All the machines on the workgroup network are equals. They all may (and probably do) function as either clients or servers. In fact, most computers in a peer-to-peer network work simultaneously as both client *and* server. While this environment is convenient, you may find that it's not practical. What happens when your colleagues are using so much of your computer's shared disk space that there's none left for you? Do you turn off disk sharing or disconnect the network cable? You could. It's your computer, right? Before your group disintegrates into a collection of separate PCs, your group should get a dedicated file server.

Using "Client/Server" and "TCP/IP" Together in a Sentence (or, Don't Believe Everything You Hear)

Client/server and TCP/IP may seem unrelated to you — after all, client/server is a style and TCP/IP is a technology, right? Why, then, does the computer industry link the two together? Because TCP/IP is a key element of many, but not all, client/server solutions. Right or wrong, comments like the following are being uttered in settings from respected trade journals to cocktail parties.

Heard at the water cooler: *"My boss said I need to learn about TCP/IP because she wants the department to be client/server-oriented."*

Heard at a cocktail party: *"Everybody who's anybody is getting TCP/IP and client/server."*

Heard at a Jazzercise class: *"You can't have open client/server computing without TCP/IP."* (This one throws in "open" as a bonus.)

UNIX has two primary lineages:

- ✔ System V, originally developed by AT&T's Bell Laboratories
- ✔ Berkeley UNIX (BSD, Berkeley Software Distribution), from the University of California at Berkeley

Both of these derivations are UNIX systems; they're just different flavors — like dark chocolate and milk chocolate (see Figure 4-2). Chocoholics will argue over which is best, but chocolate is still chocolate (except maybe for white chocolate).

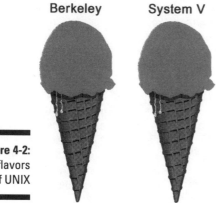

Berkeley   **System V**

Figure 4-2:
Two flavors
of UNIX

Back when DARPA was building what became The Internet, DARPA paid for the development of TCP/IP on Berkeley UNIX. The university began to use TCP/IP to connect the computers across the campus, as well as to hook up to other college and university campuses across the United States. When Ethernet was introduced in the early 1980s, TCP/IP quickly hopped on that bandwagon. Because many scientific organizations were using UNIX as their operating system, the UNIX, TCP/IP, and Ethernet combination stimulated the growth of large networks of workstations.

TCP/IP, UNIX, and networking in general have been tied together in people's minds ever since. In fact, UNIX vendors include the TCP/IP protocols as part of the operating system without extra charge. If UNIX is the parent operating system for TCP/IP, it now has many cousins who recognized a good thing. The same people who think client/server requires TCP/IP may also think it automatically requires UNIX, too. It doesn't — nevertheless, for many client/server solutions, the UNIX operating system is the right choice.

From the Littlest Laptop to the IBM Mainframe

Today, UNIX is not the only operating system that bundles TCP/IP; many vendors are including TCP/IP with their operating systems. TCP/IP is accepted as the protocol that links computers not just to each other, but to all the different computers and servers in the world, from the littlest laptop to the mighty mainframe. TCP/IP makes all of them candidates for clients or servers.

The PC TCP/IP market is growing by leaps and bounds. The International Data Corporation in Framingham, Massachusetts, cites these nifty facts:

- The number of PCs using TCP/IP grew 112% between 1992 and the end of 1993, to almost 4.5 million.
- At the end of 1994, there were about 8 million PCs using TCP/IP.

Bundles of joy: Operating systems with TCP/IP built in

Here are some of the desktop operating systems that include TCP/IP as a standard feature:

Microsoft Windows for Workgroups

Microsoft Windows for Workgroups is an extension of Microsoft Windows that lets small groups of PCs join together in a workgroup to share disks, files, and printers. The members of the workgroup can share and communicate using built-in PC protocols or TCP/IP.

Microsoft Windows NT Workstation and Server

Microsoft Windows NT is Microsoft's portable operating system for client/server computing. It comes in two flavors: Windows NT Workstation and Windows NT Server. Both have built-in TCP/IP for communicating across a LAN or WAN. With Windows NT Workstation, up to ten PCs can join together in a workgroup to share resources, as they do with Windows for Workgroups. Windows NT Server facilitates the connecting of very large numbers of PCs in a domain that is ideal for client/server and distributed computing.

Microsoft Windows 95 ("Chicago")

"Chicago" is the code name for Microsoft Windows 95, the successor to Windows 3.1 and Windows for Workgroups. Today, you still need to buy special software if you want to communicate from Windows to The Internet or any WAN. With Windows 95, TCP/IP is built in free of charge, and your personal computer can also be a member of a Microsoft Windows NT domain. Chicago also includes tools for browsing The Internet.

Macintosh System 7.5

Appletalk is the traditional networking protocol for Macintosh computers. With System 7.5, Apple Computer built in TCP/IP, as well. With TCP/IP, Mac users can connect to computers that do not speak Appletalk; they can also now connect to The Internet without paying for an extra network software package.

IBM OS/2 Warp

OS/2 is IBM's operating system for PCs that competes with Microsoft's offerings. In fact, early versions of OS/2 were developed by Microsoft for IBM. Now that Microsoft and IBM are divorced, they still talk via TCP/IP. Warp, also known as OS/2 Version 3, is the latest version of OS/2. Before Warp, the built-in protocols for OS/2 did not let you go beyond your LAN. You had to buy extra software to do wide-area communicating, including connecting to The Internet.

UNIX

Check out the "UNIX and TCP/IP Symbiosis" section earlier in this chapter.

Please Sir, May I Have Some More?

If you have an operating system or client/server solution that leaves you hungry for TCP/IP, remember that you can buy TCP/IP packages for almost any computer and operating system. For example, there are over two dozen versions of TCP/IP for Microsoft Windows. Do not despair if TCP/IP is not built in to your computer's operating system. You'll find TCP/IP vendors out there who will be glad to take your money and make your WAN connectable with TCP/IP. The hard part is deciding which vendor you want to do business with.

Oh . . . Now I Get It!

In the chapters to come, you'll study many more client/server subjects — including TCP/IP's own components, some popular services, and the basics of programming your own applications. Until then, remember that client/server is like sex:

- It's on everyone's mind most of the time.
- Everyone's talking about it.
- Everyone thinks everyone else is doing it.
- Everyone thinks they're the only ones not getting any.
- Everyone brags about their success.

Chapter 5

Luscious Layers

. . . .

In This Chapter

▶ All about OSI — the International Standards Organization's protocol for open systems

▶ The difference between OSI and TCP/IP

▶ The OSI protocol's seven-layered architecture

▶ How TCP/IP's layers compare to OSI's

. . . .

*B*efore you can really understand the components of TCP/IP, we need to show you the basis for their design. To do this, we'll compare them with the components of another standard for network architecture and protocols: OSI.

ISO OSI — Am I Dyslexic or Is That a Palindrome?

ISO, the International Standards Organization, specifies worldwide standards for different types of computing. (ISO is pronounced *eyeso* — *eyesore* without the *ore.*) ISO sets standards for networking, database access, and character sets, among other things. There are lots of other standards organizations besides ISO, by the way. One of these is ANSI, the American National Standards Institute, which often cooperates with ISO to standardize the standards!

In order to support the idea of open systems, the products of major hardware and software vendors must comply with standards. As far as networks and protocols are concerned, ISO's goal is for all vendors to use a standard network architecture for their hardware and software products, thereby making all of us network users able to communicate happily and easily regardless of what computer products we happen to have.

ISO's most visible effort in this network and protocol compatibility dream is OSI, Open Systems Interconnect, which defines a network architecture and a full set of protocols. (OSI is pronounced *oh ess eye.* Very often it is referred to as ISO OSI, pronounced *eyeso oh ess eye.* We know it's not consistent, but don't blame us.) You first read about OSI in Chapter 2.

The ImpOSIble Dream?

Not surprisingly, attaining this dream of overall compatibility has been somewhat difficult to bring about. Maybe ISO should have named itself Parad*ISO*, after its goal!

ISO is not the first organization to define a network architecture — sometimes called a *model* — and protocols to go with it. Indeed, listed in Table 5-1 are three names we think will sound vaguely familiar to you, and the proprietary network architectures and protocols they defined for themselves.

Table 5-1: Some Vendor-Defined Protocols

Vendor	Architecture/Protocol
IBM	System Network Architecture (SNA)
Digital Equipment Corp.	Digital Network Architecture and DECnet
Apple Computer	AppleTalk

The difference between these vendor-defined standards and those of the ISO is that the ISO OSI (have your eyes crossed yet?) enables *interoperability* between the various vendors. The goal of ISO's interoperability standards is to allow all parts of your network to work together, regardless of which suppliers you bought them from. Toward this goal, OSI divides network functions into layers and specifies how the layers should interact. Theoretically, then, OSI is blissful Paradise for network users.

Okay, so far this makes sense. Even the United States government liked OSI. (Maybe we should have worried when we heard that.) As mentioned in Chapter 2, the U.S. government first became interested in using OSI to connect government installations. The government's OSI profile was called GOSIP.

But in the late 1970s, when ISO was just beginning to recommend the development of OSI as a standard for multivendor networking, TCP/IP had already been in use for years (for the federal government as well as others), as a standard on the ARPANET and the other networks around the world that evolved into The Internet.

Trouble in ParadISO?

Today, very little of OSI is in production as compared to TCP/IP. One reason is that the OSI specification is extremely complicated, and it's taking too long to implement all the functionality. Another reason is that TCP/IP is already here and in use. During the long (and seemingly never-ending) trip to ParadISO, people realized that their computers could work together by using TCP/IP's set of already existing protocols.

The United States government was one of the last groups to figure this out, but now — having been communicating via TCP/IP for years — they are recommending TCP/IP as an alternative to the OSI network protocols. They've decided to let TCP/IP be a standard, as well.

Taking a Modular Approach to Networking

The best things to come out of OSI, so far, are its aim to support very large networks without running out of addresses, and the idea of a structured, layered network model. We can thank ISO for clearly delineating network layers and services through which applications, especially client/server applications, can communicate. When the OSI model was born, it defined the "right" way to design network protocols and applications, and in this case, "right" meant *modular*.

TCP/IP, as well, uses the concept of layers. Indeed, its notion of five layers predates the ISO OSI Reference Model (see next section) by nearly 10 years, but TCP/IP's concept wasn't firmly entrenched. Today, new developments in TCP/IP follow the OSI example of modular layers and clean interfaces. Internet committees that direct the evolution of TCP/IP watch ISO's efforts and the OSI Reference Model's layered approach. IPng borrows some of OSI's goals and plans.

The ISO OSI seven-layer cake

There are seven layers in what is officially called the ISO OSI Reference Model. We, however, are predisposed to more satisfying things like desserts and snacks, so we call it a *seven-layer cake*.

Each layer of the cake depends on the layers below it; that is, each layer provides services to the layer above it. When two peer computers are communicating, each computer has its own set of layers. When you send a message to another computer on the network, your data starts at the top layer of your computer, travels down all the layers to the bottom of the cake, and jumps across to the other computer. When your data gets to the other computer, it starts at the bottom layer and moves up the cake to the application in the top layer. Technically, the seven layers are called a *stack*. Figure 5-1 illustrates these layers.

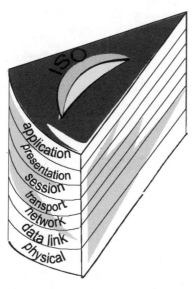

Figure 5-1: In the ISO OSI Reference Model, messages eat their way through the seven-layer cake.

What are all these layers for?

Creamy white cake, raspberry filling, sugary frosting . . . mmmmmm . . . er, sorry. You wanted to know what the layers are for, didn't you. Here we go: Each layer has a special function. The lowest layers are hardware oriented. The highest layer does user stuff, such as e-mail and file transfers. Starting with Layer 1 at the bottom of the cake, let's examine each layer.

Layer 1: The physical layer

The physical layer is pure hardware, including the cable, satellite, or other connection medium, and the network interface card. This is where electrical signals move around, and we try not to think too hard about how it works.

Layer 2: The data link layer

This is another layer we don't want to strain our brains trying to figure out. Again, hardware is involved. This is the layer that splits your data into packets to be sent across the connection medium. Here's where Ethernet or token ring wiring get handled. Once the data is on the wire, the data link layer handles any interference. If there is heavy sunspot activity, the data link layer works hard to make sure the interference does not garble the electric signals.

Sunspot activity and solar flares tend to disturb all sorts of transmissions, not just network signals. Your cellular telephone and television reception, for example, can degrade during solar episodes. Even with cable TV, the television channels still have to be broadcast from the networks to your cable company. Wouldn't it be nice if television broadcasts had a data link layer like ISO OSI's to fix the poor reception? ■

Layer 3: The network layer

Here's the first place on the OSI Model where a TCP/IP protocol fits into the equation. IP is the TCP/IP protocol that works at this layer. This layer gets packets from the data link layer (Layer 2) and sends them to the correct network address. If more than one possible route is available for your data to travel, the network layer figures out the best route. Without this layer, your data would never get to the right place.

Layer 4: The transport layer

Though the network layer routes your data to its destination, it cannot guarantee that the packets holding your data will arrive in the correct order or that they won't have picked up any errors during transmission. That's the transport layer's job. TCP is one of the TCP/IP protocols that work at the transport layer; UDP is another one. (Chapter 6 explains what these protocols do.) The transport layer makes sure that your packets have no errors and that all the packets arrive and are in the correct order. Without this layer, you couldn't trust your network.

Layer 5: The session layer

The other protocols that make up TCP/IP sit here on Layer 5 and above. This layer establishes and coordinates a *session*, which is simply the name for a connection between two computers. You have to have a session before two computers can even think about actually moving data between them.

Layer 6: The presentation layer

The presentation layer works with the operating system and file system. Here's where files get converted from one format to another, if the server and client use different formats. Without the presentation layer, file transfer would be restricted to computers with the same file format.

Layer 7: The application layer

This is the layer where you do your work, such as sending e-mail or requesting to transfer a file across the network. Without the application layer, you couldn't create any messages or data to send, and your computer wouldn't know what to do with any data that someone else sent you.

Fitting TCP/IP into the Seven-Layer Cake Format

The protocols of TCP/IP stack up in layers, too, similar to the OSI Reference Model. But TCP/IP has fewer layers. As you can see in Figure 5-2, the TCP/IP cake is five layers high. Notice that the fifth (top) layer is a rich one. Though it's called the application layer, it combines OSI's session, presentation, and application layers. TCP/IP's third layer is The Internet layer, but it's analogous to OSI's network layer.

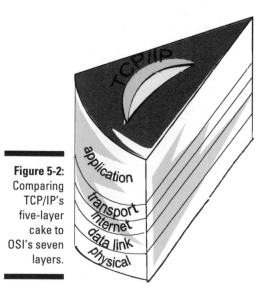

Figure 5-2:
Comparing
TCP/IP's
five-layer
cake to
OSI's seven
layers.

The ISO OSI's physical and data link layers are included in the TCP/IP layer cake in Figure 5-2, even though they have nothing to do with TCP/IP. TCP/IP is software that is independent of the underlying hardware, but we didn't want you to forget that the hardware is still part of the total solution.

We all know that cake alone is yummy but not very nutritious. For the main course, from soup to nuts, read Part II, where we explain the set of TCP/IP protocols and show the many applications that run over those protocols. That way you'll have a healthy, balanced meal.

The 5th Wave   By Rich Tennant

"NO SIR, THIS ISN'T A DATING SERVICE. THEY INTRODUCE PEOPLE THROUGH A COMPUTER SO THEY CAN TALK TO EACH OTHER IN PERSON. WE INTRODUCE PEOPLE IN PERSON SO THEY CAN TALK TO EACH OTHER THROUGH A COMPUTER."

Part II

TCP/IP from Soup to Nuts to Dessert

The 5th Wave — By Rich Tennant

"WE SORT OF HAVE OUR OWN WAY OF PREDICTING NETWORK PROBLEMS."

In This Part...

Hold on to your forks! Part II delves into the ingredients of the TCP/IP suite: the protocols themselves. You'll see how the protocols fit into the network layer cake and get a chance to become familiar with most of them. Using the TCP/IP "dinnerware" you'll be able to serve up The Internet's goodies. With TCP/IP applications and protocols you can take advantage of everything from reading news to exchanging e-mail and online conversation with other users to copying good stuff like games, technical articles, and even TCP/IP itself.

Is your computer underpowered? In this part you'll learn how you can "borrow" processing power from across the network. It's a piece of cake!

Last but not least, you'll find out how The Internet uses TCP/IP to organize its own client/server structure.

Chapter 6

Do You Have a Complete Set of TCP/IP Dinnerware?

In This Chapter

▶ Most of what you need to know about protocols but were afraid to ask

▶ How many protocols are there in TCP/IP, and what do they do?

As you learned in Chapter 1, a protocol is the set of agreed-upon practices, policies, and procedures used for communication. In this book, we're concerned with TCP/IP as the protocol for communication between two or more computers. But TCP/IP is actually a large suite of pieces that work together.

The TCP/IP Protocol Suite

What's a suite, you ask? In a hotel, a suite is a collection of rooms that are treated as a single unit. Similarly, the TCP/IP suite is a collection of protocols, named after two of the original pieces, TCP and IP.

Now you might say, "A suite is too big. Can I just rent a room?" Nope. Sorry. The protocols in the TCP/IP suite move the data from one network layer to another and interact with one another. You couldn't really have a functional network with just one of the TCP/IP protocols.

Remember the layer cakes from Chapter 5? Figure 6-1 shows the TCP/IP five-layer cake with some of the protocols drawn on the layers. You don't need every protocol on the cake to run a network application, but you need at least a taste from each layer. So even though you may not use all the rooms in the suite, you will definitely need more than one.

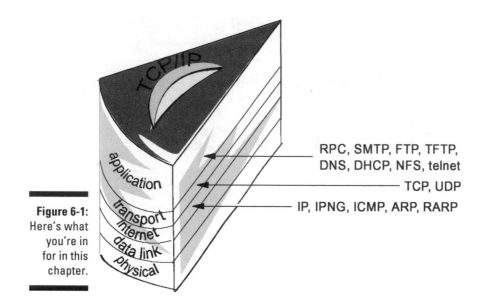

RPC, SMTP, FTP, TFTP,
DNS, DHCP, NFS, telnet

————————— TCP, UDP

————————— IP, IPNG, ICMP, ARP, RARP

Figure 6-1:
Here's what
you're in
for in this
chapter.

Getting the picture? Good, but don't get too pleased with yourself — this is as far as we're going in comparing TCP/IP to a hotel room. That's because you need to know that there's more to TCP/IP than just TCP and IP. To help you understand, we're going for an analogy that will let you compare all the pieces to something more familiar. Read on . . .

Many people try to compare the TCP/IP protocol to a Swiss Army knife, which has cutting blades of various sizes, a corkscrew, scissors, nail file, and so on. The analogy works pretty well except for one thing. The really cool Swiss Army knives, with all those clever and handy pieces, are too big to have with you all the time. The first thing they'll do is poke a hole in your pocket!

So we have a different analogy for you. TCP/IP is like a complete set of dinnerware: plates, bowls, glasses, forks, spoons, and yes, even knives. And TCP/IP continues to expand, which means we can also include cups and saucers, wine glasses, the cream pitcher, finger bowls, and matching salt and pepper shakers. When we say complete, we mean complete!

Okay, okay. We're getting carried away with the dinnerware idea, maybe. We suspect you probably eat off paper plates as often as we do. But TCP/IP doesn't know or care whether your plates are paper, stoneware, or bone china. A plate is a plate.

TCP/IP bowls you over

Many pieces of the TCP/IP suite function as protocols, applications, *and* services (Figure 6-2). In this and the next six chapters, as we talk about all the great things you can do with TCP/IP, we'll keep you well informed of whether you're using a TCP/IP protocol, a network service, or an application — and highlight the places where the same name applies to one or more of these things.

To kick off the TCP/IP dinnerware analogy, imagine a large bowl. That one bowl can be used in various roles, in more than one room:

✔ To mix a cake batter (a mixing bowl in the kitchen)

✔ To hold Seinfeld-sized portions of your favorite cereal, or tonight's soup, or the cat's dinner (a serving bowl in the dining room)

✔ To hold flowers (a vase in the living room)

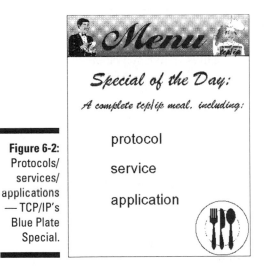

Figure 6-2:
Protocols/
services/
applications
— TCP/IP's
Blue Plate
Special.

TCP/IP's modular, layered design makes it easy to innovate and add new components. If you envision a new network service, as you go about designing the server and client applications, you can simultaneously design a new protocol to add to the TCP/IP suite. The protocol will enable the server application to offer the service and will let the client application consume that service. This elegant simplicity is a key advantage of TCP/IP.

When you do create a new protocol/application/service combination for your network, be sure to follow the RFC (Request For Comments) process described in Chapter 2. Follow the instructions in Appendix A, and get a copy of RFC 1543, "Instructions to RFC Authors." ■

Protocol . . . application . . . service . . . What's the difference?

In the fabric of a network, you'll find the protocol/application/service relationship is so tightly woven together that it may be very difficult to distinguish the threads in the cloth. Let's use FTP as an example. FTP stands for file transfer protocol, but it's not just a protocol. FTP is also a service and an application. The FTP service, application, and protocol work together so that you can move files around the network.

✔ FTP is a *service* for copying files. You connect to a remote computer offering this service, and you are able to "pull" and "push" files from or to that computer.

✔ FTP is also an *application* for copying files. You run a client application on your local computer to contact the FTP server application on the remote computer. Your client application is usually called FTP, the file transfer *program*. The server application is often called FTPD, the file transfer protocol *daemon*. (The term daemon comes from UNIX. Think of friendly demons haunting the computer to act on your behalf.) You tell the client what you want to do — pull or push files — and it works with the server to copy the files.

✔ Finally, FTP is a *protocol* for copying files. The client and server applications both use it for communication to ensure that the new copy of the file is, bit for bit and byte for byte, identical to the original.

So FTP is three, three, three things at once! Most of the time you'll know from the context whether someone is referring to the service, the application, or the protocol. If you can't quite tell, maybe it doesn't really matter.

And now, on to the protocols!

The Protocols (And You Thought There Were Only Two!)

Hold on tight, here come the pieces in the TCP/IP protocol suite, listed in no particular order.

IP: Internet Protocol

The Internet Protocol, IP, is responsible for basic network connectivity. IP is the plate in a basic place setting. When you're eating, you need a plate to hold your food. When you're networking, you need a place to put (send and receive) data — that place is a network address.

The core of IP works with internet addresses (you'll find the details about these addresses in Chapter 13). Every computer on a TCP/IP network must have a numeric address. The IP on your computer understands how and where to send messages to these addresses.

While IP is taking care of addressing, there's a lot more to do to make sure that your data gets to where it's going, correctly and in one piece. IP doesn't know or care when a packet gets lost and doesn't arrive. So, we need some other protocols to ensure that no packets and data are lost, and that those packets are in the right order.

TCP: Transmission Control Protocol

Once the food is on your plate, you need something to get it into your mouth without dropping it all over your lap. In our place setting, this is the spoon. Yeah, sure, you *could* use a fork, and some of you can probably even eat your peas from a knife without losing any, but a spoon is the most reliable implement for most foods. Try eating soup with a fork!

TCP, the Transmission Control Protocol, is our network spoon. No matter what kind of data you have, TCP makes sure that nothing is dropped. TCP uses IP to deliver packets to those upper-layer applications and provides a reliable stream of data among computers on the network. Error checking and sequence numbering are two of TCP's more important functions. Once a packet arrives at the correct IP address, TCP goes to work. On both the sending and receiving computers, it establishes a dialog to communicate about the data that is being transmitted. TCP is said to be "connection oriented," because it tells the network to resend lost data.

Theoretically, you could have TCP without IP. Some other network mechanism besides IP could deliver the data to an address, and TCP could still verify and sequence that data. But in practice, TCP is always used with IP.

UDP: User Datagram Protocol

As mentioned just above, your TCP network spoon does the best job on that homemade cream of mushroom soup. In contrast, the User Datagram Protocol,

You've Got to Have Connections . . . Or Do You?

TCP/IP communicates among the layers in different ways. These methods are either *connectionless* or *connection oriented*.

Connection oriented communication is reliable and pretty easy to understand. When two computers are communicating with each other, they "connect." Each understands what the other one is doing. The sending computer lets the receiving computer know that data is on the way. The recipient acknowledges receipt of the data (called *ACKs* for short) or denies receipt of the data (negatively acknowledges, or *NACKs*). This ACKing and NACKing is called *handshaking*.

Suppose you send a fax to your friend Ken in Tokyo. If you want to be sure he gets it, you might call and say, "I'm faxing you the baseball results now. Call me when you get it." Once the fax comes in and Ken checks it over to make sure it is readable, he calls you and says, "Thanks. I'm thrilled to hear that the Cubs won the World Series." That's connection-oriented communication.

But suppose you send the fax without first notifying your friend. And, for some reason, it never gets there. Ken doesn't know to expect anything, so he doesn't know that anything is lost. That's *connectionless* communication. When connectionless data are sent, the computers involved know nothing about each other or the data being sent. If you're on the receiving end, no one tells you that you're about to get anything. If you're sending data, no one bothers to mention whether or not they got it or if it was totally garbled.

With this in mind, you might wonder why any data communications would be done in connectionless mode. But there's a time and place for everything. First of all, communication is faster without the ACKs and NACKs. Secondly, not every network message needs to be as accurate as your e-mail. Finally, some applications do their own error checking and reliability processing, so they don't need the connection-oriented overhead of TCP.

UDP, is like your fork. You can do a pretty good job of cleaning your plate with a fork, and though it's not as reliable as TCP, UDP nevertheless gets a lot of data across the network.

UDP uses IP to deliver packets to upper-layer applications and provides a flow of data among computers. UDP provides neither error checking nor sequence numbering, although these features can be added by the application that has chosen to use UDP. This protocol is said to be "connectionless," because it does not provide for resending data in case of error.

UDP is used by the Network File System (NFS), the Domain Name System (DNS), and the Remote Procedure Call (RPC) application programming interface. These are discussed in detail in Chapters 10, 11, and 20, respectively.

Figure 6-3 shows the relationship between IP, TCP, and UDP, and the applications at the upper layers. All the applications shown are provided with TCP/IP. If you write your own TCP/IP applications, you can draw those in on the picture, too.

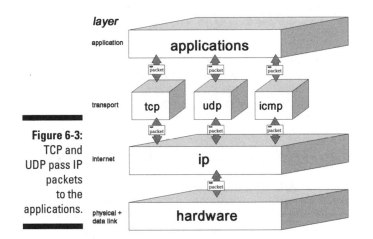

Figure 6-3:
TCP and
UDP pass IP
packets
to the
applications.

ICMP: Internet Control Message Protocol

The Internet Control Message Protocol, ICMP, reports problems and relays other network specific information, such as an error status from some network device. IP detects the error and passes it to ICMP. A very common use of ICMP is the echo request generated by the Ping command (see Figure 6-4).

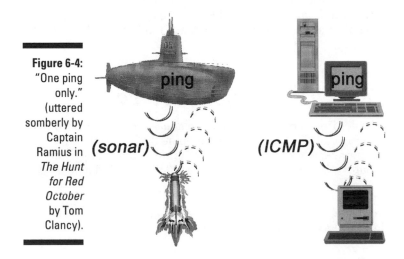

Figure 6-4:
"One ping
only."
(uttered
somberly by
Captain
Ramius in
*The Hunt
for Red
October*
by Tom
Clancy).

ICMP is like your crystal water glass, the one that "pings" so nicely when you accidentally hit it with the fork you're waving around to emphasize your point in that argument about the greenhouse effect.

ARP: Address Resolution Protocol

When all you know is the TCP/IP address of the remote computer, it's the job of the Address Resolution Protocol, ARP, to find that computer's network interface card hardware address. ARP is like your salad plate. With its load of addresses for the devices on the network, ARP is closely allied with IP, the dinner plate. (See Chapter 13 for more on TCP/IP addresses.)

RARP: Reverse Address Resolution Protocol

When all you know is the network interface card hardware address of a remote computer, the Reverse Address Resolution Protocol, RARP, will find the computer's TCP/IP address. RARP is your salad fork, because it goes with your salad plate. We don't mean to suggest any relationship to the UDP dinner fork, however. Hey, there are places where we have to stretch the analogy a little, okay?

FTP: File Transfer Protocol

The File Transfer Protocol, FTP, is like your knife. Not a special steak knife or a little butter knife, just the regular dinner knife. It's FTP that helps you copy files between two computers. You use your FTP knife to either "pull" the files from the remote computer (known as *downloading*) or "push" them to the remote computer (known as *uploading*). As described earlier in this chapter, FTP is also the name of an application and a service, so we'll be looking at it again (and again).

TFTP: Trivial File Transfer Protocol

The Trivial File Transfer Protocol, TFTP, is used to *down-line load* files from a TFTP server. Another use of TFTP is in Digital Equipment Corporation's remote installation service, where you install a computer's operating system from another computer's files via the TFTP protocol. This is called a *network installation*.

TFTP is your butter knife, a smaller version of the FTP dinner knife. You can see why we needed to be a little specific about your FTP knife.

SMTP: Simple Mail Transfer Protocol

The Simple Mail Transfer Protocol, SMTP, transfers e-mail messages among computers. The messages may go directly from the sender's computer to the recipient's, or the messages may proceed through intermediary computers in a process known as *store and forward*.

SMTP is like your wine goblet. Again, a disclaimer is in order: We don't mean to suggest any relationship to the ICMP water glass, which you managed to knock over anyway as that discussion heated up.

E-mail, of course, is one of the Big 3 network applications (along with file transfer and signing on to remote computers), and many vendors have their own mail protocols. SMTP is the mail transfer protocol for The Internet. UNIX mail understands SMTP, but other operating systems do not. When users of SMTP-ignorant computers need to get out to the outside world, aka The Internet, a special SMTP gateway must be established for that communication.

Chapter 7 tells you more about SMTP gateways and e-mail in general. ∎

NTP: Network Time Protocol

The time-of-day clocks that computers maintain are synchronized by the Network Time Protocol, NTP. Time-stamping is important in all sorts of applications, providing everything from document creation dates to network routing date/time information. NTP gets the time data from a time-server computer, which gets it from an official source, such as the United States National Institute of Standards and Technology. In continental Europe, ISO provides a time service used with banking transactions and stock transfers.

NTP is like your seafood fork. You know, the tiny one you use (or try to, anyway) to get the lobster meat out of the claw. NTP is a special-purpose tool, just right for the job it's made for.

NNTP: Network News Transfer Protocol

NNTP, for Network News Transfer Protocol, enables the efficient transfer of articles between news servers, and between a news server and its news clients. NNTP is the gravy boat; it's perfectly shaped to handily carry a lot of stuff that can get really messy.

BOOTP: Boot Protocol

When you acquire a new computer, it needs an operating system. If the computer has no disks for storage, you can download the operating system into your computer's memory from another computer on the network. When you do, your diskless computer uses the Boot Protocol, BOOTP, to load its operating system (or other stand-alone application) via the network. *Booting* means loading the operating system.

If you do have disk storage on your new computer, you should install your own local operating system. Some vendors, Digital Equipment Corporation, for instance, let you perform a remote installation from another computer on the network. The remote installation copies all the operating system files to your computer's disk; from that point on, you can boot the operating system locally.

BOOTP is the carving knife you need to slice the roast beef. And this time we *do* mean to suggest a relationship to FTP, your dinner knife, and to TFTP, your butter knife, because all these "knives" move files around the network.

RIP, OSPF: Numerous Gateway (Router) Protocols

Under your network place settings are a tablecloth made of gateways and routers, which have various gateway and router protocols to allow them to exchange network topology and status information. Here are the two most popular ones:

- Routing Information Protocol, RIP
- Open Shortest Path First, OSPF

Chapter 18, "The Dreaded Hardware Chapter," has much more on gateways, routers, and other hardware devices.

DHCP: Dynamic Host Configuration Protocol

We couldn't not consider you housekeeping haters out there in putting together the TCP/IP dinnerware. We knew you'd want a recyclable paper plate. DHCP, the Dynamic Host Configuration Protocol, is that paper plate. This protocol is a client/server solution for sharing numeric IP addresses.

The DHCP paper plate (a DHCP server) maintains a pool of shared addresses — and those addresses are recyclable. When a DHCP client computer wants to use a TCP/IP application, that client must first request an IP address from the DHCP server. The server checks the shared supply, and if all the addresses are in use, the client is notified that it must wait until another client finishes its work and releases an IP address. If an address is available, the DHCP server sends a response to the client that contains the address.

This shared-supply approach makes sense in environments where computers don't use TCP/IP applications all the time, or where there are not enough addresses available for all the computers that want them.

And Many, Many More . . .

There are many more pieces of TCP/IP, and new ones are being developed this very minute! The ones described in this chapter are the most important, the most visible, and the most common.

And now, starting in the next chapter, we look at the wonderful things you can do with TCP/IP.

Chapter 7

E-Mail and Beyond — Shipping and Handling Included

. . . .

In This Chapter

▶ E-mail: Is it a TCP/IP application or not?

▶ How to find out someone's e-mail address

▶ How to have aliases without getting your picture on the wall in the police station

▶ What SMTP (Simple Mail Transfer Protocol) does to/for your messages

▶ When do you need to install an SMTP gateway?

▶ Using MIME to pretty up a basic e-mail message

▶ Online newsgroups and chatting: How to spend all your waking hours hanging out on The Internet

. . . .

*A*t the restaurant at the end of the network, the e-mail, file transfer, and remote login choices are the Big 3 favorites on the TCP/IP plate. And of these, e-mail is the most popular. In this chapter we'll find out more about the e-mail banquet — it has several courses.

But before we do, let's get some education on the difference between a plain-vanilla application and a TCP/IP application.

The Medium Is the Message (Sometimes)

When we talk about services and applications in this chapter, remember that we are talking about TCP/IP services and applications for the most part. It's important to understand what is and what is not a TCP/IP application. It may be different from what you think.

Let's use e-mail as an example. When you start a session to compose and send an e-mail message, the program you use to *create* the message is an application, but not a TCP/IP application. In modern e-mail terminology, you are using a *mail user agent* (MUA) to create your message. The UNIX applications called mail and Mail are examples of MUAs. Because the UNIX operating system is case sensitive, mail and Mail are two different programs.

When you *send* the e-mail message, the MUA hands it to a *mail transfer agent* (MTA). Sendmail, with implementations for various operating systems, is the most common MTA. The MTA is the TCP/IP application, and it uses the TCP/IP protocol SMTP (Simple Mail Transfer Protocol). The MTA takes responsibility for delivery of the message and passes it to another MTA. The message moves from MTA to MTA until it gets to the addressee's computer. The addressee then uses the MUA to read the message.

The communication between an MUA and an MTA does not have to be and is usually not TCP/IP, but the communication between MUAs is. Figure 7-1 illustrates the relationship between the MUA, MTA, and the SMTP protocol.

Remember, the SMTP protocol and all the other protocols in the TCP/IP suite are described in Chapter 6. ∎

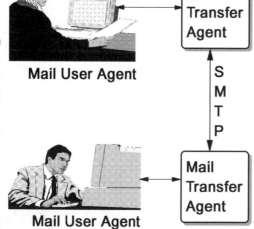

Figure 7-1: Neither rain nor snow nor gloom of night can stop the mail user agents (MUAs) and mail transfer agents (MTAs).

Mail User Agent

Mail Transfer Agent

Mail User Agent

Mail Transfer Agent

S
M
T
P

Call my medium

There are many different mail user agents available, including some that are free (public domain). The UNIX operating system has included an e-mail system since day one, and some of the popular MUAs on UNIX are mail, Mail, and mailx. (Note that, since UNIX is case sensitive, mail and Mail are two different MUAs.)

Several other operating systems, such as Microsoft Windows for Workgroups, include e-mail. Other vendors' software products, such as Lotus cc:Mail, bring the joy of e-mail to the operating systems that don't include it, as well as providing alternatives for those that do.

It doesn't matter whether your MUA is a UNIX application, a Microsoft Windows application, an X Window System application, a Macintosh application, or any other vendor's application. Just remember that whatever e-mail application you choose to use has the ability to talk to the TCP/IP application and protocol. The TCP/IP applications, which you can't see, are those other agents, the MTAs.

Casper, the friendly MTA

Now don't get nervous here. It's okay that the mail transfer agents and TCP/IP are invisible to you. Your MUA can see the TCP/IP application and service and that's what matters. Think of TCP/IP as a friendly ghost, only visible to certain beings. You can't see the ghost with your eyes, but you can communicate with it through your MUA medium.

So e-mail is a kind of electronic seance, where you need an intermediary to get you to TCP/IP. This paranormal approach is not true of every application. You do have direct contact with certain TCP/IP applications, such as FTP. Whether you get to talk to TCP/IP directly or have to go through a medium depends on what you are trying to do (e-mail or file transfer or something else).

And Now . . . On to the Restaurant at the End of the Network

Once you get started with e-mail — Number 1 of the Big 3 — you'll wonder how you ever lived without it. You'll complain every time you have to pick up a pen and paper to write a real, old-fashioned letter. Okay, so you don't write letters anyway, but aren't those *#!*@$&% long-distance telephone charges annoying! (When *will* our parents get on The Internet?!)

One other thing before we dive into the e-mail banquet: We've warned you before that talking about TCP/IP without talking about The Internet is impossible — it would be like discussing gasoline without talking about cars. So again in this chapter you'll find lots of references to The Internet as we describe the things that TCP/IP lets you do.

The E-mail Course at the TCP/IP Banquet

Electronic mail is the first network application most people meet. (File sharing is the other contender for this prize, but sometimes people don't realize file sharing is even happening, much less that it's a network service.) E-mail has been around so long that many of us forget some folks still don't have it yet.

So let's take a look at everything in the e-mail banquet. And wait 'til you read about MIME, a delicious dessert TCP/IP gives you — at no extra charge.

E-mail addresses: @ marks the spot

To send or receive e-mail, you and your correspondent each need to have an e-mail address. (You first saw an e-mail address in this book in Chapter 2.) These addresses take the form

```
username@address
```

The first part, *username,* is a username on a computer. The @ character is always there. Then comes the address: the computer name and some information about the computer's location on the network, separated by periods. Here's a sample (fictitious) e-mail address:

```
smith@abc.university.edu
```

In this address, *smith* is the username, *abc* is the computer name, *university* is where the computer is located, and *edu* is a domain name that represents educational institutions.

Don't worry yet about all these pieces of the address. Chapter 13 explains all you need to know about Internet addresses and domains.

How can I find out someone's e-mail address?

Looking up someone's e-mail address is similar to finding a home address. Wanna take a date to the e-mail banquet? You have several choices for getting hold of that person, and sometimes the simplest way is the best. Here are some ways you can find out where that smart-looking redhead with the cool tortoise shell eyeglasses lives on The Internet:

1. Use the telephone. Sometimes the phone number is right there on the person's business card. Or you might even find it in the phone book or by calling Directory Assistance (though this last alternative costs a quarter in the United States! %!@$*#!&$!).

2. Get the e-mail address from an e-mail message sent by the cute redhead to you or someone you know. The sender's address is there. If you don't believe us, go read it again and see.

3. Look up the redhead electronically in The Internet phone book, which is maintained by the InterNIC — the Internet information center we told you about in Chapter 2. Not everyone is listed (see the next section), but it may be worth checking. Figure 7-2 shows a session with the InterNIC. We connected with the telnet command (more on telnet in Chapter 8), and used the whois command to look up the addresses for the InterNIC itself and a major online service.

4. Politely ask the appropriate postmaster — each electronic organization has one. The postmaster is responsible for managing the e-mail environment, and is normally very busy, but a friendly request for assistance may get you the address you need.

Who's more important, Bill Clinton or Bill Gates?

Not everyone on The Internet is registered in the InterNIC directories referred to in choice #3 above. For example, the President of the United States is at president@whitehouse.gov, but we could not find him in the InterNIC directory. On the other hand, when you use the whois command to look people up, you might have to page through dozens of entries. Try looking up the name Bill with whois, and you'll find over 140 entries for various people and organizations named Bill, but not a thing for a certain bespectacled young billionaire, bill@microsoft.com. And nothing for Bill Clinton, either. Does this mean that these two people are equally important? Or unimportant?

When using the InterNIC, we suggest you stay flexible and keep trying! ■

SMTP: The Meat and Potatoes

As you have read, SMTP (Simple Mail Transfer Protocol) is the part of the TCP/IP protocol suite that MTAs use to communicate. SMTP defines how messages move from one computer's MTA to another's MTA, but not what path each message takes. A message may go directly from the sender's computer to the recipient's, or it may proceed through intermediary computers, via the *store and forward* process.

```
leiden@max: ~ $ telnet internic.net
Trying 198.41.0.5...
Connected to internic.net.
Escape character is '^]'.

SunOS UNIX 4.1 (rs) (ttyp0)

*************************************************************************
* -- InterNIC Registration Services Center --
*
* For wais, type:              WAIS <search string> <return>
* For the *original* whois type:  WHOIS [search string] <return>
* For referral whois type:     RWHOIS [search string] <return>
*
* For user assistance call (703) 742-4777
# Questions/Updates on the whois database to HOSTMASTER@internic.net
* Please report system problems to ACTION@internic.net
*************************************************************************
Please be advised that use constitutes consent to monitoring
(Elec Comm Priv Act, 18 USC 2701-2711)

6/1/94
We are offering an experimental distributed whois service called referral
whois (RWhois). To find out more, look for RWhois documents, a sample
client and server under:
gopher: (rs.internic.net) InterNIC Registration Services ->
        InterNIC Registration Archives -> pub -> rwhois
anonymous ftp: (rs.internic.net) /pub/rwhois
Cmdinter Ver 1.3 Tue Apr 25 22:36:15 1995 EST
[vt100] InterNIC > whois internic
Connecting to the rs Database . . . . . .
Connected to the rs Database
InterNIC Registration (INTERNIC-BLK) INTERNIC-BLK1  198.0.0.0 - 198.255.255.0
InterNIC Registration (NETBLK-INTERNIC-BLK4) INTERNIC-BLK4
                                             206.0.0.0 - 206.255.255.0
Whois: whois internic-blk
InterNIC Registration (INTERNIC-BLK)
    Network Solutions
    505 Huntmar Park Drive
    Herndon, VA 22070

    Netname: INTERNIC-BLK1
    Netblock: 198.0.0.0 - 198.255.255.0

    Coordinator:
        Network Solutions, Inc.  (HOSTMASTER)  HOSTMASTER@INTERNIC.NET
        (703) 742-4777 (FAX) (703) 742-4811

    Record last updated on 18-Jan-95.
Whois: whois compuserve
CompuServe Incorporated (COMPUSERVE2-DOM)                  COMPUSERVE.NET
CompuServe Incorporated (NET-COMPUSERVE) COMPUSERVE          149.174.0.0
CompuServe Incorporated (NET-COMPUSERVE-NET) COMPUSERVE-NET1   198.4.4.0
CompuServe Incorporated (NET-COMPUSERVE-NET2) COMPUSERVE-NET2  198.4.5.0
CompuServe Incorporated (NET-COMPUSERVE-NET3) COMPUSERVE-NET3  198.4.6.0
There are 10 more matches.  Show them? y
CompuServe Incorporated (NET-COMPUSERVE-NET4) COMPUSERVE-NET4  198.4.7.0
CompuServe Incorporated (NET-COMPUSERVE-NET5) COMPUSERVE-NET5  198.4.8.0
CompuServe Incorporated (NET-COMPUSERVE-NET6) COMPUSERVE-NET6  198.4.9.0
CompuServe Incorporated (NET-COMPUSERVE-NET7) COMPUSERVE-NET7  198.4.10.0
CompuServe Incorporated (NET-COMPUSERVE-NET8) COMPUSERVE-NET8  198.4.11.0
CompuServe Incorporated (NETBLK-COMPUSERVE-BLK) COMPUSERVE-BLK
                                      205.156.192.0 - 205.156.223.0
CompuServe, Inc. (COMPUSERVE-DOM)                          COMPUSERVE.COM
CompuServe, Incorporated (ASN-COMPUSERVE) COMPUSERVE                4183
Compuserve Incorporated (DUB-IMG--HST) DUB-IMG-1.COMPUSERVE.COM  198.4.9.1
Tsohan, Colleen (CT00)        Compuserve@75310            415-445-6403
Whois:
```

Figure 7-2:
Contacting
the InterNIC
to find an
e-mail
address.

In store and forward, as each message travels through the network on the way to its destination, it may pass through any number of intermediate computers, where it is briefly stored before being sent on to the next computer in the path. This is sort of like a weary traveler stopping to rest occasionally before continuing the trip across the network galaxy (Figure 7-3).

The SMTP protocol is strictly about moving messages from one computer to another. Though SMTP does not care about the content of an e-mail message, it does limit the formatting attributes of the message. SMTP can only transfer ASCII text. It can't handle fonts, colors, graphics, attachments, or any other of those fancy e-mail features that some of you may already know and love.

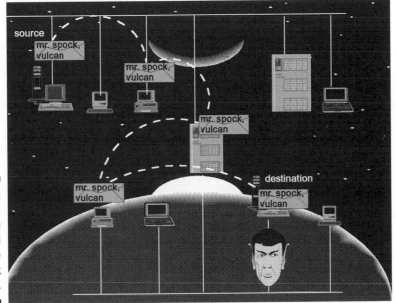

Figure 7-3:
A message is stored and forwarded across the network galaxy.

RFC Alert: *RFC822, Standard for the format of ARPA Internet text messages,* describes the format of a mail message. Specifically, it defines the syntax for the header lines (such as From:, To:, Date:, and so on) and the free-form, text-only body.

Why You Can't Find Bill Clinton Using the InterNIC

There used to be one central whois database that served as the directory for the whole Internet. All you had to do to be listed was register by sending e-mail to the InterNIC (admin@ds.internic.net). As The Internet grew, however, it became impossible to maintain and update the whois database. So now if you try to register, the InterNIC politely replies that they are no longer taking changes or additions, and tells you why not. Research is currently underway to find a method of providing Internet directory services using multiple distributed whois servers. Stay tuned.

MIME Means a Lot More Than Marcel Marceau

To enhance the body of an e-mail message so that it can be used to carry fonts, colors, and so forth, some good-deed doers (RFC writers, as described in Chapter 2) invented MIME, Multipurpose Internet Mail Extensions. MIME is pronounced the way you might expect, as "spoken" by Marcel Marceau. If the SMTP is the meat and potatoes of e-mail, MIME is dessert. And a meal isn't complete without dessert, is it?

> *RFC Alert:* MIME is described in two RFCs — *RFC1521, MIME (Multipurpose Internet Mail Extensions) Part One: Mechanisms for Specifying and Describing the Format of Internet Message Bodies*; and *RFC1522, MIME (Multipurpose Internet Mail Extensions) Part Two: Message Header Extensions for Non-ASCII Text.*

One of the most important features of MIME is that it allows the body of e-mail messages to have all those cool enhancements such as fonts and colors, while still allowing it to be delivered by SMTP (which, as explained above, couldn't care less about anything but ASCII text).

"How do they do that?" we hear you asking. Well, it requires that you must use a *MIME-compliant* mail user agent — that is, your MUA must know how to generate MIME message bodies. When you compose your sophisticated e-mail message, your MIME-compliant MUA encodes the deluxe features into a text-only representation that SMTP can transfer. The message can then pass through the necessary intermediary computers as usual, and none of them needs anything special to process your enhanced message.

When the message arrives at its final destination, your correspondent also needs a MIME-compliant MUA in order to decode the fancy features. Without a MIME-compliant MUA, the recipient of your message may not be able to do much with it.

How an SMTP Gateway Works

Because of the long-standing relationship between UNIX and TCP/IP, the UNIX mail system uses SMTP. The same cannot be said, however, about most other e-mail products. Those other e-mail systems need an *SMTP gateway*.

An SMTP gateway is software that translates e-mail messages between RFC822/MIME format and the format of another e-mail system. For example, let's say your organization uses Lotus Notes and its built-in e-mail system, which does not use SMTP. In order to exchange e-mail with people who do use an SMTP mail system, your organization needs an SMTP gateway. The gateway converts outbound mail messages into RFC822/MIME format, and inbound mail messages into Lotus Notes format.

Every SMTP gateway has to deal with the fact that no two e-mail systems are exactly alike, no matter how similar their features. Some things just won't match up when the gateway translates the message formats. The simple elegance of SMTP means that its mail system usually appears less sophisticated than other systems, though MIME does help narrow the gap.

"Alias Smith and Jones"

Mail aliases are the after-dinner drinks of the e-mail/SMTP/MIME meal — they're sometimes nice to have, but definitely not required. Mail aliases are a standard feature of SMTP mail systems.

One convenience mail aliases provide is a handy way to forward e-mail to another address. Suppose you'll be working at a branch office for a month. Instead of connecting to the home office each day to read your e-mail, you can have your e-mail forwarded to a computer at the branch office. Figure 7-4 shows a mail alias forwarding Marshall Wilensky's e-mail from the main office to the branch office, where he works one day a week. The postmaster at the main office has created a mail alias on the main office computer to forward Marshall's e-mail to the branch office computer.

There are two different kinds of mail aliases: private and public (though they do similar things).

main office   **branch office**

Figure 7-4:
With a
mail alias,
Marshall
can get his
e-mail even
when he's
out of town.

mwilensky@lotus.com   marshall@branchoffice.lotus.com

> ✔ The mail aliases *you* create are private; no one else can use them. To
> find out how to create your private mail aliases, consult the manual for
> your MUA. (On a UNIX system, you normally define them in the file
> named .mailrc located in your home directory.)
>
> ✔ The mail aliases that a *postmaster* creates are public; everyone can use
> them. The operating system and e-mail environment dictate how public
> aliases are created and maintained. (On a UNIX system, the postmaster
> normally defines them in the file /usr/lib/aliases.)

Neat things you can do with mail aliases

Mail aliases can also provide assistance to e-mail users in the following ways:

Mailing lists

In e-mail parlance, a *mailing list* is one e-mail address that sends your message
to multiple recipients. For example, the alias

```
tcpip_for_dummies_authors
```

could translate to these two addresses:

```
mwilensky@lotus.com
leiden@tiac.net
```

Most mailing lists are provided by means of public aliases (although you can
also create your own *distribution lists* by creating private aliases). You send
e-mail to the parties on the list in the same way, regardless. Mailing lists are
sometimes called *exploders,* because one e-mail message "explodes" into
many more.

Friendlier or more standard addresses

It's fairly obvious that this address:

```
Marshall_Wilensky@crd.lotus.com
```

takes more effort to type than this alias:

```
mwilensky@lotus.com
```

By means of public aliases, a postmaster can create and implement a consistent, more user friendly naming convention for your organization.

A way to reach people with unspellable names

A lot of people have trouble spelling Marshall's last name, so in a case like his, the postmaster might define this public alias:

```
mwilenski@lotus.com
```

for this address:

```
mwilensky@lotus.com
```

(Look closely; the *i* in Wilenski has been changed to a *y*.) Now Marshall will get the e-mail whether you spell his name correctly or not.

Some boring e-mail examples

Here is a message sent to a regular username, with no alias:

```
% mail marshall_wilensky@crd.lotus.com
Subject: Hello there
This message is to user marshall_wilensky. No alias. The sender had
to type a long address and know how to spell Marshall's name (2 "l"s
and a "y" at the end).

This message was written using the UNIX mail user agent, Mail. SMTP
got this message from the mail transfer agent and delivered it
across the network.

That's all. Bye for now.
.
Cc:
%
```

Here is a mail message sent to an alias. This looks the same whether the alias is public or private.

```
% mail wilenski@lotus.com
Subject: Hello there
This message is to the same person, but to his mail alias. And I
didn't even have to know how to spell his name. Hard to tell the
difference just by looking, isn't it?

This message was also written using the UNIX mail user agent, Mail.
 SMTP got this message from the mail user agent and delivered it
across the network.

That's all. Bye for now.
.
Cc:
%
```

Usenet News: Sharing Info over Lunch at the Network Table

If e-mail is the Number 1 dinner choice on the TCP/IP plate, then news is Number 1 for lunch. News via TCP/IP is known by various names, including Usenet news, netnews, and Network News. We'll call it Usenet news in this book.

Usenet news is a TCP/IP service consisting of a worldwide collection of online *newsgroups.* Each newsgroup is an electronic conversation group about a particular topic. Topics range from Disney to Star Trek, from home repair to gay and lesbian rights. Anyone on The Internet can post an article stating an opinion and/or asking for information. You've heard the stories of people meeting on line through newsgroups and falling in love, sight unseen — it really happens!

There are over 8,000 different Usenet newsgroups, and new ones are being created every day. We mentioned rec.arts.disney in an earlier chapter. Newsgroups are categorized by interest areas, and the pieces of a newsgroup name are the hierarchy for those interest areas, separated by dots (periods). The first part of the name is the most general topic, and each subsequent part of the name gets a little more specific. Newsgroup names look somewhat like the part of an e-mail address on the right-hand side of the @ sign, but it's just a coincidence.

The following table lists the main newsgroup hierarchies that you'll see often in newsgroup names.

Hierarchy	*Subject*
comp.	Computers and related topics
misc.	Miscellaneous
news.	Usenet news subjects, not the evening news or the newspaper
rec.	Recreation and the arts
sci.	Science
soc.	Society/sociology; sometimes relevant, sometimes wildly theoretical
talk.	Discussion; often controversial
alt.	"Alternative"; weird and serious stuff, as well

There are many other special or regional categories, as well, such as

Hierarchy	*Subject*
ne.	New England and the northeastern United States
biz.	Business
bionet.	Biology

Newsgroups to Help Newcomers

If you are new to Usenet news, there are a few newsgroups that are devoted to helping you learn how to read and write articles. Here are three of the most useful ones.

✔ news.announce.newusers: The articles in this newsgroup are about Usenet news features.

✔ news.newusers.questions: You can post articles here asking questions about how Usenet news works.

✔ news.answers: The articles here list the most frequently asked questions (FAQs) from the most popular newsgroups. This newsgroup is a fascinating catchall of useful and useless trivia.

See *The Internet For Dummies* for more information on news. ■

How to use newsgroups to learn more about TCP/IP

There are several newsgroups about TCP/IP. In the following list, many of the newsgroups are categorized by operating system. If a newsgroup is operating-system specific, its name appears in boldface italic, like this: *os2*.

comp.os.***ms-windows***.networking.tcp-ip

comp.os.***os2***.networking.tcp-ip

comp.protocols.tcp-ip

comp.protocols.tcp_ip.domains

comp.protocols.tcp-ip.***ibmpc***

relcom.tcpip

uiuc.sw.***pc***tcp

bit.listserv.***ibm***tcp-1

Look at the next list to see how many newsgroups there are about the VMS operating system alone. (VMS is one of the operating systems from Digital Equipment Corporation.) The reason there are so many discussions about TCP/IP in these VMS-specific groups is that several vendors have TCP/IP products that run on VMS. This is one of the reasons why there's a separate hierarchy called vmsnet. All of the following are vendor specific, except for the .misc group:

vmsnet.networks.tcp-ip.cmu-tek

vmsnet.networks.tcp-ip.misc

vmsnet.networks.tcpip.multinet

vmsnet.networks.tcpip.tcpware

vmsnet.networks.tcpip.ucx

vmsnet.networks.tcpip.wintcp ■

Newsgroups come and go, and sometimes an existing newsgroup becomes inactive (no more articles are written for it). Our lists of TCP/IP-oriented news-groups is current as of this writing, but as you look around on The Internet, you may see the list grow or shrink. ■

With so many interesting electronic discussions out there, you could spend all your waking hours chit-chatting on The Internet. And you wouldn't even have to shower and dress, since no one can see or smell you. You *Saturday Night Live* fans out there know what we mean, right?

rn tin tin: the dog's breakfast the morning after the TCP/IP banquet

The end-user application for accessing Usenet news is called a *newsreader*. It's similar to the MTA for e-mail: The newsreader passes your requests on to the TCP/IP service. You do not communicate directly with any TCP/IP components; it's all done invisibly for you by the newsreader. Whether news is stored on your own computer (as in older technology) or on a server (the newer client/server technology), you use a newsreader to read articles, post follow-ups or new articles, mail a response directly to the article's author, forward an article via e-mail to another person, and so on.

Newsreaders come in all shapes, sizes, and flavors. Many are free (public domain). You may have several to choose from on your computer. Some of the more popular ones are

rn

trn (see Figure 7-5)

xrn (for the X Window System)

nn

tin

Every newsreader needs to keep track of which articles you have already read. A good newsreader helps you by organizing the articles by *discussion thread*. Sometimes this means the newsreader looks at the article's Subject: or Summary: line to see if it's similar to other articles. Without this kind of feature, you're stuck reading articles in the chronological order in which they arrived on your computer or the server.

```
% trn comp.protocols.tcp-ip
Unread news in comp.protocols.tcp-ip                    567 articles
Unread news in comp.protocols.tcp-ip.domains            74 articles
Unread news in comp.protocols.tcp-ip.ibmpc            510 articles


====== 567 unread articles in comp.protocols.tcp-ip — read now? [+ynq] y
Getting overview file..
comp.protocols.tcp-ip #36318 (385 more)
Newsgroups: comp.protocols.tcp-ip.ibmpc,comp.protocols.tcp-ip,alt.        [1]
+          winsock,comp.os.ms-windows.networking.tcp-ip,alt.answers,
+          comp.answers,news.answers
From: aboba@netcom.com (Bernard Aboba)


comp.protocols.tcp-ip.ibmpc Frequently Asked Questions (FAQ), part 1 of 3
Followup-To: poster
Summary: Frequently Asked Questions (and answers) about TCP/IP on
+       PC-Compatible Computers
Keywords: TCP/IP, IBM PC, SLIP, PPP, NDIS, ODI
Organization: MailCom
Date: Mon Dec 26 15:00:25 ESI 1994
Lines: 3220


Archive-name: ibmpc-tcp-ip-faq/part1


comp.protocols.tcp-ip.ibmpc:
FAQ Posting, part 1, 1/1/95



################   Legalese ################


This document is Copyright (C) 1993,1994,1995 by Bernard Aboba, except where
the copyright is retained by the original author(s). This document
may be distributed non-commercially, provided that it is not
modified in any way. However, no part of this publication may be
sold or packaged with a product for sale in any form without the
prior written permission of Bernard Aboba.


This FAQ is presented with no warranties or guarantees of ANY KIND
including correctness or fitness for any particular purpose. The
author(s) of this document have attempted to verify correctness of the
data contained herein; however, slip-ups can and do happen.  If you use
this data, you do so at your own risk. While we make every effort to
keep this FAQ up to date, we cannot guarantee that it is, and we will
not be responsible for any damages resulting from the use of the information
or software referred to herein.


Unless otherwise stated, the views expressed herein are my own.  Last
time I looked, I had not been appointed official spokesperson of any
of the following:
```

Figure 7-5:
Here's a
sample
session
with trn, a
character-
based
newsreader.

```
                    The Planet Earth
                    The U.S.Government
                    The Internet
                    Microsoft, IBM, Sun or Apple
                    The State of California (not so good)
                    The University of California, Berkeley
                    The City of Berkeley (bringing you Riot of the Week(SM))
                    Addison-Wesley
                    Publisher's Group West
                    Any major or minor breakfast cereal (not even oatmeal!)


    This FAQ will be posted monthly. In between it will be
    available as:
    ftp://ftp.netcom.com/pub/ma/mailcom/IBMTCP/ibmtcp.zip


    Please note the change in the archive address!


    ############# This FAQ is on the Web ##############


    After each posting, this FAQ is automatically
    converted to HTML by Ohio State, and made available
    on the Web. This means that if you have a WWW browser,
    you can read the FAQ online, and click on links
    to download individual files.


    This is how I read the FAQ myself, and it is
    highly recommended. To get at the HTML version, try:
    http://www.zilker.net/users/internaut/update.html


    ################# Citation entry  ################


    This FAQ may be cited as:


      Aboba, Bernard D.(1994) "comp.protocols.tcp-ip.ibmpc Frequently
      Asked Questions (FAQ)" Usenet news.answers, available via
      ftp://ftp.netcom.com/pub/ma/mailcom/IBMTCP/ibmtcp.zip,
      57 pages.



    ################# Change History  ################


    Changes from 11/1/94 posting:
    Updated commercial stack entries, cleaned up broken
    links reported by readers (thanks!). New entries
    sport a "*"


    ################# Related FAQs ################
```

Figure 7-5:
(continued)

There is a FAQ available on features of TCP/IP
Packages for DOS and Windows. This is available at:
ftp://ftp.cac.psu.edu/pub/dos/info/tcpip.packages.

The Windows Sockets Faq is posted to alt.winsock, and
is available at:
ftp://SunSite.UNC.EDU/pub/micro/pc-stuff/ms-windows/winsock/FAQ

The PC-NFS FAQ is available at:
ftp://seagull.rtd.com/pub/tcpip/pcnfsfaq.zip
ftp://ftp.york.ac.uk/pub/FAQ/pcnfs.FAQ

The SNMP FAQ is regularly posted to news:comp.protocols.snmp

The TCP/IP FAQ is posted to news:comp.protocols.tcp-ip, and is
maintained by mailto:gnn@netcom.com.

The Windows NT FAQ is available from
Steve Scoggins, mailto:sscoggin@enet.net

An NT Web FAQ is available from:
http://www.luc.edu/~tbaltru/faq/

The "How To Get It" FAQ on the Crynwr packet driver
collection is irregularly posted to news:comp.protocols.tcp-ip.ibmpc
by Russ Nelson, mailto:nelson@crynwr.com.

################# Book info #################

A bunch of you have requested information on the
book I am working on. Here is the basic info:

Title: The PC-Internet Connection, TCP/IP
Networking for DOS and Windows
Authors: Bernard Aboba
Pages: 600 (estimated), 8.5" by 11"
Distributor: Publisher's Group West
ISBN: 1-883979-00-5
Price: $32.95 (est), includes CD-ROM with
Chameleon Sampler software, WS-Gopher, PC-Eudora,
Etherload, EtherDump, much more.
Estimated release: No date set (yeah, it slipped a
few months)

To look at sample chapters from the book, check out
the following WWW page:
http://www.zilker.net/users/internaut/forth.html

Figure 7-5:
(continued)

```
I'm currently working on incorporating comments
from the first beta release, finishing the index
and generally cleaning it up, so the second beta
release won't be out for at least another month.
Until the second beta is out, I will not be accepting
review requests. Sorry!

########## COOL WWW PAGES relating to TCP/IP ##########

http://www.charm.net/ppp.html (Cool home page with lots of pointers to
TCP/IP stuff)
http://www.zilker.net/users/internaut/update.html (This FAQ, in HTML)
http://www.crynwr.com/crynwr/nelson.html  (Crynwr Software Home Page)
ftp://ftp.biostat.washington.edu/ftp/pub/msdos/network.setups

################ EXAMPLE CONFIG FILES  ################

Many thanks to Dave Fetrow (fetrow@biostat.washington.edu)
for creating an archive of setup files. The archive is
particularly oriented toward sets of applications that
are somewhat tricky, such as combinations involving
different driver sets, mixtures of NetWare, TCP/IP,
and W4WG, etc.

Please include not only the setup and configuration files
but some directions. Comments included with the setup files
are highly desirable. The files can include your name if you
desire.

Please mail submissions to mailto:ftp@ftp.biostat.washington.edu.

The archive itself is located at:
ftp://ftp.biostat.washington.edu/ftp/pub/msdos/network.setups

Late breaking development: the archive has crashed, and
files have been lost.


TABLE OF CONTENTS

A. Components of a TCP/IP solution

A-1. What do I need to run TCP/IP on the PC?
A-2. What are packet drivers?  Where do I get them?
A-3. What is Winsock?  Where can I get it?
A-4. What is Trumpet Winsock? How do I get it to dial?
A-5. What publicly distributable TCP/IP applications are there
     for DOS?  Windows?
```

Figure 7-5:
(continued)

A-6. What software is available for doing SLIP? Compressed SLIP?
     PPP? For DOS? For Windows?
A-7. What about the software included with various books?
A-8. What diagnostic utilities are available to find problems with
     my connection? Where can I get them?
A-9. Is there a CD-ROM with the software included in this FAQ?
A-10. Does Windows NT support SLIP? PPP?
A-11. Where can I get Microsoft TCP/IP-32?
A-12. How do I get my BBS to run over TCP/IP?
A-13. Are there graphical TCP/IP servers out there?
A-14. What methods of dynamic address assignment are available?
A-15. How can I set up PPP server on a UNIX host?
A-16. What is WinSNMP? Why doesn't my TCP/IP stack support SNMP?
A-17. What HTTP proxies are available for use with NCSA Mosaic?
A-18. Why doesn't my Web browser support direct WAIS queries?
A-19. What is SOCKS? What TCP/IP stacks support it?
A-20. How can I handle authentication on my NNTP server?
A-21. What is SLIPKnot?
A-22. What is TWinSock?

B. Questions about drivers

B-1. What do I need to know before setting up SLIP or PPP?
B-2. How do I configure SLIPDISK?
B-3. How do I install packet drivers for Windows applications?
B-4. When do I need to install WINPKT?
B-5. How to do I run both WinQVT and ODI?
B-6. Is it possible to use BOOTP over SLIP?
B-7. How do SLIP drivers work?
B-8. When do I need to install PKTMUX?
B-9. Can NDIS be used underneath multiple protocol stacks of the same type?
B-10. Is there an NDIS over packet driver shim?
B-11. How do I run NetBIOS over TCP/IP?
B-12. How do I run NFS and another TCP/IP application?
B-13. How do I run Trumpet Winsock along with KA9Q or NFS?
B-14. I am trying to run Netware and TCP/IP at the same time, using
     PDETHER. How do I do this?
B-15. Sample Stick Diagrams
B-16. Strange and wonderful configuration files submitted by readers

C. KA9Q Questions

C-1. What version of KA9Q should I use and where do I get it?
C-2. What do I need to run KA9Q? Why won't it do VT-100 emulation?
C-3. How do I configure KA9Q as a SLIP dialup connection?
C-4. How do I configure KA9Q as a router?
C-5. How do I get KA9Q to support BOOTP?
C-6. How do I get KA9Q to support PPP?

Figure 7-5:
(continued)

C-7. How do I get KA9Q to support SLIP dialin?
C-8. Can I use KA9Q as a packet filter?
C-9. Can I use KA9Q as a BOOTP server?
C-10. Where can I get a manual for KA9Q?
C-11. Is there a way to prevent KA9Q from listening to ICMP redirect
      packets? RIP packets?
C-12. Will KA9Q route source-routed packets? If so, is there any way to
      turn off this (rather undesirable) behavior?
C-13. I'm trying to use the TextWin version of KA9Q as a SLIP router
      and it isn't working. What's wrong?

D. PCROUTE and PCBRIDGE

D-1. How do I get PCROUTE set up?
D-2. I want to use MS TCP/IP-32 to contact a host over a serial link,
     but have no SLIP or PPP driver. What do I do?
D-3. How do I get PCBRIDGE to use a SLIP or PPP driver?
D-4. Can I get PCROUTE to switch off RIP?

E. Hints for particular packages

E-1. How do I get DesQView X to run over the network?
E-2. Why is NFS so slow compared with FTP?
E-3. Where can I get information on running NetWare and TCP/IP
     concurrently?
E-4. What NetWare TCP/IP NLMs are out there and how do I get them
     to work?
E-5. How do I get a telecom package supporting Int 14h redirection
     to work?
E-6. I am having trouble running Netmanage Chameleon apps along with
     WFW TCP/IP-32. What do I do?
E-7. How do I get Windows For Workgroups to work alongside NetWare?
E-9. How come package X doesn't support the AppleTalk packet driver?
E-10. NCSA Telnet doesn't reassemble fragments. What should I do?
E-11. I am trying to configure a Macintosh to set its parameters automatically

     on bootup, but it isn't working. What's wrong?
E-12. I've heard that DHCP is a potential security risk. Is this true?
E-13. What is TIA?
E-14. What PC TCP/IP implementations support recent advances?
E-15. What network adapters have on-board SNMP agents?
E-16. What is the easiest way to get WFW and Novell Netware to coexist?
E-17. I'm trying to use packet driver software alongside WFW v3.11 and
      am having a hell of a time. What should I do?
E-18. What proxy software is available for those concerned about security?
E-19. How do I mount ftp.microsoft.com on the desktop using file manager?
E-20. I am having trouble connecting to a Windows NT PPP server. What should
      I do?

Figure 7-5:
(continued)

```
F. Information for developers

F-1. What publicly distributable TCP/IP stacks are there that I can
     use to develop my own applications?
F-2. Where can I get a copy of the Windows Sockets FAQ?



——————— - FAQ Begins Here ——————-

A. Components of a TCP/IP solution

A-1. What do I need to run TCP/IP on the PC?

To run TCP/IP on the PC you will need:
```

[**Stuff Deleted**   ]

Figure 7-5:
(continued)
We've
abridged it
here to
shorten it.

```
End of article 36318 (of 36884) — what next? [npq] q

======   74 unread articles in comp.protocols.tcp-ip.domains — read now?
[+ynq]   q
%
```

Watch out: Reading news articles in chronological order can give you mental indigestion! For example, suppose a news user in Honolulu posts an article. As the article flows via The Internet around the world and toward you, another news user in San Francisco reads it and posts a response. The response, too, flows via The Internet around the world and toward you. It's entirely possible that the response will arrive before the original article arrives. If the original article was a question and the response is an answer, you might see the answer before the question! This confusing situation is quite common on The Internet, so get used to it. ▪

By the way, if you are in a network environment in which the news articles are stored on a server, that news server is running NNTP, the Network News Transfer Protocol. (NNTP is pronounced by saying the letters *N N T P*.) NNTP moves articles from server to server and from server to newsreader (client). NNTP is another invisible part of TCP/IP. ▪

Talking the Talk

E-mail and Usenet news carry messages among users that are separated by space and time. Two other Internet services, talk and Internet Relay Chat (IRC), carry online messages among users that are separated only by physical space.

You'll recall seeing talk listed in the table of popular newsgroup topics earlier in the chapter. Don't confuse the talk service with the Usenet newsgroups that are in the talk. hierarchy. The Internet talk service is live interaction between two people. ■

Private line only

Using talk, you can actually make "telephone calls" via TCP/IP. Both you and the other person (the talkee) must be on line at the same time. Talk provides a private, one-to-one connection. There are no party lines or conference calls. (See the following section on IRC for multiparty conversations.)

Why use talk?

- ✔ You *can't* use the phone. It's broken, or your kids are using it, or maybe you have only one telephone line and you're using it for a dial-up connection to the Internet or for a fax transmission. So, instead, why not use a network connection to carry your "voice" message?

- ✔ You don't *want* to use the phone, maybe because you don't want long-distance telephone charges to appear on your phone bill. The advantage of using a talk session, instead, is that its cost is built into the cost of your network connection.

- ✔ You want to check to see if someone is actually there before you use the phone.

- ✔ The person you want to speak to is in a different-from-usual location, and you don't know the phone number. Perhaps the person has dialed in from a remote site (another office location or a hotel room).

- ✔ One or both of you is hearing impaired.

Have you already guessed that talk involves a client, a server, and a TCP/IP protocol?

There are no answering machines on talk, so if you want to leave a message at the tone, send e-mail instead. ■

When you are "talking" to someone, your screen gets split into two sections; your words appear in one half, and your talkee's words show up in the other half. What you type gets sent across the network immediately. That means your talkee sees exactly what you type, including mistakes and "mistalks," so think before you type! ∎

See *The Internet For Dummies* for more detailed information on talk.

Internet Relay Chat (IRC): TCP/IP's version of CB radio

Internet Relay Chat, IRC, is the citizen's band (CB) radio of TCP/IP. (You pronounce IRC by saying the letters *I R C.*) Chatting was created to overcome the primary limitation of talk — namely, that only two people at a time can communicate. IRC provides a party-line environment.

Chatting is done on *channels*, which are named rather than numbered. Each channel is supposed to be for a specific topic, but you'll have to judge the situation for yourself when you're connected. Chatting is a pretty "loose" environment, although discussions can be scheduled in advance for a specific time, topic, and channel. Each channel has at least one operator, who cannot moderate the discussion but can disconnect individual chatters. On the other hand, since the chatters can simply sign in again, disconnecting them may not help keep the discussion focused and free of unruly behavior.

As you might expect by now, for chatting you use an IRC client, which communicates with IRC servers via a TCP/IP protocol. The client helps you communicate with the IRC server, connect to the channel of your choice, and chat with the other users. The servers keep track of the chatters and the channels, and exchange the messages so that all the chatters see all of the chatting.

Not all TCP/IP implementations include IRC. If party-line chatting is important to you, check out several TCP/IP packages before you buy, to make sure you get a version that contains IRC. ∎

See *More Internet For Dummies* for more information on IRC.

Both talk and IRC let you communicate live with people anywhere in the world. There's still no reason for you to bathe or put on clean clothes. No one will ever know that you're in your pajamas.

So far in the TCP/IP banquet, we've looked at messaging applications, services, and protocols: e-mail, Usenet news, talk, and IRC. You can run the applications on your own computer or on another computer on the network without having to get up and go to that computer. The next chapter is about sharing computers across a TCP/IP network.

Chapter 8

Over There, Over There, Do Some Stuff, Do Some Stuff, Over There

· ·

In This Chapter

▶ Using someone else's computer from a distance — a l-o-o-n-n-g-g distance

▶ Telnet versus rlogin: the same, but different

▶ How to be trustworthy in a network environment

▶ Using the X graphical user interface (note that we did not say X rated!)

· ·

The Crepe Place / In Paris = TCP/IP?

Suppose you're hungry, craving a big juicy burger, but for some reason, you aren't going to use your own stove to grill it. Maybe you're out of meat, or maybe your studio apartment only has a pathetic little hotplate without the necessary heat to charbroil half a pound of prime ground beef. No problem — you can get what you want from your favorite neighborhood burger place. It's not far away and no big deal to walk over and place your order.

You can do that with computers too. If you're lucky, when your computer is too weak to do what you want (not enough memory, speed, or software), you can wander down the hall and borrow a colleague's computer for a while.

But what if it's not a burger that you crave? What if you want some of those fabulous crepes suzette that you can only get in Paris? In that case your favorite restaurant is slightly less accessible! And it's the same with computers. It's not always easy or convenient to find a computer that you can borrow to do what you need for as long as you need to do it.

So what *do* you do if the computer you need to access is in Paris, and you're in Scranton, PA? It's time to order in. And here's where TCP/IP is a lot more accommodating than the best restaurant in Paris. If you ask that restaurant to deliver your crepes to Scranton, probably the best you can do, at great expense, is overnight delivery — and you'd have to reheat them, which would ruin them, anyway.

But with TCP/IP, accessing that big, powerful computer in Paris is just as easy as if it were at your desk, and you can do it in fractions of a second. And better yet, if your colleagues need to use the Paris computer as well, lots of you can share it at the same time without even getting up from your desks.

Sharing Other People's Computers

In a network environment, the computers within your organization are often shared resources. In Chapter 4, we introduced the client/server concept of a *compute server,* a computer with CPU cycles it is willing to share. In this section, we'll look at some of the TCP/IP tools you can use to access a compute server.

You say you want me to steal a Harley?

Sharing a computer's CPU resources is called *cycle stealing*. No, we're not talking about going out to a biker bar and committing a felony. In this case, we're talking about stealing *computer processing cycles.* The computer component that does the processing is called the central processing unit (CPU). A CPU cycle occurs each time a computer's internal clock ticks. (Those clocks tick a lot faster than your alarm clock, by the way.) So, when you are cycle stealing, you are using the CPU power of another computer. ▪

To handle the distribution of computer power in an organized way, many businesses set up compute servers for you to steal from or share with. A compute server is a powerful computer that is configured especially for sharing among many users. When you steal CPU cycles from a compute server, there's no need to feel guilty.

In this chapter you'll learn how you can cycle steal with TCP/IP, but computer etiquette requires that you always do it with permission. After all, if you cycle steal from a computer that has an underpowered CPU, you are stealing from someone who can't afford to share, and processing for both of you will be slower as a result. Besides, if your victim is a techie, she will know how to detect your theft, and you might wind up in worse shape than if you *had* tried to steal some big biker's Harley. ▪

You can't steal a moped

Not every computer can be a compute server. Some operating systems cannot provide this service; others are set up so they will not. Neither the Macintosh (when it runs the Macintosh operating system) nor personal computers running DOS and Microsoft Windows can provide compute services for other network users. They are designed to be used by only one person at a time. (Why do you think they're called *personal* computers?)

A *multiuser operating system, regardless of the computer running it*, is designed to be used by more than one person at a time. Most multiuser, timesharing systems, such as UNIX, are capable of providing compute services, although they may not offer them. The person responsible for keeping the computers running (the system manager) may have purposely set up a particular computer in that way. There are many techniques for doing that, and the choices depend on the operating system itself.

Microsoft Windows NT is an interesting operating system example because it's a hybrid. Only one user can log in interactively to a computer running Windows NT, but many users can still share the CPU power by using TCP/IP tools.

But let's deal with the positive. You *know* there is a computer somewhere on your network that you can use to steal more power. Luckily, for you to borrow some compute cycles from another computer, that computer does not need to have the same operating system you have. In fact, this is one of the big benefits of telnet and rlogin (remote login), two TCP/IP applications for cycle stealing. You will see them in action a bit later in this chapter.

Why did the hungry user steal cycles? To get to the restaurant on the other side of the network.

There are various uses to which you can put your stolen cycles. Suppose you have a Macintosh without much CPU power, and you need to do some major calculations about weather systems. You don't need to tie up your Mac, grinding them out. Instead, you can telnet to the big supercomputer at the central office, and use the remote CPU to do your math in seconds rather than minutes or hours.

Does your organization maintain a large database? or even several? Say you've got access to one that tracks restaurants. To use it, you don't need to install a database management system on your PC. When you're hungry, you telnet over to the computer and read through the information on restaurants in your area. (You didn't think we'd let you get away without a food example in this section, did you?)

Another common use for telnet is in research. There are public telnet sites that give you access to libraries around the world.

But even if you're not interested in supercalculations or researching exotic butterflies in the rainforests, don't forget that telnet can help you with your everyday life. One simple example is in getting your e-mail forwarded to you while you're on a business trip. Instead of having it forwarded, you can use telnet or rlogin to connect to your home office and read your mail remotely.

Using telnet or tn3270 to Borrow Processing Power

Telnet is both a TCP/IP application and a protocol for connecting to a remote computer and using it interactively. The computer you are using — maybe you are sitting in front of it right now — is the *local computer*. The *remote computer* is the other one, the one farther away from you.

The telnet application's role is to act as a *terminal emulator*, making your expensive, high-powered computer act just like an old-style computer terminal. Whatever commands you type on your local keyboard are sent across the network for execution by the remote computer.

Oldies But Goodies

Most telnet applications emulate a Digital Equipment Corporation (DEC) VT100 terminal. In its time, starting in the early 1980s, a VT100 was *the* thing to have, and its fancier successor models were equally state of the art. You needed a VT100 in order to use the large, central computer shared by you and everyone near you. Once personal computers became popular, VT100 terminals and their descendants were virtually eliminated outside of the DEC environment. These days, instead of a dedicated dumb terminal, most people use a terminal emulator application running on a smart computer.

Another standard in its day was the IBM 3270 terminal. A special version of telnet, called tn3270, emulates an IBM 3270. (The *tn* is short for telnet.) If you are connecting to an IBM mainframe computer, you will probably need to use tn3270 rather than telnet.

What you need to know before starting telnet

Before using telnet to grab those cycles, you need the name of the computer to which you want to connect, or at least its numeric TCP/IP address. If in your environment you're only using e-mail addresses, the computer name is the part right after the @ sign. For example, in smith@abc.university.edu, the computer name is abc.university.edu. See Chapter 13 for the full discussion of TCP/IP names and addresses.

Next, since you're connecting to a multiuser operating system, you need to know a username and password for the remote computer. One way a system manager can restrict access to a compute server, or prevent a computer from acting as a compute server in the first place, is not to disclose any valid username and password for the computer.

On The Internet, there are public telnet sites (that is, remote sites accessible via telnet), where the username and password for log-in are published. And there are some really public sites that don't require a username and password at all.

Once you have the computer name (or numeric address) and a username and password, or know that you are connecting to a public site, you're ready to start.

Number, please . . . Whenever you're asked for a computer's name, you can supply that computer's numeric TCP/IP address instead. From now on in this book we'll just say "computer name," but you can give either the name or the numeric address. (For more about computer name-and-address translation, see Chapter 11.) ■

Telnet tutorial

1. Run the telnet program on your local computer.

   ✔ This usually means typing the command **telnet**, followed by the computer name you are accessing. After you type the name, telnet opens a connection to the remote machine for you.

   ✔ Or, if your computer has a graphical user interface (GUI), click on the icon to start telnet. Connect to the remote computer by clicking on other commands, for example, the Open command on the File menu. Then you'll enter the remote computer's name.

2. Pay attention to the telnet messages about your connection that appear on your screen. You will see the numeric address of the remote computer and its name, as TCP/IP tries to make your connection.

What is your Escape character? When you read the telnet connection messages, take special note of what the telnet application tells you about the Escape character (you can see examples in Figures 8-1 and 8-2). You may need to use this character later if you want to interrupt your remote computer session temporarily and issue some additional commands to telnet itself. More on this later. ▪

3. Log in to the remote computer using the username and password that you have determined in advance. You may then see some messages from the remote computer. In Figure 8-1, the messages are from a UNIX operating system on a Sun Microsystems computer. Here the system manager has chosen to display a security warning message as part of the log-in process. In Figure 8-2, telnet is being used from a PC running Microsoft Windows for Workgroups and TCP/IP.

4. Now you can start typing the commands you want to use in your remote work session. In Figure 8-1, the commands appear preceded by a percent sign (%), the UNIX operating system's command prompt.

In our sample telnet session in Figure 8-1, our computer has taken care of the terminal emulation mode automatically by setting us to be a VT100. Terminal emulation tells the remote computer how we need to see data displayed on our local computer. (VT100 is the most common terminal emulation mode.) On some computers, however, you may have to set your own terminal emulation mode. If all you see on your screen when you type are nonsense characters, you probably are in an incorrect terminal emulation mode. If everything looks fine on the screen, you can enter any command that works on the remote computer's operating system.

Pay careful attention to any security messages that the remote computer displays. It is a federal offense to break ("hack") into a computer you are not allowed to share. All kinds of law enforcement agencies will track you down, and people have gone to jail for hacking. ▪

Figure 8-1:
Here we're connecting to a remote computer using telnet.

```
% telnet frodo ─────────────────── Start telnet and open connection to frodo.
Trying 130.103.40.225 ... ─────── TCP/IP address of frodo.
Connected to frodo.
Escape character is '^]'. ──────── Remember your Escape character!


SunOS UNIX (frodo)

login: student9 ─────┐           Logging in. Remote computer is running
Password:          ──┘           the UNIX OS. Username is student9.
```

```
Last login: Fri Jan 20 17:17:03 from 130.103.40.224
SunOS Release 4.1.3 (FRODO) #1: Fri Oct 8 10:27:11 EDT 1993

****************************************************************************

                          UNAUTHORIZED USE PROHIBITED!

This system is for the use of authorized users only.

Individuals using this computer system without authority,
or in excess of their authority, are subject to having
all of their activities on this system monitored and
recorded by system personnel.

In the course of monitoring individuals improperly using
this system, or in the course of system maintenance, the
activities of authorized users may also be monitored.

Anyone using this system expressly consents to such
monitoring and is advised that if such monitoring reveals
possible evidence of criminal activity, system personnel
may provide the evidence of such monitoring to law
enforcement officials.

****************************************************************************
```

Security warning message

```
% ls ──────────── This is a UNIX command to list the files on the remote computer's directory.
.Xauthority   .aliases    .logout      .xinitrc.mwm  notes
.Xdefaults    .cshrc      .mwmrc       Notes         notes.tmp
.Xpdefaults   .login      .xinitrc     jbigram.id
% logout
Connection closed by foreign host. ──────── The telnet connection is automatically closed
%                                            when you log out of the remote computer.
```

Figure 8-1:
(continued)

Figure 8-2:
Here we're
connecting
to a remote
computer
using telnet
and a
graphical
user
interface.

```
─ Mem: 42.9 Mb  User: 82% GDI: 52%   Telnet - [None]        4/26/95  11:25 PM ▾
 Connect  Edit  Terminal  Help
  Remote System ...

  Exit            Alt+F4
                          ─            Connect
                           Host Name: candace|        ±
                           Port:      telnet          ±
                           TermType:  vt100           ±
                               Connect       Cancel
```

The great escape

You did remember to make a note of the Escape character message when you logged in to the remote computer, didn't you? Now we're going to tell you what to do with it.

By pressing the key(s) that represent the Escape character in your telnet application, you can switch from issuing operating system commands to issuing telnet commands. Here are some useful telnet commands:

Telnet Command	Function
open	Initiates a connection to a remote computer.
close	Terminates your connection to a remote computer. If you started telnet with a computer address, close will also quit telnet. If you used the open command to start your remote connection, the close command will close the connection, but telnet remains active so you can open a connection to another computer.
quit	Terminates your connection and quits telnet.
set echo	If the characters you are typing are not appearing on screen, set echo may help fix the problem.

The IBM mainframe connection

If you need to connect to an IBM 3270-type mainframe computer, tn3270 is the TCP/IP application for you. It works like telnet but sets the terminal emulation mode to work with your mainframe.

R you Ready foR moRe Remote log-ins?

An alternative to telnet is rlogin. Though not available on every operating system, rlogin is almost always there on UNIX systems. Though they provide the same kind of functionality, telnet and rlogin were implemented by separate groups of people, and each works differently at the bit and byte levels.

The rlogin application is one of the *r utilities,* a group of network utilities developed at the University of California at Berkeley for accessing remote computers. The utilities in the group all start with the letter *r.*

Who do you trust?

When you rlogin to the remote computer, you may or may not be prompted for a username and password. You will not be prompted for this information if the remote computer *trusts* you or the computer from which you are logging in. The notion of trust in this discussion comes from UNIX and the TCP/IP environment that grew up with it. When two UNIX computers are set up so they trust each other, all the users on one computer are allowed to use the other computer.

Trust is not automatically reciprocal: Just because computer A trusts computer B (and all of computer B's users) that doesn't mean that computer B trusts computer A and all its users. Nevertheless, it is quite common for trust to be defined in both directions. Figure 8-3 shows an rlogin session on an untrusted computer, so the user has to type a password. After the password is entered, the user can list the files in the remote computer's directory and send e-mail.

```
$ rlogin max

+=================================================================+
|                 Welcome to The Internet Access Company          |
|             Data: (617) 275-W331 Voice: (617) 275-2221          |
||To sign up for a SHELL account, type 'new' at the login: prompt|
||To sign up for SLIP or PPP accounts, call (617)275 2221.       |
||For general information, send email to 'info@tiac.net'.         |
+=================================================================+

Password:
Last login: Mon Feb 13 16:37:33 from bed-1p3
Copyright (c) 1980, 1983,1986,1988,1990,1991 The Regents of the University
of California.  All rights reserved.

Mail will be restored 2/13/95

$ ls
ACTIVE          News            ftp.example     mbox
Mail            dog-biscuits    mail            trn.txt
$ mail
No mail for leiden
$ mail fay@cookie.enet.dec.com
Subject: Hi. This mail is from an rlogin session.
```

Figure 8-3:
Here we are
accessing
a remote
computer
with rlogin.

Stealing Cycles with rsh, remsh

Sometimes you need to connect to a remote computer and work interactively to perform a variety of tasks, as with rlogin or telnet. At other times, you simply have just one thing to accomplish. The University of California at Berkeley's r utilities include rsh, short for *remote shell*. With rsh, you can tell a remote computer to execute one command.

When you use rsh, the command you enter must include the following three elements, separated by spaces:

- The rsh command itself
- The name of the remote computer you want to use
- The command to perform on the remote computer

Here is the syntax:

rsh *remote_computer command_to_execute_there*

So a sample command looks like this:

```
rsh max ls
```

Watch out: For rsh to work smoothly, the remote system must trust you. (See the description of trust in the previous section.) Figure 8-4 illustrates what happens if you try to use rsh to connect to a computer that does not trust you and your computer.

If you can rlogin to a remote computer without being prompted for a username or password, you can use rsh. ■

```
$ rsh max ls
Permission denied.
```

Figure 8-4:
A cycle stealer tries to list files on a remote computer that does not trust him.

On some computers, rsh stands for *restricted shell,* not *remote shell.* A restricted shell limits the operating system commands available to the user. On those computers, the remote shell command is remsh. ■

What? They Don't Trust You? No Problem: It's rexec to the Rescue.

Another r application, rexec, is like rsh and remsh — it allows you to connect to a remote computer to issue one command at a time. Rexec is different from rsh and remsh, however, because you must know a valid username and password for the remote computer.

Before it attempts to execute your command, rexec always prompts for a username and password. Your password is encrypted before it is sent "across the wire" to the server (see Chapter 18 for more information about encryption and other security issues). Rexec uses the TCP/IP service, rexecd.

Though rsh is quicker because it does not involve thorough log-in processing, rexec is more secure because it does. Take your pick.

X Marks the GUI: The X Window System

We've used the term *graphical user interface* (GUI, pronounced "gooey") several times already in this chapter. Most of you are already familiar with this term — it refers to all the graphics and other screen elements you click on with a mouse as you communicate with the computer, rather than typing in commands.

Microsoft Windows is an example of a graphical user interface that is layered on top of a nongraphical operating system, MS-DOS. The Apple Macintosh has a graphical operating system. In the Mac, you cannot separate the GUI from the operating system itself; they are tightly integrated.

The UNIX operating system is nongraphical, like MS-DOS. In a UNIX system, the GUIs (there can be several to pick from) are all built on a technology known as the X Window System, which was developed at MIT, the Massachusetts Institute of Technology. (Other than the word *Window,* there is no connection at all between the X Window System and Microsoft Windows.) Many people (lazily) refer to the X Window System by these nicknames:

- X
- X11, meaning version 11
- X11R4 or X11R5, meaning version 11, release 4 or 5

The X Window System is the technology beneath the following enhanced user interfaces, among others:

Motif, from the Open Software Foundation and other vendors

Open Windows, from Sun Microsystems

DECwindows, from Digital Equipment Corporation

AIXwindows, from IBM

Open Desk Top, from the Santa Cruz Operation

Visual User Environment, from Hewlett-Packard

The X Window System is not limited to UNIX. It is the GUI for several other nongraphical operating systems, such as VMS. No other GUI has matched one very significant feature of the X Window System: its ability to run an application on one computer and send the display to another computer or dedicated X Window terminal.

X Window System tutorial

The following code segment shows the steps you follow on a UNIX system to use the local computer for X display and the remote computer to run the application. When using a remote computer, you use the setenv DISPLAY command to identify your local computer as the display computer.

```
rlogin remote_UNIX_computer

setenv DISPLAY local_computer:0

run graphical_application
```

In the example above, the setenv command is for the UNIX C shell. UNIX has many different command interfaces called shells. If you use a shell different from the C shell, here's what you need to do:

```
set DISPLAY=local_computer:0

export DISPLAY

run graphical_application
```

Once you have executed these commands, the entire user interface of the application appears on your local computer, such as a Sun workstation, which must be capable of receiving and displaying X output. ∎

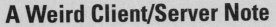

A Weird Client/Server Note

When you run an application on a big computer and use your little workstation to display X Window System graphics, you are running a client/server application over the network. But which is the client and which is the server? Usually, we think of big computers as the servers, and less-powerful computers such as PCs and UNIX workstations as the clients. But with X, the little computer that handles the X Window System GUI is functioning as the display server.

In this chapter, we told you how to log in to another computer and work remotely. What if you need to edit a file stored on that other computer? You could telnet or rlogin to the remote computer to read and edit the file across the network, but all those characters streaming over the network from the compute server to your client and back will affect network performance and may make reading the file very slow. The next chapter shows how you can bring the file to your own computer and read and edit the file locally.

The 5th Wave   By Rich Tennant

"You know, I liked you a whole lot more on the Internet."

Chapter 9

Share and Share Alike

● ●

In This Chapter

▶ Copying files with FTP

▶ Getting good stuff — free! — from The Internet, using Anonymous FTP

▶ Getting files by e-mail with ftpmail

▶ Do you trust rcp? Does it trust you?

● ●

*I*n Chapter 8, you checked out some ways to access remote computers, with telnet or rsh or rlogin. Once you sign on to a remote computer, you can look at files on that computer. But, of course, once you sign off again, you can no longer read those files. And in many cases, you may not be trusted enough to get in to the remote computer in the first place. Remember that untrustworthy cycle stealer in Figure 8-4?

In this chapter, you'll see ways to share files on remote computers, with and without explicitly logging in across the network.

Using FTP to Share Files across a Network

Making a copy of a file is often the simplest way to share it. With a personal computer, you can copy the file onto a floppy disk (also called a diskette) and easily share it that way. Of course, in order to do this, both computers must

✔ Have a floppy disk drive.

✔ Use the same size floppy disk. (The most common size now is 3.5", but 5.25" was very popular in its time and you may still have some. Do you remember 8" diskettes?)

✔ Support the same recording densities. (The 3.5" floppy disks normally hold 1.44 megabytes of data; 5.25" diskettes normally hold 1.2 megabytes.)

✔ Support the same formatting method. PCs and Macs both use 3.5" disks, but each computer type stores data on the disks in completely different ways.

Personal computers always have a floppy drive, but larger computers rarely do. Certainly you could choose any other medium that the computers have in common — magnetic tape, for example. But this book is about TCP/IP, not media. So let's look at the ways available to copy files *over the network*.

The FTP Blue Plate Special

In Chapter 6 we first told you about FTP, the protocol/service/application for copying files to and from a remote computer. (Remember, the computer you are actually using is the *local computer*. The *remote computer* is the other one farther away from you.) Recall that you use the FTP client application to connect to a remote computer that is providing the FTP service. The FTP protocol comes into play when you actually (finally) ask the application to transfer the files.

Figure 9-1 shows FTP on the menu as appetizer, main course, and dessert.

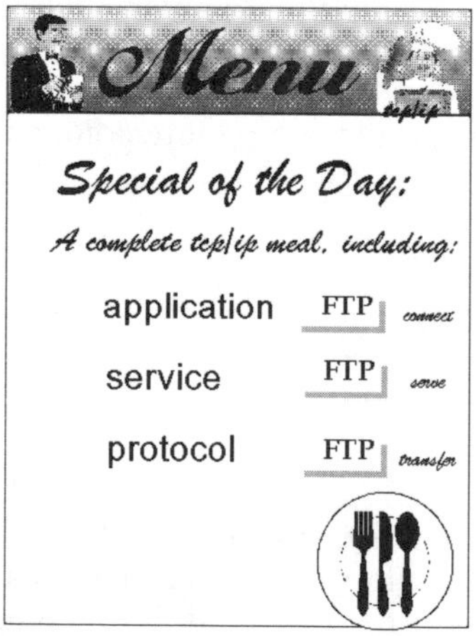

Figure 9-1: FTP is served at each course of the TCP/IP meal.

You don't have to go to China for egg rolls

Suppose it's dinnertime, and you're hungry for egg rolls, Hungarian goulash, and crepes suzette, with an Alka Seltzer chaser. You have some choices:

✔ Travel around the world to China, Hungary, and France to assemble your meal. If the egg rolls are cold and greasy before you get to eat them, well, that's life in the multicultural world. And you do have the Alka Seltzer to get you through the night.

✔ Order in. Get on the phone or fax to China, Hungary, and France and talk to the best restaurant in each country. Have everything shipped to you at the same time by the fanciest messenger service you can find. The egg rolls may even still be warm when your doorbell rings.

It works the same way with computers and files. If you want files from three different computers, you can travel to each one and get what you need. Or, you can stay put and use FTP. It's the next best thing to being there.

With FTP, you don't have to care what operating system is on those remote computers, because they all have TCP/IP. This ability to transfer files to and from computers running different operating systems is one of the best benefits of FTP. For example, suppose your local computer runs DOS with Microsoft Windows, and you need a file that's on a UNIX system. No problem. Start up the FTP client application on your PC, connect to that UNIX system, and *get* or *put* your files.

Get? Put? What are we talking about, you ask. Relax — these are FTP commands, and you'll see them in action shortly. ■

How to Use FTP

You're about to get the lowdown on using one of the handiest TCP/IP goodies around. But first . . .

Before you start

Here are a few things you must have ready before you start the FTP client application:

✔ The name of the remote computer or its TCP/IP address

✔ Your account name and password — these are what get you access to the remote computer

Anybody Home?

There are lots of ways to find out who or what is out there on the networks, including The Internet. Four of the tools you can use are finger, rwho, ruptime, and ping. These are explained in more detail for you in Chapter 14, but here is a brief description of what they do. We think you'll find their names ranging from mildly amusing to slightly perverted. Most of them came from UNIX. Need we say more?

✔ The **finger** utility displays plenty of information about network users, including their current plans. Finger is good for finding out someone's e-mail address. This utility is amazingly thorough — it'll even tell you how many cold sodas are in a machine in Pittsburgh, PA.

✔ The **rwho** utility tells you all the users currently logged in to computers on your network. You can find out if someone is signed on before you try to talk to them electronically (see Chapter 7).

✔ The **ruptime** utility lists all the computers on the network. This one is useful to see if a computer is available before you use ftp or rcp to transfer files to or from it.

✔ The **ping** utility lets you find out if a specific computer is up and running on the network. When you already know the name of the computer you want, ping is a lot more efficient than ruptime.

If possible, you should also know in advance:

✔ The names of the files you're interested in.

✔ The locations of the files. If they're your files that you're moving to the remote computer, you'd better know where they are! If you're retrieving the files from a remote computer, you can browse around to find them.

✔ Whether the files contain anything besides plain text. If they do, you must transfer them in binary mode rather than the default ASCII mode.

By the way, be sure to scan every file you transfer for viruses. You never know what's contagious. ■

Tutorial: Using FTP to transfer files

There are six basic steps to follow if you want to transfer files using FTP:

1. Start your FTP client application.

   If you have a GUI, such as Microsoft Windows, this step may be as simple as clicking your mouse on an FTP icon (see Figure 9-2). Without a GUI, you'll need to type the **ftp** command. In Figure 9-3, an FTP session is started from a command line.

2. Tell the FTP client application the name (or numeric address) of the remote computer that's holding the files you want. You can add this item to the ftp start-up command, as was done in Figure 9-3. Or you can use the FTP open command at the ftp> prompt to connect with the remote computer, as shown here:

```
ftp> open candacel
```

3. When you're prompted, tell the remote computer your account name and password.

   The prompt from FTP lists your computer name, followed by a colon and your username in parentheses. If you have an account on the remote system with that name, just confirm the prompt as is by pressing Enter. Otherwise, type a valid username. As an extra security precaution, when you type the password, nothing appears. Here's what all this looks like:

```
** Name (candy:leiden):
331 Password required for leiden.
Password:
230 User leiden logged in.
```

If you don't know a valid account name for the remote computer, you can try entering the username *anonymous.* Anonymous FTP is discussed later in this chapter. ■

4. Use the FTP dir command to find the files you need. At the ftp> prompt, type **dir**:

```
ftp> dir
```

5. If you need to move to another directory on the server, use **cd** (the change directory command) followed by the name of the directory. If you're not sure where you are on the remote computer, use **pwd** to print the working directory on the screen.

```
ftp> cd pub
ftp> pwd
```

6. Now you can transfer the files you want. Use the **get** command to copy files from the remote computer to your computer. Use the **put** command to copy files from your computer to the remote computer.

```
ftp> get file1
ftp> put file2
```

If you want the new copy of the file to have a different name, add it to the end of the get or put command, like this:

```
ftp> get file1 newfile1
ftp> get file2 newfile2
```

In fact, renaming may be required when you copy files between two different operating systems that have different file-naming capabilities. For example:

```
ftp> get pretty-long-UNIX.file.name DOSFILE.txt
```

In the above commands, *file1, file2, newfile1,* and so on stand for the real names of the files that you type in. Be sure to type the filenames in the correct case. Under DOS and Windows there's no difference between file1, File1, FILE1, FiLe1, and fIlE1. But under UNIX those are five different files! ■

7. Exit from FTP when you're done, as follows:

```
ftp> quit
```

Microsoft TCP/IP-32

FTP   TELNET   Microsoft TCP/IP-32 Help   Release Notes

Figure 9-2:
Clicking on
the FTP icon
starts the
FTP client
application
on a PC.

Mix-and-Match Commands: If you have spent any time at all working on a UNIX or MS-DOS system, some of the previous commands will look familiar to you. DOS stole some commands, such as cd, from UNIX, so some of the commands are the same on both operating systems and have been used by many applications, including FTP. There are some differences; for instance, dir will be familiar to you DOS folks, but only UNIX people will recognize pwd. If you're not sure what FTP command to use in any situation, type **help** or **?** at the ftp> prompt to get a list of FTP commands, as shown in Figure 9-4. ■

```
% ftp frodo
Connected to frodo.
220 frodo FTP server (SunOS 4.1) ready.
Name (bilbo:wilensky): student9
331 Password required for student9.
Password:
230 User student9 logged in.
```

Figure 9-3: No GUI on your system to do pointing and clicking? Type ftp to start your FTP client application, followed by the address of the remote computer.

```
─ Mem: 43.0 Mb  User: 80% GDI: 63%              FTP                   4/27/95  10:27 PM  ▼ ▲
─  File  Edit  State  Window  Help                                                        ▲
                                                                                          ▼
Ftp> ?
Commands may be abbreviated.  Commands are:

?                debug          ls             put            status
append           dir            mdelete        pwd            trace
ascii            disconnect     mdir           quit           type
bell             get            mget           quote          user
binary           glob           mkdir          recv           verbose
bye              hash           mls            remotehelp
cd               help           mput           rename
close            lcd            open           rmdir
delete           literal        prompt         send
Ftp>
Ftp> open frodo




─────────────────────────────────────────────────────────────────────────────────────────
Running    Input pending in Stdin/Stdout/Stderr
```

Figure 9-4:
Using the help (?) command to see the valid FTP commands.

Beyond the Basics (Just a Little)

What if you want to move more than one file? You can always do multiple gets or puts — not too bad if you only need a couple of files, but it can be downright painful if you want to transfer a bunch of files.

And how about specifying file types? So far, our examples have shown how to transfer ASCII text files, but if you want that neat new computer game, it's going to be stored as a *binary file*. Binary files are made up of 0s and 1s instead of letters so they can be executed by your computer, but to us they look like transmissions from outer space.

A file's filename extension gives you a clue as to whether the file contains ASCII text or binary code. ASCII files usually have names that end with the extension .TXT. Files in binary have names that end with various extensions, such as .EXE, .DOC, .ZIP, and .TIF. ■

Let's take a look at how to manage these tasks with FTP.

ASCII and ye shall receive

Unless you tell it otherwise, FTP assumes that you are moving plain old ASCII text files. But if you want to transfer something a bit more exotic, like that new game or maybe a zipped file with a special format, FTP has the binary option to take care of that. ("Zipping" is one form of file compression; see "Smart FTP Tricks" later.)

To switch to binary mode, type **binary** at the ftp> prompt any time before you type **get** or **put**. Then, after transferring your binary file, you can easily switch back to ASCII transfer mode by typing **ascii**.

If you transfer a file in the "wrong" mode, you may not be able to use it. This is especially true if you copy an application in ASCII mode. You'll have to redo the copying operation in the correct mode. The FTP client application doesn't warn you when you're doing it wrong, because it doesn't know that something might be wrong. It can only do what you tell it to do.

Shortcuts for multiple files

If you want lots of files, FTP has two commands, **mget** and **mput** (for multiple get and multiple put), that allow you to transfer groups of files. Just name the files right after the command, like this:

```
ftp> mget file1 file2
ftp> mput file3 file4
```

Here *file1, file2,* and so forth stand for the names of the files you want. The only catch is that the list of files has to fit on one line. (See "Using Wildcards" just below.)

You can't rename the files you copy with mget and mput, so you may have to use multiple get and put commands.

Turning Off Prompt: By default, FTP asks you to confirm the copy before it transfers each file. If this gets on your nerves, you can turn it off by typing the **prompt** command before typing the mget or mput command, like this:

```
ftp> prompt
```

The prompt command is a "toggle," which means each time you enter it, it turns prompt mode either on or off. So if you turn prompt mode off, just type the command again to turn it back on again. ∎

Using wildcards

If you want to copy a group of files large enough that all their names don't fit on the command line, you can use *wildcard characters* to condense the string of names.

For example, to copy the files that contain account records for multiple customers whose names start with *smit,* you would use an asterisk (*) wildcard, attached to a partial filename, like this:

```
ftp> mget smit*
```

This tells ftp to get all the files whose names start with the characters preceding the *.

If you want to copy every file in the directory, it's even easier: Just use a single * with the mget or mput command. For example, to put all the files from your local directory into the remote computer's directory, type

```
ftp> mput *
```

To see all this in action, take a look at the sample ftp session in Figure 9-5.

```
% ftp frodo
Connected to frodo.
220 frodo FTP server (SunOS 4.1) ready.                          You already know
Name (bilbo:wilensky): student9                                  this signing-on part
331 Password required for student9.
Password:
230 User student9 logged in.
ftp> dir                                                         Your first command
200 PORT command successful.
150 ASCII data connection for /bin/ls (130.103.40.225,1109) (0 bytes).
total 36
-rw------  1 student9 users        0 Mar  1  1994 .Xauthority
-rw-r--r-- 1 student9 users      579 Feb 18  1994 .Xdefaults
-rw-r--r-- 1 student9 users    13888 Jan 26  1994 .Xpdefaults
-rw-r--r-- 1 student9 users      449 Feb 18  1994 .aliases
-rw-r--r-- 1 student9 users      793 Jan 26  1994 .cshrc      UNIX
-rw-r--r-- 1 student9 users      790 Feb 18  1994 .login      directory
-rw-r--r-- 1 student9 users        6 Dec 13  1993 .logout     listing of
-rw-r--r-- 1 student9 users     4340 Dec 13  1993 .mwmrc      files on
lrwxrwxrwx 1 student9 users       27 Feb 18  1994 .xinitrc -> the server
/usr1/student9/.xinitrc.twm
-rw-r--r-- 1 student9 users     1221 Jan 26  1994 .xinitrc.mwm
-rw-r--r-- 1 student9 users      459 Feb 18  1994 Notes
-rw-r--r-- 1 student9 users     3027 Jan 27  1994 jbigram.id
drwxr-xr-x 4 student9 users     3072 Jan 27  1994 notes
-rw-r--r-- 1 student9 users     1490 Jan 10  1994 notes.tmp
226 ASCII Transfer complete.
939 bytes received in 0.074 seconds (12 Kbytes/s)               Techie message from ftp
ftp> bin                                                        Your command to do a binary transfer
```

Figure 9-5:
A user transfers files with FTP.

```
200 Type set to I. ──────── Another ftp message
ftp> get jbigram.id ──────────────────── Finally, the transfer of the file from frodo to bilbo
200 PORT command successful.
150 Binary data connection for jbigram.id (130.103.40.225,1110) (3027 bytes).
226 Binary Transfer complete.
local: jbigram.id remote: jbigram.id
3027 bytes received in 0.0014 seconds (2.1e+03 Kbytes/s)
ftp> ascii ──────────── Your command to do an ASCII file transfer    More messages
200 Type set to A.
ftp> put dead.letter                                                  Transfer a file
200 PORT command successful.                                          from bilbo to
150 ASCII data connection for dead.letter (130.103.40.225,1111).      frodo
226 ASCII Transfer complete.
local: dead.letter remote: dead.letter
1097 bytes sent in 0.0022 seconds (5e+02 Kbytes/s)
ftp> quit
221 Goodbye.
%
```

Figure 9-5:
(continued)

"Looking at" a file

Want to check out the contents of a file without actually transferring it? Just specify an output filename of hyphen (-). For example:

```
ftp> get README -
```

This command gets the README file transferred to your screen. It doesn't matter which operating system you're using; the hyphen always means the screen. The file is not saved in any way. If you like the contents of the file and want a copy of your own, get it again without the hyphen. ■

Using Anonymous FTP to Get Good Stuff

On The Internet, there are a large number of publicly accessible FTP servers. These are known as *Anonymous FTP sites* or *archives,* because when you connect to them, you specify **anonymous** as the account name. When you are challenged for a password, enter your own e-mail address. Actually, you can enter *any*thing here, except *no*thing (you have to enter *some*thing) — but the *right* thing to do is provide your e-mail address.

Some Anonymous FTP sites are provided by companies such as Microsoft, Novell, and IBM. In fact, we used Anonymous FTP to get a copy of TCP/IP from Microsoft. (The catch-22 in this was that we had to use a computer already set up with TCP/IP and connected to The Internet.) Other sites are provided by universities and numerous other good-deed doers.

Anonymous FTP sites are like snowflakes — no two are identical — but ALL of the sites contain files that you can retrieve for free. Some have megabytes and megabytes of public-domain software and shareware. Others hold graphics files and text, and still others contain weird and wonderful things too numerous to mention. (Did that get your interest?)

Although all Anonymous FTP sites are "publicly readable," only a very small percentage are "publicly writeable." You can connect to any of them and retrieve all the files you want, but most don't allow you to place files there.

In any case, Anonymous FTP is both fun and valuable. Let's all say a great big thank you to the wonderful people who provide Anonymous FTP sites. THANK YOU!

How to use Anonymous FTP

Start your FTP client application just as you did before for any regular FTP session. Once you're logged in as anonymous, go ahead and use the cd and dir commands to discover what's available at the remote site. Many directories have files named README or some variation thereof, such as README-FIRST. If you spot those files, use them as needed for help in navigating through the archives of directories and files.

If you see a directory named pub in an anonymous site, look there first. Many sites put the good *public* stuff in pub. ■

When you log in as anonymous, you may see a message from the site's manager asking you to copy files only during evening hours. This is because each FTP request chews up system resources on the remote computer, and if there are lots of you out there connecting to that remote computer, it slows down the people who work there. So, be nice.

Anonymous isn't ubiquitous

Don't assume that you can copy files from just anywhere on The Internet, or on your organization's internet. The system or network administrator at the remote site must have configured the system to allow the use of Anonymous FTP. If the remote system doesn't accept anonymous, you're out of luck. In that situation, you need a valid account's username and password if you want to use FTP to copy files to and from that computer.

Watch out: That naked lady has no PG rating

If you're parents of cyberkids, you will want to monitor what they retrieve via anonymous FTP. They can get great stuff, such as a copy of a U.S. Supreme Court decision to use in a school report. Dream on, you say? OK, let's be more realistic — they can get lots of free computer games. But watch out for those games. Some of them are more violent than what you would like your kids to see. More significantly, be aware that, although Anonymous FTP is a great source for just about anything, among that "anything" is a wide selection of pornography. ■

Here's that dog-biscuit recipe we promised you

Did you think we were kidding in the Introduction when we said you could get a recipe for dog biscuits on The Internet? Check out Figure 9-6. But beware; this is an edited version of the recipe. You'll have to get on The Internet to have the complete one.

```
% ftp gatekeeper.dec.com
Connected to gatekeeper.dec.com.
220- *** /etc/motd.ftp ***
      Original by:  Paul Vixie, 1992
      Last Revised: Richard Schedler, April 1994

Gatekeeper.DEC.COM is an unsupported service of Digital Corporate Research.
Use entirely at your own risk - no warranty is expressed or implied.
Complaints and questions should be sent to <gw-archives@pa.dec.com>.

      EXPORT CONTROL NOTE: Non-U.S. ftp users are required by law to follow
U.S. export control restrictions, which means that if you see some DES or
otherwise controlled software here, you should not grab it.  Look at the
00README-Legal-Rules-Regs (in every directory, more or less) to learn.
(If the treaty between your country and the United States did not want
you to respect U.S. export control restrictions, then you would have
Internet connectivity to this host.  Check with your U.S. embassy
if you want to verify this.)

Extended commands available via: quote site exec COMMAND
Where COMMAND is one of:
index PATTERN   - to glance through our index (uses agrep).
```

Welcome message from the FTP site

Figure 9-6: You can use Anonymous FTP to get a recipe for dog biscuits!

```
example:
        ftp> quote site exec index emacs
locate STRING   - like "index", but faster and without RE support.
ex:
        ftp> quote site exec locate updatedb

This FTP server is based on the 4.3BSD-Reno version.  Our modified
sources are in /pub/DEC/gwtools.

If you are connecting to gatekeeper from a VMS system running a
version of earlier than V2.0, a bug in UCX will prevent the automatic
login from working. To get around this, wait for the message that says:
        %UCX-E-FTP_LOGREJ, Login request rejected and then log in by
hand with the "login" command at the "FTP>" prompt.  You should also
 consider upgrading to the latest version of UCX.
```

Welcome message from the FTP site

```
220 gatekeeper.dec.com FTP server (Version 5.97 Fri May 6 14:44:16 PDT 1994)
ready.
Name (gatekeeper.dec.com:leiden): anonymous
```
Anonymous FTP
```
331 Guest login ok, send ident as password.
Password:
```
Type your e-mail address
```
230 Guest login ok, access restrictions apply.
Remote system type is UNIX.
Using binary mode to transfer files.
```
Interesting . . . FTP server is assuming binary
```
ftp> dir
200 PORT command successful.
150 Opening ASCII mode data connection for /bin/ls.
total 27641
```
This is a huge site with lots of subdirectories
```
dr-xr-xr-x  4 root     system      512 Jan 19 06:13 .0
dr-xr-xr-x  5 root     system      512 Jan 19 06:13 .1
dr-xr-xr-x  7 root     system      512 Jan 19 06:15 .2
dr-xr-xr-x 10 root     system      512 Jan 19 06:19 .3
dr-xr-xr-x  2 root     daemon     2048 May  8 1992 .4
dr-xr-xr-x  2 root     daemon     2048 Feb 21 1992 .5
dr-xr-xr-x  2 root     daemon     2048 Mar  3 1992 .6
dr-xr-xr-x  2 root     daemon     2048 Jun  8 1992 .7
dr-xr-xr-x 11 root     system      512 Jan 19 06:35 .8
dr-xr-xr-x  6 root     system      512 Jan 19 06:37 .9
dr-xr-xr-x  2 root     daemon     4096 Jan  8 1993 .a
dr-xr-xr-x 23 root     system      512 Jan 19 07:02 .b
drwxr-xr-x  2 root     system      512 Dec 28 12:37 .c
dr-xr-xr-x  2 root     daemon     2048 Feb 19 1993 .d
dr-xr-xr-x  2 root     daemon     2048 Feb 19 1993 .e
drwxr-xr-x  4 root     system      512 Mar 11 1994 .f
-rw-r--r--  1 root     system        0 Jan 19 07:05 .fnd
dr-xr-xr-x  4 root     system      512 Mar 10 1994 .g
dr-xr-xr-x  5 root     system      512 Jan 17 16:13 .h
drwxr-xr-x  2 root     system      512 Dec 28 12:37 .i
dr-xr-xr-x  2 root     daemon     4096 Nov 17 1993 .j
drwxr-xr-x  2 root     system      512 Dec 28 12:37 .k
```
This FTP site is a UNIX system; all the d's at the beginning of each line mean directory

Figure 9-6:
(continued)

```
-r—r—r—  1 root      system           858 Dec 11   1992 00README-Legal-Rules-Regs
-r—r—r—  1 root      system         33298 Apr 28   1994 GATEWAY.DOC
-r—r—r—  1 root      system           211 Sep  6   1989 GATEWAY.DOC;1        Do what
-r—r—r—  1 root      system         51925 Apr 28   1994 GATEWAY.PS            it says
-r—r—r—  1 root      system      10894531 Jan 20 05:04 Index-byname
-r—r—r—  1 root      system       1974469 Jan 20 05:03 Index-byname.Z
-r—r—r—  1 root      system      10894531 Jan 20 05:15 Index-bytime
-r—r—r—  1 root      system       2207675 Jan 20 05:21 Index-bytime.Z
-r—r—r—  1 root.     system          4037 Jan 20   1994 README.ftp
-r—r—r—  1 root      system          4156 Nov 12 15:35 README.nfs
-r—r—r—  1 root      system          4152 Apr 13   1994 README.nfs~
-r—r—r—  1 root      system          6002 Jan 20   1994 README.www
-r—r—r—  1 root      system           647 Aug  5   1993 US-Legal-Regs-ITAR-NOTICE
-r—r—r—  1 root      system         13265 Dec 30 01:29 archive.doc
-r—r—r—  1 root      system         13279 Sep 27   1993 archive.doc~
dr-xr-xr-x 3 root    system           512 Dec 30 10:05 bin
drwxr-xr-x 7 root    system           512 Oct 27   1992 contrib
dr-x—x—x  2 root     system      512 Dec 28 12:57 dev
dr-xr-xr-x 2 root    system      512 Dec 28 12:57 etc
lrwxr-xr-x 1 root    system            30 Jan 16 01:18 gatekeeper.home.html ->
hypertext/gatekeeper.home.html
-r—r—r—  1 root      system         33298 Jan  7 06:51 gateway.doc
-r—r—r—  1 root      system         51925 Jan  7 06:51 gateway.ps
lrwxr-xr-x 1 root    system            20 Dec 31 14:12 home.html ->
gatekeeper.home.html
dr-xrwxr-x 8 root    system           512 Jan 16 01:41 hypertext
lrwxr-xr-x 1 root    system             9 Dec 28 12:57 index.html -> home.html
lrwxr-xr-x 1 root    system            30 Dec 28 12:57 info.html ->
pub/DEC/DECinfo/html/home.html
-r—r—r—  1 root      system       2012839 Jan 19 05:57 locate.database
dr-xr-xr-x 2 root    system          8192 Dec 28 12:36 lost+found
lrwxr-xr-x 1 root    system            11 Dec 28 12:58 private -> .1/.private
dr-xr-xr-x 2 root    system          1024 Dec 28 12:58 pub
dr-xr-xr-x 2 root    system           512 Dec 28 12:58 rom
226 Transfer complete.
ftp> cd pub ──────────────── Move to public directory
250 CWD command successful.
ftp> dir ──────────────── See what files are in it
200 PORT command successful.
150 Opening ASCII mode data connection for /bin/ls.
total 38
lrwxr-xr-x 1 root    system            11 Dec 28 12:58 Alpha -> ../.b/Alpha
lrwxr-xr-x 1 root    system             9 Dec 28 12:58 BSD -> ../.0/BSD
lrwxr-xr-x 1 root    system             9 Dec 28 12:58 DEC -> ../.2/DEC
lrwxr-xr-x 1 root    system             3 Dec 28 12:58 Digital -> DEC
lrwxr-xr-x 1 root    system             9 Dec 28 12:58 GNU -> ../.8/GNU
lrwxr-xr-x 1 root    system            10 Dec 28 12:58 Mach -> ../.b/Mach
```

Figure 9-6:
(continued)

```
lrwxr-xr-x  1 root      system        10 Dec 28 12:58 NIST -> ../.b/NIST
lrwxr-xr-x  1 root      system        13 Dec 28 12:58 UCB -> ../.0/BSD/UCB
lrwxr-xr-x  1 root      system         9 Dec 28 12:58 VMS -> ../.b/VMS
lrwxr-xr-x  1 root      system         9 Dec 28 12:58 X11 -> ../.9/X11
lrwxr-xr-x  1 root      system        17 Dec 28 12:58 X11-contrib ->
../.b/X11-contrib
lrwxr-xr-x  1 root      system        12 Dec 28 12:58 athena -> ../.b/athena
lrwxr-xr-x  1 root      system        10 Dec 28 12:58 case -> ../.b/case
lrwxr-xr-x  1 root      system        10 Dec 28 12:58 comm -> ../.b/comm
lrwxr-xr-x  1 root      system        17 Dec 28 12:58 conferences ->
../.8/conferences
lrwxr-xr-x  1 root      system        10 Dec 28 12:58 data -> ../.b/data
lrwxr-xr-x  1 root      system        14 Dec 28 12:58 database -> ../.8/database
lrwxr-xr-x  1 root      system         9 Dec 28 12:58 doc -> ../.b/doc
lrwxr-xr-x  1 root      system        13 Dec 28 12:58 editors -> ../.b/editors
lrwxr-xr-x  1 root      system        12 Dec 28 12:58 forums -> ../.b/forums
lrwxr-xr-x  1 root      system        11 Dec 28 12:58 games -> ../.b/games
lrwxr-xr-x  1 root      system        14 Dec 28 12:58 graphics -> ../.8/graphics
lrwxr-xr-x  1 root      system        10 Dec 28 12:58 mail -> ../.8/mail
lrwxr-xr-x  1 root      system        10 Dec 28 12:58 maps -> ../.b/maps
lrwxr-xr-x  1 root      system        11 Dec 28 12:58 micro -> ../.f/micro
lrwxr-xr-x  1 root      system        10 Dec 28 12:58 misc -> ../.8/misc
lrwxr-xr-x  1 root      system        16 Dec 28 12:58 multimedia ->
../.b/multimedia
lrwxr-xr-x  1 root      system         9 Dec 28 12:58 net -> ../.3/net
lrwxr-xr-x  1 root      system        10 Dec 28 12:58 news -> ../.8/news
lrwxr-xr-x  1 root      system        10 Dec 28 12:58 plan -> ../.9/plan
lrwxr-xr-x  1 root      system        15 Dec 28 12:58 published ->
../.b/published
lrwxr-xr-x  1 root      system        13 Dec 28 12:58 recipes -> ../.2/recipes
lrwxr-xr-x  1 root      system         8 Dec 28 12:58 sf -> ../.b/sf
lrwxr-xr-x  1 root      system        15 Dec 28 12:58 standards ->
../.b/standards
lrwxr-xr-x  1 root      system        12 Dec 28 12:58 sysadm -> ../.b/sysadm
lrwxr-xr-x  1 root      system        10 Dec 28 12:58 text -> ../.8/text
lrwxr-xr-x  1 root      system        12 Dec 28 12:58 usenet -> ../.b/usenet
lrwxr-xr-x  1 root      system        12 Dec 28 12:58 usenix -> ../.9/usenix
226 Transfer complete.
ftp> cd recipes
250 CWD command successful.
ftp> dir
200 PORT command successful.
150 Opening ASCII mode data connection for /bin/ls.
total 1646
-r--r--r--  1 21        30            1903 Feb 12  1987 apple-crisp
-r--r--r--  1 21        30            2127 Jul  3  1986 apple-pie-1
-r--r--r--  1 21        30            2544 Oct 23  1986 apple-pie-2
-r--r--r--  1 21        30            1970 Jan 22  1987 banana-bread
```

You could get some new games

Move down another level of subdirectories

What recipe files are there?

recipes
Soup to nuts in here

Figure 9-6:
(continued)

```
-r-r-r-   1 21      30        2895 Sep 24  1987 biscuits-1
-r-r-r-   1 21      30        3820 Sep 25  1986 bread
-r-r-r-   1 21      30        3717 Oct 31  1986 bread-rye
-r-r-r-   1 21      30        3199 Nov 20  1986 bread-stuff-1
-r-r-r-   1 21      30        2793 Apr 21  1988 bread-white-1
-r-r-r-   1 21      30        4197 Mar 19  1987 brownies-1
-r-r-r-   1 21      30        2173 Nov  5  1987 brownies-2
-r-r-r-   1 21      30        2143 May 19  1988 carrot-bars
-r-r-r-   1 21      30        4975 Jun 10  1986 carrot-pudding
-r-r-r-   1 21      30        2930 Jul  9  1987 carrotcake-1
-r-r-r-   1 21      30        2474 Jan 22  1987 carrotcake-2
-r-r-r-   1 21      30        2086 Dec  3  1987 carrots-gratin
-r-r-r-   1 21      30        3924 Jan 11  1987 cheesecake-1
-r-r-r-   1 21      30        3164 Apr 26  1986 cheesecake-2
-r-r-r-   1 21      30        1923 Apr 26  1986 cheesecake-3
-r-r-r-   1 21      30        2623 Jun  5  1986 cheesecake-4
-r-r-r-   1 21      30        2297 Feb 11  1987 cheesecake-5
-r-r-r-   1 21      30        3291 Feb 11  1987 cheesecake-6
-r-r-r-   1 21      30        4620 Mar 19  1987 cheesecake-7
-r-r-r-   1 21      30        2832 Apr  7  1988 cheesecake-8
-r-r-r-   1 21      30        2626 Oct 15  1987 chicken-lime
-r-r-r-   1 21      30        2126 Jan 15  1987 chicken-macad
-r-r-r-   1 21      30        1922 Jan 15  1987 chicken-marnar
-r-r-r-   1 21      30        2117 Jun 13  1986 chicken-micrn
-r-r-r-   1 21      30        4520 Nov 15  1986 chicken-mole-1
-r-r-r-   1 21      30        2031 Jun 19  1986 chicken-mole-2
-r-r-r-   1 21      30        1906 Jan 29  1987 chicken-peanut
-r-r-r-   1 21      30        3375 Oct 15  1986 chili-1
-r-r-r-   1 21      30        1969 Jun 14  1986 chili-2
-r-r-r-   1 21      30        3374 Jan 11  1987 chili-3
-r-r-r-   1 21      30        2348 Aug 14  1986 chili-4
-r-r-r-   1 21      30        3329 Jan 11  1987 chili-5
-r-r-r-   1 21      30        1689 Nov 30  1986 chili-6
-r-r-r-   1 21      30        3462 Nov 19  1987 chili-7
-r-r-r-   1 21      30        2614 Jan 11  1987 choc-cake-1
-r-r-r-   1 21      30        2960 Jan 15  1987 choc-cake-2
-r-r-r-   1 21      30        3179 Jan 29  1987 choc-cake-3
-r-r-r-   1 21      30        2401 Feb 19  1987 choc-cake-4
-r-r-r-   1 21      30        2323 Jul 23  1988 choc-cake-5
-r-r-r-   1 21      30        3005 Dec  1  1986 choc-chip-1
-r-r-r-   1 21      30        2199 Jun 12  1986 choc-chip-2
-r-r-r-   1 21      30        2283 Apr 26  1986 choc-chip-3
-r-r-r-   1 21      30        3124 Apr 26  1986 choc-chip-4
-r-r-r-   1 21      30        2171 Jan 22  1987 coco-chips
-r-r-r-   1 21      30        1869 Jun  9  1987 coconut-drops
-r-r-r-   1 21      30        2201 Jun  9  1987 coconut-joys
-r-r-r-   1 21      30        2759 Jan  1  1987 coconut-shrimp
-r-r-r-   1 21      30        2277 Jan 13  1987 cod-pudding
```

You can never have too many of these

Lots of free recipes

Should we have a bake-off?

Figure 9-6:
(continued)

```
-r—r—r—  1 21      30        2657 Jun 14  1986 coffee-cake-1
-r—r—r—  1 21      30        3320 Apr 16  1987 coffee-cake-2
-r—r—r—  1 21      30        2561 Jul  5  1986 crab-butter
-r—r—r—  1 21      30        4190 Dec 11  1986 cranb-bread-1
-r—r—r—  1 21      30        2102 Jun 10  1986 cranb-chicken
-r—r—r—  1 21      30        2241 Oct 29  1987 cranb-cookies
-r—r—r—  1 21      30        2715 Dec 14  1987 cranb-quiche
-r—r—r—  1 21      30        2567 Nov 20  1986 cranb-relish
-r—r—r—  1 21      30        3717 Jan 11  1987 cranb-relish-2
-r—r—r—  1 21      30        1979 Jul  3  1988 cranb-relish-3
-r—r—r—  1 21      30        1832 Nov 20  1986 cranb-sauce-1
-r—r—r—  1 21      30        2682 Sep 24  1987 dandelions
-r—r—r—  1 21      30        2773 Mar 26  1987 dog-biscuits
-r—r—r—  1 21      30        1721 Aug  5  1988 drunk-leeks
-r—r—r—  1 21      30        1916 Dec  1  1986 egg-mousse
-r—r—r—  1 21      30        1888 Jun 19  1987 eggnog1
-r—r—r—  1 21      30        2170 Dec 18  1986 eggnog2
-r—r—r—  1 21      30        6000 Nov 15  1986 eggnog3
-r—r—r—  1 21      30        3408 Jul  4  1988 meat-pie-1
-r—r—r—  1 21      30        3481 Jul 10  1986 meat-pie-2
-r—r—r—  1 21      30        2545 Jul 10  1986 meat-pie-3
-r—r—r—  1 21      30        4244 Jul  7  1988 meat-pie-4
-r—r—r—  1 21      30        2651 Jun 12  1986 meatballs-1
-r—r—r—  1 21      30        2066 Mar 12  1987 meatballs-2
 r  r—r—  1 21      30        ?541 Oct 19  1986 meatloaf-1
-r—r—r—  1 21      30        1888 Aug 22  1986 meatloaf-2
-r—r—r—  1 21      30        2667^O
ftp> get dog-biscuits
200 PORT command successful.
150 Opening BINARY mode data connection for dog-biscuits (2773 bytes).
226 Transfer complete.
2773 bytes received in 0.367 secs (7548 bytes/sec)
ftp> quit
221 Goodbye.
%
```

Aha!
Here's
the one
we want

Type Ctrl+O to suppress
the rest of the list

Nothing's too good for Fido

Maybe this should have been
transferred in ASCII mode.
Remember, they warned us
up front about binary.

Figure 9-6:
(continued)

Smart FTP Tricks

FTP . . . transferring files . . . get and put . . . sounds pretty basic, doesn't it?
But what if you've copied a compressed file — can you use it? And what
about those people out there who would love to use FTP, but whose connection to the outside world provides only e-mail? Are they out of luck?

Following are a couple of smart FTP tricks you can use to make life on The
Internet easier.

✔ How to decompress compressed files

✔ How to work around your connectivity problems to receive files from FTP archives when you can't open an FTP connection

FTP can squeeze you in

Disk space is nearly always a problem for almost everyone. The unwritten rule is, the more you have, the more you fill it up — and there is *never* enough. To save space and make even more files available to you, many FTP sites *compress* their files. Once you find the file you want, your job is to uncompress it so you can use it. Here's where you have to get smart.

Unfortunately, there's no neat little utility called FTP Unzip to get you by. So your first task is to determine what compression method was used on the file. There are literally dozens of (and maybe more) ways to compress files. That's why we think dir will become one of your favorite FTP commands — because dir is the command you use to find the README files. We're not kidding. Read the README first, and it will probably tell you how the files were compressed and where to get the decompression utility. Most compression/decompression programs are in the public domain (which means they're free or very cheap).

Sometimes you can tell what compression software was used by looking at the file type. The file type is represented by a period and some letters following the filename. You DOS users know this as a *filename extension.* Table 9-1 lists some of the most widely used file types and the compression method used.

Table 9-1: Popular File Compression/Decompression Methods

File Type	Operating System	Compression Utility
.zip	MS-DOS	PKZIP/PKUNZIP
.z or .Z	UNIX	compress/uncompress
.tar	UNIX and many others	Actually this is a personal backup utility that groups one or more files into an archive. Tar stands for "tape archive," but you frequently find tar archives on disk (that's UNIX for you . . .).
.gz	UNIX	GNU Zip. GNU stands for "GNU's Not UNIX"; the fact that the definition includes the acronym again is cyclical on purpose. (Another clever UNIX name . . . who needs to be funny when we have UNIX?)
.sit	Macintosh	StuffIt

Beating the system with ftpmail

If you don't have an FTP client application on your computer, don't despair. It's a little harder and takes a couple of days, but yes, Virginia, there is still an FTP for you. It's called ftpmail. You send e-mail to one of many ftpmail sites on The Internet, requesting the files you want, and a couple of days later (or less if you're lucky), you have your files.

Table 9-2 lists a few ftpmail servers.

Table 9-2: Some Favorite ftpmail Sites

ftpmail Site	Country Served
decwrl.dec.com	United States
ftp.uu.net	United States
doc.ic.ac.uk	United Kingdom
cs.uow.edu.au	Australia
ieunet.ie	Ireland
ftp.uni-stuttgart.de	Germany

Once you choose your site, follow these steps to use e-mail to simulate FTP:

1. Send an e-mail message to this address:

   ```
   ftpmail@some.site
   ```

   where *some.site* is the ftpmail site you've chosen.

2. In the body of the message, put the appropriate ftpmail commands. Table 9-3 lists the most useful ones. Basically, you use the same commands you would use if you actually had FTP access to The Internet.

Table 9-3: Commands to Use with ftpmail

Command	What It Tells ftpmail
reply *your e-mail address*	Where to e-mail the files you request.
connect *anonymous ftp site*	The Internet address of the site that has the files.
chdir *directoryname*	The name of the directory holding the file. Your message can have multiple chdir commands.
get *filename*	The file to get from the directory. Your message can have multiple get commands.
ascii/binary	What file transfer method to use.
help	You want complete ftpmail instructions for this site e-mailed to you.
quit	You're done.

Remember, you'll have to wait for your files. The ftpmail site sends you a reply that it got your message, and your files follow shortly.

Using rcp (Yet Another Copy Command)

An alternative to FTP is rcp (pronounced by saying the letters *r c p*), another of the Berkeley UNIX r utilities for remote access. (This utility is not provided on all computers that use TCP/IP, however.)

The rcp utility is a little more lightweight than FTP, and therefore faster. For one thing, you don't explicitly log in with a username and password. For another, there is no anonymous rcp variation.

Here are the three ways to use rcp, with the syntax and a sample command for each.

- ✔ To copy a file from your computer to a remote computer across the network:

    rcp *local_file remote_computer:remote_file*

    ```
    rcp profits1 candace1:profits1
    ```

- ✔ To copy a file from a remote computer on the network to your local computer:

    rcp *remote_computer:remote_file local_file*

    ```
    rcp candace1:profits2 profits2
    ```

- ✔ To copy a file from one remote computer to another:

    rcp *remotecomputer_a:remotefile remotecomputer_b:remotefile*

    ```
    rcp marshallcomp:profits3 candace1:profits3
    ```

Do you remember the discussion of trust in Chapter 8? If not, or if you haven't read it yet, you should check it out. Trust is essential for rcp. ■

And now, on to Chapter 10, where we'll go fishing for information on and about other networks.

Chapter 10

Sharing Loaves and Fishes: NIS and NFS

● ●

In This Chapter

▶ Information sharing with NIS

▶ Your introduction to domains

▶ Still more clients and servers

▶ File sharing with NFS

● ●

*N*ow that you've read Chapter 9, you're no longer a file-sharing novice. You know how to use FTP and rcp to copy files across the network. You know how to log in to remote computers using telnet and rlogin so you can use files that are in place on other computers in your network or The Internet. Once you know where to find the files, you have the tools to access them.

So what more could there be? Two other network sharing services, that's what. First we'll look at NIS, the Network Information Service, and then we'll get acquainted with NFS, the Network File System. Together, these services let you do even more sharing of your network's bounty.

Fishing for Information with NIS

NIS, the Network Information Service, is a client/server environment that lets computers — primarily UNIX systems — share system and user account information over a TCP/IP network. You pronounce NIS by saying the letters *N I S.* (Some people think it rhymes with *hiss,* but we don't.)

What's in a Name?

NIS was developed by Sun Microsystems, Inc. The service was originally called Yellow Pages, but British Telecom owns the rights to that name, so Sun changed it to NIS. Some people and some computers still refer to NIS by its old initials, YP. Apparently British Telecom doesn't own the abbreviation.

In the NIS environment, an NIS client issues queries for the information stored in the NIS servers. An NIS server acts on the query and sends a response to the client. That response is either the requested information or an indication that there is no information. (Do you have any Threes? Go Fish!)

Since NIS is for sharing system files, it is mainly useful to system managers. Users, as well, can benefit from NIS when they have accounts on several different computers. If you're only interested in sharing user files, skip ahead to the NFS section of this chapter.

By the way, you may be wondering how this shared information differs from FTP-shared files as described in Chapter 9. In this case, you share the information without making extra copies of the files.

What kind of info can I get with NIS?

Nifty as NIS is, the information distributed via NIS is almost exclusively specific to the UNIX operating system. NIS organizes its information into *maps*, including

- UNIX user accounts
- UNIX group definitions (a component of UNIX security)
- TCP/IP computer names and addresses (see Chapter 13)
- Mail aliases (see Chapter 7)

There is one small exception to the general UNIX flavor of NIS: Some versions of TCP/IP for Microsoft Windows can query NIS servers for computer name-and-address information. But your PC cannot be a full-function NIS client.

Why NIS is so popular

Who needs NIS? The NIS information sharing service is extremely valuable to

✔ Users, because they can easily work on more than one computer without having to remember the different usernames and passwords for every computer to which they sign on. They may not even know that NIS is running. They'll just know that life is easier because each user only needs to remember one username and one password.

✔ System managers, because they can more easily take care of multiple computers, and they don't have to reproduce as many files across the network. NIS can save system managers enormous amounts of time.

The technical specifications for NIS are freely available, and the source code has been licensed to every UNIX operating system vendor. Specifications and source code are important if you're planning to write your own version of NIS, but very few of us are. We're customers and we want to buy and use the tools that vendors build for us.

What's Domain Idea?

An *NIS domain* is the collection of computers in your organization that share the information contained in the maps. The *domain name* is the key that unlocks the data for the members of the domain.

The term domain is used by several networking products, including Microsoft Windows NT Server, Lotus Notes, and Novell NetWare. But be aware that domain has a different meaning in each and every product that uses it. As you work through this chapter, set aside any other domain definitions you might know and concentrate on NIS domains as defined just above. ■

Master of your domain

In every NIS domain there is one, and only one, *master server*. One of the computers in your organization must be selected to fill this role. The NIS master server holds the data files that feed the maps. Whenever a map's data needs to be changed, the UNIX system manager edits the proper data file on the master server.

The NIS master server answers queries from NIS clients and periodically supplies the *slave servers*, if any, with copies of the map data.

The role of slave servers

In the NIS domain there may be slave servers; they are optional, and there are no hard-and-fast rules about how many to have. The fundamental role of slave servers is to help the master server answer client queries. NIS clients don't care which server answers a query, as long as the answer is correct.

Every NIS slave server answers queries from NIS clients and periodically gets copies of the map data from the master server.

The role of the clients

In an NIS domain, there are only three roles. If a participating computer is not the master server or a slave server, it is simply a client. The client issues queries and eagerly awaits the answers from any available server. The master server and any slave servers are technically clients too, but they normally handle their own needs.

As an end user, you can log in to the master server, a slave server, or a client computer. Your account information is available throughout the domain. The system manager may choose to limit access to the servers since they're usually pretty busy.

Figure 10-1 illustrates a domain where the master server is updating maps for two slave servers. Two clients are looking up user account information on the master, and one other client is accessing account information on one of the slaves.

Domain Octopussy

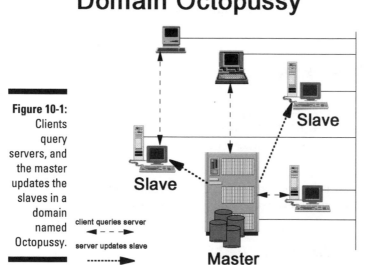

Figure 10-1:
Clients query servers, and the master updates the slaves in a domain named Octopussy.

Slave

Slave

client queries server

server updates slave

Master

NIS in Action

Let's look at a famous fictitious fish and mollusk distributor, Odd Octopus Pies and Sushi, OOPS. The company has 20 computers distributed throughout its international branch offices. All of the computers run the UNIX operating system. Traveling salespeople have accounts on all 20 computers and can log in to any available computer at whatever site they happen to be visiting for the day.

How does NIS serve this company?

Behind the scenes at OOPS

On UNIX systems, user account information is stored in a file called /etc/passwd. (The directory part, /etc/, is pronounced "slash *E T C* slash"; or "slash etsee slash." The passwd part is generally pronounced "passwid"; get a Boston native to say it for you). This file holds usernames, passwords, home directories, and other general user information. So, if OOPS has 20 computers, that means someone has to store and update 20 passwd files.

The OOPS problem

Employment at OOPS is volatile. After all, selling octopus products can be quite lucrative, but the demand is limited to only a few parts of the world. The system manager, Clem Chowder, keeps plenty busy maintaining those 20 passwd files, and he never has time to do any research on toxicity studies and local dredging regulations — much less sample his company's wares. OOPS needs to find a way to share one copy of the passwd file across all 20 of the computers.

The OOPS solution

Ta da! It's NIS to the rescue. Since NIS is part of UNIX, Clem doesn't need to purchase or install it. He's already got NIS. So Clem decides to create an NIS domain for the 20 OOPS computers. He chooses Octopussy as the domain name and picks one computer to be the master server. The other 19 computers join the Octopussy domain as NIS clients.

Clem then stores the information from all 20 computers in files on the master server. Those files feed the NIS maps. When Clem learns about new employees, he only has to update the central files. Now he has time to eat all the octopus pies he wants.

When an OOPS employee logs in to any of the company's 20 computers, the log-in process requests account information from the master server via the UDP and IP protocols (described in Chapter 6).

OK, NIS Is Great. Are There Any Pitfalls?

There are three areas where NIS sometimes is difficult:

✔ Configuration and administration
✔ Performance
✔ Security

Let's return to our fictitious fish factory to examine these challenges and some ways to meet them.

Configuration and administration

System administrator Clem Chowder may have a lot of work ahead of him when he initially sets up NIS. He needs to change from a local file model with multiple copies of the password and system files, to a single, central set of files replacing or supplementing the local files. This task is not simply a matter of deleting the local files and creating the central NIS files. Rather, it's a question of deciding how much information (if any) to keep local and how much to share across the network. So, the initial setup to deploy NIS may take a long time — but it's worth it to gain the benefits of easier management in the future.

Some UNIX operating system vendors provide a tool to set up NIS. For example, Digital Equipment Corporation gives you nissetup. These tools do all the work of editing files and configuring computers as servers or clients. If he uses a tool, Clem doesn't have to flounder <grin> around in a sea <second grin> of configuration files.

OOPS's files on the master server are only as good as the most recent update, so Clem has to be careful to take care of updates immediately. Happily, with NIS he has only to update the central files, and that's a lot less work than having to maintain 20 copies as in the pre-NIS system.

Performance

The queries from the clients (the main school of OOPS's computers) to the master and slave servers result in increased network traffic, and the larger the domain (that is, the more computers in the domain), the more a network's response may slow down.

Also, if OOPS has just one master server and no slaves, when all the clients hit on the master at the same time, the performance of the master server will slow down everyone in the domain. Using slave servers helps reduce the load on the master, but they put another, different burden on the master server: keeping the slaves' maps up to date.

The master server, then, is a single point of failure. If the master server is out of action and there are no slave servers, the clients' queries are not answered. The client application that issued the query remains waiting — conceivably forever — for the answer, unless the user can abort the program's request. NIS queries are such a common part of the normal operation of the client that the computer will ultimately be incapable of completing any processing for any user. The client doesn't crash, but it seems to freeze solid, or "hang." We think you can see the value of having at least one slave server on the network.

If the master server is out of action, the slave servers answer queries, but they can't continue forever. To keep their maps up to date, the slave servers issue periodic queries to the master server. When these go unanswered, the slave servers eventually hang, and then the clients hang.

There is no automatic way to convert a slave server into a replacement master server. So Clem, if he's wise, keeps backup copies of the data files in safe places and maintains a plan for manually converting one of the slave servers into a temporary master server. OOPS needs at least one slave per network segment.

Security

Using NIS may open up some holes in the security of the OOPS network. Clem cannot restrict membership in the NIS domain — any computer can join the domain at any time and access all the information in the maps. The only piece of information that an OOPS employee needs to add a client to the domain is the domain name, Octopussy. To add a slave server, an employee needs only the domain name and the name of the master server. If the employee were to set up another master server for the Octopussy domain, the slave servers wouldn't use it because they know the name of the master server, but the clients would accept the responses from the phony server.

It is possible for a malicious person to add a client to the domain, take the UNIX account information from the passwd map, and attempt to break into users' accounts. Someone *really* evil could add a bogus master or slave server that replies to queries with incorrect data.

What should OOPS do to prevent any of this? One option might be NIS+, which is described next. Clem and his contemporaries should also check out the security information in Chapter 19.

NIS+ — a fine kettle of fish

Sun Microsystems created NIS+, a new generation of NIS. The old NIS maps become NIS+ tables, but their function is the same — to store in central locations information about user accounts and computers, network addresses, and system configuration data.

NIS+ offers improved performance features for large domains, as well as tighter security, but the new product is not yet available from all the UNIX vendors. Until it is, Odd Octopus Pies and Sushi must accept the security risks as the price they pay for a useful service.

Using NFS to Share Fishes . . . er, Files

Sharing disk space is one of the most common reasons to link computers via a network. (Sharing printers and sending e-mail are at the top of the list, too.) You've just finished reading about NIS maps — one example of sharing system files. But what about user files, such as documents, spreadsheets, text, and word processing documents? If Ms. Selena Sushi, a user in the OOPS domain, can log in to any computer, can she see her files there? Or will she have to copy them from her home computer to the computer at which she is logged in for the day?

In Chapter 9 you learned how FTP and rcp are used for copying files, so if Ms. Sushi has to copy her files, she's got the tools. But if she copies files, she'll be using twice the disk space, and if she updates any files, she'll have to be careful to copy those updates back to her home computer. Otherwise, her files will be out of sync. There must be an easier way for Ms. Sushi to stay in touch with her files, you say? Without copying them all over the company as she travels?

You're right — there is. It's called NFS, the Network File System (pronounced by saying the letters *N F S*). NFS uses the UDP and IP protocols (discussed in Chapter 6). NFS is extremely common on UNIX systems and is also supported on most other operating systems.

NFS = Nifty File Sharing

NFS is a client/server environment that allows computers to share disk space, and users to see their files from multiple computers without having to copy the files to those computers. It's file sharing in place.

In the NFS environment, computers that have disk space they are willing to share are NFS servers, and computers borrowing disk space are NFS clients. A given computer can be

- ✔ Either an NFS server or an NFS client
- ✔ Both a server and a client simultaneously
- ✔ Neither a server nor a client

Most operating systems provide the NFS client portion, but some do not provide the server.

Who needs NFS? The NFS disk sharing service is extremely valuable to

- ✔ Users, because they can access much more disk space
- ✔ System managers, because they can more easily provide disk space to the users and more easily back up the users' files

NFS was originally developed for UNIX by Sun Microsystems, Inc. (also the creator of NIS, as mentioned earlier). The technical specifications are easy to get, and the source code has been licensed to every UNIX operating system vendor. Specifications and source code are important if you're planning to write a version of NFS yourself, but very few of us are. We're customers and we want to use the tools that vendors build for us.

Why is NFS so great?

One of the best things about NFS is that it is "transparent." With NFS, the OOPS employees cannot tell the difference between local disk space (connected directly to a particular computer) and shared disk space coming from an NFS server.

With NFS, Selena Sushi can work at any participating computer and still have access to her files. The files "follow" her from computer to computer, including to laptop and notebook computers when they're connected to the network. A file is a file is a file, no matter where she is logged on.

Is your computer broken? Find out who is absent today and you can use theirs. With NFS, your files are there. Do you need to use a different operating system instead of your regular one? Log in to a computer that is running what you need. With NFS, your files come with you.

Your home away from home

With NFS, it is entirely possible that your home directory will not be located on your home computer. And because file access via NFS is so transparent, you might not even know it.

What About Performance?

The NFS client/server environment is very flexible, in that any computer can play the role of client and server simultaneously. But system administrator Clem Chowder should think about the trade-offs between flexibility and performance when he sets up the servers. For example, if the most frequently used file is Charlie Tuna's inventory file, it should be placed on a fast disk on the most powerful computer for quick retrieval.

For best performance, Clem can dedicate a computer to be an NFS server and limit the other services provided by that computer. Everyone's files get stored on the NFS server, and the users' computers become clients that access the files on the server. A dedicated NFS server also makes it easier for Clem to back up all the OOPS employees' files, because all files are on one computer. Clem can and should dedicate as many computers as he needs. He's not limited to just one.

If OOPS employees are working on a really big project, such as editing a large document, they can reduce network traffic (and therefore work faster) by logging in to the server to work on the file locally. On the other hand, with a dedicated server, Clem may not be too happy about letting everybody log in directly to the server — and in fact may not even allow them to, unless they have a very good reason such as a long edit session on that large document.

Getting in one another's way

Because NFS maintains a single copy of files, sometimes more than one person will access the same file. If you're all just reading the file, there's no problem. But if you're trying to update the same file simultaneously, that's when the fun begins. Figure 10-2 shows three users trying to update simultaneously the file that holds the all-time scoring record, changing a piece of data called *x*.

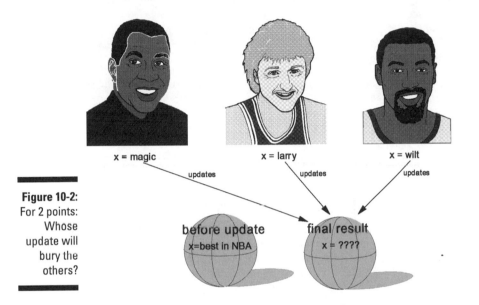

Figure 10-2:
For 2 points:
Whose
update will
bury the
others?

Which of the three updates wins? There's no way to tell. What you *can* be sure of is that in the world of NFS, just like the NBA, the winner will bury the losers' updates. Unlike the NBA, however, none of the NFS users will know what happened. It will be as if two of the updates never occurred.

Some operating systems have file systems with *locking features* (also called *concurrence control*) to avoid the problem of buried updates. The first user who grabs the data gets a lock on it, which prevents other users from updating the data. When the first user is done, the next user gets the lock and will be assured of seeing the first user's update before deciding whether to bury it or not. But you can't count on such file system locks in an environment of heterogeneous computers, operating systems, and file systems. Each computer on the network may be running a different operating system, which may or may not provide concurrence control.

Don't Buy Your Network Solutions from the Trunk of Someone's Car

When you think about performance, you have to consider hardware, ugly as that may be. As an NFS client, you're accessing files across the network. That means cables, and packets traveling across wires, and network controllers, and maybe even things like gateways and routers.

The quality and robustness of the hardware you use has a significant effect on NFS performance. If the network interface card inside your computer is old and slow, don't expect to see files as quickly as your neighbor, who's got

the latest and greatest, does. If some of the hardware in your network is cheap and unreliable, the NFS server may not always be up and running. And that means your files (and a lot of other people's) won't be at the ready.

The good news is that there are reliable, redundant hardware and software solutions to performance problems. When it comes to network hardware and server/file availability, you get what you pay for.

We're not trying to scare you away from NFS. It really is an excellent solution for sharing files and saving disk space. Many environments never encounter the "buried update" problem because most users are reading files, not updating the same shared files at the same time. If buried updates become worrisome, Clem should make sure that the operating systems and file systems both support locking. Or, OOPS can establish policies and procedures for collaborative efforts.

Mixing and Matching

TCP/IP's prized interoperability is another strength of NFS. The operating system for the server does not have to match the operating systems of the clients. That means Selena Sushi can use her PC or anybody else's PC to access files stored on a UNIX server, if that's what's been set up by Clem Chowder. On the other hand . . .

There's interoperability and then there's interoperability

There may be a few NFS surprises in a mixed operating system environment, because each operating system uses a different file format. For example, say Ms. Sushi's PC runs DOS, and she's trying to edit a file on the UNIX server. The UNIX file might appear to Selena's PC editor as one long sentence. That's because of the way the different file formats treat the ends of lines in a file.

On the DOS file system, the end of each line is marked by a two-character combination of a carriage return <CR> plus a line feed <LF>. On the UNIX file system, the end of line is marked by just one character, the line feed <LF>. And that difference confuses some PC editors and word processing products, as well. ■

Something else OOPS users (and you) must be aware of when using DOS clients is the difference in filename conventions. DOS only allows 8.3 file specifications; that is, 8 characters for the name, a . separator, followed by 3 optional characters designating the file type. UNIX allows long filenames — some versions allow them to be as long as 255 characters (although would you really want to have to type a filename that long, much less remember it?). Anyway, the best thing for the OOPS folks to do is to name files stored on the server according to the "lowest common denominator," which in most cases is DOS.

Will I Get Arrested for Automounting?

Before you can understand the *automounter* for NFS, you need to know about *mounting* in general. (And if you consider yourself an expert on mounting, please be advised that we mean mounting file systems here. Ahem.)

On UNIX, files and directories flow seamlessly together in a tree structure with a root at the top, not the bottom. (Aw, c'mon, give us a break here. This is computer science, not Earth science.) The system administrator *mounts* directories onto the tree. The users on a UNIX system do not need to know what disk device holds their files. They only need to know the files' location in the directory tree.

Figure 10-3 shows a typical UNIX directory tree. At the top is the familiar forward slash (/) representation of the root directory, meaning the top of the tree. The UNIX help directories, man1 through man8, lie on the path named /usr/man (please excuse the UNIXism).

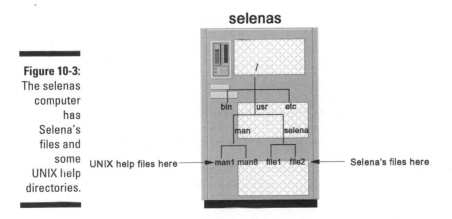

Figure 10-3:
The selenas computer has Selena's files and some UNIX help directories.

With NFS, Mr. Chowder the system administrator mounts *remote* directories on the tree. The technical term for this is "NFS mounting." The files look local to the users, even though the files exist physically on the remote computer.

Figure 10-4 shows two computers, each with a directory tree. Although the trees look exactly the same, some of the files exist only on one of the computers. The charliet computer does not have very much free disk space, so the system manager NFS-mounted the UNIX help directories there, leaving the physical directories and files residing on the selenas computer. Users on the charliet computer access the help files just as if they were local. Even the directory path name is the same, /usr/man/man1. Clem then does the same with Selena's files. When Selena is logged in to the charliet computer, she can access her files in exactly the same way as when she is on the selenas computer.

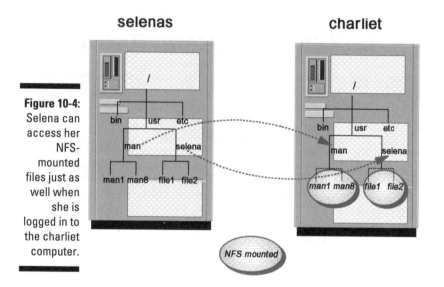

Figure 10-4: Selena can access her NFS-mounted files just as well when she is logged in to the charliet computer.

Now do I get to find out what the automounter is?

Yes, now you do. Consider this: Selena usually does not sign on to the charliet computer; only occasionally does she need to see her files there. Keeping that in mind, Clem Chowder does not want to have Selena's files always mounted on charliet. Nor does he want to be at Selena's beck and call to mount the files on charliet whenever Selena decides she needs them. Clem is, after all, a busy person.

Enter the automounter — an enhancement to NFS. It automatically mounts the disk space you need when you need it. This is called *dynamic mounting*. Automountable disk space is registered in an NIS map (see the discussion of NIS earlier), so the participating computers know about all of that space. The automounter is very fast; you should never notice the delay in getting to the disk space. But even if you do, the benefit is worth the tiny performance penalty.

Using the automounter is a handy option for system managers like Clem Chowder, who manage file systems that are inactive for large amounts of time. The automounter keeps a timer for each of the mounted disk spaces, so it knows when you aren't using them any more. When a timer expires, the automounter dismounts the disk space. When you need it again, the disk space is mounted again.

NIS and NFS Together

NFS and NIS are completely independent of each other, but are very often used together. As you have seen, NIS allows the information in system files to be shared; NFS allows user files themselves to be shared. When NIS and NFS are used together, Selena Sushi has only one username and one password that work on every NIS client.

When she logs in to a computer that is also an NFS client, all of her files are there waiting for her. If the computer is an NIS client only, Selena has access only to the files stored on that computer. In this case she may wind up having files stored on every computer in the NIS domain.

If the computer is an NFS client only, Selena has a separate account on every computer, and each has a unique username and a unique password — but at least she has only one set of files to worry about.

When NIS and NFS are used together, they hide the location details of remote files from you. As far as you are concerned, your account and files automatically follow you as you go from one computer to another on the network.

One computer can be both an NFS server and an NIS server (master or slave). ■

Are NIS and NFS Used on The Internet?

Re NIS: In case you haven't figured it out for yourself yet, let us be blunt — NIS is *not* used to tie The Internet together. Who would control the one master server? What would happen if it failed? How could any number of servers handle the load from the enormous number of clients? On the other hand, many of the organizations that are connected to The Internet use NIS every day. They couldn't run their networks without it.

Re NFS: Yes, there is some use of NFS on The Internet. Many of the organizations connected to The Internet also use NFS every day and couldn't run their networks without it.

Still More File Sharing

NFS is very popular, but it is not the only file-sharing system out there. Some companies offer add-on products that implement file sharing. For example, Digital Equipment Corporation's Pathworks implements file sharing with or without TCP/IP.

Another file-sharing system is RFS, the Remote File System, from AT&T (no, not the phone company part). RFS, pronounced by saying the letters *R F S,* only works on UNIX System V operating systems with no interoperability options.

A Novell NetWare file server can also be accessed via TCP/IP. The NetWare system manager must first install a product such as Novell's NetWare IP.

In this chapter we explored the client/server environments of NIS and NFS. They don't have to be used together, but the combination is quite common in organizations using UNIX. In the next chapter, you'll learn about a client/server solution used on The Internet: DNS, the Domain Name System.

Chapter 11

Fishing in a *Really* Big Pond

· ·

In This Chapter

▶ How DNS keeps The Internet's myriad computers organized

▶ The DNS version of client/server

▶ The DNS version of domains . . . Or, why your e-mail address has so many parts

▶ More about whois, and a look at nslookup

▶ A lot of technical information that you should probably forget about

· ·

*I*n Chapter 10 you went fishing for information with NIS, which lets computers that are grouped fairly close together on a network share system and user information. Well, that was small fry. That was an appetizer, a sardine, compared to the main course in this chapter.

Here you'll learn about another service: the Domain Name System (DNS, pronounced by saying the letters *D N S*). But when you fish for information with the DNS rod and reel, you are fishing not just around your own network but on The Internet.

By the way, at this point in our journey writing this book, we got full. We lost our appetite. We gained 10 pounds and decided to go on a diet. Actually, we ran out of food metaphors as the technical pace of our subject matter picked up. So, though we promise to keep you entertained right on through the appendix and the glossary, you won't find any more references to chocolate, cherries, cheesecake, or china — for a while anyway.

Getting to Know DNS

A *name service* translates (or *resolves*) a computer name into a numeric address. The Domain Name System, DNS, is the name service for The Internet, and it translates computer names into TCP/IP numeric addresses. (You'll be learning more about computer names and addresses in Chapter 13.)

If your organization's network is connected to The Internet, you *must* use DNS. If your organization has a private internet, you *may* use DNS to provide the name service for your network.

DNS was created specifically to handle the requirement that each computer needs to be uniquely named on the network. By adding some pieces to your computer name to make it unique, DNS solves the problem of duplicate computer names.

DNS = Does Nifty Searches

DNS is a way for computers to share information about computer names and addresses over a TCP/IP network. On a large network (such as The Internet), that's a lot of information.

In techie terms, DNS is the *name-and-address resolution service* used on The Internet. In more straightforward terms, DNS is a kind of directory service. It searches for and finds the numeric Internet address for a computer name, and vice versa. (Of course, if we could remember those complicated numeric addresses, we wouldn't need a name-and-address resolution service, but brain cells being what they are . . .)

Unlike NIS, which is primarily used by computers running the UNIX operating system, DNS is used by all operating systems.

Speaking of The Internet . . .

Computers on a TCP/IP network, and that includes The Internet, have both a name and a numeric address. Most of us mere mortals prefer to call our computers by name, and the network is nice enough to accept either names or numbers. When you use a name, it gets translated into numbers behind the scenes.

To be unique, a computer name has multiple parts separated by periods — that is, the . character. Though it looks like a period, the computer world calls it "dot." Take the e-mail address

```
candace@max.tiac.net
```

for example. It is pronounced "candace at max dot teeack dot net." We've run this format down for you in earlier chapters, so you'll recall that the first piece of this address, max, is the computer's name; and the last piece of the computer name on the right, net, represents a domain name — a DNS domain name. The intermediate pieces represent things like company names. ∎

Do You Drive a Lotus or Just Work There?

Remember back in Chapter 2, where you read about the ARPANET, predecessor to The Internet? Imagine a time (long ago!) when there were only a few computers on that network. Those computers had ordinary names of just one word. A computer named lotus, for example, didn't need any other names to identify it because it was the only lotus on the network. With millions of computers partici-pating on The Internet, finding unique names is more difficult. Today you'd wonder if the computer, lotus, belongs to the software vendor or the car manufacturer. And if you send e-mail to user Smith on computer lotus, will it go to your friend at the car company or to someone you never heard of at the software company?

Client/Server Again — You Can't Get Away From It

DNS is a client/server environment. Queries are issued by the clients (application programs such as telnet, FTP, etc.), asking a *name server* for a computer name to numeric address translation. If the name server can answer the query, it responds with the requested information, and all is well.

If it cannot supply the information, two things may occur, based on whether the name server is or is not *responsible for* the information (more on this shortly).

- ✔ If the name server is responsible for the information, the answer to the client is that there is no information. (Do you have any Fives? Go Fish!)

- ✔ If the name server is not responsible for the information, it forwards the query to, or at least toward, the name server that is responsible. (The name server knows to do this based on how the system manager has set things up.) When the answer comes back, it travels all the way back down the chain to the client.

If the client "times out" — gets tired of waiting for a response — that's the same as receiving a "No Information" answer from the queried name server.

If at this point *you* have timed out, too, hang in there. We're going to explain this "responsibility" thing next.

Who's responsible?

So what does it mean to be "responsible for" the name and address information? The DNS term for responsibility is *authority*. There are several different types of name servers that may be deployed in your environment. In the DNS world there is no single master server, as there is with NIS. Instead, there are *primary name servers* that know, via the DNS database, the names and addresses of the computers in your organization. These name servers are *responsible for* this information, and the answers they give to client queries are said to be *authoritative*.

Because DNS is a distributed, that is, decentralized, no one computer has to have all the information about all the addresses. Can you imagine the size of the disk you'd need to hold the addresses of all the computers on The Internet? Not practical, even if possible. Therefore, multiple name servers work together to translate a name to an address.

Name Servers and Resolvers

One of the pieces of DNS is the *name server program* that responds to queries for a resolution of a name to an address. The name server program may or may not be included in your TCP/IP product. If you need to set up and run your own name server, make sure you have the program.

Another piece of DNS is a library of programs called a *resolver,* which takes the client program's request to get address information and converts it into a query to the name server. (The resolver is part of every TCP/IP product. You need it; you have it. Don't worry.) More specifically, when a programmer writes an application that needs to know a computer's address, the application contains a call to the resolver routines. For example, this request in a program, "Open an FTP connection to computerx," generates a DNS query for the address of computerx. ∎

Figure 11-1 shows the resolver communicating with the name server on behalf of a client application.

DNS's pieces and parts

As you can tell from what you've read so far, there are lots of bits and pieces that work together for DNS, including hardware, software (programs and some TCP/IP protocols), data files, and people. Here is a summary, including the ones you've just learned about:

✔ The distributed database, which holds information about computers in domains on The Internet or on your internet

✔ Domains: logical collections of computers whose requests for network address lookups are all handled by the same server(s)

✔ Name servers: programs that access information from the database and respond to client queries

✔ Clients: programs that request network address information from the name servers

✔ The resolver, which works on behalf of the client applications to get network address information from the name server

✔ System managers and network administrators, who set everything up and maintain the databases

In the next few sections, we'll take a closer look at these pieces.

Figure 11-1:
The resolver asks the name server to answer an address query.

Another Definition of Domain: The Internet's

You'll remember reading, in our discussion of NIS in Chapter 10, that the term *domain* is used by various products and applications to mean different things. Here we go with a new one, and since Domain is the first word in the DNS name, it's a good place to start.

The Internet is so huge that it organizes its participating computers into groups of administrative units; these units are called domains. The domains themselves are organized hierarchically into a tree structure, as illustrated in Figure 11-2.

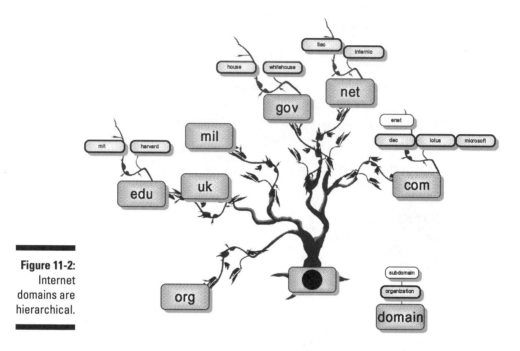

Figure 11-2:
Internet domains are hierarchical.

The Internet's tree structure has branches extending from the *top-level domains.* Your computer sits in the leaves, at the edge of this hierarchy of domains. The InterNIC establishes and maintains the domain at the root of this tree. Just above the root is the set of top-level domains, the kingfishes of The Internet.

In the United States, the top-level domains have the generic organization types listed in the following table. (You may recognize the three-character designators in the first column as the last part of many Internet addresses.)

Organization Type	*Definition*
com	Commercial enterprise
edu	Educational institution
gov	United States government
org	Organization
mil	Military service
net	Network services provider ∎

In the United States, if you want your organization to be on the Internet, you must register it with the InterNIC. Most Internet access service providers (such as NEARnet) are empowered to do this for you. When you register, either directly with the InterNIC or via the access provider, your organization is assigned to one of the top-level domains listed above.

Subdomains

The top-level domains branch out into *subdomains*, which are usually named after your organization. A subdomain is any subdivision of a domain. So a subdomain of a top-level domain is a second-level domain. If your organization is large, it may further create its own subdomains for administrative purposes; these are third-level, fourth-level, and so forth. You can see a few second-level domains in Figure 11-2 (such as mit.edu and lotus.com), and a third-level domain (enet.dec.com).

The internationalization of The Internet

Outside the United States, the rightmost piece of the Internet address is the two-character country code specified by ISO standard 3166; a few of these top-level domains are listed in the following table. So an Internet address in one of these countries would be something like oops.co.uk.

ca	Canada
in	India
uk	United Kingdom (Actually, the ISO code is GB, but it's hard to make a long story short about whether a country is in Great Britain or the UK.)
us	United States

The Subdomains, They Are A-Changin'. When you communicate with someone outside the United States, be aware that the subdomains might (or might not) have different names. In Australia, they use the same style as in the U.S. (com.au, edu.au, and so on). But in the UK, their administrative domains are named differently, as in co.uk (corporation) and ac.uk (academic community). So don't assume anything about subdomain names outside the U.S.; always look them up. As world geography changes rapidly in the 1990s, The Internet has been unable to keep pace. For example, the top-level domain yu still exists on The Internet, even though Yugoslavia no longer exists on the world map. ■

What Did The Internet Say to the Domain?

F Q. Before you say "Hey! Same to you!", please read on. We explained earlier that a DNS domain is the collection of computers in an organization that are the responsibility of the same DNS servers. If your organization is using DNS, it has at least one DNS domain, and the name of the domain is the key that unlocks the data for the domain members. Let's take a closer look at these domain names.

You have already seen some DNS domain names used in this book. (They can be part of e-mail addresses.) For example, when you send mail to mwilensky@abc.university.edu, the university.edu part of this address is the domain name. Each DNS domain has a unique name. This name is so important that it actually becomes part of each computer's name. The result is called a *fully qualified domain name,* or *FQDN,* pronounced by saying the letters *F Q D N.*

Here are some examples:

> ✔ The computer named **hbs** is part of the DNS domain named **harvard.edu**, yielding the FQDN **hbs.harvard.edu.**
>
> ✔ The mythical computer named **viper** is part of the mythical DNS domain named **support.lotus.com** yielding the FQDN **viper.support.lotus.com**.

Figure 11-3 shows what these two FQDNs look like on the Internet tree.

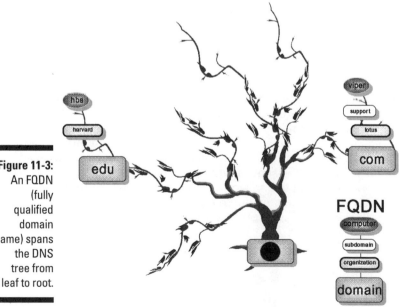

Figure 11-3:
An FQDN (fully qualified domain name) spans the DNS tree from leaf to root.

FQDNs are so long! Are there any shortcuts?

Yes, there are — depending on where you're sending e-mail from. If you send mail to mwilensky@abc.university.edu, the mail will reach him no matter where you are when you send it. On the other hand, that's a pretty long address to have to type. To make things easier, you don't always have to use an FQDN. If you don't, TCP/IP assumes the domain is the same as yours.

So if you, too, are on computer abc, you can simply send mail to the user-name mwilensky, and save some typing. If you're on a different machine, say computer xyz, but your computer is also in the university.edu domain, you can leave out the domain name and just send to mwilensky@abc.

These shortcuts are not limited to e-mail. ■

Servers, Authority, and Other Techie Stuff

There are three types of servers you can have in your DNS domain:

- ✔ The primary name server
- ✔ The secondary name server(s)
- ✔ The caching name server(s)

Before we examine their roles in the scheme of things, be sure you know your authority figures. Read on . . .

Who's in charge here?

In the DNS environment, a name server — any kind of name server — can be one of three different states when queried by the client:

- ✔ It knows the answer *authoritatively*. That means it has the answer in its data files. This is the same as being responsible for the data.
- ✔ It knows the answer, but *not authoritatively*. That means it has stored (*cached*) in memory the data it learned from some previous query.
- ✔ It doesn't know the answer and has to ask another server. ■

You'll see examples of authoritative and nonauthoritative answers later in Figure 11-11.

Primary name servers are the authority for their *zone*. A zone is often the same as a domain, but not always (see the later sidebar, "Zoning Out . . . "). A primary name server can delegate authority to a *secondary name server,* to lessen the primary's workload and to give it a backup. (Is this starting to sound like life at the office? To relieve stress, delegate!)

When the primary name server delegates authority, it ships the truth, in the form of the database, to the secondary name server. The more the primary can delegate, the more stress relief it gets. Each domain should have a primary and at least one secondary name server.

Caching name servers also help relieve stress, but they're not entirely trustworthy, since they don't have the real truth in the form of database files on disk. Caching name servers have what they "believe" to be the truth, in the cache. (It's sort of like an office intern or apprentice — they're eager to help out, but do you trust them to do the tough stuff?)

All servers do caching, especially of the data for which they are not responsible. Caching servers do *only* caching, since they have no data files and are not responsible for any information.

The primary is master of the domain

The primary name server is the "big" one. It has authority for its whole domain. That means the master stores the databases for its zone. It can also delegate authority to secondary name servers. The primary server is the ultimate repository of truth — at least as far as the names and addresses in the domain are concerned.

By the way, please don't confuse the DNS primary name server with an NIS master server. (You do remember NIS from the last chapter, don't you?)

The secondary name servers

In school, the little kids in primary school look up to the big kids in secondary school. But on The Internet, it's just the opposite: Secondary name servers download copies of name/address information from a primary or another secondary name server.

The more secondary name servers your organization has, the less chance there is of clogging up the primary name server, and the better protected you are from a failure of the primary. Secondary name servers are the backups for the primaries, and if the primary delegates authority, the secondary can answer address queries from any other name server in its zone.

The big difference between a primary name server and a secondary name server is where they get their information. The primary gets it from the database files; the secondary gets it loaded in from a primary or another secondary name server. Figure 11-4 shows a primary/secondary/caching server configuration.

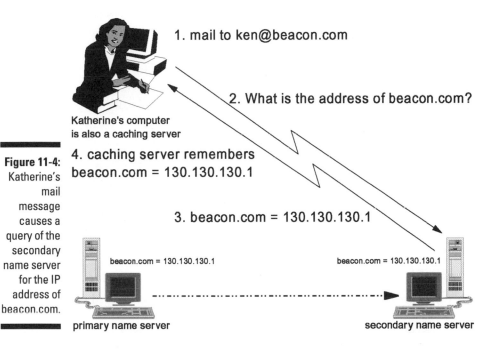

1. mail to ken@beacon.com

2. What is the address of beacon.com?

Katherine's computer
is also a caching server

Figure 11-4:
Katherine's
mail
message
causes a
query of the
secondary
name server
for the IP
address of
beacon.com.

4. caching server remembers
beacon.com = 130.130.130.1

3. beacon.com = 130.130.130.1

beacon.com = 130.130.130.1   beacon.com = 130.130.130.1

primary name server   secondary name server

Caching servers

Caching servers have no authority in a DNS arrangement and do not store any databases on their disks. They depend on the kindness of other name servers for information. The caching servers query other servers for name/address information and keep (i.e., cache) it in memory for users who are geographically close.

If Katherine sends mail to ken@beacon.com, her local caching server will look up beacon.com in the DNS and hold on to the information. (In Figure 11-4, you can see that beacon.com is 130.130.130.1.) When Katherine sends Ken another mail message, beacon.com's IP address is now quickly available from the caching server, and her request for the name-to-address translation is spared a long trip across the network.

Figure 11-5 shows how a caching server saves time and steps.

1. mail to ken@beacon.com

Katherine's computer
is also a caching server

There's only 1 step now since
the caching server remembers
beacon.com = 130.130.130.1

Figure 11-5:
The numeric
address of
beacon.com
is stored by
a caching
server.

beacon.com = 130.130.130.1   beacon.com = 130.130.130.1

primary name server   secondary name server

What could possibly go wrong?

Take a close look at Figure 11-6. It seems that beacon.com has been renumbered; the address on the primary name server is now 130.130.130.2. But Katherine's caching server is holding the old address information. To avoid this problem, the cached data in a name server expires periodically.

To manage this expiration procedure, the administrator of the authoritative name servers (the ones responsible for knowing the truth) sets a Time To Live, TTL, value for the name/address data. Think of the TTL as a timer that limits how long any name server can cache the data. When the timer runs out, the cached data must be discarded. Without the TTL, no updates would ever replace old information. Remember that the resolver issues a query for computer name to address translation every time you go out on the network, regardless of the application you are using.

Smaller TTL values mean that the data cached by nonauthoritative name servers (including the caching servers) is updated more often. The trade-off is that those name servers must query more frequently. Larger TTL values reduce network traffic but increase the likelihood that old, possibly incorrect, data is still alive. ■

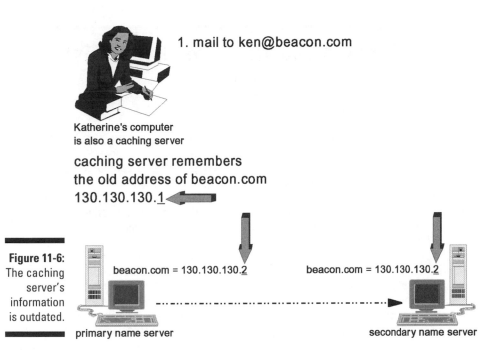

Figure 11-6:
The caching server's information is outdated.

1. mail to ken@beacon.com

Katherine's computer
is also a caching server

caching server remembers
the old address of beacon.com
130.130.130.1

beacon.com = 130.130.130.2   beacon.com = 130.130.130.2

primary name server   secondary name server

Servers, lies, and videotapes

We lied. There are no videotapes. And there are more than three name server types.

Now that you're a name server expert, there are two more types you should know about: *slave name servers* and *forwarding name servers.* Though not as widely used as primary and secondary and caching name servers, they have their uses.

A slave name server can function as a primary or secondary or as a caching name server. The difference is that the slave has no direct contact with The Internet. If a slave name server does not have the information it needs to resolve an address query, it sends the query to a forwarding server. The slave server contains a list of the numeric addresses of the forwarding servers to use. It queries the forwarding servers in the list, in order, until it receives an answer or reaches the end of the list.

A forwarding name server is any server except a slave. The server (primary, secondary, or caching) that receives the slave's query is the forwarding server.

Zoning Out (and You Will If You Read This)

We mentioned earlier that zones and domains can be the same. But since name servers are assigned to zones, not domains, you may want to understand the difference in the relationships among domains, zones, and name servers.

Imagine domain ALPHA, a big domain with 26 subdomains named (imaginatively) A–Z. Let's say domain ALPHA delegates authority for subdomains X, Y, and Z to some other department in the company. (For example, the MIS department might delegate some authority to the Research and Development department.) Delegating authority for subdomains means that a different name server is responsible for subdomains X, Y, and Z. To add to the confusion, there's also zone ALPHA. Zone ALPHA has only 23 subdomains. Figure 11-7 shows the relationship of domain ALPHA to its subdomains and

the two servers, and of zone ALPHA to those elements, as well.

When zone ALPHA's name server is queried for information about computers in the X, Y, or Z subdomains, that name server replies with the name of the name server that has authority for X, Y, and Z. In this case, zone ALPHA holds data for domain ALPHA and ALPHA's first 23 subdomains, and a pointer to the name server for subdomains X, Y, and Z.

Domain ALPHA contains the ALPHA domain data, plus all data for subdomains A–Z. Zone ALPHA contains ALPHA domain data and data for subdomains A–W. Since name servers are zone based, it takes at least two name servers to be responsible for all subdomains in domain ALPHA — one server for zone ALPHA, and another server for X, Y, and Z's zone (aptly named Other).

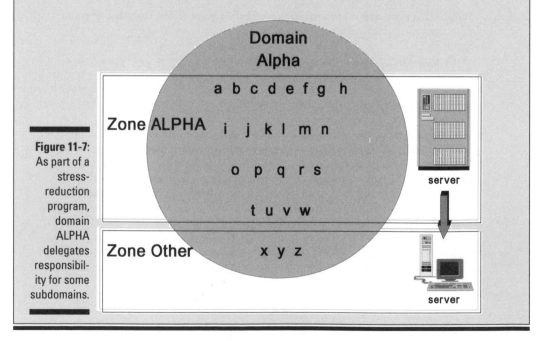

Figure 11-7: As part of a stress-reduction program, domain ALPHA delegates responsibility for some subdomains.

DNS versus NIS

You've been introduced, now, to both DNS and NIS. Both are naming services. Both provide lookup services for groups of computers called domains. DNS provides name/address lookups and translation. NIS works with smaller groups of computers, providing name/address lookups, plus UNIX system and account information.

DNS has a strategic advantage over NIS. Although both use a tree structure, NIS is a mountain with a pointy top and DNS is a butte with a flat top, as shown in Figure 11-8. The top of the NIS mountain is the single master server in the domain and thus the single point of failure. DNS's "flattened" top is formed by a set of name servers, where no one server can be a single point of failure. That makes the DNS environment extremely robust — robust enough to serve The Internet.

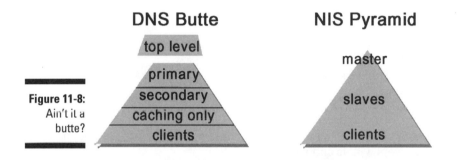

Figure 11-8:
Ain't it a
butte?

In the Beginning There Were Hosts Files

Long ago, before The Internet was even a gleam in anyone's eye, keeping track of the names and addresses of a group of computers wasn't a big deal. A text file containing the addresses and names of the computers was the perfect solution. This was the *hosts file*, and each computer kept a local copy. *Host* normally means computer, but it can also refer to any other device connected to the TCP/IP network, including routers, bridges, and terminal servers (see Chapter 17). Local hosts files are still in use today. If your com-

puter needs to communicate with only a small number of other computers, it's easy to list them in your own local hosts file.

Every TCP/IP product on every operating system knows how to look in a local hosts file to resolve a computer's name into its numeric address. Every TCP/IP product on every operating system knows how to query DNS servers. Only UNIX systems and a few TCP/IP Windows products know how to query NIS servers for address resolution (see Chapter 10).

When to use DNS

You'll want to use DNS in the following circumstances:

- ✔ If your own computers are connected to The Internet
- ✔ If you're a system manager or network administrator responsible for more than a few computers
- ✔ If many of your computers run an operating system other than UNIX, which means that NIS won't help you

When you have a large private internet, DNS is the best choice because it eases your maintenance burden. Manually updating and synchronizing local hosts files on all your computers is tedious, time consuming, and risky. Moreover, those local hosts files can be enormous if your organization has thousands of computers, and each one needs its own copy. With DNS, if and when you do attach your organization to The Internet, your domain will be ready to go.

Finding Information About Domains and Name Servers

There are two tools that can help you find information about DNS domains and name servers: whois and nslookup.

Don't believe everything you read about whois

In the past you could use the whois command to look people up on The Internet. You may still read that this is so in some older books about UNIX and/or about The Internet. But the whois database no longer contains people, as discussed in Chapter 7. There are just too many of them on The Internet. Nevertheless, the database is still a good source of "what is" data about domains and servers, although we said "people and organizations" back in Chapter 7.

Figure 11-9 shows the results of asking for whois information about the domain lotus.com.

```
% whois -h rs.internic.net lotus.com
Lotus Development (LOTUS-DOM)
    55 Cambridge Parkway
    Cambridge, MA 02142

    Domain Name: LOTUS.COM

    Administrative Contact, Technical Contact, Zone Contact:
        Sanderson, William J.  (WJS2)  wsanders@ccmg.lotus.com
        617-693-1115

    Record last updated on 20-Oct-94.

    Domain servers in listed order:

    NIC.NEAR.NET                 192.52.71.4
    BU.EDU                       128.197.27.7
    NOC.CERF.NET                 192.153.156.22

The InterNIC Registration Services Host contains ONLY Internet Information
(Networks, ASN's, Domains, and POC's).
Please use the whois server at nic.ddn.mil for MILNET Information.
%
```

Figure 11-9:
The whois
command
tells you
about
domains
and servers.

Your fishing pole: nslookup

To query a DNS server manually, you can use the nslookup utility (pronounced by saying _N S lookup_). Most TCP/IP products include this program.
Because nslookup calls the same resolver routines as every other TCP/IP
application, it's also a basic troubleshooting tool.

So why would you want to query a DNS server manually (that is, instead of
from some application)? You say your applications take care of that for you?
OK — but inquiring minds want to know. And if you want to, you can use
nslookup to

  ✔ Troubleshoot network connections

  ✔ See if the data in the name server's cache is current

  ✔ See how mail messages actually get where they're going

All the nslookup commands that you use for manually querying a name
server are shown in Figure 11-10.

Be careful as you enter nslookup commands. Any typographical error is
treated as a request for DNS information, so watch those typos. For example,
if you want to set a timeout value, but you type "sit timeout=5" instead of "set
timeout=5", nslookup will ask the name server for information about a computer named "sit." ∎

```
% nslookup ———————————————— Manually query a DNS server.
Default Server:  dnsp.lotus.com
Address:  130.103.48.124 ————————— The server we're querying announces itself.

> ? ————————————————————— Ask for online help.
Commands:          (identifiers are shown in uppercase, [] means optional)

NAME               - print info about the host/domain NAME using default server
NAME1 NAME2        - as above, but use NAME2 as server
help or ?          - print help information
exit               - exit the program
set OPTION         - set an option
    all            - print options, current server and host
    [no]debug      - print debugging information
    [no]d2         - print exhaustive debugging information
    [no]defname    - append domain name to each query
    [no]recurse    - ask for recursive answer to query
    [no]vc         - always use a virtual circuit
    domain=NAME    - set default domain name to NAME
    root=NAME      - set root server to NAME
    retry=X        - set number of retries to X
    timeout=X      - set time-out interval to X
    querytype=X    - set query type to one of A,CNAME,HINFO,MB,MG,MINFO,MR,MX
    type=X         - set query type to one of A,CNAME,HINFO,MB,MG,MINFO,MR,MX
server NAME        - set default server to NAME, using current default server
lserver NAME       - set default server to NAME, using initial server
finger [NAME]      - finger the optional NAME
root               - set current default server to the root
ls NAME [> FILE]   - list the domain NAME, with output optionally going to FILE
view FILE          - sort an 'ls' output file and view it with more
>
> exit ——————— All done!
%
```

Figure 11-10: These are the only nslookup commands. Anything else is a DNS query.

These are the commands. Anything else you type (that means typos!) is interpreted as a query re an address to be resolved.

Working with nslookup

When you start nslookup, it connects to a default name server — the same one your computer normally uses for DNS queries. You can explicitly switch to another server any time you need to, using the server and lserver commands.

By default, nslookup only asks for address information. To find other kinds of information, use the set type= command, followed by a record type listed in Table 11-1. Figure 11-11 shows a real-life nslookup session.

Table 11-1: DNS Record Types to Use with Set Type= Command

DNS Record Type	Description
A	Address information (the default)
CNAME	Canonical name, also known as common name or alias
HINFO	Host information, such as computer model and operating system
MX	Mail eXchanger, a computer that receives mail on behalf of a computer and/or forwards it further on
any	I don't care; give me any and all information

```
% nslookup ─────────────── Manually query DNS server
Default Server:  dnsp.lotus.com
Address:  130.103.48.124 ──── Server we're querying announces itself

>
> set type=any ──────────── Report any kind of data you know about
>
> mail.lotus.com.
Server:  dnsp.lotus.com            First query (mail.lotus.com)
Address:  130.103.48.124           has authoritative response,
                                   even though it's not
                                   announced that way
mail.lotus.com  internet address = 130.103.46.2
>
>
> hp.com
Server:  dnsp.lotus.com
Address:  130.103.48.124

Non-authoritative answer:
hp.com   inet address = 15.255.152.4
hp.com   origin = relay.hp.com
        mail addr = hostmaster.hp.com
        serial=1002204, refresh=10800, retry=3600, expire=604800, min=86400
Authoritative answers can be found from:
NS.INTERNIC.NET inet address = 198.41.0.4
AOS.ARL.ARMY.MIL        inet address = 128.63.4.82
AOS.ARL.ARMY.MIL        inet address = 192.5.25.82
AOS.ARL.ARMY.MIL        inet address = 26.3.0.29
NS1.ISI.EDU     inet address = 128.9.0.107
C.PSI.NET       inet address = 192.33.4.12
TERP.UMD.EDU    inet address = 128.8.10.90
```

Figure 11-11:
A sample
nslookup
session.

```
NS.NASA.GOV      inet address = 128.102.16.10
NS.NASA.GOV      inet address = 192.52.195.10
>
>
> hpl.hp.com ─────────────── Query to resolve this address
Server:  dnsp.lotus.com ┐
Address:   130.103.48.124 ┘── This server . . .

Non-authoritative answer:
hpl.hp.com       nameserver = hplns3.hpl.hp.com
hpl.hp.com       nameserver = hplabs.hpl.hp.com
hpl.hp.com       nameserver = hplns26.hpl.hp.com
hpl.hp.com       nameserver = pub.hpl.hp.com
hpl.hp.com       nameserver = hplb.hpl.hp.com
hpl.hp.com       nameserver = hplms26.hpl.hp.com
hpl.hp.com       preference = 20, mail exchanger = hplms2.hpl.hp.com
hpl.hp.com       preference = 23, mail exchanger = mlhub26.hpl.hp.com
hpl.hp.com       preference = 25, mail exchanger = hplms26.hpl.hp.com
hpl.hp.com       preference = 30, mail exchanger = hplabs.hpl.hp.com
hpl.hp.com       preference = 35, mail exchanger = hplb.hpl.hp.com
hpl.hp.com       origin = hplns3.hpl.hp.com
        mail addr = ns-admin.hplabs.hpl.hp.com
          serial=854, refresh=10800, retry=3600, expire=604800, min=86400
Authoritative answers can be found from:
hplns3.hpl.hp.com        inet address = 15.0.48.4
hplabs.hpl.hp.com        inet address = 15.255.176.47
hplns26.hpl.hp.com       inet address = 15.9.144.4
pub.hpl.hp.com  inet address = 15.255.176.10
hplb.hpl.hp.com inet address = 15.255.59.2
hplms26.hpl.hp.com       inet address = 15.255.168.31
hplms2.hpl.hp.com        inet address = 15.0.152.33
>
> hpl.hpl.hp.com ─────────────── Another query
Server:  dnsp.lotus.com
Address:   130.103.48.124

@ dnsp.lotus.com can't find hpl.hpl.hp.com: Non-existent domain ──┐
>
> hplms2.hpl.hp.com
Server:  dnsp.lotus.com
Address:   130.103.48.124

Non-authoritative answer:
hplms2.hpl.hp.com        inet address = 15.0.152.33
Authoritative answers can be found from:
hplns3.hpl.hp.com        inet address = 15.0.48.4
hplabs.hpl.hp.com        inet address = 15.255.176.47
hplns26.hpl.hp.com       inet address = 15.9.144.4
```

. . . delivers this infor- mation

There is no information for this address

Figure 11-11: *(continued)*

```
pub.hpl.hp.com  inet address = 15.255.176.10
hplb.hpl.hp.com inet address = 15.255.59.2
hplms26.hpl.hp.com      inet address = 15.255.168.31
>
> set type=mx ─────────────────── Report only Mail Exchange data
>
> hpl.hp.com
Server:  dnsp.lotus.com
Address:  130.103.48.124

Non-authoritative answer:
hpl.hp.com      preference = 20, mail exchanger = hplms2.hpl.hp.com
hpl.hp.com      preference = 23, mail exchanger = mlhub26.hpl.hp.com
hpl.hp.com      preference = 25, mail exchanger = hplms26.hpl.hp.com
hpl.hp.com      preference = 30, mail exchanger = hplabs.hpl.hp.com
hpl.hp.com      preference = 35, mail exchanger = hplb.hpl.hp.com
Authoritative answers can be found from:
hplms2.hpl.hp.com     inet address = 15.0.152.33
mlhub26.hpl.hp.com    inet address = 15.9.144.132
hplms26.hpl.hp.com    inet address = 15.255.168.31
hplabs.hpl.hp.com     inet address = 15.255.176.47
hplb.hpl.hp.com inet address = 15.255.59.2
hplns3.hpl.hp.com     inet address = 15.0.48.4
hplns26.hpl.hp.com    inet address – 15.9.144.4
pub.hpl.hp.com  inet address = 15.255.176.10
>
> exit
%
```

NOTE: This is a subset of the data returned in earlier response

Figure 11-11:
(continued)

This chapter has described how the name of a computer gets resolved into a numeric address that TCP/IP understands. So you can just live with computer names and forget about the numbers — because name resolution, as done by DNS or the hosts file, takes care of it for you. (If you really want to worry about those numeric addresses, Chapter 13 will run the numbers for you.) In the meantime, let's look at some more information-finding services in Chapter 12. These are especially popular on The Internet. (By the way, all of the services in Chapter 12 use DNS invisibly, to translate computer names into addresses.

Chapter 12

Feasting on Information

● ●

In This Chapter

▶ Information services and what they can do for you

▶ Hypertext and hypermedia

▶ The World Wide Web and browsers

▶ Meals on The Internet: Gopher Goulash, Web Wingdings, and malts with Archie and Veronica

▶ How to get free Internet browsing software

● ●

So you've learned how to set your table with TCP/IP dinnerware. You've been fishing around your own internet to see who and what are there, and you know how to dig into domains on The Internet. The riches of The Internet have been opened to you through FTP, telnet, and DNS. You've seen how to access The Internet by connecting to remote hosts and copying files across a network. And you also know that the data inside all those files are the really important ingredients of The Internet feast. You can't wait to take that raw Internet data and bake it into succulent tidbits of information, using all the latest tools in your information management repertoire — outlining, cross-referencing, indexing, summarizing, and condensing — all without having to copy the files to your own host. Connection established and mouse at the ready, you stop dead — uh . . . now what?

There is an absolute glut of information and files available on The Internet — so much that you may feel overwhelmed. Even when you know what you want, it can be really hard to find it. The information services described in this chapter will help you navigate the Net.

When you're finished reading this book, you're sure to want more of The Internet's information, and you can continue your exploration with *The Internet For Dummies* and *MORE Internet For Dummies*. ∎

Surfers' Paradise

Cruising around The Internet to see what's out there is often called *surfing the Net*. Vinton

Cerf is known as the Father of The Internet. So shouldn't it be Cerfing the Net?

How Do Info Services Help Me?

In the last few years, a number of new information services have been developed and deployed on The Internet. When you go to that big TCP/IP banquet at Internet Hall, the tools introduced in this chapter represent the frills of the dinnerware set: the lobster picks, fruit knives, and demitasse cups that you don't even know you need until you sit down to eat.

Like most of the applications and services you have read about in this book, the Internet information services are client/server environments. You use a client application — either as software on your own computer or by connecting to a host that is running the client application — to communicate with a server.

Some of these information exploration tools have a GUI (graphical user interface), so to take full advantage of their features you need to run them from a Windows, Motif, or Macintosh computer. Other tools have just a plain-character interface that you can run from a DOS/PC or even a dumb terminal. But whatever the user interface, there's usually a TCP/IP protocol in there somewhere. And the information you can access is much more than just plain text.

Using <u>Archie</u> to Search FTP <u>Archives</u>

Archie is a client/server environment that helps you find out which Anonymous FTP archives hold the things you're looking for on The Internet. Archie is like a card catalog to the world's FTP libraries.

Archie is just a finder. Once you've found the location of what you're looking for, you have to go get it. So your next step is to use Anonymous FTP to transfer the files you want to your own computer. ■

Advice for Betty: Ways to talk to Archie

The most efficient way to use Archie is to install a copy of Archie client software on your computer. Then you can connect to Archie servers all over the world. Even if you don't have an Archie client program, you can still talk to the Archie servers by using telnet or e-mail. These methods are much slower, but they get you in. You'll see examples of all these methods at work shortly.

To get your own Archie client software, use telnet or e-mail to access an Archie server. Perform an Archie search for the word *archie*. The results of the search will show you which Anonymous FTP servers have Archie software. Then go get it with FTP. You do remember how to do that, right? (If you don't, take another look at Chapter 9.)

Using Archie client software on your computer

Following is an example of the fastest choice for Betty to get in touch with Archie — by using Archie client software. In Figure 12-1, a UNIX client is accessing Archie. Betty has typed the command

```
archie -h archie.sura.net ipng
```

to select a specific Archie server and perform a search. Let's look at the elements of this command:

- ✔ The first *archie* is the UNIX operating system command to launch a nongraphical Archie client.

- ✔ The *-h archie.sura.net* means "connect to the Archie server on that host."

- ✔ The *ipng* (for IP Next Generation protocol) is the subject about which Betty wants to search for information.

```
% archie -h archie.sura.net ipng

Host beta.xerox.com

     Location: /pub
          DIRECTORY drwxrwxr-x      1536  Oct  5 11:38  ipng

Host cnri.reston.va.us

     Location: /iesg
          DIRECTORY drwxrwxr-x       512  Sep 19 14:50  ipng

Host ftp.cis.ohio-state.edu

     Location: /internic/iesg
          DIRECTORY drwxr-xr-x       512  Sep 22 01:25  ipng

Host ftp.isi.edu

     Location: /iesg
          DIRECTORY drwxr-xr-x       512  Sep 20 04:58  ipng

Host munnari.oz.au

     Location: /iesg
          DIRECTORY drwxr-xr-x       512  Sep 20 06:37  ipng

Host nic.ddn.mil

     Location: /iesg
          DIRECTORY drwxr-xr-x       512  Jan 22 1994  ipng

Host nic.switch.ch

     Location: /mirror/current-ietf-docs
          DIRECTORY drwxrwxr-x       512  Mar 25 1994  ipng
```

Figure 12-1: An Archie client asks the server to search for information on the IPng protocol.

Using telnet

You can also telnet to an Archie server and log in as user archie, as Betty
has done in the session illustrated in Figure 12-2. Betty is not asked for a
password. That's because Archie servers are public.

```
% telnet archie.internic.net
Trying 192.20.239.132...
Connected to ds.internic.net.
Escape character is '^]'.
              InterNic Directory and Database Services

Welcome to InterNic Directory and Database Services provided by AT&T.
These services are partially supported through a coooperative agreement
with the National Science Foundation.

First time users may login as guest with no password to receive help.

Your comments and suggestions for improvement are welcome, and can be
mailed to admin@ds.internic.net.

AT&T MAKES NO WARRANTY OR GUARANTEE, OR PROMISE, EXPRESS OR IMPLIED,
CONCERNING THE CONTENT OR ACCURACY OF THE DIRECTORY ENTRIES AND
DATABASE FILES STORED AND MAINTAINED BY AT&T. AT&T EXPRESSLY
DISCLAIMS AND EXCLUDES ALL EXPRESS WARANTIES AND IMPLIED WARRANTIES
OF MERCHANTABILITY AND FITESS FOR A PARTICULAR PURPOSE.

DS2 will be rebooted every Wednesday morning between 8:00AM and 8:30AM

SunOS UNIX (ds2)

login: archie
```

Figure 12-2:
Betty
telnets to an
Archie
server and
logs in as
user archie.

Using e-mail

Another way to get to Archie is to send an e-mail message that contains an
archie command to an Archie server. (You'll find a collection of Archie commands later in Table 12-1.) Remember ftpmail, which we talked about in
Chapter 9? This is a similar situation — let's call it "Archiemail." Figure 12-3
illustrates an e-mail message to the Archie server archie.rutgers.edu.

When you send your Archiemail, make sure the Archie commands start in
column 1 of the message. For instance, in Figure 12-3, the Help command
automatically mails you the Archie help guide. ■

Archie on a platter

So you've decided to give Archie a try. You've acquired Archie client software, or you're going to telnet to an Archie server, or you have an e-mail message ready to go to a server. Before you can go any further, you need to know
the names of the Archie servers. The screen in Figure 12-4 contains a list of a
few Archie servers around the world.

Archie servers come and go on The Internet, but you can get the most current
list by using Archie's servers command. ■

Once you know where the servers are, you can search them for information
about topics that interest you. Archie's whatis command lets you search for

a list of references about any topic. Want to read articles about FTP? See Figure 12-5 for an example of the what is command.

```
& mail archie@archie.rutgers.edu
Subject:
help                                E-mail is sent to the Archie server.


From archie-errors@dorm.rutgers.edu Thu Feb 23 14:58:47 1995 ── The response starts here.
To: Candace Leiden <leiden@max.tiac.net>
From:  (Archie Server)archie-errors@dorm.rutgers.edu
Reply-To:  (Archie Server)archie-errors@dorm.rutgers.edu
Date: Thu, 23 Feb 95 14:57 -0500
Subject: archie [help] part 1 of 1
X-Status:


>> path Candace Leiden <leiden@max.tiac.net>

>> help
                Archie Email Help (Version 3.2)

HELP for this archie email server, as of 11 April, 1994.

To perform an archie search via email, send mail to

        archie@<archie_server>

where <archie_server> is the name of an archie host, some of which are listed
below.

The "Subject:" header in mail sent to archie is treated as part of the
message body.

Command lines begin in the first column. All lines that do not match a valid
commands are ignored.

Empty messages are treated as "help" requests (this file). If no command
in a particular message can be recognized, the message is treated as
"empty" and this file will be returned.

The current (and complete) list of archie servers can be found with the
"servers" command (described below). A sample list is:

    archie.au                 139.130.4.6      Australia
    archie.edvz.uni-linz.ac.at 140.78.3.8      Austria
    archie.univie.ac.at       131.130.1.23     Austria
    archie.uqam.ca            132.208.250.10   Canada
    archie.funet.fi           128.214.6.102    Finland
    archie.univ-rennes1.fr    129.20.128.38    France
    archie.th-darmstadt.de    130.83.128.118   Germany
    archie.ac.il              132.65.16.18     Israel
    archie.unipi.it           131.114.21.10    Italy
    archie.wide.ad.jp         133.4.3.6        Japan
    archie.hana.nm.kr         128.134.1.1      Korea
    archie.sogang.ac.kr       163.239.1.11     Korea
    archie.uninett.no         128.39.2.20      Norway
    archie.rediris.es         130.206.1.2      Spain
    archie.luth.se            130.240.12.30    Sweden
    archie.switch.ch          130.59.1.40      Switzerland
    archie.nctuccca.edu.tw                     Taiwan
    archie.ncu.edu.tw         192.83.166.12    Taiwan
    archie.doc.ic.ac.uk       146.169.11.3     United Kingdom
    archie.hensa.ac.uk        129.12.21.25     United Kingdom
    archie.unl.edu            129.93.1.14      USA (NE)
    archie.internic.net       198.49.45.10     USA (NJ)
    archie.rutgers.edu        128.6.18.15      USA (NJ)
    archie.ans.net            147.225.1.10     USA (NY)
    archie.sura.net           128.167.254.179  USA (MD)


If you do not get mail back within 1 day or so, try using the "path"
command described below.

Mail destined for the ADMINISTRATION of individual servers should be
addressed to:

        archie-admin@<archie_server>

where <archie_server> is one of the hosts listed above. If you are having
a problem with a particular server, try sending mail to its administrator
first before contacting the general archie contact address below. They
may already be aware of the problem.

To request the ADDITION or DELETION of a site from the archie database,
send mail to:

        archie-admin@bunyip.com

To contact the IMPLEMENTORS of archie, send mail to:

        archie-group@bunyip.com
```

This is from the Archie help guide Candace requested.

Figure 12-3:
Here we're sending e-mail to Archie, asking for help.

```
archie> servers
-----------------< List of active archie servers >---------------

    archie.au                  139.130.4.6      Australia
    archie.edvz.uni-linz.ac.at 140.78.3.8       Austria
    archie.univie.ac.at        131.130.1.23     Austria
    archie.cs.mcgill.ca        132.206.51.250   Canada
    archie.uqam.ca             132.208.250.10   Canada
    archie.funet.fi            128.214.6.102    Finland
    archie.univ-rennes1.fr     129.20.128.38    France
    archie.th-darmstadt.de     130.83.128.118   Germany
    archie.ac.il               132.65.16.18     Israel
    archie.unipi.it            131.114.21.10    Italy
    archie.wide.ad.jp          133.4.3.6        Japan
    archie.hana.nm.kr          128.134.1.1      Korea
    archie.sogang.ac.kr        163.239.1.11     Korea
    archie.uninett.no          128.39.2.20      Norway
    archie.rediris.es          130.206.1.2      Spain
    archie.luth.se             130.240.12.30    Sweden
    archie.switch.ch           130.59.1.40      Switzerland
    archie.nctuccca.edu.tw                      Taiwan
    archie.ncu.edu.tw          192.83.166.12    Taiwan
    archie.doc.ic.ac.uk        146.169.11.3     United Kingdom
    archie.hensa.ac.uk         129.12.21.25     United Kingdom
    archie.unl.edu             129.93.1.14      USA (NE)
    archie.internic.net        198.49.45.10     USA (NJ)
    archie.rutgers.edu         128.6.18.15      USA (NJ)
    archie.ans.net             147.225.1.10     USA (NY)
    archie.sura.net            128.167.254.179  USA (MD)
archie>
```

Figure 12-4:
The servers
command
lists
worldwide
Archie
servers.

```
archie> whatis ftp
DNSEmulator             Shell scripts using nslookup to simulate Domain Name
                        Service (for ping, telnet, and ftp) under SunOS.
RFC 1068                DeSchon, A.L.; Braden, R.T. Background File Transfer
                        Program (BFTP). 1988 August; 27 p.
RFC 238                 Braden, R.T. Comments on DTP and FTP proposals 1971
                        September 29; 1 p. (Updates RFC 171, RFC 172; Updated
                        by RFC 269)
RFC 412                 Hicks, G. User FTP documentation 1972 November 27; 10
                        p.
RFC 414                 Bhushan, A.K. File Transfer Protocol (FTP) status and
                        further comments 1972 December 29; 5 p. (Updates RFC
                        385)
RFC 438                 Thomas, R.; Clements, R. FTP server-server
                        interaction 1973 January 15; 5 p.
RFC 448                 Braden, R.T. Print files in FTP 1973 February 27; 4
                        p.
RFC 458                 Bressler, R.D.; Thomas, R. Mail retrieval via FTP
                        1973 February 20; 2 p.
RFC 463                 Bhushan, A.K. FTP comments and response to RFC 430
                        1973 February 21; 3 p.
RFC 468                 Braden, R.T. FTP data compression 1973 March 8; 5 p.
RFC 475                 Bhushan, A.K. FTP and network mail system 1973 March
                        6; 8 p.
RFC 478                 Bressler, R.D.; Thomas, R. FTP server-server
                        interaction - II (Not online) 1973 March 26; 2 p.
RFC 479                 White, J.E. Use of FTP by the NIC Journal 1973 March
                        8; 6 p.
RFC 480                 White, J.E. Host-dependent FTP parameters 1973 March
                        8; 1 p.
RFC 506                 Padlipsky, M.H. FTP command naming problem 1973 June
                        26; 1 p.
RFC 520                 Day, J.D. Memo to FTP group: Proposal for File Access
                        Protocol (Not online) 1973 June 25; 8 p.
RFC 532                 Merryman, R.G. UCSD-CC Server-FTP facility 1973 July
                        12; 3 p.
```

Figure 12-5:
The whatis
command
gives you
information
about FTP.

Archie commands

When you use Archie to explore what's available, you only need a few simple commands to get around. You've already seen a couple of them in action in previous sections. Table 12-1 lists some of the Archie commands. For a complete list, access Archie and use the help command.

Table 12-1: Archie Commands

Archie Command	Function
servers	Displays a list of available servers worldwide.
prog	Does the actual search according to search types you establish with the set search command (see below). The prog command is the heart of Archie, and works just like find.
find	Works the same as prog.
set search exact set search sub	Lets you specify how you want to search for information in a file, before you start the prog or find search. Set search exact tells Archie to look for filenames that exactly match search criteria. For example, prog malt will find *malt*, but not *Malt* or *malt_shop*. Set search sub tells Archie to look for filenames that contain the characters you specify. For example, prog malt will find *malt*, *Malt*, *Malt_shop*, and *malt_shop*.
show search	Displays the search method currently in use.
whatis *subject*	Searches for files about *subject*, and descriptions of them (as in Figure 12-5), but doesn't tell you where to find them. Use the find or prog command to display the files' location.
manpage	Displays the entire manual — the big, BIG manual about Archie.
help	The most important command of all.
mail *e-mail address*	Sends the search results via e-mail to the address you provide.

What Are Hypertext and Hypermedia?

You may have heard the terms *hypertext* and *hypermedia* used in conjunction with the latest and greatest Internet tools. However, both hypertext and hypermedia have been around for a long time and are used not only for "middle-aged" Internet tools such as Gopher, but also for applications not related to TCP/IP and The Internet, such as Hypercard on the Macintosh. In this chapter you'll read about the middle-aged Gopher, as well some pretty popular toddlers: World Wide Web browsers. Gopher and browsers are hyperbased.

Hypertext is text that contains in-line pointers to other text in the same file or another file. A common example of hypertext is the Microsoft Windows help system, where you click a highlighted word or icon or button, and you get more information about what you clicked on. The linked, multipage information you click around in is hypertext.

Hypermedia extends the hypertext concept beyond just text and into multimedia. In hypermedia applications, a pointer can take you to a sound byte, or a graphic image, even a video clip. These days, there's much more to life on The Internet than just text!

In a hypermedia document about Switzerland, for instance, you might click a pointer and see a picture along with explanatory text, and hear a yodeler in the background (see Figure 12-6). About the only thing hypermedia can't do is give you a taste of nutty Emmentaler cheese or a sniff of heavenly milk chocolate . . . yet! We figure it's only a matter of time until they come up with something called *hypersensory*! An April Fool's joke on The Internet recently was that vendors were selling "smell boards" for PCs.

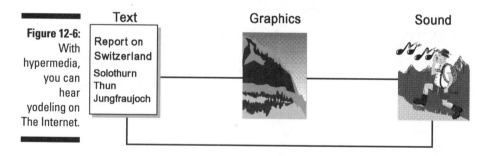

Figure 12-6: With hypermedia, you can hear yodeling on The Internet.

Text

Report on Switzerland

Solothurn
Thun
Jungfraujoch

Graphics

Sound

The newest use of hypermedia on the Internet — and one with which you may already be familiar — is the World Wide Web. Later in this chapter you'll be reading about Gopher, the Web, and browsers, which help you handle the terabytes of information available on the Net, as well as Net navigators that are not hyperbased.

Gophers Go-fer Internet Gold

Gopher is a client/server rodent for burrowing through The Internet. As you travel through the tunnels of Gopherspace, you see menus that help you find the information you want. Gopher menu choices often take you to other menus, allowing you to work your way around, up, down, across, and through The Internet feast. One of the best features of Gopherspace is that when your choices take you from one gopher server to another, you travel painlessly and almost invisibly.

Gopher works harder than Archie. When you want to bring the information you've found into your own computer, Gopher displays the information and then automatically starts telnet or FTP or whatever TCP/IP application that you need to deliver the information. This is a big advantage over Archie, which finds the files but makes you fetch them yourself. ■

How to start Gophering

You can get into Gopher with the same three methods you use for Archie:

- ✔ Use Gopher client software on your computer (the most efficient choice, once you have the software).

- ✔ Telnet to a Gopher server and log in as user gopher. The username is usually gopher, but Table 12-2 lists a few other usernames you can try.

- ✔ Send e-mail to a Gopher server (GopherMail). We'll give you details on this in an upcoming section. (So now we have ftpmail, Archiemail, and GopherMail . . .)

Just as you do for Archie, you need to know the names of Gopher servers. Table 12-2 lists a few Gopher servers to try if you don't have Gopher client software. By the way, the first server listed, consultant.micro.umn.edu, is the original gopher hole at the University of Minnesota . . . home of the Golden Gophers . . . and probably the most crowded Gopher site.

Table 12-2: A Selection of Public Gopher Clients Worldwide

Gopher Server Address	Username	Geographic Location
consultant.micro.umn.edu	gopher	United States
pubinfo.ucsd.edu	infopath	United States
scilibx.ucsc.edu	infoslug	United States
info.anu.edu.au	info	Australia
finfo.tu-graz.ac.at	info	Austria
nstn.ns.ca	fred	Canada
gopher.sunet.se	gopher	Sweden
gan.ncc.go.jp	gopher	Japan

Getting Gopher going

Gopher menus differ from server to server, but all have the same basic role: pointing you to more menus and information. Figure 12-7 shows the top Gopher menu at sunsite.unc.edu at the University of North Carolina.

Figure 12-7:
Gopher
burrows
around The
Internet to
find and get
what you're
looking for.

```
              Internet Gopher Information Client 2.0 p110

                  Root gopher server: sunsite.unc.edu

-->  1.  About Ogphre/
     2.  Sun and UNC's Legal Disclaimer.
     3.  Surf the Net! - Archie, Libraries, Gophers, FTP Sites./
     4.  Internet Dog-Eared Pages (Frequently used resources)/
     5.  Worlds of SunSITE -- by Subject/
     6.  SUN Microsystems News Groups and Archives/
     7.  NEWS! (News, Entertainment, Weather, and Sports)/
     8.  UNC Information Exchange (People and Places)/
     9.  The UNC-CH Internet Library/
    10.  UNC-Gopherspace/
    11.  UNC-Gopherspace (new home on usit)/
    12.  What's New on SunSITE/
    13.  Search the UNC Gopherspace with Jughead <?>


Press ? for Help, q to Quit                          Page: 1/1
```

The Up Arrow and Down Arrow keys are the most convenient way to move through Gopher's menus. When something you want is highlighted, you press Enter, or you can type the number of your choice and then press Enter.

The all-important Help command is ?. Two other commands you might need are u for Go Up one menu level and q for Quit.

In Figure 12-8 you can see what Gopher has retrieved from the Dog-Eared Pages area. The Dog-Eared Pages are a collection of frequently used information about The Internet, maintained at the University of North Carolina server. Later, in Figure 12-9, you will get a glimpse of the Dog-Eared Pages menu, behind the displayed "Rock n Roll Lyrics . . . " search box.

Gopher search and retrieval is not just for serious stuff like technical information and news. You can use Gopher to ferret out everything from poetry to religious treatises to song lyrics to . . . well, you get the idea. Ever wonder how many rock songs mention Satan? Just for fun, Figure 12-9 shows the Rock n Roll Lyrics for Searching feature in action. You can search this database for any words you like, and then transfer files containing the lyrics of your favorite songs.

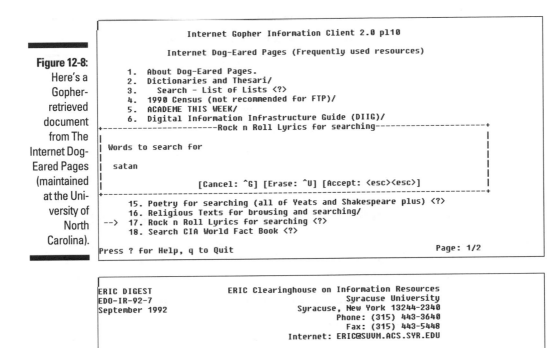

Figure 12-8:
Here's a
Gopher-
retrieved
document
from The
Internet Dog-
Eared Pages
(maintained
at the Uni-
versity of
North
Carolina).

Figure 12-9:
The devil
made me
do it.

Gopher bookmarks

Gopher delves through a series of complex, interconnected tunnels and
worldwide servers. Once you've found something, wouldn't it be nice to
leave a trail of bread crumbs in case you want to return? Your Gopher client
software lets you do just that. These placemarkers are called *bookmarks*.
Each client does bookmarks differently; on UNIX, you can use the bookmark
commands listed in Table 12-3.

Table 12-3: Gopher Bookmark Commands (UNIX)

Command (on UNIX)	Function
A	Marks the current directory
a	Marks the current item
v	Views your list of bookmarks
d	Deletes a bookmark from your list

GopherMail for the poorly connected

When you have to use e-mail to get in touch with Gopher, send your message to a GopherMail server. GopherMail servers come and go on The Internet. Table 12-4 lists some GopherMail servers around the world as of this writing.

Table 12-4: GopherMail Servers

E-mail Address	Location
gophermail@mercury.forestry.umn.edu	Minnesota, USA
gophermail@eunet.cz	Czech Republic
gopher@earn.net	France
gopher@ftp.technion.ac.il	Israel
gopher@nig.ac.jp	Japan
gopher@dsv.su.se	Sweden

To get a help guide for using Gopher, send e-mail to a GopherMail server, and enter **help** as the subject of the message, similar to what was done in Figure 12-4 for Archie. ■

Here are the steps for using GopherMail:

1. Locate the GopherMail server you want to use. Send an e-mail message to that server, leaving the body of the mail message blank.

2. Wait for GopherMail to respond to your e-mail. The response will include a Gopher menu.

3. Follow the directions and mark the menu items you want GopherMail to return to you. Mail the updated menu back to the GopherMail server.

4. Again, wait for GopherMail's response. You may have to repeat steps three and four to continue burrowing through menus to the source of the items you want. ∎

You need a lot of time and patience when working with GopherMail, because you have to get things a menu at a time. If your response to the initial GopherMail menu is to select an item that leads to another menu, Gopher-Mail sends the next menu. Then you respond with your selection on that menu, and so forth, until you finally get through all the submenus and are able to select a file. ∎

Gopher a WAIS Down The Internet

The Wide Area Information Service (WAIS), pronounced like the word *ways,* is yet another client/server environment. This one is for searching the wide range of databases available across The Internet. The databases — maintained by those good-hearted volunteers you read about in Chapter 2 — function as libraries about specific topics, from computers and networking, to aeronautics, to spanakopita (Greek spinach pie, as you Internet foodies probably know).

When you run WAIS, it looks in the databases you named and lists the *documents* (usually articles and books) that contain the subjects you asked about. Using WAIS is kind of like using the index at the back of a book. WAIS can also display the documents themselves.

Archie Goes-fer Veronica

Veronica is a tool for zooming through Gopherspace looking for specific directories and files. You probably think it's named for Archie's girlfriend, but actually it stands for Very Easy Rodent Oriented Networkwide Index to Computerized Archives (whew!). Veronica takes your favorite Internet files and builds you a personal (but temporary) Gopher menu of them, so you can avoid having to repeat long Gopher searches.

To use Veronica, you get into an upper-level Gopher menu and check for an entry that mentions "search" or "Veronica." (For example, in Figure 12-10, item 3 of the second menu says, "Search titles in Gopherspace using Veronica.") Next, when you get to the Veronica menu, look for the item about Frequently Asked Questions (FAQ), which offers basics about using Veronica.

Veronica is very popular, like her comic-book namesake. Sometimes Veronica is extremely slow to respond. She has been known to accept so many dates for the same day that she has to tell you she's got too many connections and to please try again later. But who needs her? You've seen ways to get through Gopherspace on your own.

You can get WAIS client software from public Internet sites using Anonymous FTP. There is even a graphical WAIS client for the X Window System GUI (most UNIX and VMS operating systems provide an X GUI). You can also access WAIS from Gopher menus, as shown in Figure 12-10.

```
gopher gopher2.tc.umn.edu

              Internet Gopher Information Client 2.0 p110

                   Root gopher server: gopher2.tc.umn.edu

        1.  Information About Gopher/
        2.  Computer Information/
        3.  Discussion Groups/
        4.  Fun & Games/
        5.  Internet file server (ftp) sites/
        6.  Libraries/
        7.  News/
  -->   8.  Other Gopher and Information Servers/
        9.  Phone Books/
        10. Search Gopher Titles at the University of Minnesota <?>
        11. Search lots of places at the University of Minnesota <?>
        12. University of Minnesota Campus Information/




Press ? for Help, q to Quit                            Page: 1/1
              Internet Gopher Information Client 2.0 p110

                   Other Gopher and Information Servers

        1.  All the Gopher Servers in the World/
        2.  Search All the Gopher Servers in the World <?>
        3.  Search titles in Gopherspace using veronica/
        4.  Africa/
        5.  Asia/
        6.  Europe/
        7.  International Organizations/
        8.  Middle East/
        9.  North America/
        10. Pacific/
        11. Russia/
        12. South America/
        13. Terminal Based Information/
  -->   14. WAIS Based Information/
        15. Gopher Server Registration. <Form>


Press ? for Help, q to Quit, u to go up a menu         Page: 1/1
```

Selecting item 8 takes you to the next menu.

By the WAIS, here's Veronica.

Here's WAIS via Gopher.

Figure 12-10: Gophering WAIS.

The World Wide Web (WWW)

The World Wide Web, WWW, is a worldwide hypermedia information service on The Internet, and it's amazingly hot these days. WWW is usually pronounced by repeating *W* three times, but saying "W W W" is such a tongue twister that many people just say "World Wide Web" or "the Web." Others say "W3" or "W cubed."

A common misconception among newcomers to the Information Superhighway is that The Internet and the Web are the same thing. Actually, the Web is a subset of the computers and information on The Internet.

Mosaic and Netscape are very popular Web clients; others include Lynx and Cello. WWW clients, which are also called *browsers,* communicate with the servers via HTTP, the HyperText Transfer Protocol.

Thanks, but I'm just looking

To use the Web, you need a browser (client) and TCP/IP. You also need a computer with a graphical interface if you want to take full advantage of the Web's spectacular features. But don't worry if you don't have a browser. You can connect via telnet to a public host that has a nongraphical browser.

In Figure 12-11 we are telnetting to a public, nongraphical browser in Switzerland, the origin of the Web. Nongraphical browsers cannot display all the Web's information, because some information is formatted with graphic tools.

```
% telnet telnet.w3.org
                        GENERAL OVERVIEW OF THE WEB

   There is no "top" to the World-Wide Web. You can look at it from many points
   of view. Here are some places to start.

   by Subject[1]          The Virtual Library organises information by subject
                          matter.

   List of servers[2]     All registered HTTP servers by country

   by Service Type[3]     The Web includes data accessible by many other
                          protocols. The lists by access protocol may help if
                          you know what kind of service you are looking for.

   If you find a useful starting point for you personally, you can configure
   your WWW browser to start there by default.

   See also: About the W3 project[4] .
     [End]


1-4, Back, Up, Quit, or Help:


                            WWW Client Software products

      WWW clients

                              W3 CLIENTS

      These programs allow you to access the WWW from your own computer. See
      also: other W3 software .

Email based browsers

   Agora
           Based on the line-mode browser. If you cannot have full access
           to the Internet. (beta)

Terminal based browsers

   Line Mode Browser
           This program gives W3 readership to anyone with a dumb
           terminal. A general purpose information retrieval tool.

   "Lynx" full screen browser
           This is a hypertext browser for vt100s using full screen, arrow
           keys, highlighting, etc.

   Tom Fine's perlWWW
           A tty-based browser written in perl.

   For VMS
           Dudu Rashty's full screen client based on VMS's SMG screen
           management routines.

   Emacs w3-mode
           W3 browse mode for emacs. Uses multiple fonts when used with
           Lemacs or Epoch. See doc .
```

Figure 12-11: Use the Web to find client software.

```
PC Running Windows

    Cello
            Browser from Cornell LII

    Mosaic for Windows
            From NCSA.

    WinWeb
            EINet's full-feature World-Wide Web client

    GWHIS for MS Windows
            Commercialized version of NCSA Mosaic from Quadralay Inc.

    Netscape
            Commercial browser

    Galahad for BIX
            An off-line access tool for the on-line Byte Information
            eXchange, that also includes a Web browser with forms
            capability.

    Quarterdeck Mosaic
            and more on Quarterdeck

    SlipKnot
            SlipKnot, a graphical World Wide Web browser specifically
            designed for Microsoft Windows users who have UNIX shell
            accounts with their service providers, has been released as
            shareware by MicroMind, Inc.

Macintosh

    Mosaic for Macintosh
            From NCSA. Full featured.

    Samba
            From CERN. Basic.

    MacWeb
            EINet's full-feature World-Wide Web client

    Netscape
            Commercial browser

X-Windows

    NCSA Mosaic for X
            Browser using X11/Motif.

    GWHIS Viewer for X
            Commercialized version of NCSA Mosaic from Quadralay Inc.

    tkWWW Browser/Editor for X11
            Browser/Editor for X11. (Beta)

    MidasWWW Browser
            From Tony Johnson. (Beta, works well.)

    Chimera
            Browser using Athena (doesn't require Motif)

    "ViolaWWW" Browser for X11
            Browser for X11. (Beta, unsupported)

    Arena
            HTML3 browser for X11. (prerelease, supported)

    Netscape
            Commercial browser
NeXTStep

    Browser-Editor on the NeXT
            A browser/editor for NeXTStep. Allows wysiwyg hypertext
            editing. Requires NeXTStep 3.0

    OmniWeb
            Working browser from Omni. Freely available.

VM

    Albert
            A full-screen WWW client for VM systems by David Nessl,
            University of Florida. Available from
            ftp://www.ufl.edu/pub/vm/www. (VM is an IBM mainframe operating
            system).

Unreleased or Unsupported

    Browser on CERNVM
            A full-screen browser for VM. Nonexistant. Use the line mode
            www. Might arrive suddenly one day.

    Dave Ragget's Browser
            Unreleased. For X11, (later PC?)

    Erwise
            X-windows early browser. Unsupported, now of historical.

    NJIT's Browser

Assumes a character-grid terminal with cursor addressing, and provides
a full-screen interface to the web.
```

Figure 12-11:
(continued)

Graphical browsers, on the other hand, are the easiest way to access the Web, and the most fun (see Figure 12-12). In the next section, you'll take a closer look at some of the features of these browsers.

If you would like to have your own browser, you can use Anonymous FTP to get one free. Table 12-5 lists some Anonymous FTP sites from which you can copy either graphical or character-cell (nongraphical) browsers. ■

Table 12-5: Anonymous FTP Sites with WWW Browsers

Anonymous FTP Site	Browser Name
ftp.mcom.com	Netscape
ftp.ncsa.uiuc.edu	Mosaic (for Macintosh)
gatekeeper.dec.com	Mosaic (for most operating systems)
ftp2.cc.ukans.edu	Lynx

Look closely at the text in Figure 12-11 and you'll see it lists both character-cell Web browsers and graphical browsers.

If you have a plain character-cell browser such as Lynx, or a line-mode browser, you'll need to know the commands listed in Table 12-6 to help you navigate.

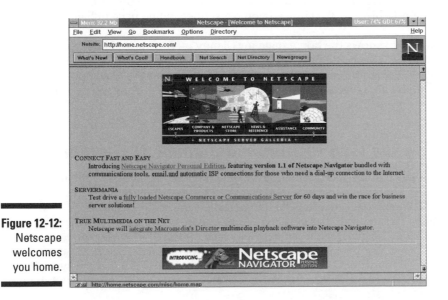

Figure 12-12: Netscape welcomes you home.

Table 12-6: Commands for Nongraphical Web Browsing

Browser Command	Function
home	Go to the home page.
recall	Review documents you've already viewed.
top	Go to the first page of the document.
bottom	Go to the last page of the document.
next	Follow the next link in the chain of information.
previous	Retrace the prior link.

Mousing across the Web

Graphical browsers really bring the Web to life. The next group of figures demonstrate some of the really neat things you can do with a graphical browser. We used Netscape for these examples, but you can do the same and similar things with any of the graphical browsers. The buttons may look slightly different, but the basic functionality is the same.

To get started, just click on the icon for your browser and you will get the *home page* — the Web term for a "welcome" screen. Typically, it explains what the service is all about and points you in the right direction for what you want to browse. We showed you Netscape's home page in Figure 12-12.

Figure 12-13 shows the home page for Disney — you know, Mickey and Minnie's home. This home page includes a multimedia show, and even tells you what kind of resources you need to have for enjoying the movie preview service. If you do, you can actually preview movies in full color and sound on your computer, by clicking on the words "Movie Plex."

Using the Web to learn more about The Internet

We've talked a lot about The Internet in this book, because TCP/IP and The Internet are really a package deal. You can't have The Internet without TCP/IP (no matter what the OSI fanatics say); nor would we have had TCP/IP without The Internet. But in the greater scheme of things, this book really only skims the general characteristics of The Internet, in order to show you the relationship between the Net and its protocols and services. So if you think you're turning into an Internet junkie (or already are and always will be), the best place to learn more about The Internet is on The Internet itself.

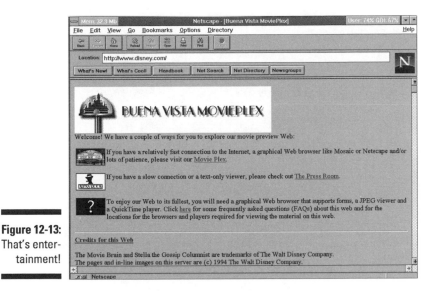

Figure 12-13:
That's enter-
tainment!

Figure 12-14 shows a page linked to Netscape's home page, this one for Internet exploration. This is a great place to start and let the Web teach you about
The Internet. You don't have to use the Netscape browser to access this Web
page. Any browser can get you here.

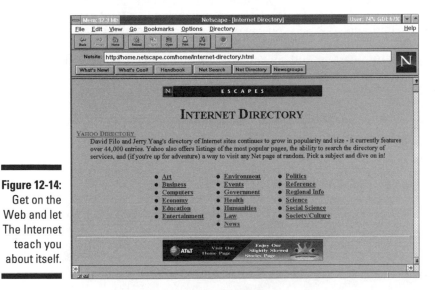

Figure 12-14:
Get on the
Web and let
The Internet
teach you
about itself.

All the news that's fit to surf

Graphical browsers also function as Usenet news readers (discussed in Chapter 7). Figure 12-15 shows an example of reading news via the Netscape
browser. To get this started, we clicked on Netscape's Newsgroups button.

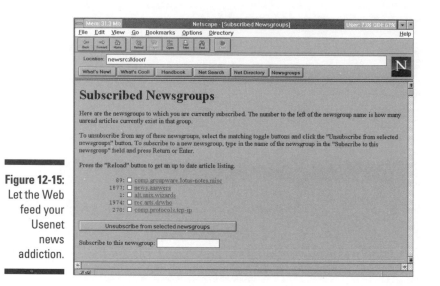

Figure 12-15:
Let the Web feed your Usenet news addiction.

Shopping and other fun

The Internet is emerging as an unlimited commercial site. In the future you may wind up spending more time at an Internet mall than you do walking through the traditional kind — the ones with hard floors, recycled air, and salespeople who spray you with perfume. The Internet mall even has a food court! It has all kinds of restaurants to which you can e-mail an order, and they deliver.

In Figure 12-16, a certain well-known database company is doing some marketing on the Web. From their home page, you can get free trial software and training information.

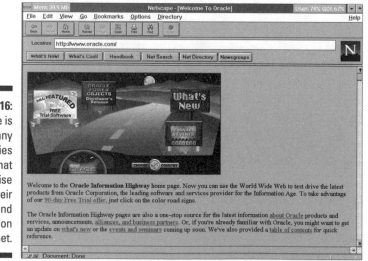

Figure 12-16:
Oracle is one of many companies that advertise their services and products on The Internet.

Everybody, Sing! "Duke, Duke, Duke, Duke of URL, URL, URL . . . "

If you've been paying attention to the cool WWW home pages we've been showing you, you probably have noticed the Location box just above the action buttons. This box has contained character strings that start with *http*. This string of characters is technically called a Uniform Resource Locator, or URL. (The acronym is pronounced both ways, by saying the letters *U R L* or by saying "earl.")

Let's take an URL apart and analyze it. We'll use

    http://www.oracle.com/

The *http* is the protocol, HyperText Transfer Protocol, that you use to access the resource. Everything following the colon is the location of the WWW resource. The location starts with //, followed by the site name. If anything follows the final /, it is a filename on that host.

Did you notice in Figure 12-15 that there's only one word, **newsrc**, in the Location box? That's because Usenet news is handled a little differently. Since it's more local, the use of NNTP is invisible.

URLs do not locate only Web resources. Here are examples of URLs that point to an Anonymous FTP site and a Gopher server:

    ftp://ftp.microsoft.com

    gopher://sunsite.unc.edu

When you're off browsing, the Web can actually take you to a non-HTTP resource such as those above.

It's likely that you could easily spend all your spare time — if not all your days and nights — browsing the wonders of the World Wide Web. But this little taste is all we're providing as part of our TCP/IP soup-to-nuts banquet. In case you missed the point of this chapter, there are literally dozens of additional information services that are available on TCP/IP networks in general and The Internet in particular. For details about these information services and about the fun and education available on The Internet, you can read *The Internet for Dummies*. And many of you will probably already be anxious to jump in and start surfing. That's probably the best way of all to learn.

Chapter 13

Nice Names and Agonizing Addresses

· ·

In This Chapter

▶ A new name for computers: hosts

▶ Why have both names and addresses?

▶ TCP/IP network addresses are classy things

▶ The parts and fields of IP addresses

▶ How to get an IP address, and an address on The Internet

▶ Subnets and supernets and why they wear masks

▶ Some math you can't even do with a calculator

· ·

*I*f your computer is already on a network, and you always call computers by name, and you don't give a fig what TCP/IP is doing to your computer's name behind the scenes, you can breathe easy in this chapter. The only thing you really need to learn here is another term for a computer — a *host* — and what it means. In other words, you can go look up the term, host, in the book's Glossary and move on to Chapter 14 or some other chapter. This whole chapter will be techno-geekism for you.

On the other hand, if you need to get your computer on the network or The Internet, or you want to know the meaning of all those strings of numbers and dots that you see when you use an application such as FTP or telnet, stay right here. Most of the information in this chapter is aimed at you — especially if you're a beginning network administrator.

What Did You Say Your Computer's Name Was Again?

You have a name. When you were born, your parents gave it to you. They did this for several reasons: to fill in the big space on your birth certificate, to give them something interesting to yell when they call you for dinner, and because "Hey you!" is sorta rude (not to mention unspecific). Ultimately, though, the idea behind your name is to identify you uniquely. Sometimes it takes your entire name to identify you: Alfred E. Newman, Smokey The Bear, Thurston Howell III. Sometimes it only takes part of your name: Einstein, Gandhi, Gilligan.

You also have a number. Most of us have more than one:

- A driver's license number
- Credit card number(s)
- A social security (or other government identification) number

You can change your name if you want. You may acquire a nickname, slapped on by one of your friends or maybe even chosen by you yourself. Maybe you write books under a pen name. If you're working as a spy, you probably assume a number of "covers." When you get married, you may elect to take your spouse's last name. You can even go to court and change your name legally.

Changing your numbers is a little harder. In most cases, you have to get some corporation or official agency to approve and make the change for you.

Getting to know you . . .

If your computer uses TCP/IP, your computer must have a name, too. If you're lucky, you may get to choose it yourself. Most likely, though, your organization has a naming policy that helps you select a name or that limits your choices. In some cases, a system manager or network administrator gets to have all the fun and assigns a name to your computer for you.

Your computer has a number, as well. That number is called the computer's *IP address,* and we'll spend the greater part of this chapter studying it. (Throughout much of this book, we've called it a *numeric address* — now you know the correct technical term.) Your computer may have more than one IP address, depending on how many networks it's connected to.

Your computer's name and IP address can change, too. It may never write a book under a pseudonym or take a married name, but it can take on nicknames, change names, and have multiple identities. (If you use it for espionage, maybe your computer has a "cover," too . . . would you believe Agent 80486?)

There are a number of reasons why a computer needs a name.

✔ You need to be able to connect to a particular computer and the services it offers. Knowing that computer's name makes it easier to link up.

✔ You want your e-mail delivered to a specific place. Without computer names and addresses, e-mail would be impossible.

✔ Humans like naming things (dogs, cats, goldfish) and can remember names. Computers like dealing with numbers, as you'll see later in this chapter.

What happens if the computer name isn't unique on the network? Do you remember the two Lotus companies we compared in Chapter 11? One makes cars; the other makes software. If you tried to connect via FTP to a computer named just lotus, would you find files about cars or software?

TCP/IP and The Internet require that each and every computer on the network, in the organization, in the world, in the solar system be uniquely identified by both name and address. To identify computer lotus, then, we need more names — kind of like first, middle, last, and maybe more. (Do you remember Princess Diana stumbling all over Prince Charles's names during their wedding ceremony? Perhaps it was an omen . . .)

Fully Qualified Domain Names (FQDNs). You'll recall from Chapter 11 that a computer's full name is called a fully qualified domain name, FQDN. (Go ahead, just *try* to say it three times fast.) So, for computer lotus, its FQDN might be

```
lotus.lotus.com
```

where computer name = lotus; organization name = lotus; and Internet top-level domain = com (short for commercial organization). Here's another example:

```
hbs.harvard.edu
```

where the computer name = hbs; organization name = harvard; and Internet top-level domain = edu (short for educational institution). ∎

What's the Local Hosts File?

We promised you'd learn a new term for a computer in this chapter, and we always keep our promises. Up to now, we've been calling a computer on the network a computer, or sometimes a system, but now we're going to get more technical and start calling it a *host*. Substitute the term *host* for *computer*, and you can then say that every host on a TCP/IP network has a name and a number.

In Chapter 11 we introduced you to the concept of a local *hosts file*. This file, residing on your own computer, lists by both name and number the hosts (computers) you want to communicate with.

✔ On UNIX, the hosts file is /etc/hosts.

✔ On the version of TCP/IP that we use with Microsoft Windows NT, the hosts file is c:\winnt\system32\drivers\etc\hosts.

✔ On non-UNIX systems, the hosts file's location varies with the TCP/IP product you're using.

Figure 13-1 shows the names and addresses in a small local hosts file.

Figure 13-1:
A local hosts file identifies each host by name and number.

```
# Copyright (c) 1993-1994 Microsoft Corp.
#
# This is a sample HOSTS file used by Microsoft TCP/IP for Windows NT
# 3.5.
#
# This file contains the mappings of IP addresses to host names. Each
# entry should be kept on an individual line. The IP address should
# be placed in the first column followed by the corresponding host name.
# The IP address and the host name should be separated by at least one
# space.
#
# Additionally, comments (such as these) may be inserted on individual
# lines or following the machine name denoted by a '#' symbol.
#
# For example:
#
#      102.54.94.97       rhino.acme.com          # source server
#       38.25.63.10       x.acme.com              # x client host

127.0.0.1        localhost
130.103.40.55    marshallw
130.103.40.12    candacel
```

If you're part of a large network, you will probably want to use a naming service to replace or supplement your local hosts file. See Chapter 10 for information on the Network Information Service (NIS) and Chapter 11 for information on the Domain Name System (DNS) to resolve (translate) host names into addresses. ∎

The Many Faces of IP Addresses

Hosts on a network are identified by their numeric IP address. Yes, you usually type in the host's name, but somewhere along the way TCP/IP resolves (that is, translates) that name into an IP address. That's the raison d'être for your local hosts file, and NIS and DNS. In the case of big networks (and can you get any bigger than The Internet?), it's DNS that does the name/address resolution.

Why bother with a number if the computer has a name?

People like names. Computers like numbers.

What's in an IP address?

The address where you live is made up of several parts. It may include any of many elements that identify you — your street name, post office box, city, region (province, state, canton, county), country, postal code, and so forth. The same is true of your computer (host). The difference is that you *know* your address, and it is mostly text with a few numbers; but you may or may not know your computer's address, which is all numbers and dots.

The IP address is a set of numbers separated by dots. It identifies *one network interface on a host.* Every device on the TCP/IP network — that is, every network interface on the network, since some devices may have more than one — needs a unique IP address. If your host is on a TCP/IP network, that host has an IP address, even if you've always called your computer by name.

You may have noticed this numeric address showing up in messages and wondered what it was. For example, telnet reports the IP address as it tries to connect to the remote host. Here's a code fragment that shows it. You connect to frodo by name, and telnet responds with frodo's IP address.

```
% telnet frodo
Trying 130.103.40.225 ...
Connected to frodo.
```

An IP address is a 32-bit number. It is divided into two sections: the network number and the host number. (You can't see the division. Wait for the section on subnet masks later in this chapter.) Addresses are written as 4 fields, 8 bits each, separated by dots. Each field can be a number ranging from 0 to 255. This style of writing an address is called *dotted decimal notation.*

All hosts on the same network must use the same network number. Each host/network interface on the same network must have a unique host number.

Figure 13-2 shows some legal combinations of network and host numbers. ■

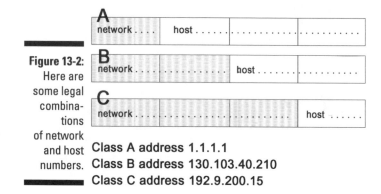

Figure 13-2:
Here are
some legal
combina-
tions
of network
and host
numbers.

Class A address 1.1.1.1
Class B address 130.103.40.210
Class C address 192.9.200.15

How Do I Get an IP Address?

Can you just pick any IP address that's unique on your network? Most of the time, the answer is no, unless you are the network administrator.

Most organizations have network administrators (known affectionately as the network police) who tell you what to use for an address so that yours doesn't conflict with anyone else's. After all, you can't just pick any ol' house on the block and move in — someone else probably already lives there, right? So, your network police officer is there to make sure nobody squats at a network address that's already in use. If the police don't do their job, and you *do* set up your computer to use an existing address, don't come whining to us that you never receive your e-mail or that you're receiving someone else's junk mail.

Only if your network isn't connected to any other network is it okay for you or your network police to pick a host address out of the blue. If your network is connected, your address must be unique across the combination of linked networks. Figure 13-3 shows what can happen if your address is not unique.

On The Internet, where many thousands of networks are interconnected, no one person actually polices to make sure each and every address is unique. The assignment of the network number portion of the IP address keeps the organizations clearly identified and separate.

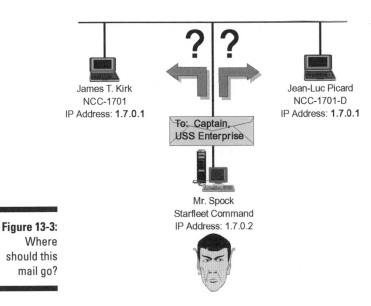

Figure 13-3:
Where
should this
mail go?

How do I get an address on The Internet?

To connect your network to The Internet, you need an official block of
addresses. The official bestower of IP addresses is the InterNIC. There are also
regional Internet *access providers* who can give you your official addresses.

How do you find out who these Internet access providers are? The best way
is by looking at lists on The Internet, but that's a catch-22 we don't want to
get into here. One of the next best ways is to ask neighboring organizations
that are already on The Internet who they use. You can also look at the ads
in almost any computer-related magazine. Many Internet starter kits in
bookstores are preconfigured to link you to an Internet access provider.

Getting Help from InterNIC Registration Services

The Registration Services part of the InterNIC
(rs.internic.net) is funded by the National Science Foundation and your U.S. tax dollars to
assist you with registering your network on The
Internet. The people at InterNIC Registration
Services work with network administrators to
register their networks and assign Internet
addresses. For help, call User Assistance Services at the InterNIC in Herndon, Virginia, 1-
703-742-4777. They will help you get the forms
you need to register your domain and to get
Internet addresses.

If you think you might want to connect your network to The Internet some day, you can save yourself a lot of work down the line by applying for IP addresses ahead of time. You can start using them locally as soon as you get them, and when you finally connect to the Information Superhighway, you won't have to renumber your network and all your hosts. ■

The Four Sections of the IP Address

An IP address looks like this:

```
field1.field2.field3.field4
```

The meaning of these fields depends on your *network class*. There are three classes of networks in TCP/IP. Whether your organization connects to The Internet or is a private internet, the classes work the same way.

Let's use the biggest internet we can think of — The Internet — to examine how network classes work.

Class A is for a few enormous networks

Theoretically, there can only be 127 class A networks on The Internet, but each one of those 127 can have a huge number of hosts: about 17 million each (16,777,216 to be exact). Only a few very large organizations need class A networks. (By the way, there is no class A network that starts with the number 0, and the entire class A network numbered 127 is reserved. This leaves only 126 class A networks.)

Class B is for lots of big networks

Although they're nowhere near as enormous as class A networks, class B networks are hefty, as well. Each class B network can have about 65,000 hosts — the size needed by some universities and larger companies. The Internet can support up to 16,384 class B networks.

Class C is for the thousands of small networks

Class C networks are much smaller, and The Internet has over 2 million (2,097,152) of these. Most of the networks connected to The Internet are class C. Each one can have only 256 hosts. (Actually, each class C network can have only 254 hosts; the numbers 0 and 255 are reserved.)

For Math Nerds Only: Biting Down on Bits and Bytes

Who decided how many hosts are in the class A, B, and C networks? And why can there only be 127 class A networks when there can be a zillion (well, almost) of class C?

It all has to do with the arrangement of the bits inside the addresses. For example, class A addresses use the first field as the network section, and the next three fields as the host section. The more fields in a section, the bigger number you get. Since class A only has one field in the network section, it can only have a small number of networks. But the three fields in the hosts part allow each of those 127 networks to have a ton of computers.

Table 13-1 shows how the four fields of the IP address are assigned to the network section and host section.

Table 13-1: The Two Sections of the IP Address

Network Class	Network Section of IP Address	Host Section of IP Address
A	field1	field2.field3.field4
B	field1.field2	field3.field4
C	field1.field2.field3	field4

The binary blues

Danger! There be math ahead. If you already understand binary numbers and how to convert from decimal to binary, skip ahead to the next section. If you don't understand binary, this section takes you back to first grade. Get ready to look at place values in a whole new way.

Figure 13-4 takes the number 127 apart to show how it's constructed in binary. A computer looks at the number 127 as an arrangement of 0s and 1s. Computers ultimately do everything in binary, base 2, so if we look at the place value columns in Figure 13-4, we don't see the familiar 1s, 10s, 100s, etc., from the decimal system. Rather, we see the 1s, 2s, 4s, 8s, 16s, 32s, 64s, 128s, etc.

(Remember, in binary, the only possible values in a column are 0 or 1. Also remember that there are 8 bits in a byte.) In the decimal system, it takes three columns — the 1s column, the 10s column, and the 100s column — to represent the number 127. To get to 127, then, our binary number has 7 columns: the 1s, 2s, 4s, 8s, 16s, 32s, and 64s. ■

Class A Network

Figure 13-4:
Binary numbers are as easy as 1, 2, 3. Oops, make that 0 and 1.

128	64	32	16	8	4	2	1	place value columns
0	1	1	1	1	1	1	1	bit values (either 1 or 0)

high order bit ◄──────────── low order bit

127 = 1+2+4+8+16+32+64

Classy Bits

In a computer, each place-value column in a binary number is represented by a bit. In the early days of computers, you could look inside the cabinet and actually see circular magnets called cores; each magnet was a bit. A core magnetized in one direction (say, clockwise) meant the bit was set to 1. The other direction (counterclockwise) meant the bit was set to 0. Today's transistors and semiconductors have replaced the magnets, so it's harder to see what's going on inside — but the computer still uses bits of 1 and 0. All numbers inside the computer, from 0 to 1 trillion and on up, are made from bits. The computer keeps adding the 1s and 0s until it reaches the total, such as 127.

If each and every bit of the class A network piece were set to 0 or 1, that would result in a higher number than the 127 allowed by The Internet. Figure it out: 128+64+32+16+8+4+2+1. But TCP/IP requires that the high-order bit for a class A network is always 0. According to this rule, when you add up the bits you get 0+64+32+16+8+4+2+1 for the number of class A networks that a 32-bit address allows. To determine how many networks and hosts were allowable for each Internet class, the maximum value was calculated for the field combinations of each section. The rules for class B state that the first two high-order bits must be 1 and 0. For class C, the first two high-order bits must be 1 and 1.

The high-order bits are the bits at the end of the number. *Which* end depends on whether your computer reads from right to left or left to right. If a computer reads from right to left, as does a PC, the high-order bits are the ones on the far left end.

Administering Subnets and Subnet Masks

Subnets divide one network into multiple smaller networks. The separate networks are normally interconnected by network devices called *routers.* (Routers, brouters, bridges, and more are explained in Chapter 17, "The Dreaded Hardware Chapter.")

Not every environment requires subnets. For example, if your organization's class C network has 254 or fewer hosts and the network lives entirely in one building, there's no reason to subnet it. But if your organization's network does expand into multiple locations, the network administrator has a couple of options.

One is to ask for another entire network number for each new facility, but this is sorta greedy if your existing network still has enough unassigned host numbers for future growth. The other option is to take your existing network and split it into pieces, one piece for each location.

When subnets are necessary, and the network administrator (this may mean you!) uses good common sense to subdivide the network, subnets do yield some advantages over one large network:

✔ Smaller networks are easier to manage and troubleshoot, even though there are more pieces.

✔ Network traffic overall is reduced, and performance may improve because most traffic is local to its subnet.

✔ Network security can be applied more easily at the interconnections between the subnets. For some mind-numbing details about network security, read Chapter 18.

Figure 13-5 shows a main network with two subnets. Each network and each host has an address. Look carefully at field3 in each address; you'll find some subtle differences.

The address for a subnet uses the address for the main network and borrows some bits from the host part to extend the network section. The borrowed bits enable each subnet to have its own unique network address. Because the subnet addresses are derived from the main network's address, you do not have to ask the InterNIC for them. These addresses already belong to your organization; you've just decided to deploy them differently.

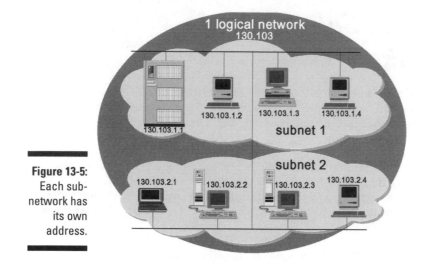

Figure 13-5:
Each sub-network has its own address.

Maskerading subnets

When the network administrator borrows bits from the main network address's host section, TCP/IP must be told which bits of the host section are borrowed to be used as the network address. The administrator uses a *subnet mask* to borrow those host bits. A subnet mask is 32 bits, just like the IP address. The bits for the network address are all set to 1, and the bits for the host address are all set to 0.

Before defining a subnet mask, the network administrator needs to figure out how many subnets to create and how many hosts will be in each subnet. This determines how many bits should be set to 1. (There's a subnetting example a few paragraphs down.)

The more bits used for the subnet mask, the fewer hosts can be on the subnet. ■

Why do I have a mask if it's not Halloween?

Your network has a subnet mask even if it doesn't have subnets. Most TCP/IP implementations supply a default subnet mask, which says, "Hi. I'm a network that is not subnetted." Figure 13-6 shows the default subnet mask for each class of network. Some TCP/IP vendors (Microsoft, for example) automatically configure the default subnet mask for you.

A   255.0.0.0

| 11111111 | 00000000 | 00000000 | 00000000 |

B   255.255.0.0

Figure 13-6:
Each class
has a
default
subnet
mask.

| 11111111 | 11111111 | 00000000 | 00000000 |

C   255.255.255.0

| 11111111 | 11111111 | 11111111 | 00000000 |

The subnet mask must be the same for each computer on the network; otherwise, the computers won't understand that they're on the same network. ■

The subnet mask is applied to the IP address in every message in order to separate the network number and the host number. For example, when your computer examines the class C address 192.9.200.15 and applies the default subnet mask of 255.255.255.0, it sees the network number 192.9.200 and the host number 15.

How do you know that this works? Hold on to your techie hats. It's done by converting nice decimal numbers like 255 to not-so-nice binary numbers like 11111111. And then, after all the numbers are converted to binary, they get XOR'd (Exclusive Or'd). XOR is a binary mathematical operation. If you are not ineXORably bORed by now, read the upcoming sidebar. Just remember, though this stuff may seem incomprehensible to you, your computer lives, breathes, and eats binary and thinks this is Really Fun! ■

P.S. The authors cannot be held responsible for any medical or mental complications that result from reading beyond this point!

Subnetting 101

Here's the subnetting example we promised you earlier. We're going to split one class C network with 256 hosts into two equal subnets of 128 hosts each. We'll change the class C default subnet mask of 255.255.255.0.

Let's use network number 192.9.202, which means the 256 hosts are numbered 192.9.202.0 through 192.9.202.255. To split the network into two parts, with one part getting addresses 0 to 127 and the other getting addresses 128 to 255, you need the custom subnet mask 255.255.255.128. The 0 becomes 128 because you borrow the high-order bit from field4. (In binary, 128 is 10000000. Refer back to the sidebar, "Classy Bits," if you need help with the math.)

TECHNICAL STUFF

Boolean Arithmetic: Exclusive Or (XOR)

In the Exclusive Or (XOR) operation, regardless of the value in the data bit, a mask bit of 0 yields a result of 0. And a mask bit of 1 preserves the value in the data bit, also regardless of the value in the data bit. Another way to say this is that the result bit is a 1 if, and only if, both the data bit and the mask bit contain 1. Otherwise, the result bit is 0. Here's a table that demonstrates this:

```
            0    1    0    1    Data
XOR         0    0    1    1    Mask
            0    0    0    1    Result
```

Let's examine how a subnet mask is used to obtain the network number part of an IP address. In your computer, the fields of the dotted decimal IP address 192.9.200.15 are already in binary as

    11000000 00001001 11001000 00001111

The fields of the dotted decimal subnet mask 255.255.255.0 are already

    11111111 11111111 11111111 00000000

The XOR operation yields the network number 192.9.200, as shown here:

```
11000000    00001001    11001000    00001111    IP address: 192.9.200.155
11111111    11111111    11111111    00000000    Subnet mask: 255.255.255.0
11000000    00001001    11001000    00000000    Result: 192.9.200.0
```

To get the host number, your computer inverts the bits of the subnet mask — each 1 becomes a 0, and each 0 becomes a 1 — and does another XOR. Easy as pi, right?

```
11000000    00001001    11001000    00001111    IP address: 192.9.200.15

00000000    00000000    00000000    11111111    Subnet mask: 0.0.0.255

00000000    00000000    00000000    00001111    Result: 0.0.0.15
```

In the 192.9.202 network, there are 128 addresses that also happen to have the high-order bit of field4 set to 0, and another 128 addresses that happen to have the high-order bit set to 1. If you thought the custom subnet mask would be 255.255.255.1, you were close, but that mask borrows the low-order bit of field4. It puts all the even-numbered hosts (0, 2, 4, 6, and up to 254) in one subnet and all the odd-numbered hosts (1, 3, 5, 7, and up to 255) in the other.

Before subnetting this example network, it was easy to say that all of the hosts were in the 192.9.202 network. They still are.

Probably the most common use of subnetting is when an organization splits its class B network into 256 class C networks. To accomplish this, every host sets its subnet mask to 255.255.255.0. ■

Expanding with Supernets and Supernet Masks

If your organization has grown, you may need to link two or more class C networks together. The result will be one larger network, although it won't be as large as a class B network. In this *supernet,* the network number part of the address lends bits to the host number part — just the opposite of what happens in a subnet.

The networks being linked into a supernet should be numerically "adjacent." The meaning of "numerically adjacent" depends on whether you're using decimal or binary numbers. Adjacent binary numbers may well have nonadjacent decimal equivalents. For example, decimal 3 is adjacent to decimal 4, but their binary equivalents, 011 and 100, are not adjacent. In this first supernet example, the two network numbers are "adjacent" in both their binary and decimal values. In the later examples they are not.

Supernet Example 1: Let's link 192.9.200 and 192.9.201. We'll skip over the 192 and 9 since they're the same in both addresses, and concentrate on the 200 and 201. Your computer already stores the decimal number 200 as the binary number 11001000, and the decimal number 201 as the binary number 11001001. Notice that the only difference is the last bit. That means we only need to borrow the low-order bit of field3. To link these two networks together, we simply change from the default subnet mask of 255.255.255.0 to the custom supernet mask of 255.255.254.0.

Supernet Example 2: This next one is harder and points out the nasty side of the "adjacent" requirement. Let's link 192.9.199 and 192.9.200. Once again, we'll skip over the 192 and 9 and concentrate on the 199 and 200. Your computer already stores the decimal number 199 as the binary number 11000111, and decimal 200 as binary 11001000. Uh oh, these binary numbers differ in all of the last 4 bits! The supernet mask that links them is 255.255.240.0 (240 in decimal is 11110000 in binary) — but that supernet mask actually links together the 16 networks 192.9.192 through 192.9.207. (Do the math yourself or just trust us. We know our binary.) So if the other 14 networks don't belong to our organization, we've just created a mess and this is not the right answer for us. If all of the networks were ours, this might be okay, depending on what we really need to do.

Supernet Example 3: Okay, one last example and we're done with this. This one shows how two networks can be adjacent in their binary numbers even though they don't look adjacent in their decimal numbers. This time, we'll link 192.9.200 and 192.9.216. As usual, we'll skip over the 192 and 9 and concentrate on the 200 and 216. Your computer already stores decimal 200 as binary 11001000, and decimal 216 as binary 11010000. Wow, the only difference is one bit, although it's in the middle — which means we only need to borrow that bit in field3. To link these two networks together, we use the supernet mask 255.255.239.0. It looks strange but has been properly calculated. ■

A bit makes more than a bit of difference

It's more important that two supernet network numbers vary by one bit than it is for them to be plus or minus 1 decimal value. That's why 200 and 216 are "adjacent," but 199 and 200 are not. Table 13-2 shows how many bits of supernet mask it takes to link networks together.

Table 13-2: Bits and Network Linkages

To Link This Many Networks:	The Network Numbers Must Differ In:
2 networks	Only 1 bit position
4 networks	2 bit positions
8 networks	3 bit positions
16 networks	4 bit positions
32 networks	5 bit positions
64 networks	6 bit positions
128 networks	7 bit positions
256 networks	8 bit positions

If you are a network administrator and need to configure subnets, a calculator that converts between binary and decimal will be one of your most valuable tools. (Or, if you're a seasoned IBM mainframer, you can look up binary-to-decimal conversions on your tattered old IBM 370 green card!) ■

Supernets: the bottom line

So what the supernet mask really does is link together separate networks into one network. By using the supernet mask value of 255, we're linking together the 256 networks numbered from 0 to 255.

Is The Internet Getting Low on Addresses?

Yes.

Will The Internet Ever Run Out of Addresses?

No. Read all about IPng — IP the Next Generation — in Chapter 2.

Back to the Comfort Zone

Congratulations. You stuck with it and made it to the end of this arduous odyssey of agonizing addresses. If you're a network administrator, you'll need to work with numbers occasionally to set up IP addresses and possibly subnets, so you may be used to this stuff anyway. If you're an end user of TCP/IP and The Internet, you've just acquired a store of valuable mathematical trivia. We doubt that you'll need to use it, however, unless you become a contestant on *Jeopardy, the Network Edition.* (Don't laugh. Digital Equipment Corporation's Users Society has actually sponsored "Network Jeopardy" at its conventions.)

In any event, no matter what your role in network fun and games, for the rest of the book you can relax. We now return to the world of host and network names (although you may recognize numeric IP addresses in some of the examples). The next chapter is useful for end users as well as network administrators, because it helps you find people and hosts — and even soda machines — on an internet or The Internet. And you can do it all with names.

Chapter 14

Is Anyone There?

*H*ow do you find someone to "talk" to? How can you look up someone's e-mail address? How many people are on your network and what hosts are available? If you want to use telnet or Gopher or Archie, how can you determine if the server is up and running? The answers to these and other questions about checking out what's happening on the network are in this chapter.

Information, Please

Maybe you just need to verify an e-mail address. Maybe you're a network administrator who needs to see how many people and machines are slowing down your network and why. For whatever reason you may need to look around an internet or The Internet, there are TCP/IP tools available to help you.

We didn't have to work very hard on the humor in this chapter. For that, we have the names of the tools themselves. Many of them originated in UNIX (which is a pretty funny name itself, especially the first time you hear it pronounced without seeing the spelling). Take a look at Figure 14-1. It shows a Microsoft Windows program group with the icons for TCP/IP services and tools, and some of them are real giggles.

If you don't have a GUI, you can use most of the same tools represented in Figure 14-1, but you'll have to do more typing because you have to start them with commands. Some of the examples in this chapter are from UNIX systems without a GUI, and some are from GUI-equipped computers, so you can see for yourself the difference in the interface.

REMEMBER

TCP/IP at Work: Remember, it's not the interface that is giving you network information; it's TCP/IP. All the tools and services described in this chapter are TCP/IP — regardless of the plain or fancy wrapping. ■

Figure 14-1:
A set of graphical TCP/IP services and tools.

Fingering Your Friends and Enemies

Take it easy . . . this isn't what you may be thinking. Nevertheless, prepare yourself for some strange-looking terms: *fingering,* for instance. *Finger* is a client/server environment for getting information about the users on a computer. It's the first application we tackle in this chapter because of the wealth of information it provides.

You use a *finger client* application to ask for information about one or more users on a computer — the computer you're on, or a remote host. If you're fingering a remote computer and the *finger server* is running there, it answers your query. If the finger server isn't running on the remote computer, you'll get an error message such as

```
connection refused
```

You have already seen an example of finger in Chapter 9, where it was listed as one way to discover someone's e-mail address. But finger can provide a lot more. Be patient, the examples are coming soon.

When you use finger, it looks in the file that holds user account information for the operating system; on a UNIX system, this is the /etc/passwd file. Finger searches this file for a match on any keywords you supply with the finger command. If you don't give any keywords, finger looks in the passwd file and returns information about every user currently using the computer.

This section gives you several examples showing the kind of information you can get with various uses of the finger command. Most of these examples were done on a UNIX system, but, to show the difference, there are also a few from a graphical version of finger running on Microsoft Windows. TCP/IP doesn't care about your interface. Whether you point and click or type commands, it looks at your request and returns the information you've requested.

Some system managers disable the finger server because they feel the information it provides might be used to break into the computer in question. In this situation, you can still run the finger client application, but there is no server to answer your request. (You get a "Connection refused" message.) You'll find more about finger and about security in Chapter 18. ■

Fingering a user

Example 1: In this first example, the unadorned finger command (that is, the command without any keywords) asks finger to look for everyone on the computer.

```
% finger
Login      Name                TTY Idle   When          Where
wilensky  Marshall Wilensky No  co         Fri 17:40
leiden    Candace Leiden          p0         Fri 17:22
jtf       cia ss.psy.emigre.in s4      3  Feb 24 14:35
pete      Pete Davis              p1 14:44  Feb 23 22:28  TIAC Suppo 617-276-7200
```

Example 2: Here, we ask finger to look for a particular user, so we get more (and more specific) information:

```
% finger wilensky
Login name: wilensky                    In real life: Marshall Wilensky
Directory: /usr1/wilensky               Shell: /bin/csh
On since Jan 20 17:40:09 on console
Mail last read Fri Jan 20 17:14:24 1995
No Plan.
```

Example 3: This time, we ask finger to look for Marshall by entering "Marshall" as the keyword. Though wilensky is actually the correct account name for Marshall's record in the passwd file, finger encounters "Marshall" in a documentation field and therefore returns the information from that record. If Candace's passwd file record had "Marshall" somewhere in it, finger would find her, as well.

```
% finger marshall
Login name: wilensky                        In real life: Marshall Wilensky
Directory: /usr1/wilensky                   Shell: /bin/csh
On since Jan 20 17:40:09 on console
Mail last read Fri Jan 20 17:14:24 1995
No Plan.
```

Fingering a user
who has projects and plans

Normally, what finger lists for a user is just the basic user information, such
as login name, home directory, real name, and when mail was last read. However, if a user has created *project* and *plan files,* finger will tell you more.

If you want to provide more information about yourself to someone who fin-
gers you, you can create a project file and/or a plan file. In these files you can
describe the projects you're working on (if they're not Top Secret), your
plans for the future, or anything else you want other people to see.

On a computer running the UNIX operating system, you name the files .pro-
ject and .plan, and store them in your home directory. (The dot in front of
.project and .plan is part of the filename.) On a computer running another
operating system, consult the finger utility's documentation to find out where
to put project and plan information. ■

Example 4: In this next example, we ask finger to look for one of your
authors, who happens to have created both a project file and a plan file.
Notice the additional information finger displays in this case.

```
$ finger leiden
Login: leiden                           Name: Candace Leiden
Directory: /home/leiden                 Shell: /bin/bash
On since Fri Feb 24 14:53 (EST) on ttyq7 from bed-1p3
New mail received Fri Feb 24 12:25 1995 (EST)
     Unread since Thu Feb 23 19:10 1995 (EST)
Project:
Coauthor a book. Learn Lotus Notes.
Plan:
Finish this book and get a life.
See more movies.
```

Fingering the users on a host

You can also ask finger to look for the information for all users on a
particular host.

Example 5: Here we ask finger to find out about everyone currently on the computer frodo:

```
% finger @frodo
[frodo]
Login      Name                   TTY Idle   When     Where
wilensky  Marshall Wilensky No  co        Fri 17:40
leiden    Candace Leiden          p0        Fri 17:22
```

Example 6: The next example is in Figure 14-2. We ask a graphical version of finger to look for information about all of the users currently on the computer named bilbo. It's similar to Example 5, but here we use a GUI.

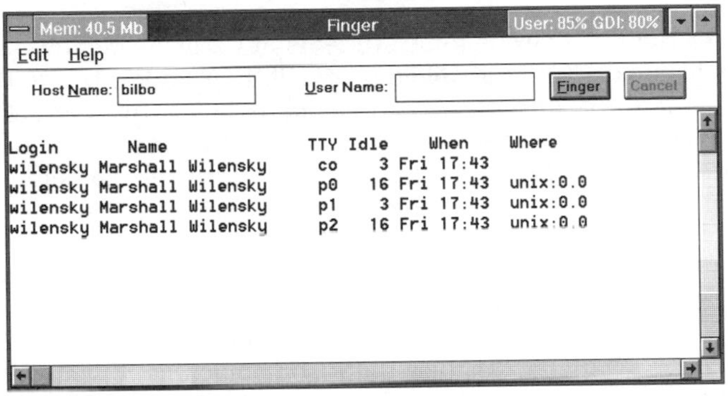

Figure 14-2:
Find out
about
everyone on
one host,
using a
graphical
finger.

Example 7: In Figure 14-3 we are again asking finger to look for everyone, but instead of specifying the host name, we give the IP address.

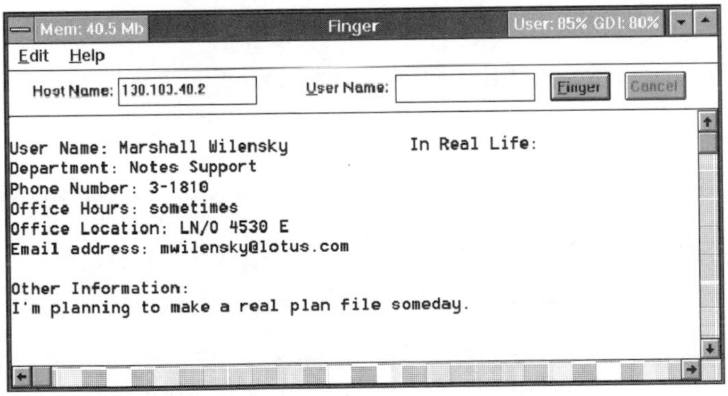

Figure 14-3:
If you don't
know the
host name,
you can use
the IP
address.

Example 8: Finally, we'll look for a specific user on frodo:

```
% finger wilensky@frodo
[frodo]
Login name: wilensky                    In real life: Marshall Wilensky
Directory: /usr1/wilensky                Shell: /bin/csh
On since Jan 20 17:40:09 on console
Mail last read Fri Jan 20 17:14:24 1995
No Plan.
```

TCP: The Cola Protocol?

Once upon a time there were some students at Carnegie Mellon University who really liked cola. And they liked it *cold*. If they made a trip to the soda machine and it was out of cola, or if the cola had recently been refilled and wasn't cold enough yet, the students were beside themselves with disappointment. To spare themselves the anguish of arriving at a below-par soda machine, they connected the machine to their network!

The students set up finger so that they could check up on the availability and temperature of the soda. And then, because they were enterprising students, they put the machine on The Internet so that, today, everyone in the world can check on the status of this particular soda machine. You never know, after all, when you're going to be in Pittsburgh and thirsty. So if you want to know how many colas are in that machine (or you just want to find out if we're pulling your leg), you can finger the machine. And if you're hungry, you can find out about these students' favorite kind of candy, as well.

In Figure 14-4 is our fingering of that soda machine — believe it or not.

Oh by the way, this is not the only soda machine on The Internet. There are dozens!

Too Much Fingering May Be Harmful to Your Network's Health

Finger is a tool to help you find out who is on your network and (possibly) what they're doing. It's also a great toy. You can discover all kinds of really cool information on The Internet by fingering computer hosts to see what they might tell you. Just remember, fingering can be addictive, and excessive use of finger can also slow down network performance. Remember to go outside and get some fresh air once in a while. After you check the cola machine.

```
% finger coke@a.cs.cmu.edu
[MAILBOX.SRV.CS.CMU.EDU]

[ Forwarding coke as "coke@l.gp.cs.cmu.edu" ]

[L.GP.CS.CMU.EDU]
Login: coke                      Name: Drink Coke
Directory: /usr/coke                    Shell: /usr/local/bin/tcsh
Last login Wed Oct 12 14:27 (EDT) on ttyp1 from PTERO.SOAR.CS.CMU.EDU
Mail came on Wed Dec 14 07:33, last read on Wed Dec 14 07:33
Plan:
Thu Sep 29 17:33:39 1994
M&M validity: 0      Coke validity: 0  (e.g. da interface is down,
sorry!)
Exact change required for coke machine.
   M & M                        Buttons
  /---\          C: CCCCCCCCCCCC............
  |    |          C: CCCCCC......   D: CCCCC......
  |**  |          C: CCCCCC......   D: CCCCC......
  |*****|         C: CCCCCC......   D: CCCCC......
  |*****|                           C: CCCCC......
  \---/                          S: CCCCC......
    |         Key:
    |          0 = warm;  9 = 90% cold;  C - cold;  . - empty
    |          Leftmost soda/pop will be dispensed next
 _.-^-_.
```

Figure 14-4:
I need a soda, a cold soda, and I need it now!

Fun with finger

It turns out that you can learn a lot about a lot of things with finger. You can learn about earthquakes, space, the Space Shuttle . . . just by fingering computers on The Internet. The next few examples illustrate some of the more interesting uses of finger.

TCP: Tremor Control Protocol?

Take a look at Figure 14-5. There you'll find the result of fingering an earthquake information system. You readers in California and Alaska will doubtless be interested in this one.

```
% finger quake@geophys.washington.edu
[geophys.washington.edu]
Login name: quake                    In real life: Earthquake
Information
Directory: /u0/quake                       Shell: /u0/quake/run_quake
Last login Wed Dec 14 16:26 on ttyi2
New mail received Wed Dec 14 15:57:51 1994;
   unread since Wed Dec 14 00:49:16 1994
Plan:
The following catalog is for earthquakes (M>2) in Washington and Oregon pro-
duced by the Pacific Northwest Seismograph Network, a member of the Council of
the National Seismic System.  Catalogs for various regions of the country can
be obtained by using the UNIX program `finger quake@machine' where the follow-
ing are machines for different regions.

gldfs.cr.usgs.gov   (USGS NEIC/NEIS world-wide), andreas.wr.usgs.gov (Northern
Cal.),
scec.gps.caltech.edu (Southern Cal.),
fm.gi.alaska.edu (Alaska),
seismo.unr.edu (Nevada),
eqinfo.seis.utah.edu (Utah),
slueas.slu.edu (Central US),
tako.wr.usgs.gov (Hawaii),

Additional catalogs and information for the PNSN (as well as other networks)
are available using the World-Wide-Web  (mosaic) system at URL:
 `http://www.geophys.washington.edu/'

DATE-TIME is in Universal Time (UTC) which is PST + 8 hours. Magnitudes are
reported as local magnitude (Ml).  QUAL is location quality A-good, D-poor, Z-
from automatic system and may be in error.

DATE-(UTC)-TIME   LAT(N) LON(W)   DEP  MAG QUAL COMMENTS
yy/mm/dd hh:mm:ss  deg.   deg.    km   Ml


94/11/03 20:48:58  46.38N 119.25W  0.4 2.1  B FELT  11.7 km NNE of Richland
94/11/09 22:25:24  46.40N 120.13W  0.0 2.1  C    35.1 km  SE of Yakima
94/11/10 09:42:41  44.36N 123.31W 19.2 2.0  B    41.3 km NNW of Eugene, OR
94/11/13 16:50:47  46.58N 119.58W 28.2 3.3  B    41.0 km NNW of Richland
94/11/15 23:11:02  48.03N 125.90W 10.0 2.2  C   114.4 km   W of Forks
94/11/17 20:29:49  42.38N 122.03W  0.1 3.9  A FELT  28.4 km  NW of Klamath Fal
94/11/17 21:40:29  45.70N 120.16W  0.0 2.7  C    64.6 km SSW of Prosser, Wa
94/11/18 00:27:28  42.36N 122.03W  8.3 2.2  A    26.9 km  NW of Klamath Falls,
94/11/19 05:50:19  42.36N 122.03W  3.3 2.0  A    28.1 km  NW of Klamath Falls,
94/11/19 07:47:11  42.36N 122.03W  6.5 2.5  A    27.4 km  NW of Klamath Falls,
94/11/19 08:21:15  42.36N 122.05W  6.0 2.0  A    27.6 km  NW of Klamath Falls,
94/11/20 02:11:22  42.36N 122.03W  7.2 2.4  A    27.0 km  NW of Klamath Falls,
94/11/21 09:20:10  47.73N 120.03W  4.4 2.5  B FELT  11.5 km SSW of Chelan
```

Figure 14-5:
Use finger
to learn
about earth-
quakes in
the United
States.

```
94/11/21 20:39:39   47.73N 119.93W    0.0 2.4   C    12.9 km SSE of Chelan
94/11/23 22:00:15   47.70N 118.16W   20.8 2.4   B    57.5 km   W of Spokane
94/11/26 07:32:06   42.35N 122.03W    8.0 2.1   A    26.6 km  NW of Klamath Falls,
94/11/29 11:56:47   47.43N 121.81W   18.9 2.9   B FELT  7.6 km SSW of North Bend
94/12/12 06:23:06   49.13N 122.45W   10.0 2.4   C    39.6 km NNW of Deming
94/12/13 04:44:39   47.41N 122.81W    0.1 2.0   B    20.8 km  SW of Bremerton
94/12/13 05:44:33   46.95N 124.13W   35.1 2.0   B    25.1 km   W of Aberdeen
```

Figure 14-5:
(continued)

Spaced out

You can learn about what's going on in space (outer space, not cyberspace) by fingering a host at the Massachusetts Institute of Technology (see Figure 14-6). Notice that the message returned also refers you to Gopher and World Wide Web servers (see Chapter 12), as well as FTP, for more information.

```
% finger nasanews@space.mit.edu [space.mit.edu]
nasanews: [space] Wed Dec 14 19:34:46 1994


                    MIT Center for Space Research


This NasaNews service is brought to you by the Microwave Subnode of NASA's
Planetary Data System.  AOL users can receive this bulletin as:
   keyword "Gopher" > Aerospace and Astronomy > Nasa News.

We also maintain an email listserver for planetary microwave information at
"pds-listserver@space.mit.edu", an anonymous ftp server at "delcano.mit.edu",
and a WWW home page at "http://delcano.mit.edu/".
If you have any suggestions for how we might improve our services, please mail
them to pdsrequests@space.mit.edu".

NASA press releases and other information are available automatically by send-
ing an Internet electronic mail message to "domo@hq.nasa.gov". In the body of
the message (not the subject line) users should type the words "subscribe
press-release" (no quotes). The system will
reply with a confirmation via E-mail of each subscription. A second automatic
message will include additional information on the service.

Questions should be directed to (202) 358-4043.

NASA bulletins are also frequently posted to the "sci.space.news" Usenet news-
group, and are also available via anonymous ftp from the "NASA.News" directory
of "spacelink.msfc.nasa.gov", or via World Wide Web from
"http://spacelink.msfc.nasa.gov/". NASA also broadcasts
NASA TV on Spacenet 2, transponder 5, channel 9, 69 degrees West.
The transponder frequency is 3880 MHz, audio subcarrier is 6.8 Mhz, and the
polarization is horizontal.
```

Figure 14-6:
Interested in the National Aeronautics and Space Administration (NASA)? Finger brings you a space newsletter.

```
                              C O N T E N T S


    1  Mon Dec 12 16:05  KSC Status Report
    2  Mon Dec 12 22:26  Crippen to Leave NASA



Date: Dec 12 16:05 UTC
Subject: KSC Status Report

KENNEDY SPACE CENTER SPACE SHUTTLE STATUS REPORT
MONDAY, DECEMBER 12, 1994 (10:21 AM EST)

MISSION: STS-63 — MIR RENDEZVOUS, SPARTAN and SPACEHAB-3

VEHICLE: Discovery/OV-103
LOCATION: OPF bay 2
TARGET LAUNCH DATE/TIME: Feb. 2, 1995 at 12:51 a.m. EST
LAUNCH WINDOW: 5 minutes
TARGET KSC LANDING DATE/TIME: Feb. 10 at 7:05 a.m.
MISSION DURATION: 8 days, 6 hours, 13 minutes
CREW SIZE: 6
ORBITAL ALTITUDE: 196 statute miles
INCLINATION: 51.60 degrees

NOTE: The decision was made today to remove and replace auxiliary power
unit no. 2 due to possible cracks in the unit+s exhaust housing. No impact
to roll out to pad B or to the launch date is expected.

IN WORK TODAY:
   * Spartan interface verification checks
   * Aft engine compartment close-outs
   * Preparations to remove and replace auxiliary power unit no. 2 (tonight)
   * Main engine checks

WORK COMPLETED:
   * Crew equipment interface test (CEIT)
   * Orbital maneuvering system pod interface verification test
   * Main engine securing and inspections

WORK SCHEDULED:
   * Complete payload interface verification checks
   * Main engine clearance and final aerosurface checks
   * Orbital maneuvering system pod crossfeed connections
   * Orbiter mid-body close-outs
   * Close payload bay doors for flight

MISSION: STS-67 — ASTRO — 2
```

Figure 14-6:
(continued)

```
VEHICLE: Endeavour/OV-105
LOCATION: OPF bay 1
TARGET LAUNCH PERIOD: early March
APPROX. LAUNCH TIME: very early morning
LAUNCH WINDOW: 2 hours, 3 minutes
KSC LANDING DATE/TIME: TBD
MISSION DURATION: 15 days, 13 hours
CREW SIZE: 7
ORBITAL ALTITUDE: 218 statute miles
INCLINATION: 28.45 degrees


IN WORK TODAY:
   * Remove and replace auxiliary power unit no. 1
   * Main propulsion system verification checks


WORK COMPLETED:
   * Stack solid rocket boosters in Vehicle Assembly Building
   * Payload premate tests
   * Functional checks of orbital maneuvering system pods


WORK SCHEDULED:
   * Mate solid rocket boosters with external tank in Vehicle Assembly
     Building
   * Install ASTRO-2 payload and interface verification checks
   * Begin aft engine compartment close-outs
   * Begin preparations to install main engines



MISSION: STS-71 — 1st MIR DOCKING


VEHICLE: Atlantis/OV-104
LOCATION: OPF bay 3
TARGET LAUNCH PERIOD: late May
APPROX. LAUNCH TIME: early morning
LAUNCH WINDOW: 5 minutes
KSC LANDING DATE/TIME: TBD
MISSION DURATION: 9 days, 20 hours
CREW SIZE: 7 up, 8 down
ORBITAL ALTITUDE: 196-245 statute miles
INCLINATION: 51.60 degrees


IN WORK TODAY:
   * Orbiter structural checks
   * Main propulsion system verification checks


WORK COMPLETED:
   * Close payload bay doors
   * Main engine pump torque checks
   * Fuel cell leak checks
```

Figure 14-6:
(continued)

```
WORK SCHEDULED:
  * Off load hypergolic reactants
  * Open payload bay doors
  * Remove and replace orbital maneuvering system thrusters
  _____

Date: Dec 12 22:26 UTC
Subject: Crippen to Leave NASA

KSC Center Director Crippen to Leave NASA Jan. 21
```

Figure 14-6:
(continued)

Knock Knock. who's There?

The who utility is a UNIX program that shows all interactive users on a host. If the fourth column (after the date and time) is filled in, that means the user has logged in to the computer from a remote host — in other words, IT'S HARLEY TIME! (For cycle stealing, that is.) You can use who to find out if someone is stealing cycles from your computer.

Though it's not a part of the TCP/IP stack, the who program returns information about who (literally) is using TCP/IP, and from what remote host. In the following example, look for the FQDN or the numeric IP addresses (the ones with four fields separated by dots). On this host, *lp* stands for local port, so the users who are designated by the letters *lp* in the right-hand column are local users.

```
$ who
sylvie    ttyp9    Feb 24 08:26    (wor-lp10)
chrispx   ttypb    Feb 24 14:18    (lwl-lp5)
lavoris   ttypc    Feb 24 13:09    (155.36.16.221)
scoman    ttyq5    Feb 24 14:29    (134.174.120.50)
kld       ttyq6    Feb 24 15:04    (132.245.33.7)
leiden    ttyq7    Feb 24 14:53    (bed-lp3)
shepard   ttyqc    Feb 24 13:51    (143.251.97.106)
chianti   ttyr8    Feb 24 13:47    (192.77.186.1)
last      ttyrc    Feb 24 13:00    (bgray.avid.com)
rogets    ttyrd    Feb 24 14:29    (192.92.110.6)
sweater   ttys3    Feb 24 13:41    (151.104.40.25)
```

w -ant to Know More?

The w utility is similar to who. (And please don't send us grammar lessons on *who* versus *whom*. This is *TCP/IP For Dummies*, not *English For Dummies*.) Not only does w tell you who (literally) on your host is using TCP/IP services, it also tells you what they are doing — for instance, running Gopher or telnet. In Figure 14-7, w reveals that most users on the host computer are running network applications and exactly which network applications they are using.

```
$ w
  3:07PM   up 1 day,  2:19, 36 users, load averages: 0.32, 0.76, 1.00 ── More UNIX
                                                                           to ignore
USER     TTY  FROM             LOGIN@  IDLE WHAT ── Network location
suixcco  p0   bed-1p3          3:02PM     0 telnet main.com 4444 ── What client the
Brianc   p2   lwl-1p5          1:23PM     0 irc (irc-2.6)            user is running
frownig  p4   lwl-1p5          2:18PM     0 irc (irc-2.6)
blnk     p5   bed-1p9          3:03PM     0 rlogin -l jolea  199.232.40.10
nifte    p7   bed-1p3          2:34PM     0 ftp
chrispx  pb   lwl-1p5          2:18PM     0 telnet lerret.cs.ohiou.edu 4000
mlspeake pf   bed-1p11         3:03PM     0 gopher marvel.loc.gov
electra  q0   bed-1p3          1:26PM     0 telnet realms.dorsai.org 1501
mcmah    q4   bed-1p3          2:10PM     0 telnet btech.netaxs.com 3056
leiden   q7   bed-1p3          2:53PM     0 script tools.txt
dirienzo q8   bed-1p11         2:35PM     0 telnet infosoc.com
shephrdr qc   143.251.97.106   1:51PM     3 tin
aerie    qe   bed-1p8          2:12PM    10 telnet 134.2.62.161 4252
JIMH     qf   bed-1p6          2:51PM     0 telnet infosoc
rrestyn  r5   bed-1p6          8:58AM     0 telnet
dogerb   rd   redpanties.gradi 2:29PM     0 gopher
teeny    s7   bed-1p12         2:40PM     0 telnet alumni.caltech.edu
kaf      s8   bed-1p12         2:41PM     0 mail baker-j@pix.netway.com
```

Figure 14-7: On this computer, people really use telnet a lot, but some people like to chat.

rwho There, You Devil?

You've seen who and w show the users on one host. Now take a look at rwho, another Berkeley r utility, which shows all the users on the network — that is, all users on computers whose system administrators allow the rwho daemon to run.

The *rwho daemon* creates a packet that lists users on the computer on which the daemon runs, and broadcasts this across the network every few minutes. The program is called a daemon because the UNIX programmers who created it were devils . . . at least, that's the opinion of some system and network administrators, because of the way rwho's broadcast packets can clog up a network.

The broadcasts aren't a problem when just a few computers are on the network, but as that number rises, so does the number of packets. Soon the network is so clogged with rwho broadcast packets that there's no room for yours. Together, the rwho daemons on *all* the network's computers keep *all* that data from *all* those broadcasts, ready to display for anyone who types in the rwho command!

Some system managers and network administrators may refuse to run the rwho daemon at all, so don't be surprised if you get no information back from your rwho command. ■

Following is a sample of output from rwho. The second column tells you where the user is signed on.

```
$ rwho
Betteb    max:ttyp2      Feb 24 13:23
JMJK      max:ttyqf      Feb 24 14:51
eve       min:ttype      Feb 24 14:24
blakbird  nec:ttys0      Feb 24 14:40
blink     max:ttyrb      Feb 24 14:28
bmunts    nec:ttyra      Feb 24 14:27
breedst   max:ttyr5      Feb 24 08:58
bryanc    millenium:ttyp6 Feb 24 13:06
bblsrt    max:ttyqd      Feb 24 14:47
chianti   max:ttyr8      Feb 24 13:47
crisped   min:ttypb      Feb 24 14:18
ddkm      max:ttys1      Feb 24 14:32 :06
oldby     max:ttyp5      Feb 24 14:42 :09
leaf      dalek:ttyp1    Feb 16 16:51
leaf      dalek:ttyp4    Feb 24 12:41 :04
```

ruptime, Cousin of rwho

The ruptime utility (that's right, it's another Berkeley r utility) displays a list of the computers that are up and running on the network, and some bonus data about them.

Like rwho, ruptime uses the rwho daemon's broadcast packets, so ruptime, too, can rupture your network in terms of performance. As in the case of rwho, system managers and network administrators may choose not to configure the rwho daemon, so you may not see every host on your network (or any information at all). ■

Here's a sample of output from ruptime. In the left-hand column is the computer name; the next column is the computer's status; next is how long it's been up and how many users are logged on. You can ignore the UNIXy techno-data on the right; it's about the load average on each computer.

```
$ ruptime
dalek    up 13+17:08,    2 users,  load 1.28, 1.28, 1.28
kickoff  up  6+16:07,    0 users,  load 0.00, 0.00, 0.00
laraby   down 2+20:40
max      up  1+02:06,   37 users,  load 1.46, 1.19, 1.13
millenia up    14:49,    7 users,  load 1.34, 1.19, 1.10
```

The World According to arp

The arp utility displays the TCP/IP Address Resolution Protocol (ARP) tables. The tables are cached in memory and are maintained automatically, for the most part. Only rarely does a system manager or network administrator have to modify a table entry manually.

The arp utility learns the physical (hardware) address of a computer's network interface card by means of an *arp request*. Your computer issues the arp request when it discovers that the ARP table does not have the physical address of the computer with which yours wants to communicate. The arp request is a broadcast message asking the computer with a specific IP address to respond with its physical address, and the response is loaded into the table for future use. Each computer on the network maintains its own ARP table, cached in memory, and benefits from the responses to all arp requests, even the ones it didn't issue.

Without the ARP tables, this process would have to be done each time you access a host. For instance, if you send frequent mail messages every day to wilensky@frodo.lotus.com, you don't want to have to go out across the network for every message to find out the physical address of frodo's network interface card. By keeping frodo's physical address in the ARP tables, the computer can speed up performance and reduce network traffic.

What's a Physical Address?
Isn't the IP Address Enough?

When you buy a network interface card, it comes with a unique hardware address, also called the physical address. This hardware address is the ultimate address (final resting place) of your computer on a network. Just as TCP/IP associates your computer's name with its IP address, the IP address is associated with a hardware address. After all, when you send e-mail, you're sending it from one piece of hardware to another. The ARP piece of TCP/IP is what provides this IP address/hardware address resolution.

To find out what IP addresses are listed in the ARP tables for your computer, use the arp utility. Figure 14-8 shows sample arp output, listing the frequently accessed IP addresses and their corresponding hardware addresses.

On The Internet, routers and gateways use routing protocols such as RIP (Routing Information Protocol) and OSPF (Open Shortest Path First) to supplement ARP. See Chapter 17. ■

```
% arp -a
cisco.tiac.net (199.0.65.1) at 0:0:c:b:a2:94        ┌── IP address
zork.tiac.net (199.0.65.2) at 0:80:29:e3:95:92
kickoff.tiac.net (199.0.65.3) at 0:40:33:21:d6:9a
lit-lp16.tiac.net (199.0.65.7) at 0:c0:5:1:13:7d
mvy.tiac.net (199.0.65.8) at 8:0:20:f:20:fa          └── Hardware address
sundog.tiac.net (199.0.65.9) at 8:0:20:b:bb:94
bed-lp13.tiac.net (199.0.65.10) at 0:c0:5:1:10:88
bed-lp1.tiac.net (199.0.65.12) at 0:c0:5:1:2:5e
bed-lp2.tiac.net (199.0.65.13) at 0:c0:5:1:4:9a
bed-lp3.tiac.net (199.0.65.14) at 0:c0:5:1:7:e5
bed-lp4.tiac.net (199.0.65.15) at 0:c0:5:1:9:e9
lwl-lp5.tiac.net (199.0.65.16) at 0:80:ad:4:d8:d3
bed-lp6.tiac.net (199.0.65.17) at 0:c0:5:1:d:ea
mvy-lp7.tiac.net (199.0.65.18) at 0:c0:5:1:1a:a9
bed-lp8.tiac.net (199.0.65.19) at 0:c0:5:1:b:d8
bed-lp9.tiac.net (199.0.65.20) at 0:c0:5:1:c:b7
boris.tiac.net (199.0.65.21) at 0:40:33:28:bc:df
millenium.tiac.net (199.0.65.24) at 0:40:33:25:c7:48
toybox.tiac.net (199.0.65.25) at 0:40:33:28:b6:51
bed-lp12.tiac.net (199.0.65.26) at 0:c0:5:1:10:6a
zima.com (199.0.65.27) at 0:40:33:21:9a:7d
bed-lp11.tiac.net (199.0.65.29) at 0:c0:5:1:10:81
bobafet.tiac.net (199.0.65.32) at 0:40:33:29:43:eb
wor-lp10.tiac.net (199.0.65.55) at 0:c0:5:1:e:db
laraby.tiac.net (199.0.65.80) at 0:40:33:2b:35:77
mar-lp15.tiac.net (199.0.65.102) at 0:c0:5:1:12:f4
t1-1.Bedford.MA.tiac.net (199.0.65.111) at 0:c0:5:0:f:c6
lwl-lp19.tiac.net (199.0.65.114) at 0:c0:5:1:17:c7
bed-lp17.tiac.net (199.0.65.121) at 0:c0:5:1:15:d5
kin-lp18.tiac.net (199.0.65.171) at 0:c0:5:1:13:96
t1-2.Bedford.MA.tiac.net (199.0.65.225) at 0:c0:5:0:13:b0
davros.tiac.net (199.0.65.235) at 0:40:33:2d:40:cc
? (199.0.65.255) at (incomplete)
%
```

Figure 14-8:
The ARP tables show a computer's "other" address — the physical address.

The nslookup Utility

Look in Chapter 11 for examples of using nslookup to look up IP addresses from a name server, as well as a list of nslookup commands.

The showmount Utility

To see which NFS clients have mounted shared disk space from an NFS server, run the showmount utility on the NFS server. Showmount is also an important tool for system managers and network administrators who are responsible for network security, and you'll find more about this utility in Chapter 18.

Reach Out and Touch Something, with ping

The ping utility, to which we introduced you in Chapter 9, lets you find out if a remote computer is available. It uses the network "sonar" — the Internet Control Message Protocol (ICMP). Ping bounces a message off a computer; if there is a reply, the computer is alive and well.

Ping is one of the first troubleshooting commands a system manager or network administrator uses when investigating system and network problems. After all, if there is a problem, you need to know if the wounded computer is dead or alive.

Below you'll find an example of ping checking a computer named millenium [sic] to see if it's alive. At the end are some summary statistics about packets sent, packets lost, and how long the ping round-trip took. Also, Figure 14-9 shows a use of a GUI version of ping on a PC, and ping's output. Notice that the PC version doesn't show the packet traffic data.

```
$ ping millenium
PING millenium.tiac.net (199.0.65.24): 56 data bytes
64 bytes from 199.0.65.24: icmp_seq=0 ttl=255 time=1.518 ms
64 bytes from 199.0.65.24: icmp_seq=1 ttl=255 time=1.624 ms
64 bytes from 199.0.65.24: icmp_seq=2 ttl=255 time=1.371 ms
64 bytes from 199.0.65.24: icmp_seq=3 ttl=255 time=2.091 ms
64 bytes from 199.0.65.24: icmp_seq=4 ttl=255 time=1.356 ms
64 bytes from 199.0.65.24: icmp_seq=5 ttl=255 time=1.326 ms
64 bytes from 199.0.65.24: icmp_seq=6 ttl=255 time=1.312 ms
64 bytes from 199.0.65.24: icmp_seq=7 ttl=255 time=1.306 ms

-- millenium.tiac.net ping statistics --
8 packets transmitted, 8 packets received, 0% packet loss
round-trip min/avg/max = 1.306/1.488/2.091 ms
```

ps, We Love You

No, we're not hitting on you. The ps utility is often thought of as a UNIX performance monitoring tool, but it also lets you see what kinds of network processes, including daemons, are running on your computer. For example, if a network administrator decides to disable the rwho daemon, ps can be used to make sure it is no longer running. Figure 14-10 shows ps output from a host with lots of network processes.

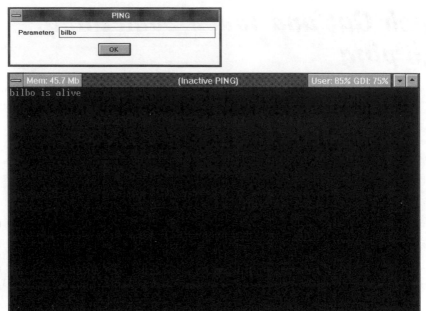

Figure 14-9:
A GUI
version of
ping is
fun, too.

```
$ ps auwx                                                      Neat! The
USER       PID %CPU %MEM   VSZ  RSS TT  STAT STARTED  TIME COMMAND        rwho
leiden   20113  3.0  0.0   348  172 p3  R+    3:06PM  0:00.04 ps auwx     daemon is
root        65  0.0  0.0  1160  992 ??  Ss   Thu12PM  1:31.58 named       running.
root        68  0.0  0.0    52  108 ??  Ss   Thu12PM  0:08.83 rwhod ──┐
root        70  0.0  0.0    60  108 ??  Is   Thu12PM  0:00.09 portmap
root        76  0.0  0.0    56   16 ??  S    Thu12PM  5:13.29 nfsiod 4
root        77  0.0  0.0    56   16 ??  I    Thu12PM  1:47.96 nfsiod 4
root        78  0.0  0.0    56   16 ??  I    Thu12PM  0:48.53 nfsiod 4
root        79  0.0  0.0    56   16 ??  I    Thu12PM  0:20.84 nfsiod 4
root        80  0.0  0.0   444  132 ??  Ss   Thu12PM  0:39.04 sendmail:
accepting connections (sendmail)
root        83  0.0  0.0    76  100 ??  Ss   Thu12PM  0:17.39 inetd
root     22947  0.0  0.0    96   72 ??  I    10:28PM  0:00.48 rlogind
patt     22948  0.0  0.0   468   76 p1  Is+  10:28PM  0:00.53 -bash (bash)
WiseGuy  27152  0.0  0.0   312   72 r6  I+   12:36AM  0:01.55 ncftp
root      5542  0.0  0.0    96   88 ??  I     8:26AM  0:23.60 rlogind
sylvan    6137  0.0  0.0   148  112 r0  I+    8:36AM  0:30.77 telnet
netcom.com
anmary    6792  0.0  0.0   568  476 p6  S+    8:52AM  0:35.11 irc (irc-2.6)
root      7004  0.0  0.0    84   88 ??  S     8:58AM  0:38.18 rlogind
root     15491  0.0  0.0   120  172 ??  I     1:00PM  0:00.35 telnetd
Bryant   16380  0.0  0.0   452  480 p2  S+    1:23PM  0:21.04 irc (irc-2.6)
root     16444  0.0  0.0    84  196 ??  S     1:26PM  0:15.52 rlogind
ellend   16534  0.0  0.0   156  260 q0  S+    1:29PM  0:07.03 telnet
```

Neat! The
rwho
daemon is
running.

Users
might
come in
via
rlogin.

Looks
like a
version of
inetd

They're
both
using IRC
to chat,
but
probably
not to
each
other.

Figure 14-10:
With ps, you
find that this
computer
has lots of
TCP/IP net-
working
going on.

```
realms.dorsai.org 1501
root      16936  0.0  0.0   120  200 ??  I    1:41PM   0:03.15 telnetd
shepherd 17449  0.0  0.0  2940  372 qc  I+   1:53PM   0:18.34 tin
ellend   17573  0.0  0.0   156  260 q0  T    1:56PM   0:00.47 telnet main.com
4444
root      17891  0.0  0.0    28  196 ??  S    2:05PM   0:00.46 comsat
deepwatr 18126  0.0  0.0  5408  592 s3  I+   2:11PM   1:08.44 trn
root      18127  0.0  0.0    96  216 ??  I    2:12PM   0:04.62 rlogind
shift     18943  0.0  0.0   276  372 p7  S+   2:34PM   0:02.70 ftp
rdf       19827  0.0  0.0   152  260 s8  I+   2:58PM   0:00.13 mail
batsoid@xx.netcom.com
root      19833  0.0  0.0   484  168 ??  I    2:58PM   0:00.06 sendmail:
server relay3.UU.NET cmd read (sendmail)
whitehed 20008  0.0  0.0   224  556 ??  S    3:03PM   0:00.40 ftpd:
dip27n8.drc.com: whitehd: RETR pgp262.zip\r\n (ftpd)
root      20033  0.0  0.0    28  232 ??  S    3:03PM   0:00.07 ntalkd
mlspeake 20060  0.0  0.0   440  356 pf  I+   3:04PM   0:00.42 gopher
```

Someone's using telnet.

Someone's getting a file via FTP.

Figure 14-10:
(continued)

In this chapter we have described the most commonly used tools for finding out many network-related facts about your computer, and about what's going on across your network. Depending on what TCP/IP product you have, there may be additional tools available to you for these information-gathering tasks. Microsoft Windows NT, for example, includes arp, finger, and ping, in addition to supplying its own graphical Performance Monitor that tracks users and processes such as daemons, and supplies dozens of network utilization statistics. Other vendors, as well, support most of the basic lookup-style tools along with their own additions and extensions.

Chapter 15

Network Files: Will Someone Please Set the Table?

• •

In This Chapter

▶ A minipreview of network security

▶ A beginner's guide to TCP/IP network administration

▶ What network files you need to have, what they do, and what they should contain

• •

*W*e started Part II by comparing the TCP/IP protocol suite to a dinnerware set, with enough pieces to serve a banquet from soup to nuts to dessert. If you're going to use all those serving pieces, you need someone who understands etiquette to set your table. (Does the seafood fork go on the left?) When it comes to TCP/IP, it's usually the network administrator or system manager who sets the TCP/IP "table" — by configuring files to work with the protocols.

This chapter describes the contents of the basic files needed to support TCP/IP.

Are the Files Already on the Table?

Some of these files are supplied with TCP/IP. Others must be created by the network administrator (you). How you do this is up to you: A text editor works just fine. Or, if you have a graphical interface to TCP/IP, you will point your mouse, click, and type some text. If you're really lucky, you have a tool that steps you through network setup in much the same way as a tutorial. Digital Equipment Corporation, for example, provides a script named netsetup that prompts you for all the required network configuration information; then it creates and maintains the files for you.

If you are using an operating system or TCP/IP product different from the ones we have on our networks, your files may vary slightly from the figures in this book. Don't worry. The files may be in a slightly different location, but the general content and the purpose of those files are the same, regardless of what directory they're stored in. If your hosts file isn't in one of the locations we've shown, search your disks for something with the word "host" in it, and then go off and look at the file. "RTFM" also applies: "Read The Fabulous Manual" that came with your TCP/IP product. ■

The Local Hosts File

Let's start with the most fundamental file that you need for communicating with other computers on your network: the local hosts file.

Back in Chapter 11, you added the word *host* to your vocabulary. That's host as in a computer on the network. If you think it's host as in "Be our guest," take a look ahead at Chapter 18, about security. ■

When you access another host by name on The Internet or an internet, your computer needs to know the remote host's IP address. You can get remote host addresses from DNS (see Chapter 11) or from your computer's local hosts file. This file lists the names and addresses of other computers (hosts) known by your computer.

When you need to know about thousands of hosts on The Internet, maintaining the hosts file is really too cumbersome a mechanism. Imagine having to spend all that time updating it as computers come and go or relocate on The Internet! In that case, you need DNS to locate remote hosts.

Performance: Let DNS and a Local Hosts File Share the Job

Many versions of TCP/IP allow you to use a combination of DNS and a local hosts file to find remote hosts. Put the most frequently accessed hosts into your local file. That way you won't have the performance overhead of accessing a DNS name server on the network to get an address for the hosts you connect to on a regular basis. Let DNS help you find addresses for hosts you access only occasionally. This is really the best of both worlds: performance and accessibility.

The location and name of the local hosts file depends on the operating system and version of TCP/IP you use. Table 15-1 lists the hosts file locations for a few implementations of TCP/IP.

Table 15-1: Popular Locations for Local Hosts Files

Location	Operating System	Vendor
/etc/hosts	UNIX	Various
c:\netmanag\hosts	Microsoft Windows	NetManage
c:\winnt\system32\drivers\etc\hosts	Microsoft Windows NT	Microsoft
c:\tcpip\etc\hosts	OS/2	IBM

How to maintain a hosts file

Your operating system or TCP/IP product provides a local hosts file to get you started. You, the network administrator, the system manager, or whoever is in charge of network configuration maintains the hosts file. If your computer runs UNIX, you get to use a plain old text editor to type in two columns of information: column 1 for the hosts' IP addresses and column 2 for the names.

If you have a computer with a graphical interface to TCP/IP, you get to point your mouse, click on menus, and fill in the blanks with the same information about hosts as what you'd enter in a text file.

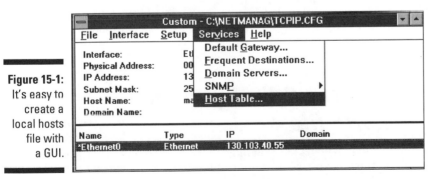

Figure 15-1:
It's easy to create a local hosts file with a GUI.

In Figure 15-1, someone is creating a local hosts file using a GUI to a PC TCP/IP product.

What's in the hosts file

Figures 15-2 and 15-3 show the contents of two different hosts files, one taken from a computer running UNIX and one from a PC running Microsoft Windows. The files have exactly the same type of information, despite their origination. One was created with a simple text editor. The other was created with a neato GUI that allowed the network administrator to click to open windows and then fill in the blanks.

Figure 15-2:
This local hosts file, created with a text editor, contains the IP address and the host name.

```
#
# Sun Host Database
#
#
127.0.0.1       localhost
#
129.103.40.1    spiderman peterparker    # M Wilensky
129.103.40.3    reddwarf                 # Marshall Wilensky
129.103.40.6    giacomo                  # Netware server
129.103.40.7    grapeleaf                # OS/2 Notes server
129.103.40.17   kerwien                  # Erica Kerwien
129.103.40.24   vogon                    # Notes NLM Server
129.103.40.53   zugspitz                 # SparcStation
```

At first you may think there are several host names on a line, but the first name is the host name and the following name(s) are nifty host name aliases. Look carefully at the entry for the host, spiderman, and you'll see a host name alias, peterparker. You can send mail to Marshall on either spiderman or peterparker. Anything preceded by a # character is for free-form comments about things like the computer's owner, location, operating system, and whatever else you think is meaningful.

In Figure 15-3, can you tell whether the file was created with a text editor or with a GUI?

Improving TCP/IP's digestion of the hosts file

Without an up-to-date hosts file, you may not be able to find other people and computers on the network, so it's important to update the file whenever a computer changes its name or address, or joins or leaves the network. It's a good idea to list the computers in most-frequently-used order. TCP/IP searches the hosts file sequentially from top to bottom until it finds the computer it is looking for, so on a big network with a large hosts file, ordering the computers appropriately gives you a performance advantage. ■

Figure 15-3:
A hosts file
created
with a GUI-
based
TCP/IP has
the same
kind of
information
as one
created
with an
editor.

```
130.103.40.52    candacel
130.103.40.50    dummy
129.103.40.1     spiderman.univ.edu peterparker
```

The Trusted Hosts File

On UNIX, the file /etc/hosts.equiv lists the other hosts on the network that your computer trusts; this is your *trusted hosts file*. This file is easy to create. It has only one column, containing the host name of each computer you trust (see Figure 15-4).

Be very careful with this file. Any remote computer listed here is a trusted host, and all of its users can log in to your computer without knowing a password. ∎

Some operating systems implement trust using other methods besides a trusted hosts file. Microsoft Windows NT Server, for example, does not use the hosts.equiv file. Instead, you set up trust relationships when you set up security policies for your computer. Trust relationships are between NT domains (groups of computers) as opposed to individual hosts.

The Trusted Hosts Print File

On UNIX you can use the /etc/hosts.lpd file to list the remote hosts that can print on the printer attached to your computer. The simplest hosts.lpd file

possible contains just one asterisk (*) character, which means any host on
the network can share your printer. If you don't have a hosts.lpd file, it's the
same as having the file with an * in it. So, if you are not prepared to be super-
generous with your printer, you'd better create one of these hosts.lpd files.

```
vogon
grapeleaf
spiderman
reddwarf
```

Figure 15-4: The hosts.equiv file lists trusted hosts.

Speaking of generosity . . . How generous can you afford to be with your
printer? If you share your printer with all hosts on your network, will the volume of remote print jobs mean you always have to wait before you can print
your own stuff? Will this same print job traffic clog up the network connection
media (the cables)? These are the questions to ask yourself before editing
your hosts.lpd file. ■

Freddie's Nightmare: Your Personal Trust File

So far in this chapter, you've read about files that are system files in system
directories. Another special (and dangerous) file that you need to be aware
of exists on a "per user" basis. You and all the other users on a computer can
create a *personal trust file* in your home directory. In UNIX environments, this
file is named .rhosts, pronounced "dot are hosts." And yes, the . is part of the
filename.

The .rhosts file holds two pieces of information: the host name and the
account name. Following are the contents of Sarah's .rhosts file in her home
directory on computer elmst. It allows Emily (from computer mainst) to have
the run of computer elmst without a password.

```
#Local host    user      comment
mainst         emily   # Let in Emily from mainst
```

Most network administrators, like Freddie, consider .rhosts files to be potential security problems. These files list trusted remote users — those who are permitted to log in to your local account without entering a password. This includes copying any files from your directories with rcp, and remotely executing any command on your computer with rsh. ■

This is scary. Why would I ever want .rhosts?

If you do a lot of work on various hosts, it's quite convenient to rlogin as yourself on all the computers on which you have accounts. Your account may be Marshall on one computer, Wilensky on another, and Mwil on a third — with three different passwords. If all of these computers have a .rhosts file that lets you in from anywhere, then you can skip remembering all those passwords.

Surprise! The curse of the network administrator lives

If Emily has been wandering all over computer elmst because Sarah lets her, Emily may get a big surprise one day when she tries to log in remotely and permission is denied. Network administrators frequently hunt down and kill these .rhosts files. Once Sarah's .rhosts file is gone, Emily needs to know a valid password in order to log in.

The Networks File

Not only do you need a hosts file (or DNS) to list the individual hosts with which you plan to communicate, along with their IP addresses, you also need a *networks file* to hold the network numbers and names with which you plan to communicate. Listing the network names lets you refer to all the hosts on the same network (or subnet) as one group. The networks file supplied with the operating system or TCP/IP product rarely needs editing.

Figure 15-5 shows a networks file. On UNIX, the network file is /etc/networks. The file can be at different locations, depending on the operating system. For example, Microsoft Windows NT Server stores the file in \winnt35\system32\drivers\etc\networks rather than in the traditional UNIX location.

Figure 15-5:
The
networks
file lists the
network
name and
its address.

```
#
# Sun customer networks
# This file is never consulted when the NIS are running
#
loopback       127
sun-ether      192.9.200    sunether ethernet localnet
sun-oldether   125          sunoldether
#
# Internet networks
#
arpanet        10           arpa
ucb-ether      46           ucbether
```

When you create your networks file, be sure to list only the network section and not the host piece of the numeric IP address. If you're not sure about this, go back and re-read about IP addresses in Chapter 13. In the file illustrated in Figure 15-5, some of the network addresses only have one piece, such as "arpanet 10." The ending 0s are assumed. You can leave them out for convenience or you can list them explicitly, as in 10.0.0. ■

The Internet Daemon Configuration File

What a mouthful! The file named /etc/inetd.conf on UNIX systems lists all the things you want the internet daemon, inetd (see sidebar), to do. The name of this file is pronounced "eye net dee dot conf." Now try it three times fast.

The inetd.conf file shown in Figure 15-6 is nearly identical to the original copy supplied with the UNIX operating system. The TFTP lines were modified slightly and the bootp line was added, to allow down-line loading of X Window terminals.

Daemons: Are We in Hell Again?

You've learned that daemons, in general, are programs that provide some sort of services. TCP/IP daemons are the servers for many of the TCP/IP client/server functions. The internet daemon program, inetd, is the heart and soul of TCP/IP services. (By the way, most daemons' names end in *d*.) Inetd supervises the other TCP/IP daemons. The internet daemon configuration file, inetd.conf, tells inetd what other servers it is responsible for.

```
# @(#)inetd.conf 1.24 92/04/14 SMI ───── This file comes with TCP/IP. Usually you don't
#                                        touch it except for good reasons.
# Configuration file for inetd(8).  See inetd.conf(5).
#
# To re-configure the running inetd process, edit this file, then
# send the inetd process a SIGHUP.
#
#
# Internet services syntax:
#   <service_name> <socket_type> <proto> <flags> <user> <server_pathname> <args>
#
# Ftp and telnet are standard Internet services.
#
ftp     stream  tcp   nowait   root   /usr/etc/in.ftpd     in.ftpd
telnet  stream  tcp   nowait   root   /usr/etc/in.telnetd    in.telnetd
#
# Tnamed serves the obolete IEN-116 name server protocol.
#
name    dgram   udp   wait     root   /usr/etc/in.tnamed    in.tnamed
#
# Shell, login, exec, comsat and talk are BSD protocols.
#
shell   stream  tcp   nowait   root   /usr/etc/in.rshd     in.rshd
login   stream  tcp   nowait   root   /usr/etc/in.rlogind   in.rlogind
exec    stream  tcp   nowait   root   /usr/etc/in.rexecd    in.rexecd
comsat  dgram   udp   wait     root   /usr/etc/in.comsat    in.comsat
talk    dgram   udp   wait     root   /usr/etc/in.talkd    in.talkd
#
# Run as user "uucp" if you don't want uucpd's wtmp entries.
#
uucp    stream  tcp   nowait   root   /usr/etc/in.uucpd    in.uucpd
#
# Tftp service is provided primarily for booting.  Most sites run this
# only on machines acting as "boot servers."
#
#####
#####    Enabled specifically for NCD X-terminals.
#####       Marshall Wilensky   Fri Feb  4 17:50:55 EST 1994
#tftp   dgram   udp   wait    root   /usr/etc/in.tftpd    in.tftpd -s /tftpboot
tftp    dgram  udp wait root  /usr/etc/in.tftpd    in.tftpd -s /usr1/ncd-install/tftpboot
bootps  dgram   udp   wait    root   /etc/bootpd        bootpd
#
# Finger, systat and netstat give out user information which may be
# valuable to potential "system crackers."  Many sites choose to disable
# some or all of these services to improve security.
#
finger  stream  tcp   nowait   nobody   /usr/etc/in.fingerd    in.fingerd
#systat  stream  tcp   nowait   root     /usr/bin/ps          ps -auwwx
```

This file comes with TCP/IP. Usually you don't touch it except for good reasons.

Security note:
This is the
original entry.

Network administrator updated this entry. Top of the directory tree for down-loading files.

Security note:
Here's where you can disable finger. Remove this entry or use # to make it a comment.

A daemon for performance monitoring

Figure 15-6:
The inetd configuration file lists TCP/IP services directed by the internet daemon.

```
#netstat    stream    tcp    nowait    root    /usr/ucb/netstat    netstat -f inet
#
# Time service is used for clock syncronization.
#
time    stream    tcp    nowait    root    internal
time    dgram    udp    wait    root    internal
#
# Echo, discard, daytime, and chargen are used primarily for testing.
#
echo    stream    tcp    nowait    root    internal
echo    dgram    udp    wait    root    internal
discard    stream    tcp    nowait    root    internal
discard    dgram    udp    wait    root    internal
daytime    stream    tcp    nowait    root    internal
daytime    dgram    udp    wait    root    internal
chargen    stream    tcp    nowait    root    internal
chargen    dgram    udp    wait    root    internal
#
#
# RPC services syntax: ——————
#  <rpc_prog>/<vers> <socket_type> rpc/<proto> <flags> <user> <pathname> <args>
#
# The mount server is usually started in /etc/rc.local only on machines that
# are NFS servers.  It can be run by inetd as well.
#
#mountd/1    dgram    rpc/udp    wait root /usr/etc/rpc.mountd    rpc.mountd
#
# The rexd server provides only minimal authentication and is often not run
# by sites concerned about security.
#
#rexd/1        stream    rpc/tcp    wait root /usr/etc/rpc.rexd    rpc.rexd
#
# Ypupdated is run by sites that support NIS updating.
#
#ypupdated/1    stream    rpc/tcp    wait root /usr/etc/rpc.ypupdated rpc.ypupdated
#
# Rquotad serves UFS disk quotas to NFS clients.
#
rquotad/1    dgram    rpc/udp    wait root /usr/etc/rpc.rquotad    rpc.rquotad
#
# Rstatd is used by programs such as perfmeter.
#
rstatd/2-4    dgram    rpc/udp    wait root /usr/etc/rpc.rstatd    rpc.rstatd
#
# The rusers service gives out user information.  Sites concerned
# with security may choose to disable it.
#
rusersd/1-2    dgram    rpc/udp    wait root /usr/etc/rpc.rusersd    rpc.rusersd
```

Programmers note: Don't forget to read Chapter 19.

Figure 15-6:
(continued)

```
#
# The spray server is used primarily for testing.
#
sprayd/1   dgram   rpc/udp   wait root /usr/etc/rpc.sprayd   rpc.sprayd
#
# The rwall server lets anyone on the network bother everyone on your machine.
#
walld/1      dgram   rpc/udp   wait root /usr/etc/rpc.rwalld   rpc.rwalld
#
#
# TLI services syntax [not yet implemented]:
#  <service_name> tli <proto> <flags> <user> <server_pathname> <args>
#
#
# TCPMUX services syntax [not yet implemented]:
#  tcpmux/<service_name> stream tcp <flags> <user> <server_pathname> <args>
#
#
# rpc.cmsd is a data base daemon which manages calendar data backed
# by files in /usr/spool/calendar
100068/2-3   dgram   rpc/udp wait root /usr/etc/rpc.cmsd   rpc.cmsd
# Sun ToolTalk Database Server
100083/1     stream  rpc/tcp wait root /usr/etc/rpc.ttdbserverd rpc.ttdbserverd
```

Figure 15-6:
(continued)

For each service, the inetd.conf file contains a line with the following fields:

- ✔ Service name: The service must also have a corresponding entry in the /etc/services file.

- ✔ Socket type: An interprocess communication mechanism that's a bit too techie for this chapter. This field usually specifies "stream" if the service uses TCP, or "dgm" or "dgram" for datagram if the service uses the UDP protocol. You might also see "raw" in this column. (For an explanation of sockets, see Chapter 19.)

- ✔ Protocol: The protocol used by the service.

- ✔ Flags: Another techno-yuck. Flags are set to either "wait" or "nowait" to specify whether inetd can accept another connection without waiting for the current server to finish.

- ✔ User: This field holds the account name that is the owner of the service. On UNIX systems, it's usually the username of the privileged user, root.

- ✔ Server path: This is the directory and filename for the daemon program.

- ✔ Arguments (args): The name of the daemon or the command that runs a tool and any other command arguments.

The Protocols File

The protocols file lists the TCP/IP protocols. You must update this file if you add protocols to your TCP/IP configuration.

Figure 15-7 shows an example of a UNIX protocols file, /etc/protocols. A similar example from a Microsoft Windows NT Server protocol file is in Figure 15-8. On Microsoft Windows NT, the file is named *protocol,* with no *s* at the end.

Figure 15-7:
On UNIX,
the /etc/
protocols
file lists
TCP/IP
protocols
used on the
network.

```
# @(#)protocols 1.9 90/01/03 SMI
#
# Internet (IP) protocols
# This file is never consulted when the NIS are running
#
IP        0      IP     # internet protocol, pseudo protocol number
icmp      1      ICMP   # internet control message protocol
igmp      2      IGMP   # internet group multicast protocol
ggp       3      GGP    # gateway-gateway protocol
tcp       6      TCP    # transmission control protocol
pup       12     PUP    # PARC universal packet protocol
udp       17     UDP    # user datagram protocol
```

Figure 15-8:
On Microsoft
Windows NT
Server, the
protocol file
is located at
\winnt35\
system32\
drivers\etc\
protocol.

```
# Copyright (c) 1993-1994 Microsoft Corp.
#
# This file contains the Internet protocols as defined by RFC 1060
# (Assigned Numbers).
#
# Format:
#
# <protocol name>  <assigned number>  [aliases...]  [#<comment>]

ip         0      IP       # Internet protocol
icmp       1      ICMP     # Internet control message protocol
ggp        3      GGP      # Gateway-gateway protocol
tcp        6      TCP      # Transmission control protocol
egp        8      EGP      # Exterior gateway protocol
pup        12     PUP      # PARC universal packet protocol
udp        17     UDP      # User datagram protocol
hmp        20     HMP      # Host monitoring protocol
xns-idp    22     XNS-IDP  # Xerox NS IDP
rdp        27     RDP      # "reliable datagram" protocol
rvd        66     RVD      # MIT remote virtual disk
```

TECHNICAL STUFF

Any Port in a Network

There are lots of services, as you can see in Figures 15-9 and 15-10. How does an application know which one it should use? Well, certainly not by name — that would be too easy, even though many applications, services, and protocols are named the same. Take FTP, for instance, which is the name of an application, service, *and* a protocol.

Applications communicate with services via an object called a *port id number.* ID numbers 1 through 255 are reserved for the most commonly used services, such as telnet and FTP.

Port numbers can also be created as needed. If you write your own TCP/IP application and service, you simply use a port number greater than 255.

When an application says to TCP/IP, "Here I am, ready to work," TCP/IP doesn't really care about the application's name. Instead, TCP/IP sees only the numbers: the Internet address of the host that provides the service, and the port number through which the application intends to communicate.

The Services File

On UNIX, the /etc/services file lists the network services being used on your computer. You don't usually have to maintain this file yourself. TCP/IP does it automatically when you enable or disable new services.

Each line in the file has these columns:

- ✔ Service name
- ✔ Port number
- ✔ Protocol (separated from the port number by a /)
- ✔ Aliases (other, optional names for the service)

Figure 15-9 is a services file from a UNIX system, and Figure 15-10 is a services file from a Microsoft Windows NT Server system. Pop Quiz: Can you see the difference? Answer: It's a trick question. Although the computers in the examples run specific services to support their users (Ingres on the UNIX system, for example), and although the file is located in different directories on the two operating systems, the basic file format is the same.

You might notice some interesting security services, including Kerberos, in Figure 15-10. Read Chapter 18 to see what that dog of a service is all about. Speaking of dogs, look for a UNIX service named biff. According to UNIX mythology, this service is named after a dog who barked at the letter carrier. Biff is, of course, the mail notification service (chuckle).

Also, now that you've read several chapters, test yourself by trying to recognize some familiar services in these examples. Can you find telnet and SMTP?

```
# @(#)services 1.16 90/01/03 SMI
#
# Network services, Internet style
# This file is never consulted when the NIS are running
#
tcpmux          1/tcp                               # rfc-1078
echo            7/tcp
echo            7/udp
discard         9/tcp           sink null
discard         9/udp           sink null
systat          11/tcp          users
daytime         13/tcp
daytime         13/udp
netstat         15/tcp
chargen         19/tcp          ttytst source
chargen         19/udp          ttytst source
ftp-data        20/tcp
ftp             21/tcp
telnet          23/tcp
smtp            25/tcp          mail
time            37/tcp          timserver
time            37/udp          timserver
name            42/udp          nameserver
whois           43/tcp          nicname         # usually to sri-nic
domain          53/udp
domain          53/tcp
hostnames       101/tcp         hostname        # usually to sri-nic
sunrpc          111/udp
sunrpc          111/tcp
#
# Host specific functions
#
tftp            69/udp
rje             77/tcp
finger          79/tcp
link            87/tcp          ttylink
supdup          95/tcp
iso-tsap        102/tcp
x400            103/tcp                         # ISO Mail
x400-snd        104/tcp
```

Figure 15-9:
A UNIX
services
file, /etc/
services.

```
csnet-ns       105/tcp
pop-2          109/tcp                           # Post Office
uucp-path      117/tcp
nntp           119/tcp        usenet             # Network News Transfer
ntp            123/tcp                           # Network Time Protocol
NeWS           144/tcp        news               # Window System
#
# UNIX specific services
#
# these are NOT officially assigned
#
exec           512/tcp
login          513/tcp
shell          514/tcp        cmd                # no passwords used
printer        515/tcp        spooler            # line printer spooler
courier        530/tcp        rpc                # experimental
uucp           540/tcp        uucpd              # uucp daemon
biff           512/udp        comsat
who            513/udp        whod
syslog         514/udp
talk           517/udp
route          520/udp        router routed
new-rwho       550/udp        new-who            # experimental
rmonitor       560/udp        rmonitord          # experimental
monitor        561/udp                           # experimental
pcserver       600/tcp                           # ECD Integrated PC board srvr
ingreslock     1524/tcp
```

Figure 15-9:
(continued)

```
#
# This file contains port numbers for well-known services as defined by
# RFC 1060 (Assigned Numbers).
#
# Format:
#
# <service name>  <port number>/<protocol>  [aliases...]    [#<comment>]
#
echo           7/tcp
echo           7/udp
discard        9/tcp          sink null
discard        9/udp          sink null
systat         11/tcp
systat         11/tcp         users
daytime        13/tcp
daytime        13/udp
netstat        15/tcp
qotd           17/tcp         quote
```

Figure 15-10:
A Microsoft
Windows
NT Server
services file,
\winnt35\
system32\
drivers\etc\
services.

```
qotd            17/udp    quote
chargen         19/tcp    ttytst source
chargen         19/udp    ttytst source
ftp-data        20/tcp
ftp             21/tcp
telnet          23/tcp
smtp            25/tcp    mail
time            37/tcp    timserver
time            37/udp    timserver
rlp             39/udp    resource      # resource location
name            42/tcp    nameserver
name            42/udp    nameserver
whois           43/tcp    nicname       # usually to sri-nic
domain          53/tcp    nameserver    # name-domain server
domain          53/udp    nameserver
nameserver      53/tcp    domain        # name-domain server
nameserver      53/udp    domain
mtp             57/tcp                  # deprecated
bootp           67/udp                  # boot program server
tftp            69/udp
rje             77/tcp    netrjs
finger          79/tcp
link            87/tcp    ttylink
supdup          95/tcp
hostnames       101/tcp   hostname      # usually from sri-nic
iso-tsap        102/tcp
dictionary      103/tcp   webster
x400            103/tcp                 # ISO Mail
x400-snd        104/tcp
csnet-ns        105/tcp
pop             109/tcp   postoffice
pop2            109/tcp                 # Post Office
pop3            110/tcp   postoffice
portmap         111/tcp
portmap         111/udp
sunrpc          111/tcp
sunrpc          111/udp
auth            113/tcp   authentication
sftp            115/tcp
path            117/tcp
uucp-path       117/tcp
nntp            119/tcp   usenet        # Network News Transfer
ntp             123/udp   ntpd ntp      # network time protocol (exp)
nbname          137/udp
nbdatagram      138/udp
nbsession       139/tcp
NeWS            144/tcp   news
sgmp            153/udp   sgmp
```

Figure 15-10:
(continued)

```
tcprepo          158/tcp    repository      # PCMATL
snmp             161/udp    snmp
snmp-trap        162/udp    snmp
print-srv        170/tcp                    # network PostScript
vmnet            175/tcp
load             315/udp
vmnet0           400/tcp
sytek            500/udp
biff             512/udp    comsat
exec             512/tcp
login            513/tcp
who              513/udp    whod
shell            514/tcp    cmd             # no passwords used
syslog           514/udp
printer          515/tcp    spooler         # line printer spooler
talk             517/udp
ntalk            518/udp
efs              520/tcp                    # for LucasFilm
route            520/udp    router routed
timed            525/udp    timeserver
tempo            526/tcp    newdate
courier          530/tcp    rpc
conference       531/tcp    chat
rvd-control      531/udp    MIT disk
netnews          532/tcp    readnews
netwall          533/udp                    # -for emergency broadcasts
uucp             540/tcp    uucpd           # uucp daemon
klogin           543/tcp                    # Kerberos authenticated rlogin
kshell           544/tcp    cmd             # and remote shell
new-rwho         550/udp    new-who         # experimental
remotefs         556/tcp    rfs_server rfs# Brunhoff remote filesystem
rmonitor         560/udp    rmonitord       # experimental
monitor          561/udp                    # experimental
garcon           600/tcp
maitrd           601/tcp
busboy           602/tcp
acctmaster       700/udp
acctslave        701/udp
acct             702/udp
acctlogin        703/udp
acctprinter      704/udp
elcsd            704/udp                    # errlog
acctinfo         705/udp
acctslave2       706/udp
acctdisk         707/udp
kerberos         750/tcp    kdc             # Kerberos authentication-tcp
kerberos         750/udp    kdc             # Kerberos authentication-udp
kerberos_master  751/tcp                    # Kerberos authentication
```

Figure 15-10:
(continued)

```
kerberos_master    751/udp              # Kerberos authentication
passwd_server      752/udp              # Kerberos passwd server
userreg_server     753/udp              # Kerberos userreg server
krb_prop           754/tcp              # Kerberos slave propagation
erlogin            888/tcp              # Login and environment passing
kpop               1109/tcp             # Pop with Kerberos
phone              1167/udp
ingreslock         1524/tcp
maze               1666/udp
nfs                2049/udp             # sun nfs
knetd              2053/tcp             # Kerberos de-multiplexor
eklogin            2105/tcp             # Kerberos encrypted rlogin
rmt                5555/tcp    rmtd
mtb                5556/tcp    mtbd     # mtb backup
man                9535/tcp             # remote man server
w                  9536/tcp
mantst             9537/tcp             # remote man server, testing
bnews              10000/tcp
rscs0              10000/udp
queue              10001/tcp
rscs1              10001/udp
poker              10002/tcp
rscs2              10002/udp
gateway            10003/tcp
rscs3              10003/udp
remp               10004/tcp
rscs4              10004/udp
rscs5              10005/udp
rscs6              10006/udp
rscs7              10007/udp
rscs8              10008/udp
rscs9              10009/udp
rscsa              10010/udp
rscsb              10011/udp
qmaster            10012/tcp
qmaster            10012/udp
```

Figure 15-10:
(continued)

Dealing with the Devil

Earlier in this chapter you learned that inetd is the father of all daemons. Following are descriptions of a few other TCP/IP daemons you should know about.

routed (here we go again)

The routed daemon manages routing tables (explained in Chapter 17). No, don't say "rowted" or even "rooted." It's either "rowt dee" or "root dee." The routed daemon uses RIP, the Routing Information Protocol (also explained in Chapter 17).

named

The named daemon is pronounced "name dee" (are you getting the hang of it yet?). This handy daemon is the one that runs on your name server to manage DNS and do the host name/IP address resolution you learned about in Chapter 11.

More handy dandy daemons

There are lots more daemons. All have a name that ends with *d* and is pronounced by saying the name of the service followed by "dee." Some of the more famous daemons are listed in Table 15-2 along with the service they provide, and Figure 15-11 shows some popular daemons running on a UNIX system.

Table 15-2: Popular Services and Their Daemons

Service	Daemon
finger	fingerd
ftp	ftpd
telnet	telnetd
rlogin	rlogind
rsh	rshd
rexec	rexecd
talk	talkd
NFS client	nfsiod
NFS server	nfsd

```
$ ps auwx
USER         PID %CPU %MEM   VSZ  RSS TT  STAT STARTED   TIME COMMAND

root          65  0.0  0.0  1160  992 ??  Ss   Thu12PM   1:31.58 named
root          68  0.0  0.0    52  108 ??  Ss   Thu12PM   0:08.83 rwhod
root          70  0.0  0.0    60  108 ??  Is   Thu12PM 5:13.29 nfsiod 4
root          77  0.0  0.0    56   16 ??  I    Thu12PM   1:47.96 nfsiod 4
root          78  0.0  0.0    56   16 ??  I    Thu12PM   0:48.53 nfsiod 4
root          79  0.0  0.0    56   16 ??  I    Thu12PM   0:20.84 nfsiod 4
root          80  0.0  0.0   444  132 ??  Ss   Thu12PM 0:17.39 inetd
root       22947  0.0  0.0    96   72 ??  I    10:28PM   0:00.48 rlogind
root       15491  0.0  0.0   120  172 ??  I     1:00PM   0:00.35 telnetd
root       20008  0.0  0.0   224  556 ??  S     3:03PM   0:00.40 ftpd
root       20033  0.0  0.0    28  232 ??  S     3:03PM   0:00.07 ntalkd
```

Figure 15-11: This computer has some of our favorite daemons running.

TIP

If you have a problem using one of the services in Table 15-2, a quick troubleshooting technique is to check and see if the daemon is started. You can do this with ps, one of the tools you learned about in Chapter 14. In the ps output, check the last column of each entry and look for the name of the daemon (ending in *d*). If you don't see the daemon required for the service, that's the problem. To use the service, you need to get the daemon started in whatever way your operating system allows. It might be as simple as clicking on an icon, or you might have to type in a command. ∎

The 5th Wave   By Rich Tennant

Part III

TCP/IP Stew: A Little of This, a Pinch of That

The 5th Wave   By Rich Tennant

IN A DISPLAY OF PERVERSE BRILLIANCE, CARL THE REPAIRMAN MISTAKES A ROOM HUMIDIFIER FOR A MID-RANGE COMPUTER BUT MANAGES TO TIE IT INTO THE NETWORK ANYWAY.

In This Part...

So far, you've seen that TCP/IP is more than two protocols. It's a whole banquet of courses, soup to nuts, with all the necessary utensils, from the sardine can opener to the Ginsu knife to the pots and pans. Part III is a stew cooked up in a big pot using some of the more esoteric TCP/IP implements and ingredients.

Chapter 16 provides some of the ingredients for our TCP/IP stew. In Chapter 17 you'll get acquainted with some of the pots and pans that are used to cook the stew, from simple signal repeaters to complex gateways. Later chapters include other elements of Part III's ragout: security considerations, and a quick look at what you need to know before you attempt to write network programs.

You don't need to read anything in this part to understand basic TCP/IP protocols, services, and applications. But if you want to go further, this is the appeteaser for the next big meal.

Chapter 16

Dial-up TCP/IP

. . . .

In This Chapter

▶ Networking by phone

▶ Choosing the right dial-up solution for you

. . . .

You may have full network access from your office, but what about from your home? Dial-up networking can give you access to remote computers, network services, and even the entire Internet.

This chapter describes three different dial-up connection offerings. The choice for you will depend on what you want to do from your "other" locations, and what capabilities are available at the site you'll be dialing in to. Will you be connecting to a UNIX system? Can you manage with limited services — just e-mail and Usenet news, for instance? Or do you need all of the network services that you have at work (telnet, FTP, NIS, NFS, DNS)?

Depending on what you're looking for, the answer may be UUCP, SLIP or CSLIP, or PPP. What do all these mean? Read on . . .

In UUCP, the U Lies and the C Misleads

UUCP is a dial-up communication protocol that is not actually part of TCP/IP but is still worth our attention in this chapter. UUCP stands for UNIX to UNIX CoPy (pronounced by saying the letters *U U C P*). But check it out: The *U* lies and the *C* deceives!

Don't let the UNIX word scare you off — implementations of UUCP exist for other operating systems, too. That's what we mean when we say that the *U* lies. For instance, one version of UUCP for personal computers is called UUPC. (Yes, we know, UUPC's only a typo away from UUCP, but we didn't pick the name, so don't blame us. Dyslexics, untie!)

And how does the *C* mislead? By underrating UUCP's role. UUCP was created in the early days of UNIX as a way to connect two computers in the same room and CoPy files between them. This was before real networks and network interface cards existed, so the communications went between the serial ports via the same kind of simple data cables normally used for terminals. It didn't take long for users to want to link machines that were further apart than just a few feet, so UUCP was enhanced to dial the telephone and work over modems. It still works that way today, and quite well, but modern UUCP does more than just copy files across the connection.

Think back — w-a-a-a-y back — to your first phone. For many of you, it was two tin cans strung together with a long string, used by you and the neighbor kids for many a private conversation through a hedge or across a creek. UUCP is the network equivalent of that homemade "telephone." Two computers use UUCP to establish a temporary point-to-point network between them. Either computer can initiate the two-way communication by calling the other.

In a modern system using UUCP, the system manager (who is also the UUCP administrator in this case) can configure the UUCP software to establish dial-up connections with many other computers, but only one connection at a time can be active on each modem. The connections are scheduled for regular, periodic intervals, but the UUCP administrator can also force a connection at any time. Two computers often share the connection initiation responsibilities in order to share any telephone charges. The connection lasts only as long as needed to perform the work. Then the computers disconnect and hang up the phones.

So what's UUCP good for?

The ability to copy files from one computer to another is certainly useful, but most network users need additional services, so UUCP also allows for the controlled execution of a small number of commands. This combination of commands plus file-transfer capability facilitates several very useful services for UUCP users, as described in the following paragraphs.

Note: For the file transfers and remote command executions to work properly in the services described below, UUCP must be installed and running on *both* computers.

E-mail

UUCP can send an e-mail message across the phone lines to another computer, where a mail program is invoked to deliver it to the recipient or send it on toward its ultimate destination. (This is an example of the store-and-forward technique you read about in Chapter 7.)

Remote printing

After the local user types the print command, UUCP sends the file to be printed across the telephone lines to the computer that has the printer, and UUCP on the remote computer invokes the print command. If the UUCP connection has not been made yet (i.e. one computer has not yet called the other), the print command is queued to wait until the UUCP connection is made.

Usenet news

UUCP sends newsgroup articles across the phone lines to a neighboring computer. There, a news program is invoked to store the article for users of that news server and to forward it to more news servers. Today, only a tiny percentage of the computers handling Usenet news run UUCP only. But if you do not have TCP/IP yet, and need access to Usenet news, UUCP is a valuable, low cost way to get news.

If you need to review Usenet news concepts, you can reread Chapter 7.

Other goodies

That's basically it for what UUCP has to offer when you establish the temporary network, except for a couple of other handy helpers. Some really creative people have teamed up with some good-deed doers around the world to make a few more-sophisticated services available to UUCP users via e-mail. The two most notable examples are ftpmail and GopherMail.

When you're running with UUCP, to take advantage of ftpmail and GopherMail you take the same commands you would issue interactively and put them into an e-mail message to an ftpmail (or GopherMail) server. Your ftpmail and GopherMail commands are packaged into an e-mail message, and UUCP sends the e-mail across the telephone connection. The server takes your commands out of the message body, executes them for you, and sends you the results by return e-mail.

For details on ftpmail, review Chapter 9. For more on GopherMail, see Chapter 12. ■

The good, the bad, and the UUCP

First the good news: UUCP is inexpensive and secure.

The UUCP software is bundled on UNIX systems, and public domain (free) versions exist for other operating systems, too. The only communications charges involved are for the phone calls, and if you can find a UUCP site close by, you'll only be making local phone calls.

Even if the site you do find is a toll call away, there are ways to cut costs. Get the computer you're communicating with to make some of the calls; then you can split the charges. You can also schedule the connections to take advantage of lower telephone rates. It's truly wonderful how many UUCP sites are willing to help you out with connection charges as much as possible.

Because the UUCP on your computer communicates only with the UUCP on the other computer, and not with the operating system or telnet or anything else, the arrangement is secure. Any unauthorized use of a telephone number, account name, or password for accounts that UUCP uses will be detected when UUCP discovers that the caller is not another copy of UUCP. (UUCP simply hangs up.)

Now the bad news: UUCP is hard to manage and hard to find.

Getting UUCP set up and keeping it running smoothly can be difficult. There are a handful of programs and configuration files to keep track of. Also, several different "dialects" of UUCP exist, and though they accomplish the same objective, their configuration and management are different. Fortunately, all versions of UUCP interoperate, regardless of their dialect. Consult your UUCP documentation for dialect specific information.

As more and more sites use real TCP/IP and real connections to The Internet, UUCP is fading away. Over time, there will be fewer and fewer sites with which to link. If you need to connect to an outside network but are not ready to deploy TCP/IP, UUCP can be an interim solution. It has been popular and quite useful, and it may be around for a long time to come — but it's no TCP/IP.

SLIP Your Way onto the Network

SLIP, Serial Line Internet Protocol, is TCP/IP over direct connections and modems — aka dial-up TCP/IP. Sometimes you'll see it written as SL/IP. In either case, you pronounce the acronym SLIP just as you do the word *slip*.

Serial for breakfast

On the back of your computer are the ports into which devices are plugged so they can run with your computer. Modems are plugged into a serial port, also called a COM port (or, to you geezers out there, an RS-232 port). Figure 16-1 illustrates two different types of serial ports, one with 9 holes and one with 25 holes to hold the pins of your device connector (in this case, a modem). ■

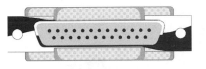

Figure 16-1:
A 25-pin
serial port
and a 9-pin
serial port.

or

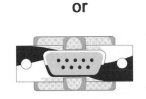

In earlier chapters, you were introduced to the ISO OSI Reference Model and
the various networks, such as Ethernet and token ring, on which TCP/IP runs.
After all the years of experience making it work over all those networks,
TCP/IP developers found it pretty easy to get TCP/IP to work over low-speed
serial links. SLIP was the result. The bulk of the changes made were at the
physical and data link layers (see Chapter 5). A serial port and a modem take
the place of a network interface card.

With SLIP, one computer can connect to another computer or to a whole network; or two networks can connect to each other, with the help of a network
device such as a router or terminal server or one of the others described in
Chapter 17. In Figures 16-2, 16-3, and 16-4, you'll see examples of the different
levels of connectivity SLIP makes possible.

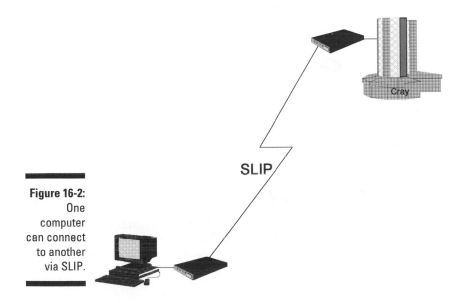

Figure 16-2:
One
computer
can connect
to another
via SLIP.

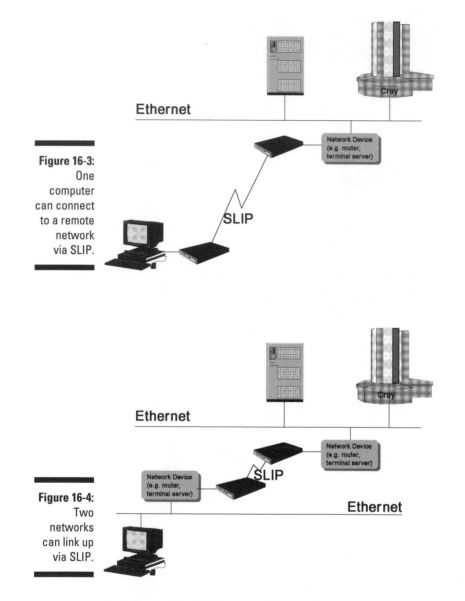

Figure 16-3:
One computer can connect to a remote network via SLIP.

Figure 16-4:
Two networks can link up via SLIP.

Is my SLIP too long?

CSLIP, Compressed SLIP (pronounced "see slip"), is an enhanced version of SLIP that reduces the amount of data that needs to be transmitted over the link. The result is more-efficient communication and therefore shorter sessions and lower telephone costs.

The designers of CSLIP studied the network traffic exchanged in SLIP connections, like those shown in Figure 16-2 especially, and saw that packets contained the same information in certain fields, such as the source and destination addresses. CSLIP minimizes this redundancy by sending only information that has changed in the packet. ■

Some TCP/IP products include only SLIP; others (such as NetManage's Chameleon for the Microsoft Windows and Windows for Workgroups operating systems) offer both SLIP and CSLIP. You cannot mix SLIP and CSLIP, however; both ends of the connection must use the same thing. Candace can speak in Latin until she's blue in the face, but since Marshall only knows Pig Latin, no real communication occurs. So if you have access to both SLIP and CSLIP, you'll have to check with the site you're calling to see which one it uses.

PPP (No, Not "The Bathroom Protocol," Silly!)

PPP, the Point-to-Point Protocol (pronounced by saying the letters *P P P*), is another dial-up network solution. PPP is a protocol that piggybacks other network protocols, and is not limited to carrying TCP/IP traffic. It can be used to carry other network protocols, too — such as SPX and AppleTalk — and can transport them all simultaneously.

The point-to-point part of PPP's name is a little misleading, since this connection method can be used to link one computer to another computer, one computer to a network, and/or one network to another network. To see the different levels of connectivity PPP makes possible, you need only look again at Figures 16-2, 16-3, and 16-4 — and substitute PPP for SLIP. The possible connections are the same for both protocols.

If the pictures look the same as for SLIP, what's the difference with PPP?

PPP is more rigidly and formally defined than SLIP or CSLIP, which means PPP requires longer for vendors to implement it, to debug it, and to offer it as part of their products. SLIP is easier to find these days, but PPP is more robust, more stable, and is multiprotocol. Microsoft Windows NT Workstation uses SLIP to implement its RAS (Remote Access Services) client. Microsoft Windows NT Server uses PPP to implement the corresponding RAS Server.

Which Dial-up Solution Is for You?

PPP is more flexible than SLIP and, because it piggybacks other protocols, can share the dial-up line with protocols such as AppleTalk. PPP also includes error correction for packet transmission. The right dial-up connection for you to use is the one that best balances the features and functionality you need, the availability of the protocol for your operating system, and the cost you are willing to pay. Use the best solution that's available — and, very important, make sure you balance your capabilities against the remote site's. Though PPP is perhaps the better protocol overall, if you need to communicate with a computer that only has SLIP, you need SLIP.

If you are able to choose from several alternatives, try to make your selection based on the following order of priority:

1. A real network connection at full bandwidth (the rate at which information can be transferred over a network)

2. PPP, used over the fastest modems you can afford

3. CSLIP, used over the fastest modems you can afford

4. SLIP, used over the fastest modems you can afford

The 5th Wave   By Rich Tennant

Chapter 17

The Dreaded Hardware Chapter

In This Chapter

▶ Pots and pans for the network banquet

▶ The marriage between hardware and software

▶ Go over the bridge and through the gateway. Repeat.

▶ Advice on when to use intelligent network devices, and when to use less-intelligent network devices and save money

*T*oday's world is divided into two kinds of people: hardware people and software people. Though very few mutants exist — people who have combined hardware and software traits — successful marriages have been known to occur between hardware and software people. Their differences, thank goodness, are complementary.

If you're reading this book, you're probably a software person (after all, network protocols *are* software). Or you may be a hardware person who wants to see how the other half lives. If you're a hardware person, you probably already know what's in this chapter and can go on to the next one if you want. And if you're wondering why a software book includes a hardware chapter at all, remember that software runs on hardware. Software can't work without hardware, and there's no point to having hardware if there's no software for it.

Network administrators usually have to configure both the hardware and the software for a network. This chapter is about the most commonly used network hardware devices, how they work to extend your network and enable it to communicate with other networks, and offers a little advice on making choices.

Are You in Charge?
or Did You Just Come to Eat?

Ever been to a big wedding reception? With separate tables for adults and children? With cocktails, the salad bar, sit-down tables, and the dessert buffet, all in different but connected rooms? With lots of round and rectangular tables big and small, holding all kinds of foods from soup to nuts?

Whoever organizes the banquet has a lot of planning to do. How many tables in how many rooms? What's the traffic pattern going to be? Will the hallways connecting the rooms be long and crowded? Or will guests be able to move smoothly from one room into another, so everyone can chow down before the food gets cold? And what about the kitchen? A banquet this size needs more than just regular dinnerware. You've got to have hardware — ranging from small sauté pans to huge kettles, soup tureens, deep fryers, roasting pans, and so forth. It's a lot of stuff that you and your guests don't want to have to think about, let alone wash up when it's over.

Like wedding receptions, networks vary in size. Maybe you're just having a party with two tables of four, and serving an appetizer, main course, salad, and dessert — nothing fancy. And you can use your everyday dishes. In network parlance, what you've got there is a small local area network (LAN) with a few hosts and some cable, but no fancy network devices or specialized hardware. But now consider The Internet and all of its miscellaneous interconnected pieces and network hardware all over the world — now there's a shindig!

If you're not a system manager or network administrator, you're probably just interested in eating from the salad bar (e-mail, copying files, and so on), so you can skip this chapter. But you system managers and network administrators out there are the caterers, so stay with us. Whether big or small, a network banquet has to be organized so that everyone gets enough to eat. That's your job. And if you're supervising the system managers and network administrators, you should definitely stay with us. Getting to know a little about network hardware will help you understand why your employees are always asking for faster, more powerful stuff.

What does hardware have to do with it?

Even though TCP/IP is software, it has to run over hardware. Like love and marriage, TCP/IP and hardware go together like a horse and carriage. And if you're responsible for a network, you can't be just "a software person" — no matter now hard you try. You need to pick up a little hardware knowledge and jargon to do your job right. Part of having a good marriage is understanding and appreciating each other's differences.

Why Doesn't This Work Anymore?

Our personal favorite excuse when anything goes wrong is, "It's a hardware problem." Try it. Say it over and over while you click your heels three times, and if you're wearing Dorothy's red shoes maybe you can get by with it. But we doubt it.

So, the answer to the question "What has hardware to do with doing a good job in network management?" is this: Network cables (and other media), along with TCP/IP software, are what link computers together so they can provide communication for and among your users. Computers are just hardware devices that happen to run some software — often, too slowly. If you're the caterer and the hot buffet is cold, your guests will be unhappy. If you're the network manager and the software runs too slowly, your users will complain. And the problem may not be with the software. Just as the caterer needs enough pots, pans, kettles, and chafing dishes, you need network hardware to satisfy guests at the TCP/IP banquet. Your network, too — unless it runs across the dining room table like ours does — needs some other hardware devices to create the infrastructure.

Remember Those Layers

You'll recall from Chapter 5 that a major benefit of TCP/IP software is that it is independent of the underlying hardware. TCP/IP protocols do, however, work *with* hardware.

Some of the hardware discussed in this chapter communicates only with the physical (bottom) layer of the TCP/IP network layer cake, and protocols are not an issue. Nevertheless, we have included information on these hardware devices. When designing or paying for a network, you may need to choose between a simple hardware device that has nothing to do with the middle (transport/internet) and upper (session/presentation/application) layers of the cake where TCP/IP is located, and a more complicated solution consisting of both hardware and TCP/IP software. We decided to include descriptions of the physical layer devices so that you can compare their features to the devices that work with TCP/IP protocols.

All of this information will help you organize your network wedding banquet with confidence, and that means building your network with the most appropriate components.

Packets chew through the network layers

Remember what you read about packets in Chapter 3? Your network message is put into packets along with some control information and sent out onto the network. Let's use the life of a packet to remind you of the layers in the network model.

A packet's life begins when an application creates it. Each packet travels down through the layers of the sending host, out across the network cables, then up through the layers of the destination host and into the appropriate application.

As the packets travel down through the layers of the sending host, control and formatting information and directions are added. When the packets reach the destination host, that information is read and stripped out as the packets move upward through each layer. For example, if you ftp a file from computer A to computer B, the data in the file is "packetized" at the application layer and sent through all the layers on computer A. By the time the packets are sent out across the wire, they have gained some weight — it's all that added network information. Once the roly-poly packets reach the destination host, they start to slim down, and when they arrive at the top layer and deposit your file, they are positively svelte again.

Figure 17-1 shows an FTP put operation; a packet travels from the application layer on computer A, out on to the network wire, and up to the application layer on computer B. You can see how the packet gains weight at each of computer A's layers, and then goes on a diet as it moves up through computer B's layers. Yo-yo dieting may be unhealthy for humans, but it works great for packets on the network.

If computer B is on a different network from computer A, a device is needed to connect the two networks. The rest of this chapter will help you understand what these devices are, how they are different, and how to decide whether you need one on your network or internet.

Use Terminal Servers to Serve Your Guests

Even in this age of networked PCs, Macintoshes, and workstations, the majority of guests at most network weddings will be terminals needing to attach to hosts. The most common terminal type is a "dumb" VT100-compatible terminal. Not all terminals are as dumb as a VT100, however. IBM terminals are smarter, and X Window terminals are really quite bright.

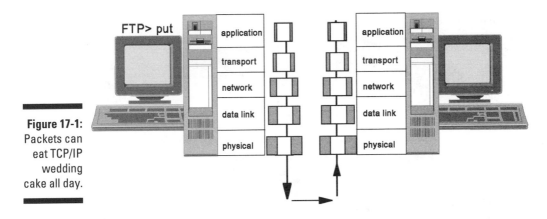

Figure 17-1:
Packets can
eat TCP/IP
wedding
cake all day.

Regardless of how smart your terminals are, the users of those terminals need to connect to the network in order to communicate with their host computers. A *terminal server* is a special device that helps terminals connect to any computer on the network.

Multiple matchmaking, network style

Figure 17-2 illustrates three different uses for terminal servers:

✔ Without a terminal server, each terminal must be attached directly to a single computer. In Figure 17-2, the terminals attached to Terminal Server 1 can connect to host A, host B, and host C.

✔ Terminal servers can also be used to create modem pools for dial-up arrangements between remote terminals and a host. The modems and telephone lines attached to Terminal Server 2 help remote terminals dial in to host A, host B, and host C. Terminal Server 2 also lets the hosts dial out to remote computers.

✔ When a terminal server is used "backwards" — that is, with its ports facing a host computer — the terminal server can be used to provide a network interface for a computer. Terminal Server 3 provides host C's network interface. Notice that the terminal server's serial ports face the host and not the users. The number of users that can connect to host C is determined by the number of serial ports linking the host and the terminal server.

Protocols? No problem. Most terminal servers on the market today are not limited to TCP/IP and can run other network protocols, too. Digital Equipment Corporation's LAT (Local Area Transport) protocol was specifically designed for terminal servers. TCP/IP, as well, is also quite skilled at carrying terminal traffic. ■

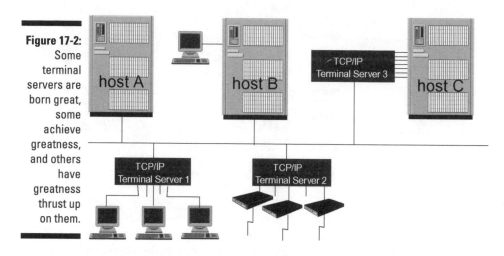

Figure 17-2:
Some terminal servers are born great, some achieve greatness, and others have greatness thrust up on them.

Do you need terminal servers? If you already have a large number of terminals attached to your computer, you probably already have terminal servers. If you are planning a network on which the hosts will have terminal users, terminal servers are a valuable asset. And when you need a modem pool or a creative solution for a network interface, terminal servers really shine.

Stretching the Network Dinner Party into a Banquet

Networks come in all sizes, shapes, and media. No matter what media your network runs on, each type has its own distance limitations. Let's use Ethernet as an example, and examine Ethernet's cable limits. Take a look at Table 17-1.

Table 17-1: Ethernet Cable Maximums for Best Signal Transmission

Cable Type	Description	Maximum Limit, in Feet/Meters
10Base5	Thick coaxial cable (Ethernet originally ran on this)	1640/500
10Base2	Thinwire cable	606/185
10BaseT	Twisted-pair wire	328/100
FDDI	Fiber-optic	Kilometers longer than wire or cable (copper media)

You'll find more stuff on cables and other connection media in Chapter 25. ■

You might be able to exceed these maximums (for instance, by using thinwire cable that is 620 feet long) and get by; the limits usually have a small amount of play built in. But remember that your data is transmitted as an electronic signal across a cable. The longer that signal has to travel, the weaker it gets. The maximums in Table 17-1 indicate the point when the signal starts to weaken.

Think about the banquet. If the kitchen is up two flights from the bar and you plan to serve the appetizers in the bar, you'd better not count on hot appetizers unless you have a dumbwaiter. Likewise, if you need to "exceed" the recommended limits for your connection media, you must use a hardware solution — the network equivalent of a dumbwaiter — to deliver your signal on time and while it's still hot.

The hardware options available for extending your network beyond the cabling limits in Table 17-1 include the following, from the simplest, least expensive to the most complex and expensive:

- ✔ Repeaters
- ✔ Bridges
- ✔ Routers
- ✔ Gateways

The next sections describe their pros and cons. Even if you are not a network support person, you'll benefit from the following discussion.

Could You Repeat Your Order, Please?

Let's say Table 17-1 shows that your twisted pair-wires, though cheap, are not long enough to extend across your building as planned. Think twice before you throw away the wire and buy some expensive optical cable, which could extend your network not just across the building, but across the county. This may extend your network, but it will also seriously shrink your budget.

Don't panic. There's another answer: a device called a *repeater* that ties two segments of wire or cable together to increase the overall length. What the repeater does is retransmit the signal so that it can travel longer distances, despite the limitations of the wires and cables. Also, when you extend a cable with a repeater, you can put more physical devices, such as computers, on the cable.

Thus you can use repeaters to extend a LAN by linking two network segments (see Figure 17-3). These segments must be of the same type. In other words, Ethernet-to-Ethernet is fine; Ethernet-to-token ring is not fine. The repeater takes the electronic signals from one network segment and retransmits them on the other segment. It never thinks about packet formats or network protocols.

Figure 17-3: A repeater makes one network longer by connecting two segments.

Although the repeater could be a potential point of failure within the network configuration, a repeater is a simple device and doesn't usually fail on its own. If you're thinking of using repeaters to extend the distance your network wires' span, be sure to consider the history of power outages in your area. Repeaters don't have built-in power-failure features such as battery backup. They are simple, inexpensive, and they do the job, but they don't have a lot of advanced options.

Keep large animals away from your network wiring! Although repeaters are durable and reliable network devices, if your pet elephant steps on one, it *will* break. ■

What happens in the TCP/IP layers?

Repeater functionality involves the physical layer of the network model only, because it's based merely on electrical signals. You simply attach the repeater to both segments of cable, and the packets flow through the repeater to the other side.

Do You Need Bridgework?

A *bridge* is a network device that extends a LAN by linking two networks that may or may not use the same media type (for example, 10BaseT cable and FDDI). The connected networks remain physically separate entities, with their own cabling limits and capacities. To the rest of your internet or The Internet, however, the bridge makes the linked networks appear as only one logical network. In Figure 17-4, one logical network consists of two separate physical networks connected by a bridge.

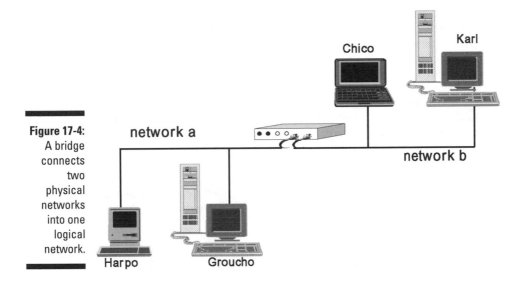

The connected networks must be geographically close, because a bridge is unable to use a modem to dial up and interconnect networks across the telephone lines. If you require this capability, you need to move up to routers, described in a later section.

The bridge reads the destination address in a packet and decides whether the packet is going to a host on the same network as the sender, or that the packet needs to go across the bridge to a network different from where the packet originated. (We hope you followed that...)

How does the bridge know where on the network the destination hardware address is located? It looks at the source hardware address and learns where things are. If it's not sure where the destination is, the bridge retransmits the packet just to be safe. The following section explains how a bridge learns.

A Note about Addresses

The address used by the bridge is not an IP address. It is the hardware address of a computer's network interface card. The bridge uses hardware addresses because it is not smart enough to understand IP addresses.

The Marx Connection

Each of the two networks illustrated in Figure 17-4 has two hosts connected by a bridge. The four hosts are named Harpo, Groucho, Chico, and Karl — they're the hosts of our well-organized network banquet. If Harpo sends a packet to Karl, the bridge knows that Harpo is on network A, but doesn't know where Karl is; so the bridge forwards the packet over to network B. If Karl sends a packet to Harpo, the bridge now knows that Karl is on network B and Harpo is on network A. The bridge learns and remembers. If Groucho sends packets to Harpo, the bridge figures out that both are on network A, and no forwarding is required. If Chico sends packets to Karl, the bridge is smart here, too, and remembers that both Chico and Karl are on network B; again, no forwarding is needed.

What's the result of all this bridgework? Each time the bridge doesn't have to forward a message, the network capacity, called *bandwidth,* is improved. There is space on the connection media for more messages.

What happens in the TCP/IP layers?

Absolutely nothing. The work done by a bridge spans both the data link layer and the physical layer.

Why the data link layer? A bridge learns the network addresses of the devices on each segment, and then it *filters* the traffic. That is, the bridge only forwards messages bound for destinations on the other network segment. The bridge is smart enough *not* to forward messages that don't need to go there.

You may be wondering why the bridge doesn't work at the internet layer. Bridges may be smart, but they're not smart enough to understand IP addresses. The bridge only understands hardware addresses on the hosts' network interface cards. If you want a network connector that is intelligent enough to work with IP addresses, you need a router (described in an upcoming section).

Don't think that having a bridge means you no longer need network protocols such as TCP/IP. The addresses in an e-mail or FTP or telnet packet are still software addresses. The bridge uses the hardware address to direct packets between networks (or to keep them on the same network), but once the bridge is done with its work, the applications take over and use the IP address. ∎

Bridging the gaps

You don't just go out and buy a bridge and position it anywhere on your network; you savvy network managers out there will have already guessed that a little design and planning is essential to this part of setting up a network. If a bridge isn't properly placed, it can't do the filtering it needs to do and must forward every packet. In that case, you either didn't need the bridge in the first place (if the distances are okay), or you could have spent less and used a repeater, instead. ■

Besides sending network messages to hardware addresses, the bridge may need to reformat the packet containing those messages. This action is based on whether the network segments are of the same type:

✔ If the network segments are of the same type, Ethernet-to-Ethernet for example, the bridge takes each packet from one network segment and retransmits it on the other segment, when necessary. By "when necessary," we mean that the transmission is only necessary when the packet is intended for a computer on the other network segment.

✔ If the network segments are not of the same type, the bridge takes the data out of the original packet and builds the correct packet type for the other network — for example, Ethernet-to-token ring, Ethernet-to-FDDI, token ring-to-FDDI, and so forth.

Bridge burps: how rude!

What if the bridge should fail? What you get then is *network bifurcation* — probably the fanciest term used anywhere in this book. You end up with two perfectly valid networks (one Ethernet and one token ring, for instance) that are no longer linked. The risk-reducing solution for this is to establish alternate paths by using multiple bridges that talk to one another. One becomes active and another one goes into standby.

✔ If you lose the standby, who cares? It wasn't doing any work in standby mode, anyway. You do want to fix it, though, and ASAP — because the active bridge is now all alone out there in the cold.

✔ If you lose the active bridge, the standby notices the lack of communication and becomes active.

This communication among bridges is not limited only to active and standby bridges. Each of them talks to all of the others, so together they can all decide which must go on active duty (no backups available) and which can be on standby. All the bridges on your internet check in periodically to make sure every thing is hunky-dory. The chatter does use up some network bandwidth, but it's worth it to keep your network traffic up and running.

Rowter or Rooter? Doesn't Matter — You Still Get to the Dessert Table

According to Webster, a *router* ("rowter") is a woodworking tool. A router ("rooter") is a sports fan with a bet on the Big Game; it's also a horse trained for distance races. In network parlance, however, you can pronounce it any way you want, so pick a side and join the battle. People pronounce it both ways and some are willing to fight for their choice. We prefer to remain nootral.

If your network suffers an identity crisis when its segments are bridged together, a router may be the therapy they need. A router extends a LAN by linking two or more network segments that may or may not use the same media type. The router permits each connected network to maintain its independent identity and address, just as a bridge does.

What makes routers special is that they are intelligent enough to understand IP addresses. In fact, the decisions the router makes about directing the packets of your data are based on the network portion of the IP address. Inside a router there is a network interface card for each segment of the network it connects. Each network interface card has a different IP address because the router itself is a member of each network.

How does routing work, anyway?

Routers work at the internet, data link, and physical layers of the TCP/IP structure.

A router resembles an octopus, whose tentacles represent all of your cabling types. Routers are smarter than bridges because they are aware of multiple paths your data packets can take across the network to their final destination. The router knows about other routers in the internet and can choose the most efficient path for the data to follow. This efficient path may change as network devices change and traffic comes and goes.

For example, on Monday, the most efficient path may be from network A to network C to network B. On Tuesday, however, the most efficient path may be from network A to network D to network B because network C is broken.

Because it knows about any problems on the network path, the router is able to detour your data when necessary.

Figure 17-5 shows a router at work as an intelligent decision-maker.

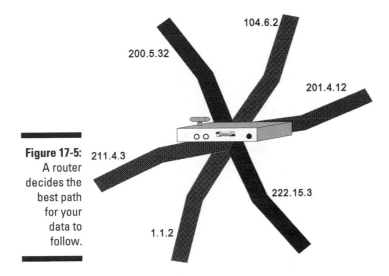

104.6.2

200.5.32

201.4.12

Figure 17-5:
A router
decides the
best path
for your
data to
follow.

211.4.3

222.15.3

1.1.2

Routers use a *routing protocol* to learn about the entire network and to determine the optimal path for sending a packet on to its destination. What is optimal? Is it the shortest path (fewest hops from one host to another)? Or the fastest path (more hops on speedier links)? Or the least congested path?

Suppose you want to go from Boston to New York City and visit the World Trade Center. Your top three choices are probably these:

1. Drive to NYC on Interstate 95 and use a city map to find the World Trade Center.

2. Drive to Boston's Logan airport. Fly to JFK airport in NYC. Take a taxi to the World Trade Center.

3. Drive to Boston's South Station. Take a train to Penn Station in NYC. Take the subway to the World Trade Center.

Figure 17-6 shows these three paths in terms of hops. Which way do you think would get you there fastest? If you've never driven to Logan airport during rush hour, most of you would guess that flying from Logan to JFK is the fastest route. However, depending on city traffic, flying may actually be the slowest way. Trust us on this. We have had the experience to prove it over and over again.

You can also see that the shortest way is not always the fastest way. Nor is the most direct route always the fastest way. And if you never go to New York City even once in your life, these facts are rules to live by on the network, as well.

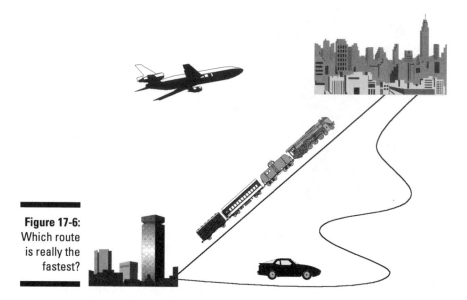

Figure 17-6: Which route is really the fastest?

Routing protocols and operating software

When you buy a router, your purchase includes proprietary software that functions as a mini-operating system which the network manager — probably you — must install and configure. The router also includes an installation guide. If you have to configure router software yourself, be sure to follow the instructions. Many routers down-line load their "operating system" software via the BOOTP or TFTP protocols described in Chapter 6.

Part of the configuration process for the router also includes selecting the appropriate routing protocol(s); these protocols, too, come with the router. There are several, but the two most prevalent routing protocols are RIP (Routing Information Protocol) and OSPF (Open Shortest Path First Protocol).

RIP (Routing Information Protocol)

RIP was developed by Xerox, which was way ahead of its time as a computer company — so ahead of its time, in fact, that it didn't catch on as a computer company. But the legacy of Xerox lives on in networking, especially Ethernet.

RIP has been part of UNIX TCP/IP since the beginning and is also a part of almost every TCP/IP product on the market today. RIP was developed before the corresponding RFC (RFC 1058), so you will find some differences in the various implementations.

Are you getting the point by now that RIP is old? Some people think it's old as in Old Reliable. Some people think it's old as in Rest In Peace. Though RIP is intelligent, and routes your packets to their destinations just fine, it is a slow learner when it comes to network changes, such as the appearance of new routers and faster paths.

OSPF (Open Shortest Path First)

The Open in OSPF is not a verb; in this case, it's *open* as in *open systems*. OSPF is a descendant of and supersedes older protocols such as IS-IS (Intermediate System to Intermediate System). OSPF is built on the concept of designated routers — that is, all routers are created equal, but some get elected to positions of importance.

If you need a refresher course in open systems, go back and look it up in Chapter 1. ∎

Brouters — Salad or Dessert?

So far, the distinction between network devices has been fairly obvious. Repeaters, bridges, and routers function at different network layers and have various levels of intelligence. Lest ye grow complacent, however, we're going to cloud the issue now with a discussion of *brouters* (never pronounced "bee-rowters" or "bee-rooters"). The *b* in brouter stands for *bridging*. A brouter is half bridge/half router. It can act as a bridge and as a router at the same time, filtering packets going to different networks.

When you come to the Jello salad on a buffet, do you consider it a salad or a dessert? Hmmm...it's got marshmallows and pineapple in it, so that makes it a dessert. But wait! Are those carrots in there next to the marshmallows? And celery, too? Maybe it's a salad after all. For similar reasons, you get to puzzle over the role of the brouter, too.

From the standpoint of intelligence and cost, a brouter falls more aptly between a bridge and a router than between a router and a gateway. In that sense, this description of brouters should probably come after the bridges section; but we've placed it here, after routers, so you'll better understand how brouters work.

How smart is a brouter?

You can put more than one network interface card inside a brouter. On the other hand, most brouters do not support as many different network interface cards as routers do. So when deciding between a brouter and a router, make sure to ask the salesperson how many interface cards your brouter can support.

In a multiprotocol internet, a brouter can route a single protocol — TCP/IP, for example. It bridges all other network protocols running on the same internet — say Novell's IPX. So in this case, with respect to IP, the brouter is quite intelligent; but it's not so smart when dealing with other protocols.

A brouter is an economical choice for a network device if you have a multiple-protocol internet and one of the protocols is used more heavily than the others. Network traffic transmitted by your most important protocol stack can take advantage of the brouter's intelligent routing capabilities. The network messages for the other protocols still get to their destinations via bridging.

Gateways: the Ultimate Interpreters

When the wine list is all French, most of us need a knowledgeable maître d' or a sommelier to help us out. To do translations on the network, you need a *gateway*. Gateways work at all the TCP/IP layers, from the bottom physical layer right up to the top application layer, to move data across networks of any type. They translate and repackage information from one application to another — even from one protocol to another.

Remember the SMTP gateway you read about in Chapter 7, for sending and receiving mail between non-SMTP sources and destinations? When a gateway does a translation, it looks at the addressing and routing information, and the data being sent, and converts it all into the format of the protocols and data on the receiving network.

Because of all the translation involved, a gateway has more work to do than the other network devices in this chapter. You can go down to a computer store and buy a repeater, then go home or to work and clamp it on your cables and put it right to work. A gateway, on the other hand, is usually a computer with two or more network interface cards, one for each culturally different network being connected. And like most computers, a gateway has to be configured with an operating system and network protocols, before you can put it to work.

A Common Gateway Myth

Many people assume that a gateway's function is to extend the size of a network. Actually, a gateway extends the *connectivity* of the network, by overcoming cultural and packet format differences between connected networks, including differences in protocols.

The Party's Over. It's Decision Time

We've discussed network devices starting with the least complex and costly and moving up the scale for both these characteristics. Table 17-2 summarizes the capabilities and features of the devices described in this chapter.

Our recommendation is to buy the simplest, most cost effective device you need. For instance, if you need to run cable up to the banquet hall's top floor, and that's a longer distance than what your cable is rated for, you need a repeater. Anything else is overkill.

 As device functions extend higher up into the TCP/IP layers, the devices themselves get smarter and more expensive. So If you are responsible for purchasing hardware, always ask yourself, "How smart a device do I need?" That way you'll make the best use of your (or your organization's) money.

Plan ahead! Suppose you decide that all you need is a repeater. Before you write the check, consider whether that repeater will still meet your needs in a month, or in six months or a year. If your network is growing, in just a few months you many need to divide it with a bridge or router. In that case, even though all you need today is a repeater, it's probably a good idea to go ahead and purchase a more complex device that will work for you later, as well. ∎

Table 17-2: Network Devices Compared

	Repeater	*Bridge*	*Brouter*	*Router*	*Gateway*
Intelligence	None	Average	Moderate	High	Genius
¹Relative Cost	*	**	***	****	*****
Configuration Complexity	Simple	Simple	Average	High	High
Network Model Layer	Physical	Physical, data link	Physical, data link, internet	Physical, data link, internet	All
Addresses Understood	N/A	Hardware	Hardware, IP	Hardware, IP	Hardware, IP

¹Relative Cost =
Inexpensive ◄─────────────────────────────────► Very Expensive
       *   **   ***   ****   *****

Chapter 18

Security: Will the Bad Guys Please Stand Up?

Security, especially network security, is a hot topic. Being connected to a network, especially The Internet, comes with some security risks. Is it worth it? For most people and organizations, the answer is yes, but a few important precautions are usually necessary.

Some of the topics in this chapter are not strictly related to TCP/IP, but are general security topics that apply to all computers and every network protocol. Before you even think about securing your network, you must secure the computers on it. As classic wisdom says, "A chain is only as strong as its weakest link." On the other hand, sometimes your network is the weak link.

Are you paranoid yet? Let's get started.

The information in this chapter is intended for everyone, but the tips are targeted at system managers and network administrators for the most part. And you'll find that we pose some questions without answering them. We do this on purpose, to get you thinking about certain issues — especially the ones that don't have easy answers. ■

What Is Involved in Network Security?

Everything:

- ✔ Hardware — the computers and other devices on the network
- ✔ Operating systems, to provide security features such as user accounts and passwords
- ✔ Software — the applications themselves
- ✔ The file system, which must offer mechanisms for protecting directories and files
- ✔ Network design — the whole kit and caboodle
- ✔ Organizational policies and procedures
- ✔ Training and education for users
- ✔ Rules and regulations, including punishments for breaking the rules
- ✔ Physical security, such as locks on computer room doors

Everyone involved in setting up security must consider a variety of questions. What are you protecting and from whom? Are the regular users on your network a greater threat than outsiders trying to break in? How much are you willing to pay, and for how much protection? How much inconvenience will legitimate users tolerate?

> **RFC Alert:** *RFC1173, "Responsibilities of Host and Network Managers; A Summary of the 'Oral Tradition' of the Internet,"* describes the security responsibilities of system managers and network administrators.

> **RFC Alert:** *RFC1244, "Site Security Handbook"* (also known as FYI8), contains a lot of good information to help your organization establish security policies and about the security risks of connecting to The Internet.

> **RFC Alert:** *RFC1147, "FYI on a Network Management Tool Catalog: Tools for Monitoring and Debugging TCP/IP Internets and Interconnected Devices"* (also known as FYI2), is a catalog of tools available to network administrators and system managers.

Who Is Responsible for Network Security?

Everyone:

- ✔ Users, who must not reveal their passwords
- ✔ System managers, who configure the services and monitor the computers

  ✔ Network administrators

  ✔ Organization management

  ✔ The organization itself, which must establish policies and procedures regarding unacceptable behavior as well as punishments for breaking the rules (We could tell you what these are, but then we'd have to kill you . . .)

  ✔ Security staff

Don't practice "security by obscurity"; that is, don't assume that users are stupid. Some users will be smarter than your assumptions, and others will make the most amazing misteaks. Here's a simple example: Leo configures his organization's Anonymous FTP server so that it is publicly writable, and assumes that no one will find out simply because he doesn't announce the change. Leo is attempting to practice security by obscurity. ■

The TCP/IP Banquet Is "By Invitation Only"

Every layer in the TCP/IP layer cake offers, and needs, different security components. Take a look at Figure 18-1 to remind yourself of the layers. Then we'll explore some layer-specific security steps.

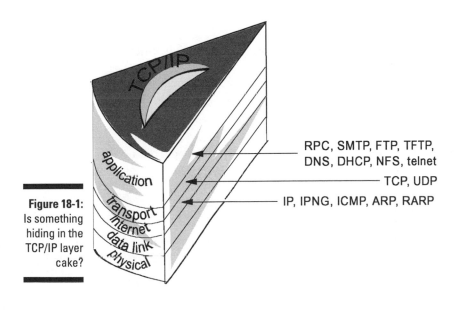

Figure 18-1: Is something hiding in the TCP/IP layer cake?

RPC, SMTP, FTP, TFTP, DNS, DHCP, NFS, telnet

TCP, UDP

IP, IPNG, ICMP, ARP, RARP

"It's Ours and You Can't Have It!"

The information on encryption we're giving you here is based on United States government practices. Other countries have their own initiatives and export controls. Much but not all of the research and development on computer security takes place in the United States. Worldwide encryption capabilities could be improved and made consistent, but the U.S. government won't allow the best U.S.-designed encryption systems to be exported. Maybe it's national ego, or paranoia left over from the cold war — but it's also true that if another country passes it, the United States will be playing catch-up in this field.

Tales from the Crypt

At the bottom of the TCP/IP structure, in the physical and data link layers, you can *encrypt* the data on the wire. This is one of the most common security techniques used in communications. Encryption, and some of the other terminology used for computer security, comes straight out of the world of secret agents. Following are definitions of some of these concepts.

Encryption

This is the process of transforming a message into code to conceal its meaning.

Cryptography

This is the process of enciphering (encrypting) and deciphering (decrypting) messages in secret code.

Encryption key

This is the essential piece of information — a word or number or combination — used in encrypting and decrypting the message, but not the algorithm (process) used for encryption.

Single key cryptography

In this coding process, the same encryption key is used both to encrypt and decrypt a message. Everyday examples of single-key cryptography are those Cryptogram word puzzles in the newspaper, and the simple coded messages children create using secret decoder rings and other gadgets from cereal boxes and toy manufacturers.

Public key/private key cryptography

In this coding process, one encryption key is used to encrypt the message, and another key is used to decrypt the message. There is a relationship, usually mathematical, between the two keys. The public and private keys are very long, prime numbers that are numerically related (factors of another, larger number). Possession of one is not enough to translate the message, since anything encrypted with one can only be decrypted with the other.

Every user gets a unique pair of keys, one that's made public and the other kept secret. Public keys are stored in common areas, mailed among users, and might even be printed in newspapers. Private keys must be stored in a safe place and protected. Anyone is allowed to have your public key, but only you should have your private key.

It works something like this: "You talkin' to me? I won't listen unless you encrypt the message using my public key, so I know no one else is eavesdropping. Only my private key, which no one else has, can decrypt the message, so I know no one else can read the message. I don't care that lots of other people have my public key, since it cannot be used to decrypt the message."

The X Files

In the middle of the layer cake, in the internet and transport layers, there is a security measure for *authentication* of computer names and addresses that an application may use.

> Knock knock.
>
> "Who's there?"
>
> "Special agent Fox Mulder, FBI."

Do you believe the breathy voice on the other side of the door and open up? Or do you authenticate him by looking at his ID? Can you really believe his ID? Do you even know what an FBI ID should look like? Do you call Federal Bureau of Investigation headquarters and try to verify his identity? What if he's really a space alien in disguise?

Pretty Good Is More Than Good Enough

PGP, which stands for Pretty Good Privacy, is an exportable, public-domain (free) software package for public key/private key cryptography. PGP is the technical underpinning for adding security to applications.

In TCP/IP, the process of authentication must be built into the applications. For example, an Anonymous FTP server does only very basic authentication. To interact with the FTP server, you need an FTP client program, a user account name (anonymous), and a password (just your e-mail address). Other applications, such as Lotus Notes, have much more stringent authentication controls.

To Catch a Thief

At the top of the TCP/IP layer cake, in the application/presentation/session layer, the applications can have their own security features.

Some network applications (FTP, rexec) employ passwords, which is a good safeguard, but the use of passwords can open up other vulnerabilities. Let's say someone is trying to break into your system by guessing passwords. On the one hand, you can run some kind of accounting or system-auditing utility, and the break-in attempts are logged so you'll know you're under attack. On the other hand, the Bad Guys are wise to that scheme. To get around it, instead of using telnet to log in directly, they may use ftp to test out their guesses. Because different implementations of ftp may or may not provide the same level of auditing that logging in does, make sure the ones you use link to the accounting/auditing system so you'll know you're under attack.

Be Aware of Security Pitfalls in Your Applications

Now let's look at some of the additional security precautions that you can apply to specific applications/protocols/services.

Put limits on TFTP

The Trivial File Transfer Protocol, TFTP, provides down-line loading and remote booting. Imagine the damage if people were using TFTP not just to download an operating system to a diskless computer, but also to grab your password file. So make a careful decision about whether you really need TFTP. If you do, configure it properly and carefully so that you limit the files that can be fetched and by whom.

Test TFTP yourself — but only on your own computers; testing other people's systems is probably illegal. Try fetching your system's critical files. If you've secured things properly, the transfer will fail.

If you don't need TFTP, don't run the daemon that enables it. ■

Be careful of what's anonymous

Since anyone from anywhere can use Anonymous FTP, configure it carefully so that you limit the files that can be fetched. As with TFTP, Anonymous FTP could be used by a miscreant to grab your password file.

When you configure Anonymous FTP, you specify the topmost directory holding the files you are offering. But that makes any subdirectories under the specified directory automatically accessible (normal file and directory permissions should still apply). So, after you configure Anonymous FTP, test it to make sure you aren't making critical files available. You'll also need to make sure that users are not able to change to a directory outside the tree you specify. Figure 18-2 shows what we mean.

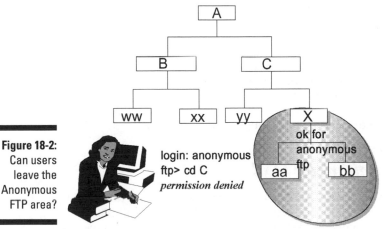

Figure 18-2:
Can users
leave the
Anonymous
FTP area?

Consider dedicating a computer to Anonymous FTP, and don't put anything on it that you're not willing to share. ■

Don't believe everything you read, part one: E-Mail

You can never be sure that an e-mail message came from the person it says it's from. Anyone who wants to send fraudulent e-mail messages can change the name of their computer and even their username. When the message goes through, SMTP doesn't verify the username, computer name, or even the sender's e-mail address. It just passes the message through with the counterfeit information. Figure 18-3 shows the SMTP dialog between the sending and receiving computers.

Figure 18-3:
The receiving SMTP computer believes what the sending computer tells it.

```
% mail -iv mwilensky@lotus.com
Subject: file to put on floopy
~rtools.txt
"tools.txt" 623/34384

.
Cc: leiden
leiden... Sent
mwilensky@lotus.com... Connecting to crd.lotus.com. (smtp)...
mwilensky@lotus.com... Connecting to lotus.com. (smtp)...
220 lotus.com Sendmail 4.1/SMI-4.10801.1994 ready at Wed, 31 May 95 09:49:27 EDT
>>> HELO max.tiac.net ──────────────── SMTP trusts that you are who you say you are.
250 lotus.com Hello max.tiac.net, pleased to meet you
>>> MAIL From:<leiden@max.tiac.net>
250 <leiden@max.tiac.net>... Sender ok ──────────── SMTP doesn't ask to see your ID.
>>> RCPT To:<mwilensky@lotus.com>
250 <mwilensky@lotus.com>... Recipient ok
>>> DATA
354 Enter mail, end with "." on a line by itself
>>> .
250 Mail accepted
mwilensky@lotus.com... Sent (Mail accepted)
Closing connection to lotus.com.
>>> QUIT
221 lotus.com delivering mail
You have mail in /usr/spool/mail/leiden
%
```

On many computers, you can't change your username or the computer's name (unless you are the system manager), but on a personal computer there are no such limitations. It's your machine and you can call it anything you want — even whitehouse.gov!

Are you worried about how trusting SMTP is? Read on.

Privacy Enhanced Mail

PEM, Privacy Enhanced Mail, is a more secure mail environment implemented by means of a new mail user agent (MUA) in conjunction with good old SMTP. (If you need to review SMTP, MUAs and MTAs, go back to Chapter 7.) PEM knows how to send and receive mail in a secure fashion, but both you and your correspondent must agree to use PEM's privacy functions. Specifically, you both must have public key/private key pairs, as well as access to each other's public keys.

For instance, Ben can't send Rachel an encrypted message, unless *both* the following requirements are met:

✔ Rachel has a public key that Ben can access. He might find it in a central repository, or she could e-mail it to him.

✔ Ben has software (especially an MUA) that can use a public key for encryption, and he knows how to use it.

Even if both these requirements are met, that is not good enough. Let's say Ben could create a public key/private key pair for Rachel and use the brand-new public key to encrypt the mail message he's sending her. Once she received the message, how would she decrypt it? Ben not only would have to give Rachel her public key but also would have to be sure that Rachel knows how to decrypt and encrypt mail. Did he keep a copy of her private key? Can Rachel trust Ben? As Johnny Carson used to say, "Who do you trust?"

Privacy Enhanced Mail may be useful, but you and your correspondents must be synchronized. ∎

Don't believe everything you read, part two: Usenet news

When you're reading Usenet news articles, you have the same lack of assurance about their authors as you do about e-mail senders. It's not impossible for a clever villain to generate deceitful news articles. To help you here, NNTP, the Network News Transfer Protocol (see Chapter 7), provides some optional authentication features.

The NNTP server can be configured so that it only accepts news articles if it can authenticate the source computer and author. For this to work, both the NNTP server and the client must use the authentication features. Most clients today are not using them, however.

Because NNTP authentication only works with the cooperation of the users (at properly configured NNTP clients), it only ensures that the good guys are who they say they are. The villains aren't going to use software that inhibits their misdeeds — at least, not voluntarily.

Usenet news articles can be trusted only if all the authentication pieces are properly coordinated. ∎

I only trust Johnny Carson and Walter Cronkite

The trust-based services (rsh, rcp, rlogin) know which computers and which users to trust, but based only on the contents of an ASCII text file. Are these files and their directories protected so only authorized users can change the contents? (On UNIX systems these include /etc/hosts.equiv, and the .rhosts files in users' home directories.)

The security of your trusted TCP/IP network services is, in reality, a function of operating system security. Any user of rsh, rcp, and rlogin, including the system manager, can open holes in security — accidentally or on purpose.

 Whenever you state a computer's name when you are using rsh, rcp, and rlogin, always specify the FQDN. Otherwise, if you say you trust lotus, you're trusting every computer named lotus everywhere on The Internet, not just the one at the car company. ■

NFS = No File Stealing!

On UNIX systems, the file named /etc/exports lists the disk space your NFS (Network File System) server is willing to share. It also allows you to limit access to only the NFS clients you name, as well as to restrict the actions of the privileged users on those NFS clients.

 Here are some tips for keeping your NFS servers safe and secure:

✔ Be specific about the disk space you are sharing. Only list the directories that need to be shared.

✔ Be specific about the NFS clients you support. Put their FQDNs in the file.

✔ Do not allow privileged users on NFS clients to have privileged access to your disk space. State (in /etc/exports) that those clients are not allowed privileged access. ■

Get help from showmount

Use the showmount command on the NFS server to see the disk space that the NFS clients are using. Here's an example:

```
% showmount -a
frodo:/var/spool/mail
frodo:/usr1/emacs
bilbo:/var/spool/mail
bilbo:/usr2/xmosaic
```

If you ever see a numeric IP address instead of the name of the NFS client, it could indicate a security problem. In means the NFS server was unable to look up the name of the client in the local hosts file, or the NIS, or the DNS.

 If you want to review NIS and NFS, look in Chapter 10; DNS (Domain Name System) is explained in Chapter 11. ■

Your money or your cola!

Finger gives away information that might be used to mount an attack against a host on your network. If you were planning a cola robbery, fingering the soda machine at Carnegie Mellon University (see Chapter 14) could give you all the information you'd need. Would you want to rob the machine when it's low on soda and full of money, or when it's full of soda and low on cash? How thirsty are you? Will you be thirsty after bagging the quarters?

Don't put really personal information in your plan or project files that could be fingered by someone with evil intentions. ■

How Promiscuous Is Your Network Controller?

Normally your network controller is only interested in looking for packets addressed to it; it ignores all the rest. Some network monitoring and management software, however, is able to place the network interface card in "promiscuous mode," making it keep and display every packet. These kinds of tools are useful for debugging network problems, but should be available to and used by authorized network administrators only.

Anyone using this software, or any network analyzer, can see the contents of any packet — perhaps even an unencrypted password or an e-mail message — as it travels by.

This network monitoring and management software is easy to get for personal computers — perhaps too easy. It may be difficult to protect yourself and your network. ■

Credit Card Shopping Risks on The World Wide Web

More and more, World Wide Web surfers want to do more than just browse published data. The Web's clients and servers, as well, need two-way communication in order to provide more sophisticated services. Corporations, especially, need this interchange in order to conduct business over The Internet. The goal is for a consumer to be able to browse a product offering, fill out an order form, and supply credit-card information (or a checking account number for electronic funds transfer, or the like). Both parties need to be sure that the transaction is done in a secure manner.

Secure HTTP is coming, soon, to address the issue of moving data across a public environment in a secure fashion. (You'll remember from Chapter 12 that HTTP is HyperText Transfer Protocol, which is how browsers communicate with servers on the Web.) The emergence of Secure HTTP should not require any changes to HTML, the language that makes the Web's pages look so good. (Although HTML, too, is getting new features, they're driven by other requirements.)

If you need secure HTTP, upgrade to new versions of World Wide Web browsers and servers as soon as they're available. ■

I Don't Do X Windows

This section covers security issues relating to the X Window System. You'll remember, from the discussion in Chapter 8, that in X environments the client/server model is "reversed." That is, you sit in front of the X Window System display server (software running on your computer), while the client applications run on remote computers.

On the X Window System display server — the machine in front of you — you can declare which remote computers are allowed to send output for the server to display. Some lazy users simply declare that they'll accept output from every computer. This is not a good idea.

Be aware that an evildoer — say, Medusa Miscreant, who lives on Code Cracker Court — might send you a fake screen that says "Enter your username and password." This method of security attack is called a *password grabber,* and it's not limited to X Window. If you unwittingly supply the information, your account is compromised, your files are in danger, and Medusa Miscreant may soon be sending e-mail messages in your name. If the fake screen exactly mimics the real operating system log-in message, you're even more likely to be fooled. ■

Avoiding this security trap is not just TCP/IP security; this precaution affects the security of your entire network. The fact that TCP/IP carried Medusa's illicit X Window message makes TCP/IP merely an unknowing accomplice, not the villain.

Never declare that you'll accept X Window output if you don't have to. If you must accept X Window output from other computers, always declare their FQDN. (On UNIX systems, you can use the xhost to do this.) Declare only the computers you really need, and only for the time interval you need. Shut them out again when you don't need them anymore.

And never type your username and password unless you're sure why you must do so! ■

Commonly Held Myths about Network Security

1. No evil people are connected to computer networks.

2. Only evil people connect to networks.

3. There are no security concerns about putting your computer on a network.

4. It is impossible to have a secure network.

5. Once your network is secure, you don't have to worry it about anymore.

6. Accounting and auditing utilities have too much overhead to be worth the expense.

Protecting Your Network

When you think about securing your network, you need to look at it from the bottom up, in this order:

✔ Connection media

✔ Computers and network devices

✔ Users

Can you protect the cables?

Are you the person who decides what devices are and are not attached to your network? Could someone illicitly attach to a network cable and "tap in" to your network?

The security of your network depends primarily on the network design and physical installation. The efforts you need to make to keep illegal devices off the network will vary with the media you employ. Here are some things to keep in mind:

✔ The cable on a traditional token ring network is shielded twisted-pair. The cable and connectors, plus the circular nature of the network, make it difficult to tap in illicitly.

✔ Traditional Ethernet coaxial cable (10Base2) can be tapped without cutting through it, but you need special tools and a transceiver to make the illicit connection.

- ✔ ThinWire Ethernet cable (10Base5) is extremely easy to tap, especially at the tee connectors and terminators. It's virtually impossible to prevent additional connections on active network segments.

- ✔ Twisted-pair Ethernet (10BaseT) cable is regular wire that you can buy in any hardware store. So to make your wiring secure, be sure to run the wires into locked communications closets.

- ✔ In all wiring closets, unused ports on hubs should be deactivated, as should the jacks in unused offices.

- ✔ Fiber-optic cable is extremely difficult to tap. The network fails completely when the cable is cut, so illicit taps announce themselves pretty clearly.

- ✔ Wireless links — including infrared, radio frequency, lasers, microwaves, and satellite dishes — are all interceptible broadcasts. How do radio and TV stations know how many people are listening/watching, you ask? And how do you know if someone is eavesdropping on your radio waves? The answer is you don't; so you'll need to encrypt the data so that eavesdroppers can't use it.

Can you detect an unauthorized host or device on your network?

To locate an unauthorized host or device on your network, you could try to ping every network address, but that's impractical on most networks — hard to automate and really boring to do manually. Plus, you're looking for things that shouldn't be there, and you'll be distracted by things that should be there and aren't. What if one node is broken or down on purpose?

In one common security attack — called a *spoof* — a miscreant replaces a valid, known host with an impostor. The miscreant turns off or otherwise disables the valid system and brings up the impostor (Ms. Medusa's own PC, possibly) with the valid system's name and IP address.

Wiring hubs may have some management controls, but you need a real network management solution based on TCP/IP's SNMP, the Simple Network Management Protocol (pronounced by saying the letters *S N M P*). Here are a few SNMP network management products:

- ✔ Hewlett-Packard's OpenView
- ✔ IBM's NetView
- ✔ Sun Microsystems's Sun NetManager

Why Fort Knox Isn't on The Internet

Automatic teller machines are not on The Internet; they are on private networks. That's why criminals yank them out of the walls to steal them and the money inside — although some evildoers have probably tried to connect to the network and tell the machines to spit out money.

Also, as an alternative to SNMP, OSI has defined CMIP (pronounced *see-mip*), the Common Management Information Protocol. CMIP really hasn't caught on, however, especially in comparison to SNMP.

Can you keep unauthorized users off your computers?

Unauthorized tapping into your physical network may be less of a problem for you than protecting your network and your computers from improper use by authorized and semiauthorized users. If your organization's network is linked to The Internet, that means anyone linked to the network — legally or illegally — can potentially reach one of your computers or any network device.

So how do you protect yourself? Don't give them access. See the sidebar, "Why Fort Knox Isn't on The Internet," and the upcoming section on firewalls.

What Is a Firewall?

Make sure you've read Chapter 17 before diving into this section. Don't say we didn't warn you. ▪

Webster's Seventh New Collegiate Dictionary defines a firewall as a "wall constructed to prevent the spread of fire." Notice it doesn't say anything about *putting out* the fire. A real firewall actually only slows the fire's movement through a building.

A *network firewall* is more like a dam with a hydroelectric power plant. The dam has a specific number of very carefully built openings and spillways that allow some of the water through in a controlled way. And "damn!" is what you may say while you try to set up a network firewall, and what your users may say when they try to do work through one. We can also compare a network firewall to the passport control and customs at an international airport.

Before you're allowed into or out of a country, you must pass a series of checkpoints. In a network firewall, every packet has to pass certain checks before it's allowed to continue on its way.

In terms of network traffic, normally you'll be more concerned with inbound traffic (from The Internet to your network) than with outbound. Letting your users out onto The Internet is more or less essential these days. Some people you simply have to trust to behave responsibly — and others you don't. You have some control over the people in your own organization, but much less control over the outsiders.

How can you identify the Medusa Miscreants? You can't, and there's no easy way to look in every packet and find out "what the heck is this for?" You have to use what's there — the source address, the destination address, and the port (the service that's being used) — to determine which services are allowed through the firewall and which are not.

How a firewall works

The firewall examines every packet and decides whether it's allowed in or out. If the firewall refuses to let it pass, the packet is thrown away. The sending system will get the idea when there is no response. Most applications will take the lack of response as bad news; they may try again or give up and go away. (What does a caller do if you don't answer your phone when it rings?)

Types of firewalls

There are many approaches you can take to establish a firewall. The following sections describe some solutions for minimal, good, and better protection against undesirable traffic, and offer suggestions for setting them up. We are not particularly recommending any of these, but simply introducing you to the basic concepts so you can decide for yourself.

If you are connected to The Internet via a commercial service provider, ask your provider about their own security precautions and the services they can extend to you. You can also hire a network consultant to help you with customized solutions. ∎

Minimal protection: "No default route"

The most common way to tell your computer how to send a message to a network number different than its own — including The Internet — is to establish a *default route* value. If you don't designate the default route, your computer can't send packets to a different network. This inability to send outbound traffic also offers some protection from inbound traffic, because almost all TCP/IP services need two-way communication.

Here's an example: If an Internet user tries to obtain one of your files with FTP, they won't be able to — because their ftp request needs your computer to answer. But your computer can't send anything out, either. Of course, this also means you can't use FTP to get a file from another computer on The Internet, because your computer can't send your request to the destination.

So with "no default route" you get protection from undesired access, but at the cost of services. Sure, boarding up the doors and windows in your house makes it more difficult for someone to break in, but you'll soon be dead because you can't go out for groceries.

This basic approach, then, is not really a true firewall; but it's cheap.

Good protection: Packet filtering by routers

A typical and more effective firewall can be established using a router on your network. A router looks at the destination address in each packet to determine where the packet goes. You build your firewall by establishing *filters*. A filter is a rule you establish on the router to train the router to drop certain packets on purpose. Nothing less intelligent than a router can do this because of the software required.

The three fields that can trigger the filters are the source address, the destination address, and the port number.

✔ The source address answers the question, "Where did this packet come from?" Remember that Medusa Miscreant can set her computer's IP address to anything she wants. Depending on how her computer is attached to the network and how its packets reach your computer, you cannot necessarily trust the validity of that source address. The DNS helps her by telling her what IP address to use for spoofing attacks. But your filter can say "I don't trust this computer at all and will not talk to it."

✔ The destination address answers the question, "Where is this packet going?" When the destination is one of your computers, you can decide whether any packet is allowed to go there at all. Your filter can say "Look, this computer does not receive packets directly from outside. Forget it. No way." Sometimes you may choose to redirect the packet to a special server. In this case your filter can say "The packet is okay, but send it over there instead." E-mail is a good example of a service that you may want to redirect. You can disallow receipt of e-mail directly from outside, arranging for all e-mail to be routed instead through a single point of contact. The DNS mail exchange records, known as MX records, are designed specifically for this.

✔ The port number answers the question, "What service is this packet destined for?" If you're not running a particular server, why should you accept any packets of that protocol? For instance, if you're not running a World Wide Web server, you can freely and safely ignore any HTTP packets. Your filter can say, "I refuse to talk about that subject."

Better protection: A gateway

Like a router, a gateway is a combination of hardware and software, but a gateway is even smarter than a router because it has a whole computer for a brain. Anything a router can do, a gateway can do better. The problem is, someone has to build the gateway software, and each one is a custom solution.

Network management considerations when setting up a firewall

A simplistic firewall is a single router that links the internal and external networks, examines every packet, and decides whether or not to let it pass. Look at Figure 18-4; you can see that there is some protection, but is it enough? In this most basic approach, there may also be a question of ownership and control: Who owns the router, you or your Internet service provider? Where is the router installed, on your premises or the service provider's?

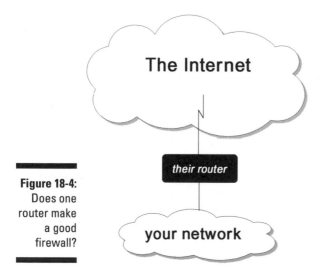

Figure 18-4:
Does one router make a good firewall?

Some organizations choose to add another router and another network segment (Figure 18-5). The Internet service provider owns one router and you own the other. Fortunately, routers are invisible to the network users. In this arrangement, you must decide carefully how the network's computers are arranged — the computers need to be placed on the correct network segment, based on their function within the network.

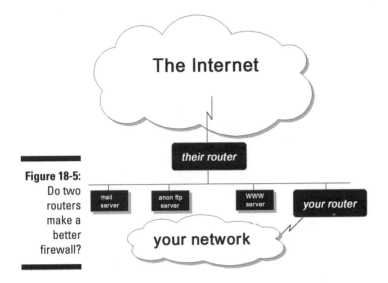

Figure 18-5:
Do two routers make a better firewall?

This intermediate approach has one major advantage: If you decide to disconnect from The Internet by turning off your own router, your organization still appears to be on the network, because some of your computers are still active even though no traffic is coming in. E-mail can be queued for later delivery inside; external users can still get to the Anonymous FTP server; and the World Wide Web server can still be browsed. On the other hand, if the service provider must turn off their router, then your organization is off the network!

Some computers, such as your Anonymous FTP server and your World Wide Web server, need to be accessible from outside your organization (that is, from The Internet side of the firewall). But do they have to be directly accessible from inside your organization (that is, from your side of the firewall), as well? You can always move files onto the servers by floppy or other external media, but how inconvenient would that be? Is the trouble worth the benefit of the extra level of security?

Some computers and services must be accessible from both inside and outside your organization in order to be useful. E-mail and telnet are prime examples.

Sometimes the firewall's protection interferes with services your own users need such as Anonymous FTP and the World Wide Web. One easy solution is to add a compute server on the network segment with your externally accessible servers. To surf the Net, your users must connect to this system first. This arrangement is somewhat annoying, however, both for the users and for the system manager, who has to create user accounts on this doorway computer. Another solution is to establish a *proxy server*, which redirects packets toward their real destination. Figure 18-6 demonstrates using Anonymous FTP with a nearby proxy server.

```
% ftp door ─────────────── Connect to the proxy server
Connected to Door.lotus.com.
220-Welcome to the Lotus FTP Proxy Server.
220-This FTP Service will allow you to access external Internet
220-Host, without the need of a direct login to host Door.
220-*********************************************************
220-At the prompt following the last line of this message ~***************~,
Enter your userid and complete hostname you wish to make a FTP connection.
220-
220-Example: To FTP into Internet Host ftp.uu.net via a anonymous login
220-
220-Enter:    anonymous@ftp.uu.net
220-Then press Enter, this will connect you via FTP to your requested Host.
220-
220-(Notice: The login prompt you may receive at the end of this message
220-depends on the FTP software you are running on your desktop.
220-Some users will see if using a UNIX system `Name(Door.lotus.com:yourloginname):
' or if using a DOS/Windows system with FTP's PCTCP, you will
220-see `Userid for loging in on Door (YourName):')
220-
220-After either of these two prompts, is were you enter your ftp host
220-userid and hostname.
220-
220-If you have problems, please report them to the IS
220-Help Desk at Ext. 31767.
220-
220-THIS SERVICE IS FOR LOTUS BUSINESS USE ONLY
220 *********************************************************
Name (door:wilensky): anonymous@gatekeeper.dec.com ─── Proxy server prompts you. You respond
331-(──GATEWAY CONNECTED TO gatekeeper.dec.com──)        with the FTP archive to access.
331-(220- *** /etc/motd.ftp ***)
331-(     Original by:  Paul Vixie, 1992)
331-(     Last Revised: Richard Schedler, April 1994)
331-(     )
331-(     Gatekeeper.DEC.COM is an unsupported service of Digital Corporate
Research.)
331-(     Use entirely at your own risk - no warranty is expressed or implied.)
331-(     Complaints and questions should be sent to <gw-archives@pa.dec.com>.)
331-(     )
```

Welcome message and instructions from the proxy server.

Welcome message from the Anonymous FTP server.

Figure 18-6:
A proxy server helps with Anonymous FTP.

```
331-(    EXPORT CONTROL NOTE: Non-U.S. ftp users are required by law to follow U.S.)
331-(    export control restrictions, which means that if you see some DES or)
331-(    otherwise controlled software here, you should not grab it.  Look at the)
331-(    file 00README-Legal-Rules-Regs (in every directory, more or less) to learn )
331-(    more.  (If the treaty between your country and the United States did not )
331-(    require you to respect U.S. export control restrictions, then you would)
331-(    not have Internet connectivity to this host.  Check with your U.S. embassy)
331-(    if you want to verify this.))
331-(    )
331-(    This FTP server is based on the 4.3BSD-Reno version.  Our modified sources)
331-(    are in /pub/DEC/gwtools.)
331-(    )
331-(220 gatekeeper.dec.com FTP server (Version 5.97 Fri May 6 14:44:16 PDT 1994) ready.)
331 Guest login ok, send ident as password.
```

Password: ─────────────────────────── **You enter your e-mail address, but it doesn't display.**

```
230 Guest login ok, access restrictions apply.
```

ftp> dir ─────────────────────────── **Your normal FTP session starts here.**

```
200 PORT command successful.
150 Opening ASCII mode data connection for /bin/ls.
total 27639
```

-r—r—r—	1 root	system	858	Dec 11	1992	00README-Legal-Rules-Regs
-r—r—r—	1 root	system	33298	Apr 28	1994	GATEWAY.DOC
-r—r—r—	1 root	system	211	Sep 6	1989	GATEWAY.DOC;1
-r—r—r—	1 root	system	51925	Apr 28	1994	GATEWAY.PS
-r—r—r—	1 root	system	10894531	Jan 20	05:04	Index-byname
-r—r—r—	1 root	system	1974469	Jan 20	05:03	Index-byname.Z
-r—r—r—	1 root	system	10894531	Jan 20	05:15	Index-bytime
-r—r—r—	1 root	system	2207675	Jan 20	05:21	Index-bytime.Z
-r—r—r—	1 root	system	4037	Jan 20	1994	README.ftp
-r—r—r—	1 root	system	4156	Nov 12	15:35	README.nfs
-r—r—r—	1 root	system	4152	Apr 13	1994	README.nfs~
-r—r—r—	1 root	system	6002	Jan 20	1994	README.www
-r—r—r—	1 root	system	647	Aug 5	1993	US-Legal-Regs-ITAR-NOTICE

Files in the top-level directory.

```
lrwxr-xr-x 1 root     system      30 Jan 16 01:18 gatekeeper.home.html
-> hypertext/gatekeeper.home.html
dr-xrwxr-x 8 root     system     512 Jan 16 01:41 hypertext
dr-xr-xr-x 2 root     system    1024 Dec 28 12:58 pub
226 Transfer complete.
3483 bytes received in 18 seconds (0.19 Kbytes/s)
```

ftp> cd pub ─────────────────────────── **Move down the directory tree.**

```
250 CWD command successful.
```

ftp> dir ─────────────────────────── **Look at files in the pub directory.**

```
200 PORT command successful.
150 Opening ASCII mode data connection for /bin/ls.
total 38
```

Figure 18-6:
(continued)

```
lrwxr-xr-x 1 root     system      11 Dec 28 12:58 Alpha -> ../.b/Alpha
lrwxr-xr-x 1 root     system       9 Dec 28 12:58 BSD -> ../.0/BSD ────── Berkeley UNIX information here.
lrwxr-xr-x 1 root     system       9 Dec 28 12:58 DEC -> ../.2/DEC
```

```
lrwxr-xr-x  1 root     system         3 Dec 28 12:58 Digital -> DEC
lrwxr-xr-x  1 root     system         9 Dec 28 12:58 GNU -> ../.8/GNU
lrwxr-xr-x  1 root     system        10 Dec 28 12:58 Mach -> ../.b/Mach
lrwxr-xr-x  1 root     system        10 Dec 28 12:58 NIST -> ../.b/NIST
lrwxr-xr-x  1 root     system        12 Dec 28 12:58 athena -> ../.b/athena
lrwxr-xr-x  1 root     system        10 Dec 28 12:58 case -> ../.b/case
lrwxr-xr-x  1 root     system        10 Dec 28 12:58 comm -> ../.b/comm
lrwxr-xr-x  1 root     system        17 Dec 28 12:58 conferences -> ../.8/conferences
lrwxr-xr-x  1 root     system        10 Dec 28 12:58 data -> ../.b/data
lrwxr-xr-x  1 root     system        14 Dec 28 12:58 database -> ../.8/database
lrwxr-xr-x  1 root     system         9 Dec 28 12:58 doc -> ../.b/doc
lrwxr-xr-x  1 root     system        13 Dec 28 12:58 editors -> ../.b/editors
lrwxr-xr-x  1 root     system        12 Dec 28 12:58 forums -> ../.b/forums
lrwxr-xr-x  1 root     system        11 Dec 28 12:58 games -> ../.b/games
lrwxr-xr-x  1 root     system        13 Dec 28 12:58 recipes -> ../.2/recipes
226 Transfer complete.
2916 bytes received in 2 seconds (1.4 Kbytes/s)
ftp> cd NIST ─────────────────────
250 CWD command successful.
ftp> dir ───────────────────────
200 PORT command successful.
150 Opening ASCII mode data connection for /bin/ls.
total 21
lrwxr-xr-x  1 root     system        31 Jan 19 06:37 00README-Legal-Rules-Regs
-> ../../00README-Legal-Rules-Regs
-r--r--r--  1 root     system     14352 Sep 26  1991 GOSIP.README
dr-xr-xr-x  2 root     system       512 Jan 19 06:37 eval_guide
dr-xr-xr-x  2 root     system       512 Jan 19 06:37 gnmp
dr-xr-xr-x  2 root     system       512 Jan 19 06:37 gosip
dr-xr-xr-x  2 root     system       512 Jan 19 06:37 gug
dr-xr-xr-x  5 root     system       512 Jan 19 06:37 oiw
226 Transfer complete.
499 bytes received in 0.34 seconds (1.4 Kbytes/s)
ftp> get GOSIP.README gosip.txt ──────────────
200 PORT command successful.
150 Opening ASCII mode data connection for GOSIP.README (14352 bytes).
226 Transfer complete.
local: gosip.txt remote: GOSIP.README
14996 bytes received in 0.97 seconds (15 Kbytes/s)
ftp> cd gosip ──────────────────────
250 CWD command successful.
ftp> dir ────────────────────
200 PORT command successful.
150 Opening ASCII mode data connection for /bin/ls.
total 2072
lrwxr-xr-x  1 root     system        34 Jan 19 06:37 00README-Legal-Rules-Regs
-> ../../../00README-Legal-Rules-Regs
-r--r--r--  1 root     system     47067 Sep 26  1991 gosip_cover.ps
```

Move down to the NIS (National Institute of Standards and Technology) directory.

List the files that relate to standards.

Copy information about OSI.

Go down to the GOSIP directory.

List the files.

Figure 18-6:
(continued)

```
-r—r—r—  1 root      system       20852 Sep 26  1991 gosip_cover.ps.Z
-r—r—r—  1 root      system        2649 Sep 26  1991 gosip_cover.txt
-r—r—r—  1 root      system        1613 Sep 26  1991 gosip_cover.txt.Z
-r—r—r—  1 root      system      958466 Sep 26  1991 gosip_v2.ps
-r—r—r—  1 root      system      215753 Sep 26  1991 gosip_v2.ps.Z
-r—r—r—  1 root      system      255271 Sep 26  1991 gosip_v2.txt
-r—r—r—  1 root      system       80603 Sep 26  1991 gosip_v2.txt.Z
-r—r—r—  1 root      system      232748 Sep 26  1991 gosip_v2.w50
-r—r—r—  1 root      system      232744 Sep 26  1991 gosip_v2.wp5
```

— Lots of OSI information here.

```
226 Transfer complete.
827 bytes received in 0.46 seconds (1.8 Kbytes/s)
ftp> cd /pub/doc
```
——————— Change to another directory.
```
250 CWD command successful.
ftp> dir
200 PORT command successful.
150 Opening ASCII mode data connection for /bin/ls.
total 643
lrwxr-xr-x  1 root      system          31 Jan 19 06:39 00README-Legal-Rules-Regs ->
../../00README-Legal-Rules-Regs
drwxr-xr-x  3 root      system         512 Jan 19 06:39 DECUS
-r—r—r—  1 root      system          75 Jun 24  1990 README
dr-xr-xr-x  3 root      system         512 Jan 19 06:39 security
-r—r—r—  1 root      system       67113 Nov 26  1989 telecom.glossary.txt
226 Transfer complete.
1221 bytes received in 0.58 seconds (2 Kbytes/s)
ftp> get telecom.glossary.txt telecom.txt
```
——————— Get another file.
```
200 PORT command successful.
150 Opening ASCII mode data connection for telecom.glossary.txt (67113 bytes).
226 Transfer complete.
local: telecom.txt remote: telecom.glossary.txt
68700 bytes received in 2.6 seconds (26 Kbytes/s)
ftp> quit
```
——————— Done at last!
```
221 Goodbye.
```

Figure 18-6: *(continued)*

When you leave the Anonymous FTP server, you are automatically disconnected from the proxy server.

You might want to look at a document that AT&T provides via their Anonymous FTP server. Connect to

```
research.att.com
```

and look for the file /dist/Secure_Internet_Gateway.ps. It contains PostScript data, so you'll need the right kind of printer. ■

Firewall protection any more sophisticated than what we've covered so far is beyond the scope of this book. For additional solutions, consult your Internet service provider or a network security consultant.

Approaching Secure Environments

Vendors and researchers in network technology are aware of today's security issues and are trying to find ways to address them. There are two dominant approaches to secure communications between separate systems.

One concept is to allow only specific activities between cooperating computers, and to ensure that they've agreed on all the details. Add security (such as encrypted data traffic), to which both sides must agree. For instance, a Lotus Notes client or server communicates only with a Lotus Notes server. Since both ends are the same application, they've agreed on exactly how to communicate in a secure manner. For another example, let's revisit our primitive network consisting of two cans connected by a string. For security purposes, the kids on that network decide to speak only in Pig Latin so their parents can't understand the conversation.

The second concept is to allow two computers to do whatever the heck they want, "safe" in the knowledge that they are who they say they are. This approach is in conflict with publicly accessible computers. If you allow open access by any random computer to a publicly accessible service (such as Anonymous FTP), how can you be sure you can trust the random computer to be who it says it is?

For your consideration . . .

The following rhetorical questions are intended to get you thinking about the security issues in your environment. Do you have to know in advance who's allowed to talk to you and how? Or are you willing to talk to anyone, anytime? If the latter is true, how do you do that in a secure manner? Can you add security to what's currently happening on the network? Can you build new applications that are aware and secure? Can you identify who the sender really is? Is the sender trustworthy?

We don't have all the answers, but we want you to understand that there are lots of questions.

Kerberos: Guardian or Fiend?

Project Athena at the Massachusetts Institute of Technology was dedicated to research into very large computing environments; "very large" meant thousands of computers. Kerberos was the security part of that research. Kerberos is also a protocol used by the component parts of a secured computing environment. It's a client/server environment (but isn't everything these days)?

The Kerberos master server — there's only one in your secured computing environment — provides an authentication service used for security in an internet (not The Internet, at least not yet!). Encrypted user-account information is stored in a database on the Kerberos master server, rather than in a local password file or an NIS map.

The secured computing environment needs coordinated time services so that all computers synchronize their *ticket expirations* properly. (Aha, that's a new piece of the pie: *tickets*. You'll hear more about tickets shortly.)

Playing at Casino Kerberos

Let's walk through what happens when you're running under Kerberos. Meet Barry, who likes to play roulette. One fine day, Barry knocks on the special door at the back of Casino Kerberos. (Barry types his username at a Kerberos-enabled computer.)

Barry asks the bouncer for permission to enter the secret inner casino. (Barry's computer asks the Kerberos master server for a *ticket-granting ticket,* which is permission to talk to the *ticket-granting server.*) The bouncer then asks Barry for the casino password. Barry gives the right response and is allowed in. (Barry's computer asks him for his password and uses it to verify the response from the Kerberos master server.)

Barry is happy. He goes to the cashier window and buys some gaming chips. He has a choice; the casino games all require different chips. The chips are only valid for a short time. When that time is up, his chips are worthless. (Barry's computer sends a request to the ticket-granting server requesting an *application service ticket.* These tickets have a limited lifetime.)

Barry is ready to play. He can now lose money at the casino game of his choice, as long as he uses the correct chips at the gaming table he chooses. If he wants to move to a different gaming table, he must have the correct chips or he must return to the cashier window to get them. (Barry's computer can now present the application service ticket to an application server, as permission to use the service.)

By the way, everyone in the casino speaks Pig Latin. (All communications — between Barry's computer and the Kerberos master server, between Barry's computer and the ticket-granting server, and between Barry's computer and the desired application — are encrypted.)

When all of this is in place and operating properly, Barry can be sure he's at the right table and that everyone else standing around the table is playing by the rules. (Barry knows he's talking to the computers and services that he wants to talk to, and the computers and services can be sure that Barry is who he says he is.) Everybody's happy, right?

Catch-22 at Casino Kerberos

Here's the bad news. There aren't very many wheelers and dealers (applications) that work in Casino Kerberos. If you want or need this level of security, you'll need Kerberos'ed applications. But these days you won't find any in the local software store.

Kerberos is all about a secure environment in which you can trust the computers and the users on them. The reason it hasn't taken off is because most environments aren't closed that way. Most are linked to other environments. Kerberos is complicated, and saddled with the catch-22 typical of computer science: Kerberos isn't widely deployed because there aren't many Kerberos'ed applications, and there aren't many applications because Kerberos isn't widely deployed.

In Greek mythology, Kerberos was a three-headed dog with the tail of a snake and snakes wrapped around his neck; he guarded the entrance to Hades. If you got past Kerberos, you were in hell. For the time being, we have to wonder if this is what MIT intended.

We're CERTainly Interested in Security

CERT, the Computer Emergency Response Team, helps organizations defend themselves from attacks. The people at CERT also maintain information on the security weaknesses of operating systems and applications, and how to repair them. We recommend you look through their Anonymous FTP archive at ftp.cert.org. ■

Chapter 19

For Programmers Only

- -

In This Chapter

▶ Sockets, but no wrenches

▶ The usefulness of Remote Procedure Calls

▶ No, repeat *no* code samples!

- -

*L*et's get one thing straight right now: You won't learn how to program in this chapter. Nor will you learn how to program TCP/IP applications. What you *will* learn about are two important facilities that you need in order to program with TCP/IP. But we're not going to teach you how to implement a new TCP/IP service, or build a TCP/IP client, or port the TCP/IP protocol suite to a new operating system. If you're disappointed in this agenda, check out the book list at the end of the chapter.

Unless you're familiar with at least one programming language — almost any one will do — you might want to skip this chapter. ▪

Still with us? Great! That means either you can already program, or you're adventurous.

In either case, get set — in this chapter we're going to cover *TCP/IP sockets, and RPCs (Remote Procedure Calls).* They're the flour, sugar, and eggs in the batter of TCP/IP applications, especially of those clients and servers you've heard so much about.

And by the way, before we forget, TCP/IP sockets are *software,* not hardware. A TCP/IP socket is not something you tighten with a wrench from your toolbox, or an electrical outlet on the wall, or a place where you put the lightbulb in a lamp (see Figure 19-1).

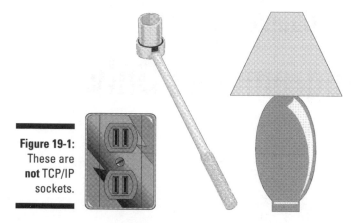

Figure 19-1:
These are
not TCP/IP
sockets.

What You Should Already Know

This section contains brief explanations of some programming terms and skills you should already have under your belt in order to make the best use of this chapter.

Functions and Libraries: To write TCP/IP applications, your programming skills must include knowledge of *functions.* Just in case you don't know about them, functions are reusable pieces of programs. You can write your own functions, or use the ones supplied by the operating system on which you run your program. An operating system's functions are stored in libraries. Some operating systems (DOS, OS/2, Microsoft Windows NT Server and Workstation, Windows 95, Macintosh) use the term *dynamic link libraries (DLLs).* Most folks pronounce DLL by saying the letters *D L L*; others pronounce it "dill," like the herb.

API: You should also be familiar with API, Application Programming Interface (pronounced by saying the letters *A P I*). An API describes the interfaces your program must use to call library functions. The TCP/IP API (provided as part of the TCP/IP software) provides some additional DLLs and a wide range of functions for you to call as part of your TCP/IP application. Every client and server program we've mentioned in this book (telnet, FTP, DNS, and so forth) calls the TCP/IP API's functions and DLLs.

Imagine an unfinished jigsaw puzzle. As shown in Figure 19-2, the pieces that are already interlocked (the DLLs) have a distinctive edge (the API), to which the missing pieces (your program) must attach.

Parameters: When your program calls a function, it must receive output, and it may need to furnish some input. This is done with *parameters.* The function also returns one value. Parameters make functions useful to many different applications. For each function, the API description tells you the following requirements:

- ✔ How many parameters must be used with that function
- ✔ The order in which the parameters must appear
- ✔ The data type of each parameter (for example, integer or character string)

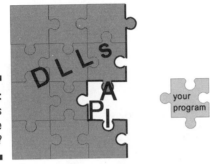

Figure 19-2:
Where does
this piece
fit?

The syntax of a function call looks something like this:

```
result = function (parameter1, parameter2)
```

Note: The above isn't code. We promised you there wouldn't be any code, and we meant it.

Here's an example of how parameters work: The TCP/IP API provides a function called *gethostbyname*. This function takes one parameter, a character string containing the name of a computer. If the computer's name and address information is in the local hosts file, or the NIS, or the DNS, then the function returns the computer's numeric IP address. If the function cannot find the computer name and address information, it returns a null value.

The TCP/IP API provides a multitude of functions. We are not going to describe them all here. We are not even going to list them. You can look them up in a book on TCP/IP programming or possibly the documentation for your TCP/IP software. ■

Sockets for Baseball Players

A network application links two computers that want to communicate, so they need a connection over which to exchange data. In TCP/IP (and some other network protocols, too) this connection is called a *socket*. Like its metal counterpart, a TCP/IP socket is a holder for something — in this case, an end-point for the connection. So it takes two sockets, one at each computer, to establish the two-way link that all communication requires.

In Figure 19-3, the pitcher and catcher are both using TCP/IP sockets: their baseball gloves. (Though the pitcher's glove is different from the catcher's mitt, we don't mean to imply any difference in the TCP/IP sockets.)

socket

Figure 19-3:
A TCP/IP
socket
helps your
computer
catch
incoming
TCP/IP
fastballs.

socket

At any given time, a computer may be communicating with any number of TCP/IP applications on any number of other computers. One socket is required for each of the connections. Each computer keeps track of the sockets it is using. Each socket contains

✔ The numeric IP address of the local computer
✔ The local port number
✔ The port number of the TCP/IP service on the remote computer

(See Chapter 16 for more information about port numbers.)

Play ball!

Here's an overview of what happens behind the scenes when you start a TCP/IP client and ask it to connect to a remote service.

1. Your client — that is, the TCP/IP application running on your computer — creates a socket that is used for the duration of the connection. The socket has a number that is unique on your computer. (Your client on Frodo says, "I need another socket for my next communication with the server application running on Bilbo. I already know my IP address. For the socket, I'll select my port number 9876; it's currently available.")

2. Your client on Frodo sends a connection request to the server application on Bilbo, asking to use the remote service. The request includes Bilbo's numeric IP address, the port number of the requested service, and the local socket number. ("Hey, Bilbo. It's me, Frodo. I want to talk to your service on port number 1234. Answer me on my port number 9876. Okay?")

3. The server application on Bilbo creates a socket, which it uses for the duration of the connection. That socket has a number that is unique on the server. (Bilbo says, "I'll answer Frodo. I already know my IP address and he wants to use my port number 1234. Frodo said to answer on his port 9876.")

4. The server application on Bilbo sends back an acknowledgment that comes to Frodo's IP address and to the socket that was created. ("Hello, Frodo. This is Bilbo speaking. I got your request to use my service on my port number 1234, and I'm answering you on your port 9876.")

5. Now that two-way communication is established, the client application on Frodo can use the service provided on Bilbo. ("Hey, Bilbo. It's me, Frodo. Got any pitchers you want to trade?" "Hello, Frodo. This is Bilbo speaking. Forget it. Try the farm teams!")

Once you're done with the remote service and you tell Frodo to disconnect, another conversation takes place behind the scenes. Frodo tells Bilbo that you're all done. The connection is closed, and both client and server applications recycle the sockets.

The TCP/IP Vendors Play Soft (ware) ball

The TCP/IP API has all the functions you need for creating sockets, opening and closing connections, and sending and receiving data. This extensive programming library was originally developed at the University of California at Berkeley as part of the development of UNIX and TCP/IP itself.

As vendors brought TCP/IP to other operating systems, they incorporated the sockets API, so that programmers like you could write new TCP/IP applications.

WinSock comes up to bat

The story is a little different for Microsoft Windows, however. At first, the TCP/IP vendors were more interested in delivering the protocol suite and the client applications than they were in delivering the API on Microsoft Windows. Finally, Microsoft and several key vendors got together and created the WinSock API. (WinSock is short for Windows Sockets.)

There are now over 30 vendors involved in the creation of the WinSock API specification. They have common goals for the WinSock API, including:

- ✔ To simplify the porting of UNIX applications to the Windows and Windows NT environments. This means all the familiar library routines are provided, and they work the same way as on UNIX.

- ✔ To provide a vendor-independent TCP/IP transport service. This means applications shouldn't know or care which vendor's TCP/IP product is installed.

If your TCP/IP for Windows product is WinSock compliant, you have the file WINSOCK.DLL on your computer. If you don't have this file, then the product is not WinSock compliant. (Or you don't have TCP/IP installed. But let's assume that you do, and it's not WinSock compliant.) Don't panic. Your client applications, such as telnet and FTP, will still work the way they should, but you will probably have trouble running other applications that want to use the TCP/IP protocols. Contact your TCP/IP vendor and ask when the product will be WinSock compliant. If you don't like the answer, you can always change to another TCP/IP product from another vendor. ■

It's early in the season for the WinSock team

The WinSock API doesn't come from a standards organization such as ANSI or ISO. It is designed by a consortium of TCP/IP vendors, and based on the Berkeley UNIX programming library. The specifications are public. That's the good news. The bad news is that parts of the specifications are not as precisely worded as they could be. The result is that not all vendors' implementations of the WinSock API work exactly the same way.

Interested in Seeing the WinSock Specs?

The specifications for Windows Sockets are available on The Internet from Microsoft's Anonymous FTP server:

```
ftp.microsoft.com in the directory /advsys/winsock/spec11
```

By the way, this Anonymous FTP server also holds Microsoft's TCP/IP product, Microsoft TCP/IP-32 for Windows for Workgroups.

Want to Be on WinSock's Mailing List?

There are three Internet mailing lists for the WinSock API. To be added to a list, send e-mail to

```
listserv@sunsite.unc.edu
```

The subject line doesn't matter. Put one or all of these commands in the message body, supplying your own e-mail address where indicated:

```
subscribe winsock your_email_address
subscribe winsock-hackers your_email_address
subscribe winsock-users your_email_address
```

Fortunately, the situation continues to improve as vendors release newer versions of their products. You may never see a problem at all, but if you do, contact the vendor or change to another product.

Calling All Procedures, Calling All Procedures. Come In, Procedures...

The TCP/IP API is an important set of programming tools, but it contains only the starting pieces for creating network applications. Sometimes you need more and larger components for your programming toolkit. Every time you want a glass of water, you shouldn't have to build it from hydrogen and oxygen. So it's *Remote Procedure Calls (RPCs)* to the rescue. (RPC is pronounced by saying the letters *R P C.*)

As the programmers at Sun Microsystems worked to develop NFS, the Network File System (see Chapter 10), they also created Remote Procedure Calls. RPCs are similar to the TCP/IP API library functions — but with an RPC, the calling program and the called routine can be on different computers! This concept is the heart of client/server applications.

As a user of TCP/IP clients and servers, you don't ever have to think about RPCs. As a programmer, however, you'll work with them often. You'll usually call the RPCs provided with the operating systems for which you write applications, but you can also create your own.

When RPCs are at work, the behind-the-scenes communication between a client and server is similar to what happens with sockets as described earlier, but the communication is optimized for better performance. The server is always waiting for incoming requests and must handle them as quickly as possible. The users, on NFS clients, are accessing files and directories stored on the NFS server as if those resources were local.

The UDP versus TCP controversy

In Chapter 6 you learned all about the protocols, including UDP, the User Datagram Protocol, and TCP, the Transmission Control Protocol. RPC communication can be carried by either of these protocols.

UDP messages are smaller and more efficient than TCP messages. UDP does not provide error checking or guarantee delivery, but these operations are handled by the applications. TCP, on the other hand, does provide these controls so that the applications don't have to — but that means the TCP messages are bigger and may be less efficient. This difference is the basis for a classic debate about small versus fast. Many of the TCP/IP services are now implemented both ways.

Ready for More?

For further exploration into the world of TCP/IP programming, you'll want to visit a bookstore and head straight for the computer section. For your convenience, we are listing a few books with which we have some experience, but we don't really intend any strong endorsement of these. Neither do we mean to imply anything negative regarding any book that's not on this list.

UNIX Network Programming by W. Richard Stevens. ISBN 0-13-949876-1. Published by Prentice Hall, Inc.

Internetworking with TCP/IP: Principles, Protocols, and Architecture by Douglas Comer. ISBN 0-13-470154-2. Published by Prentice Hall, Inc.

The Design and Implementation of the 4.3 BSD UNIX Operating System by Samuel J. Leffler, Marshall Kirk McKusick, Michael J. Karels, and John S. Quarterman. ISBN 0-201-06196-1. Published by Addison-Wesley Publishing Company.

The C Programming Language by Brian W. Kernigan and Dennis M. Ritchie. ISBN 0-13-110163-3. Published by Prentice Hall, Inc.

Programming in C by Stephen G. Kochan. ISBN 0-672-48420-X. Published by Hayden Books.

C Primer Plus by Mitchell Waite, Stephen Prata, and Donald Martin. ISBN 0-672-22090-3. Published by Howard W. Sams & Co., Inc.

Part IV
The Part of Tens

The 5th Wave   **By Rich Tennant**

"IT TURNED OUT TO BE A TWO HOUR LECTURE ON A NEW COMMUNICATIONS PROTOCOL."

In This Part...

At the network buffet, these chapters are the TCP/IP nuggets, with your choice of dipping sauce. Tasty little morsels of trivia and silliness with some valuable information thrown in for flavor.

As you work through Part IV, you may notice that ten does not always equal 10 — that's computer math for you . . .. Are we talking decimal numbers or binary? Hex, maybe? In octal, 10 means 8. In binary it means 2, and in hexadecimal it means 16. We reserve the right to count in whatever base we like.

Chapter 20

Ten Types of Networks That Use TCP/IP

In This Chapter

▶ "Ether" the packets collide or they don't.

▶ You need a token to ride *this* network.

▶ Ask a Psychic Friend what kind of network you need.

TCP/IP runs over most of the networks listed in this chapter. It's one of the strengths of TCP/IP: independence — in this case, cabling independence.

Television

You're probably familiar with several different television networks: ABC, NBC, CBS, ZDF, CANAL+, Fox, and many more. (Fox is the only one that named a series character after the network — Fox Mulder in *The X Files.*) What you may *not* know is that, if you have cable TV, you may be watching these networks on the same kind of connection media that facilitate TCP/IP.

Daisy Chain

Daisy chaining is a way to connect computers and network devices. In a daisy chain arrangement, device 1 is chained to device 2, which is chained to device 3, and so on and so forth. One of the most common daisy chain network types works with devices called *hubs,* or *concentrators*. The computers connect to the hubs, and the hubs are daisy chained.

Figure 20-1 shows daisy-chained hubs.

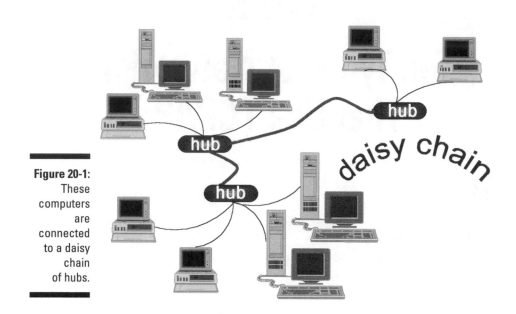

Figure 20-1:
These
computers
are
connected
to a daisy
chain
of hubs.

Ethernet

Ethernet is probably the most popular TCP/IP network technology in the world. It is an international standard, designated by the IEEE as 802.3. IEEE is pronounced "eye triple e" and stands for Institute for Electrical and Electronic Engineers.

Ethernet uses CSMA/CD (Carrier Sense Multiple Access/Collision Detection) transmission strategy. When you take apart this fancy terminology, you find a pretty simple concept:

- The CS (Carrier Sense) is about the signal that goes on the wire.

- The MA (Multiple Access) means that all hosts can send data across the wire whenever they want. They don't have to take turns.

- The CD (Collision Detection) part helps out the MA part. Because the hosts don't have to take turns, sometimes they try to send at the same time and bump into one another. So, with CD, you have a lot of "After you!" "No, after you!" politeness protocol. When there is a collision, the hosts try again at different times. In other words, when data is transmitted onto the cable, all the hosts get the signal at the same time. The host who is supposed to get the message grabs it from the cable, and all the other hosts ignore it.

The bottom line: A lot of The Internet is Ethernet, and TCP/IP runs on it.

Token Ring

Token ring is probably the second most popular TCP/IP networking technology. Like Ethernet, token ring is a wiring-and-access strategy, and it is an international standard, IEEE 802.5.

Token ring technology's principle difference from Ethernet is that token ring makes the hosts take turns transmitting. A token moves past each host on the cable until a host grabs the token. The host that wants to send data actually modifies the token, saying, "This token is mine. No one else can send now." Once the host sends its message, it modifies the token to "OK for someone else to send." The token travels along the cable waiting to be used by a host that wants to send a message. This way, there are no collisions to detect.

Token ring networks, too, are connected to The Internet, and TCP/IP runs on them, as well.

LAN

A local area network (LAN) can be founded on various technologies, such as Ethernet and token ring. Whatever the technology, a LAN operates over short distances (no more than a few miles) at high-speed data rates (from 2 to 100 megabits per second, depending on how crowded your LAN is). You can connect multiple LANs to make an even bigger network, known as a WAN.

WAN

A wide area network (WAN) can connect computers spanning the world and beyond. To communicate, WANs use long-distance connections such as telephone lines and satellite links. The Internet — the world's most famous WAN — is actually a combination of LANs and WANs.

Because their hardware requirements are different, LANs and WANs work differently at the data link layer, but we don't care because both use IP at the internet layer. IP thoughtfully hides from us the dreaded hardware specifics at the data link layer.

Wireless

Is this the two-tin-cans-and-a-piece-of-string network? Close . . . but no, it's not. Instead of a piece of string (the wire/cable), wireless networks use radio or infrared waves, as well as lasers and microwaves, as connection media.

Don't worry — if you heat up your coffee in the microwave oven, you'll ruin the flavor of the coffee, but you won't be sending it across the network (although there *is* a coffee pot connected to The Internet; see Chapter 24).

A wireless network isn't really totally wireless. For example, you can have a bunch of Ethernet LANs hooked together by wireless technology into a WAN, giving rise to the famous proverb, "No LAN is an isLANd."

Old Boy

Unfortunately, even as we strive to be gender-unspecific and politically correct, the Old Boy network still exists — although a few of the "old boys" these days are women. And if the old boys, male or female, are network savvy, they may chat via IRC and TCP/IP.

Psychic Friends

If you have cable TV and keep odd hours or have insomnia, you surely know about the Psychic Friends network. We're not sure their crystal ball is working, though, because they didn't let us know how long it would take to write this book. And if they're really psychic, why do they need TV? We suspect psychic waves travel over TCP/IP like most everything else — even if the crystal ball readers won't admit it.

Chapter 21
Ten RFCs Worth Tasting

In This Chapter

▶ Getting answers to commonly asked questions about The Internet

▶ How to register your network with the InterNIC

▶ Who's in charge? Or at least important enough to have a biography in an RFC?

▶ What do Martians think of TCP/IP?

▶ What is The Internet, anyway? If you don't know yet, here is the definitive answer.

*T*he RFC process described in Chapter 2 is the cornerstone of TCP/IP and of Internet development and growth. There are over 1,750 RFCs, and many of them function as excellent sleep aids — but the ones we've listed in this chapter and the next are of at least marginal interest.

Since The Internet and TCP/IP are so closely intertwined, many RFCs here in Chapter 21 refer to the protocols as well as to the Net. Chapter 22 lists ten more RFCs, which relate strictly to the TCP/IP protocol suite.

There are various ways to get RFCs. We connected to a public FTP server and used Anonymous FTP, as illustrated in Figure 21-1. RFCs are also available via Gopher on the World Wide Web; via ftpmail; and sometimes even by regular mail.

Appendix A tells you how to get the current list of all the RFCs that are available. For some strange and funny ones, get the RFC index and look for the RFCs dated April 1. ■

The Hitchhiker's Guide

RFC 1118: The Hitchhiker's Guide to the Internet. This RFC was written to help new Internauts understand how The Internet came to be and where it's going. You'll also find guidance on how to find online information about using The Internet and being a good Interneighbor. It's an excellent introduction for newcomers to TCP/IP, as well, because the development of The Internet and TCP/IP are symbiotic.

```
$ ftp nic.ddn.mil
Connected to nic.ddn.mil.
220-*****Welcome to the DOD Network Information Center*****
     *****Login with username "anonymous" and password "guest"
     *****You may change directories to the following:
       ddn-news          - DDN Management Bulletins
       domain            - Root Zone Files
       gosip             - DOD GOSIP Registration and Information
       internet-drafts   - Internet Drafts
       netinfo           - NIC Information Files
       rfc               - RFC Repository
       scc               - DDN Security Bulletins
       std               - Internet Protocol Standards
220 And more!
Name (nic.ddn.mil:leiden): anonymous
331-Please be advised that all INTERNET Domain, IP Network Number, and ASN
       records are now kept at the Internet Registry, RS.INTERNIC.NET.
       Please also be advised that better serving RFC repositories exist
       for internet users. Get file, "netinfo/ways_to_get_rfcs" and
       RFC 1400 for more details.
331 Guest login ok, send "guest" as password.
Password:
230 Guest login ok, access restrictions apply.
Remote system type is UNIX.
Using binary mode to transfer files.
Ftp> cd rfc
250 CWD command successful.
Ftp>
```

Figure 21-1:
You can find all the RFCs at nic.ddn.mil and many other sites.

How Do I . . . ?

RFC 1594: FYI On Questions and Answers — Answers to Commonly Asked "New Internet User" Questions. If you're new to The Internet and you have a question, read this RFC. Odds are good your question has already been asked and answered.

RFC 1594 is a special type of RFC called an FYI (For Your Information). Rather than a proposed standard or a comment on a proposal, an FYI's purpose is to inform and educate. RFC 1594 is also known as FYI 4.

What Is a . . . ?

RFC 1208: A Glossary of Networking Terms. Do you want to know more about routers, protocols, cables? Some of the simpler terms, such as modem, are not included in this RFC, but many of the terms we use in Chapter 17 are listed.

Who's in Charge?

RFC 1251: Who's Who In the Internet. If you want to know who's who in The Internet, this RFC has biographies of members of The Internet Activities

Board (IAB), Internet Engineering Steering Group (IESG), and Internet Research Steering Group (IRSG). If you only read about one person, be sure to read "father of The Internet" Vinton Cerf's biography. RFC 1251 is also known as FYI 9.

What's in a Name? Plenty.

RFC 1178: Choosing a Name for Your Computer. A lot of you think it's more important to spend time choosing a name for your dog than for your computer (and some of us agree with you). However, when you are ready to settle down to the task of picking your computer's moniker, and you plan to connect to The Internet, this RFC offers some important do's and don'ts. For instance, you don't want to pick something that's similar to NIC, or you'll get enough "wrong number" e-mail to fill up your hard disk. Similarly, you'll want to avoid names such as mail, ftp, gopher, and www.

RFC 1178, also known as FYI 5, was originally published as an article in *Communications of the ACM,* a prestigious computer science journal.

An Apple a Day

RFC 1742: AppleTalk Management Information Base. If anything can prove that TCP/IP is not just for UNIX, this is it. RFC 1742 is about Macintosh computers and the AppleTalk protocol. Written by the AppleTalk/IP Working Group, it's about using AppleTalk objects with TCP/IP's Simple Network Management Protocol.

How Do I Get Connected?

RFC 1400: Transition and Modernization of the Internet Registration Service. RFC 1400 identifies the latest form to fill out and a new telephone number to call to get your site's network registered with the InterNIC, so that you can connect your private internet (or computer) to The Internet. We say "the latest" and "new" because The Internet and all its related parts are constantly growing and changing; what's true today may be different tomorrow — see the sidebar, "How to Get a Copy of an RFC by Regular Mail (Maybe)." If you want to register with the InterNIC, be sure to study the entire RFC and any RFCs that might supersede it by the time you read it.

If you're not registered yet, you can get this RFC by ftpmail, from a friend or colleague with Internet access, from an Internet service provider (especially one that you're considering using for access), and maybe even by regular mail (see sidebar).

Trust No One?

RFC 1244: Site Security Handbook. This RFC has some guidelines in managing security for computers on The Internet. It's a good beginning for network administrators and security officers to use in creating their organizations' policies and procedures.

This RFC is oriented toward security practices in the United States. If you're managing a network elsewhere, the ideas and concepts in this RFC are useful, but many of the resources listed are only available in the U.S. ■

Some of the topics in RFC 1244 include the following:

✔ Why have security policies?

✔ Overview of instituting security policies and procedures

✔ Deciding what resources need to be protected

✔ What to do if security policies are violated

✔ Monitoring unauthorized activity and break-ins

✔ Responses to unauthorized activity and break-ins

How to Get a Copy of an RFC by Regular Mail (Maybe)

You may notice that we have not told you how to get an RFC sent to you by regular mail (that is, via the Postal Service). On the day we wrote this chapter, we had a published telephone number of a service you could call and order RFCs by mail. We called the number to check it out and were told that as of the previous day, the service no longer existed, and there had been no decision made about a replacement service. How's that for timing?

The bottom line is that we have no phone number to give you to get RFCs by mail. One of the challenges of writing, speaking, and teaching about TCP/IP today is the brisk rate at which everything is changing. TCP/IP is in transition mode, with major work being done on the new address formats and the next generation of IP. Many of the procedures are also changing.

The Truth Is Out There

RFC 1462: What Is the Internet? This is another FYI-type RFC, also known as FYI 20. It's written by the User Services Working Group of The Internet Engineering Task Force (IETF); this group comprises more of those good-hearted people we mentioned in Chapter 2. Although there is no definitive answer to the question "What is The Internet?", this RFC is the best we've got. It discusses the Net's three components:

- ✔ The network of networks connected by TCP/IP
- ✔ The people who develop and use those networks
- ✔ The software, files, and documents available on those networks

This RFC also discusses commercial opportunities on The Internet. Commercialization of the Net is one of the hottest Internet topics today, and this RFC has some information about the origins and directions of commercial use.

A View from Mars

RFC 1607: A View from the 21st Century. This RFC is really entertaining. It's written by Vinton Cerf (Big Daddy of The Internet) as a series of letters from someone working on Mars, circa 2023. You'll find it a humorous treatment of the history of Internet growth as it might appear to people in the not-so-distant future. Some of Cerf's comments about The Internet running out of addresses are very funny, especially in light of the work being done on IPng and the new IP address space. We will be dealing with *that* headache soon enough.

Chapter 22

Ten RFCs about the TCP/IP Suite (The Dish Ran Away with the Spoon)

. . . .

In This Chapter

▶ Getting hold of the really technical details about the protocols

▶ How to get practical information about using TCP/IP applications

▶ How to get practical network administration information

▶ What's on the IP plate for the future?

. . . .

*C*ables, telephone lines, fiber optics, and satellites are the physical spine of the Internet, but the TCP/IP protocol suite is truly The Internet's nervous system. And for TCP/IP, the RFCs are the equivalent of Gray's Anatomy. They range from handbooks with practical information about managing TCP/IP, to extremely detailed descriptions of the protocols, to entertaining humor and silliness. In this chapter you'll find pointers to practical management RFCs and protocol specifications.

For each protocol that we listed in Chapter 6, there is an RFC that defines the standard. After reading this book and examining this chapter, if you're hungry for the highly technical details that are available for the protocols, read the RFCs. We have pointed you to some of them in this chapter.

Appendix A tells you how to get the current list of all the RFCs that are available. ■

Planning the TCP/IP Banquet

RFC 1000: *The Request for Comments Reference Guide.* This RFC is historical. It tells a tale of the birth of the protocols and how the RFC process came to be. It also lists the various categories in which an RFC may be classified, because not all RFCs define standards.

Nitty-Gritty TCP

RFC 793: *Transmission Control Protocol.* If you're the type who lives for the really technical stuff, don't read a book. Go to the source: Read the RFC.

RFC 793 documents TCP itself. The information is quite technical. It includes the TCP header format; how TCP interfaces with the network layers above and below it; how TCP implements reliable delivery; packet resequencing; and recovery of lost and damaged packets.

See also RFC 1122. ■

Nitty-Gritty IP

RFC 791: *Internet Protocol.* As described above for TCP, this RFC contains the really technical stuff about IP. So don't bother with a book — go to the source and read the RFC.

RFC 791 spells out how Internet *datagrams* (packages of bits) are delivered from the source host to the destination; how the IP layers at both source and destination interpret an IP address; and how datagrams may be fragmented and reassembled as part of the delivery process between IP layers.

See also RFC 1122, just below. ■

The Basics: Plate, Spoon, and Fork in One Setting

RFC 1122: *Requirements for Internet Hosts — Communication Layers.* This RFC discusses what goes on at the data link, IP, and transport layers of the network model. You get a walkthrough of how the lower-layer protocols work, including IP, TCP, ARP, ICMP, and UDP. The requirements in this RFC were published to help vendors implementing TCP/IP software understand how the protocols work together.

RFC 1122 is a companion to RFCs 793 and 791. ■

The Accessories That Make It Fun

RFC 1123: Requirements for Internet Hosts — Application and Support. This very technical RFC is all about the protocols, services, and applications that reside on the upper layers of the network layer cake: DNS, telnet, SMTP, FTP, and TFTP.

In Chapter 7 you read about how e-mail works with the Simple Mail Transfer Protocol (SMTP) and SMTP gateways. If you're interested in the inner workings of e-mail and want to know more, this RFC walks through the circuitry of SMTP, including data structures and algorithms.

Just to prove that RFCs do not live by technical bread alone, one whimsical topic in this RFC is "Sorcerer's Apprentice Syndrome." ■

How to Get Invited to All the Best Places

RFC 1635: How to Use Anonymous FTP. For the majority of users, file transfer is the meat of TCP/IP, and this document is for FTP novices. It describes FTP in general and has a tutorial for using Anonymous FTP. It also lists the various file-compression methods used to store FTP archives efficiently on disk, and explains how to decompress those compressed files once you get them. This RFC is the product of a joint venture from a group consisting of members of the academic community and some hardware vendors.

Many RFCs provide practical, how-to hints. RFC 1635 is an example of the tutorial-type information that can be found in many RFCs. ■

The Cookbook

RFC 1180: A TCP/IP Tutorial. This is a technical tutorial explaining the step-by-step path followed by an IP datagram as it moves from the source host to the destination via a router. If you're writing a TCP/IP application or implementation, this RFC is invaluable. ■

Beware of Eating Soup with a Fork

RFC 768: User Datagram Protocol. This RFC explains why UDP has less overhead than TCP: Since UDP doesn't guarantee the delivery of your bits, it doesn't do as much verification and checking as TCP does. You'd need a pretty thick data soup to guarantee that no bits fell off the UDP fork. In fact, this RFC recommends using TCP when reliable delivery is required.

RFC 768 is the standard specification for UDP, so there is plenty of very techie information in here, including the user datagram header format and the difference between datagram format and packet format. ■

Advice for Subnetters

RFC 1219: On the Assignment of Subnet Numbers. If you think our subnet explanation in Chapter 13 is complicated, and you're not subnetting anyway, don't bother with this RFC. On the other hand, if you are managing subnetted networks, you may find RFC 1219 interesting. It suggests procedures for assigning subnet numbers within your organization's main network.

This RFC is a comment on RFC 950, the standard for subnet masks.

Hire a Caterer to Manage the Whole Meal

RFC 1147: FYI on A Network Management Tool Catalog: Tools for Monitoring and Debugging TCP/IP Internets and Interconnected Devices. This RFC contains practical information for network administrators. It catalogs several tools for network management and performance monitoring and tells where to get them. Most of the tools are public domain (free), and FTP sites are listed. Our favorite tool name in here is SpiderMonitor.

This RFC dates from 1990. Some of the tools may have become obsolete or moved to different locations. Nevertheless, it's still a good source of information for network administrators. ■

Nouvelle Cuisine

RFC 1752: The Recommendation for the IP Next Generation Protocol.
What's new on the TCP/IP menu? IPng! There's a whole new addressing style
cooking out there, and this is one of the RFCs about it.

Be careful, though. IPng beat out several other proposed solutions, but all of
their RFCs live on. If you're browsing information about IPng, make sure you
look at the winning solution and not the also-rans. ■

Chapter 23

Ten Frequently Asked Questions about TCP/IP and The Internet

• •

In This Chapter

▶ TCP/IP software for eunuchs . . . er, UNIX

▶ There's "on the internet" and there's "On The Internet"

▶ Specials rates for news subscribers

▶ A few useful e-mail addresses

• •

*T*his chapter contains straightforward answers to some common questions. In some cases, the discussion is a summary of chapters you've already read — unless you're still standing in the bookstore and haven't bought this book yet! (If that's you and you like what you see here, just wait until you spend some time in the other chapters . . .)

What Software Do I Need to Get on The Internet?

TCP/IP. That's all you need to get on the Net. For actually working and navigating on The Internet, you may need some additional software. The TCP/IP protocol suite includes FTP and telnet client applications. If you want some of the fancier tools, such as Archie or Mosaic, check with your TCP/IP vendor. Some TCP/IP products include them and some do not. If you don't get the tools you want from your vendor, you can use FTP to transfer most of them from other Internet sites.

Do I Need UNIX to Run TCP/IP?

Absolutely not. The reason TCP/IP supports The Internet is that TCP/IP runs on practically any operating system. Yes, it started out on UNIX back in the early days, but it has migrated everywhere. You can count on UNIX to include TCP/IP, and many other operating systems are starting to do this as well. Did you pay attention to the examples in this book? Some of them were done on various UNIX systems, and some were done on assorted PC client and server operating systems.

How Do I Get on The Internet?

Register your network. Contact The Internet Registry (IR), an organization that assigns and registers IP network numbers. It is part of the InterNIC, and is referred to as *registration services (rs)*. This part of the InterNIC is located at

Network Solutions, Inc.
505 Huntmar Park Drive
Herndon, VA 22070 USA
703-742-4777

The IR also delegates some authority to regional registries (such as ncc@ripe.net and apnic-staff@apnic.net).

Can I Get on The Internet If I Don't Have a Network?

Sure. You can pay an Internet access provider to be a part of its network. In fact, this is the best solution small businesses and for you as an individual or for your family.

Look for advertisements for Internet access providers in many computer-related magazines and some daily newspapers. In typical catch-22 style, how-ever, the best lists of providers are maintained on The Internet! One such list for the northeastern United States is available on the World Wide Web. With a Web browser, access this URL:

```
http://www.pn.com/providers.html
```

Actually, this isn't really a catch-22 when you consider than many people have Internet access at work or school and now want it at home. Other folks are considering changing service providers and need to know about their options.

How Do I Get a Usenet News Feed?

If your system manager or network administrator has already set up a Usenet news feed, all you need is a newsreader client, like the ones mentioned in Chapter 7.

If you don't have access to a Usenet news feed, you have a little more work to do. First, get Usenet server software, which is available for many operating systems via Anonymous FTP. You also need to find an existing Usenet site that is willing to support a connection to your computer. Often, this "connection" is nothing more than some extra traffic over existing Internet access channels.

One well-known Anonymous FTP archive site that has the software you need, as well as more information about Usenet, is ftp.uu.net. Look for a news directory that contains subdirectories for the software. ∎

To Get a Newsgroup, Do I Need to Subscribe?

No. There is no "subscription" mechanism per se. The NNTP server either gets the newsgroup from a neighboring server or it doesn't. If you want a particular newsgroup that the server doesn't get, ask the system manager or network administrator to try to get it.

If your newsreader does use the terms *subscribed* and *unsubscribed,* they are merely declarations of whether or not you want to see the articles that have been posted to the newsgroup. Your interests are sure to change over time; this way you can easily tell your newsreader not to bother showing you some newsgroups (unsubscribed) and to concentrate on the ones you want (subscribed).

News.announce.newusers is a good newsgroup to start with, since it helps new users get oriented to The Internet.

If you're also interested in traditional newspaper and magazine articles — which are altogether different from Usenet news articles — that will help you learn about Internet topics, don't neglect the computer section of your local bookstores and newsstands. For example, try publications such as *Internet World* and *Online Access.* ∎

Can I Send Mail to Other Networks Besides The Internet?

Several networks are accessible via e-mail from The Internet, but many of these networks do not use the same addressing that's used on The Internet. Often you must route mail to these through specific gateways, as well, thus further complicating the address. Following are a few conventions you can use for sending e-mail from The Internet to users on certain networks.

From Internet to Internet

```
username@hostname.subdomain.toplevel.domain
```

For example:

```
marshall_wilensky@crd.lotus.com
leiden@tiac.net
```

From Internet to BITNET

```
user%site.BITNET@BITNETgateway
```

For example:

```
pebbles%bedrock.BITNET@cunyvm.cuny.edu
pebbles%bedrock@cornellc.cit.cornell.edu
```

where cunyvm.cuny.edu and cornellc.cit.cornell.edu are running BITNET-to-Internet gateways.

From Internet to UUCP

Depending on your setup, use one of the following:

```
user%host.UUCP@uunet.uu.net
user%domain@uunet.uu.net
```

From Internet to SprintMail

Depending on your setup, use one of the following:

```
/G=Yogi/S=Bear/O=co.abc/ADMD=SprintMail/C=US/@SPRINT.COM
/PN=Yogi.Bear/O=co.abc/ADMD=SprintMail/C=US/@SPRINT.COM
```

The above examples are case sensitive. Personally, we'd rather call Sprint-Mail users on the telephone than try to type in these addresses! ∎

From Internet to CompuServe

Replace the comma in the user's CompuServe ID (represented in the example with *x*'s) with a period, and add the compuserve.com domain name.

```
xxxxx.xxx@compuserve.com
```

For example, this address was published in *People* magazine as actor Ed Asner's:

```
72726.357@compuserve.com
```

From Internet to MCIMail

These syntax formats are all equivalent:

```
accountname@mcimail.com
mci_id@mcimail.com
full_user_name@mcimail.com
```

Can I Use TCP/IP with Novell NetWare?

Most NetWare clients access NetWare file servers by means of Novell's SPX/IPX protocol, but TCP/IP can be used in addition or instead. The NetWare server administrator must first install a TCP/IP product such as Novell's NetWare IP.

Using TCP/IP, What Computers Can I Connect Together?

All of them. Well, almost all of them. Definitely all the ones we know of that you can buy today. TCP/IP products exist for every well-known model and operating system on the market. For some old, obsolete computers, however, TCP/IP solutions may not be available.

Who Owns The Internet?

No single organization owns or controls the entire Internet. At home, you own your computer. Schools, companies, and other organizations own the computers and networks at their locations. The companies that provide connections to The Internet own the pieces that make up their service offerings. All of these interconnected pieces form The Internet and benefit us all.

See also "Who Owns TCP/IP?" in Chapter 2.

Chapter 24

Ten Strange but Real TCP/IP Network Devices (No Kidding!)

· ·

In This Chapter

▶ Thirsty or hungry? Check the Internet pantry.

▶ Sleepless in Seattle? Check the traffic and drive around town.

▶ Not everything on The Internet is a host.

▶ Just because you can do a thing, doesn't mean that you should. There are some mighty strange things connected to The Internet.

· ·

*T*his chapter offers some fun stuff on the Internet — a few that are down-right silly — for you to check out. Although you can access the devices in this chapter with any World Wide Web browser, it's almost certain that you'll be happier with graphical browsers such as Mosaic or Netscape. (In Chapter 12 you saw some Netscape screens.)

To get to the appropriate Web page, just type in the URL (Universal Resource Locator; see the "Duke of URL" sidebar in Chapter 12). You can also use other TCP/IP applications and services, such as telnet and finger, to play with these toys. Don't forget that things change rapidly on the Internet, so some of these devices may have taken a powder or may be hanging out elsewhere.

Soda Machine

Engineering students are a thirsty bunch and don't like making unsuccessful forays for quenching, so they have a long-standing tradition of hooking vend-ing machines to the network. That's right — in addition to the one we told you about at Carnegie Mellon University (Chapter 14), there are several soda machines on The Internet. They can be examined by various clients, including finger, telnet, and even Web browsers. Figure 24-1 shows the status of the one at Carnegie Mellon. To get a first-hand look, access this URL with your Web browser:

```
http://www.cs.cmu.edu/afs/cs.cmu.edu/user/bsy/www/coke.html
```

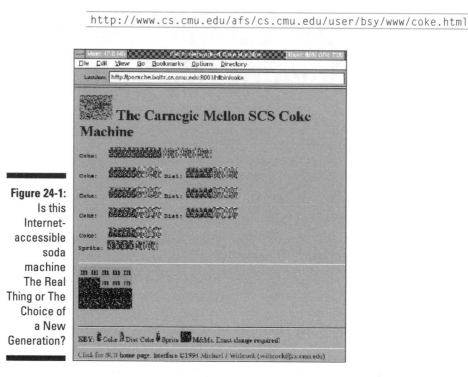

Figure 24-1: Is this Internet-accessible soda machine The Real Thing or The Choice of a New Generation?

Candy Machine

Some people think nothing goes with a nice cold soda better than some candy. But why walk all the way to the vending machine if there's nothing there? Did you notice the status of the CMU candy machine in Figure 24-1?

Toasters

Network toasters are a favorite device of vendors for showing the capabilities of their SNMP management stations. (We discussed SNMP, the Simple Network Management Protocol, in Chapter 19.) With the right connections between the host and the toaster, it's easy to control the darkness of the toast and the amount of time your bread or muffin is inside.

We couldn't find any toasters that are permanently connected to The Internet, so look for them at trade shows and technical conferences.

Coffee Pot

What's toast without some coffee? In Cambridge (in the United Kingdom, not Massachusetts), there's a coffeemaker that's on The Internet. Well, actually, they cheat just a little — there's a video camera *pointed at* the coffeemaker, and the images collected by the camera are available on The Internet. With your Web browser, access this URL:

```
http://www.cl.cam.ac.uk/coffee/coffee.html
```

Other Video Goodies

Video is used to put all kinds of things on The Internet, in addition to the above coffeemaker, including a toilet:

```
http://www.wps.com/toilet/index.html
```

an office:

```
http://www.netsys.com/sunvideo.html
```

and some fish:

```
http://www.mcom.com/fishcam/fishcam.html
```

Refrigerator

Paul Haas (paulh@hamjudo.com) has connected sensors to parts of his spare refrigerator. (It's for sale, by the way.) As you can see from Figure 24-2, a computer monitors the sensors and reports the

- Temperature in the refrigerator
- Temperature in the freezer
- Temperature of a can of Diet Coke (no, it's not in the freezer)
- Status of the light bulb
- Status of the door

If you have a World Wide Web browser, you can check the refrigerator yourself, at

```
http://hamjudo.com/cgi-bin/refrigerator
```

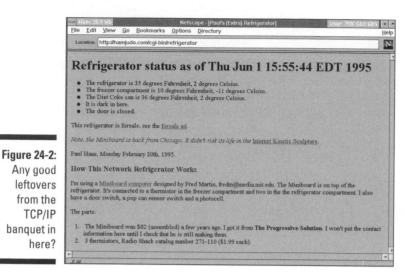

Figure 24-2:
Any good
leftovers
from the
TCP/IP
banquet in
here?

Hot Tub

Paul Haas is at it again, this time with his hot tub. Figure 24-3 shows the conditions but neglects to say whether it's in use. There's no video camera here — perhaps we should be grateful? — so you might want to send e-mail to Paul (paulh@hamjudo.com) before dropping by. If you're browsing the Web, the hot tub is at

    http://hamjudo.com/hottub_notes.html

Figure 24-3:
After eating,
wait at least
an hour
before
going in the
hot tub.

> ## Tub status as of Thu Mar 2 16:02:10 EST 1995
>
> Paul's hottub is a bit cool at about 97 degrees Fahrenheit. It is really cold outside at about 22 degrees Fahrenheit. The ozone generator is working. The cover is closed. The backup battery is Ok at 9.2 volts (this will still work down to 6 volts)
>
> **Try the refrigerator!**
>
> This hottub is brought to you by Paul Haas, paulh@hamjudo.com. I will be available starting January 1st, 1995. See my resume. For more information see my home page: Paulh's home page
>
> Comment about this server
> list comments this server

The Streets of Seattle

There are electronic sensors embedded in the roads of Seattle, Washington, to monitor the flow of traffic on the city's streets. The sensor information is linked to a map in order to display the traffic in a user-friendly format. We haven't been to Seattle, so the map doesn't mean much to us, but you can look for yourself at

```
http://198.238.212.10/regions/northwest/
```

Weather Station

Weather data is collected constantly by instrument packages around the world. We considered telling you about the one at the University of Washington, so you could decide whether or not to take that drive around downtown Seattle. But instead, why don't you investigate the ones in Norway:

```
http://www.uit.no/homepage-english.uit.no.html
```

or Sweden:

```
http://www.ausys.se/weather/weather.exe?medium+eng
```

IBM PC

It's true! These days, an original IBM PC — with 64K of RAM, two 5.25" floppy drives, and no hard disk — is considered a "pretty strange" network device. And these old fogies are still out there, we guarantee it. Just ask Candace's sister.

Chapter 25

Ten Network Connection Media

• •

In This Chapter

▶ More information for hardware junkies

▶ A couple of forms of TCP/IP media that may surprise you

• •

The connection media that carry the signals on a network are not limited to copper and fiber optic cables. The signal that goes out on the media is the electrical pattern of bits that make up your data. Connection media are usually rated and priced based on the following characteristics:

✔ Maximum distance they can carry a signal

✔ Transmission speed (speed at which the signal moves)

✔ How well shielded they are against interference (from things like garage door openers, sunspots, and UFO transmissions)

This chapter lists some common, and not so common, connection media. Be sure you have also digested Chapter 17 about the hardware/software marriage banquet. ▪

Thick Coaxial Cable (10Base5)

Ethernet originally ran over 10Base5 cable. This thick cable — and the newer "thinwire" cable described in the next section — are coaxial cable, like the stuff cable TV runs on. Thick 10Base5 has a maximum length of 500 meters for one segment. In the early days of Ethernet, you could see this fat yellow or blue cable snaking all over buildings. Digital Equipment Corporation liked orange cables; it made for some colorful offices!

10Base5 (also known as "thickwire") is a lot cheaper than optical fiber (FDDI), but more expensive than thinwire or twisted-pair. That's why, today, the thickwire is usually what forms an Ethernet backbone, hidden in ceilings, walls, and floors — while the cable segments that radiate out from the backbone are thinwire or twisted-pair. Figure 25-1 shows the similarity between a building's backbone and your spine and ribs.

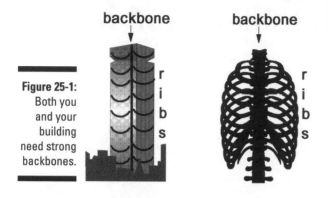

Figure 25-1:
Both you
and your
building
need strong
backbones.

Thin Coaxial Cable (10Base2)

Also called "thinwire," 10Base2 is the next generation of network coaxial cable, and is thinner and less expensive than thickwire (but not as thin or as cheap as twisted-pair). However, thinwire and twisted-pair can't carry the signal as far as thickwire, which is one reason the thickwire continues to be used as Ethernet backbone. The maximum length for thinwire is 185 meters — not even half the maximum for the thicker coaxial cable.

Twisted-Pair (10BaseT, UTP, STP)

You have twisted-pair wiring all over your house. You can buy it at hardware and home-repair stores. It's also your telephone wire. Twisted-pair is named that because it consists of two insulated wires twisted around each other, with additional insulation around the pair. Sets of twisted pairs are bundled together to make various cables. Twisted-pair is an inexpensive medium for average-length, lower-speed networks.

When unshielded twisted-pair wiring (UTP) is used for Ethernet, it is called 10BaseT. The maximum length for a 10BaseT twisted-pair segment is only 100 meters, good for wiring a football or soccer field, but usually too short for most office buildings unless the cables are run into centralized wiring closets. Shielded twisted-pair, STP, has extra metal shielding around it as protection against interference. Shielded twisted-pair is widely used in token ring networks.

Because of the low cost, small size, and flexibility of twisted-pair cable, there is substantial ongoing research and development of higher-speed networks running over this type of cable. Examples are 100BaseVG and 100BaseT, which are both "Fast Ethernet," running at 100 megabits per second over ordinary voice-grade telephone wires. 100BaseVG and 100BaseT are two different proposed standards, both of which run on the same physical cabling.

If you are using either one of these, make sure your cables, network interface cards, and smart hubs are all compatible. Check and double-check with your salesperson, and read the specs that come with your hardware. ■

Fiber Optic Cable

If you need fast transmission speeds, how about the speed of light? Optical fiber uses light instead of electricity to transmit the signal. A laser generates pulses of light along a bundle of glass (or synthetic glass or plastic) fibers. The transmission speed of fiber optic is lightning fast, and this type of cable is typically used as the backbone of large, long-distance networks. Needless to say, it costs a lot more than coaxial cable or twisted-pair.

FDDI, Fiber Distributed Data Interface, is a network standard rated at a transmission speed of 100 megabits per second. Typical use for FDDI is as the backbone of a network with Ethernet and token ring segments connected to it. There are special FDDI/Ethernet and FDDI/token ring bridges that connect the Ethernet and token ring pieces (which run over one of the traditional cable types) to the optical fiber backbone.

Ham Radio

We're not kidding. KA9Q is an implementation of the TCP/IP protocols for amateur radio systems. In the United States, you need a radio operator's license from the Federal Communication Commission in order to broadcast radio signals. We're not sure if you still need to know Morse code to pass the test, though . . .

Cable TV

CATV companies may be the carriers of the future. Today, a few cable TV companies have two-way cables with the speed and capacity to carry data. The cable TV and telephone companies are poised to fight it out over which will be your data network carrier.

Microwave

If your house or office has a clear view over the trees and buildings in your city or town, you can get special microwave hardware to be part of your network. The microwaves you use for data transmission are similar to the ones that heat up your food.

On the other hand, the microwave dishes you need for your network are nothing like the ones that fit inside your microwave oven. These microwave dishes, as small as 18 inches in diameter, are parabolic reflectors with a built-in transmitter and receiver. The catch in this case is that the microwave dishes only work on "line of sight." That is, if there's a straight line between the microwave dishes, everything is okay. But if obstacles are in the way, you need to use towers or additional dishes to work your way around the barriers.

Laser

Microwave isn't the only wireless transmission method. You can also link your network segments with beams of laser light. The lasers are smaller and usually cheaper than microwave dishes. Like microwave, lasers as well are limited to "line of sight" connections. Lasers cover less distance than microwaves but are often the right choice for crossing chasms or busy city streets.

Satellite

For *really* wide area networks, satellites are the answer. By "really wide area" we mean networks that span over 500 miles. When you use a satellite link, the distance from the earth to the satellite is included. Companies such as COMSAT sell satellite services. If your company is really big, like Chrysler Corporation or Wal-Mart, you can launch your own satellite system.

Here's an example of a network situation calling for satellites. Remember OOPS, our fictitious fish factory from Chapter 10? Let's say OOPS has grown and now has LANs in New York, Vancouver, Tokyo, and Vienna. System manager Clem Chowder quit to go work for Chowdas R Us, Inc., and Selena Sushi — now International Data Communications Manager — is installing satellite dishes for each OOPS location.

She plans to install them on roofs as shown in Figure 25-2, or in a corner of a parking lot. Each dish needs a cable running into one building, and that wire will connect to a bridge or router. Off go the OOPS packets, launched into space. Believe it or not, it takes less than a second for the signal to run out into space and back to the earth. Of course, for some applications, the Earth-to-space-to-Earth time is considered slow.

Figure 25-2:
Are satellite dishes microwave safe?

Chapter 26

Ten Reasons to Use TCP/IP

....

In This Chapter

▶ Fun things you want to make more time for

▶ A couple of work-related necessities

....

TCP/IP provides the most heterogeneous level of network connectivity you can get. This is reason enough for many organizations to use TCP/IP. If you're looking for a concise list of convincing arguments for deploying TCP/IP throughout your organization and connecting to The Internet, start with this list and look in the related chapters for more information.

You Need E-Mail

For many of us, a day without electronic mail is a day without sunshine. For others, a day without e-mail nowadays is a miracle, or a clue that something's wrong with the network. Of course, there are still those (our technical editor, for one) who believe that "no news is good news."

Why do you need e-mail? Professor Irwin Corey always said that these complex questions require multipart answers. Why? Because!

Do you need e-mail? Yes, so that you can

- ✔ Keep in touch with your friends who live far away — but for much less than the price of a telephone call.

- ✔ Tell your boss that you're taking vacation in the middle of a big project, because you don't have the nerve to tell her face to face.

- ✔ Correspond with an electronic pen pal. Some e-mail acquaintances fall in love before they ever meet in person.

- ✔ Order a deli platter when you don't have time to go out for lunch.

> ✔ Contact the President of the United States.
>
> ✔ Send your Christmas wish list to Santa Claus.

All sorts of interesting people have e-mail addresses. Try fingering the stars to see whose e-mail addresses you can find. See Chapter 14.

You Live to Shop

The Internet Mall. It's really here...24 hours a day. We'd tell you more, but we have to log in and pick up a few things.

You Want to Run Programs on Other People's Computers

Definitely a very significant TCP/IP bonus! If you have a pathetically powered computer without enough disk space to hold all the programs, games, and tools that you want, rlogin and telnet are an answer to your prayers. They let you steal cycles from all over the world (see Chapter 8). We'd tell you more, but we have to rlogin to get in our daily game workout.

You Want Someone to Play With

Life shouldn't be all work and no play. Although The Internet offers innumerable ways for people to work together, it also gives you lots of opportunities to play — by yourself and with others. For example, MUD (Multi-User Dungeon) is an online computer game for more than one player. At any time, there may be many MUDs going on simultaneously on The Internet. Because the players can interact aggressively as well as cooperatively, the dynamics of the game change constantly as players arrive and depart.

Sneakernet Is Wearing You Out

Have you ever used Sneakernet? That's when you copy files from a computer onto a floppy disk or tape and run down the hall to another computer and load them up. Then you realize you brought the wrong floppy disk or copied the wrong file, so you run back to the other office, where you realize you left the...well, you get the picture.

If you don't have all the computers in your workplace or other environment linked together by TCP/IP, this runaround may be the aerobic portion of your day. Who needs Jazzercise? But once you have TCP/IP on all the computers, you can relax, get comfortable in your chair, and transfer files to your heart's content — and only get up to go to the junk food machine...or the Jazzercise class that you now need!

Remember the soda and candy machines that are on The Internet? See Chapters 14 and 24. If you network your vending machines with TCP/IP, you can check if they are loaded up with your favorite brand before you lift yourself out of the chair.

You Have Files to Procure

While you were in the bookstore to purchase *TCP/IP for Dummies*, you may have accidentally looked at some other computer books. (We forgive you.) Did you notice that some books come with diskettes or CD-ROMs? Much of that software is available for free on the Internet. You get it via Anonymous FTP (see Chapter 9).

You Want to Gopher Broke

The World Wide Web and its browsers (see Chapter 12) may be getting all the attention these days, but Gopher is still a very valuable tool and is easy to use. Sure, it's a text-only tool, but that means you don't have to wait for all those huge graphics files to be transferred. You can use Gopher over an Internet connection of any speed, and you don't even need client software of your own. That means it's inexpensive, too.

You Dream of Untangling the Web

Face it; the World Wide Web is the place to be. The price of admission to this part of cyberspace is a little higher, though, than Gopherspace. You need

- ✔ A good connection to the Internet — a SLIP connection, at least.
- ✔ A Web browser. Netscape and Mosaic are the front-runners, but there are many more to choose from.
- ✔ Lots of spare time.

Your browser has some built-in starting points for getting caught up in the Web, and we've suggested others (in Chapter 12). Web pages come and go, so don't get angry when you find some changed or gone. That's part of the fun.

Once you get started, it's hard to stop. But please don't forget to bathe and eat periodically. Thanks.

You've Always Wanted to Hear a Free Rolling Stones Concert

On November 18, 1994, the Rolling Stones broadcast part of a concert on The Internet (see Figure 26-1). Both audio and video signals were transmitted to over 60,000 sites. For details, surf to the Stones' own World Wide Web home page at this URL:

```
http://www.stones.com
```

Who knows, maybe you'll find the schedule of the next broadcast!

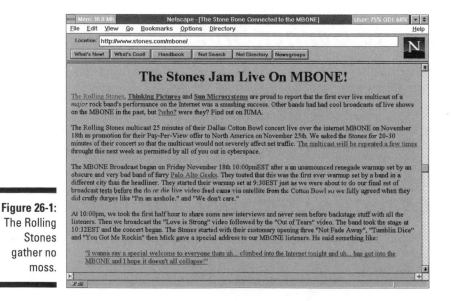

Figure 26-1:
The Rolling
Stones
gather no
moss.

Chapter 27

Ten Synonyms for The Internet

● ●

In This Chapter

▶ Some cute ways to refer to The Internet

▶ Some silly ways to refer to The Internet

▶ A political way to refer to The Internet

● ●

*B*reakfast, lunch, brunch, dinner, supper, banquet, and feast are just some of the words available to describe the eating experience. The Internet has its own keywords, starting with its name. Here are some of the more common terms you may hear.

The Net

Most people are a little lazy and prefer to say "The Net" rather than "The Internet." You'll have to infer by the context that the speaker means The Internet as opposed to a local internet — some organization's network. (The abbreviation gets even shorter for the World Wide Web. Most people just say "the Web.")

Information Superhighway

The term *Information Superhighway* is perhaps the most common synonym for The Internet, probably because most people can understand the relationship between vehicles on a roadway and information on an electronic information highway. How do you drive from Cairo, Egypt to Paris, France? We don't know exactly, but we'd want a good map. How do you "surf" from Cairo to Paris? Easy — just point and click. The auto club map would probably be out of date before you unfolded it anyway.

Infobahn

Infobahn is the keyword of choice for the internationally aware. *Info,* of course, is short for information; and *bahn* is German for highway. Infobahn is also popular because it has fewer syllables than "information superhighway".

National Information Infrastructure (NII)

The United States government has a goal to update the national network: NII, the National Information Infrastructure. That's the most common term, but you may also hear references to the following:

- HPPCI, the High Performance Computing and Communication Initiative
- NREN, the National Research and Education Network
- IITF, the Information Infrastructure Task Force
- FTSC, the Financial Services Technology Consortium

Some interesting conflicts have arisen between the private sector, which wants to run the national network for profit, and the public sector, which wants the U.S. government to pay for it but knows that it will be mismanaged.

The Network of Networks

Network of networks is truly an accurate term, since that's what The Internet is, and that's what the word *internet* means.

Cyberspace

Cyberspace borrows from the science term *cybernetic,* which refers to electronic computers. The electronic links among computers let people interact in virtual communities. They have no real physical manifestations, so cyberspace is the way to refer to these invisible towns.

A company called Control Data Corporation used to make a supercomputer called the Cyber. Other than an indication of how much room a CDC Cyber took up, cyberspace has nothing to do with that machine.

A Place to Meet and Greet

The Internet may never totally replace your neighborhood tavern, but a coffee shop in Cambridge, Massachusetts, is on The Internet. For the price of an expensive cup of coffee, you can surf for over 10 minutes. We already told you that some couples have met, dated, and become engaged via the Net. We're pretty sure that they actually had to get married in person, though.

The Outer Limits

There are some pretty strange things going on on The Internet, sometimes. It's too bad those Outer Limits aliens aren't in control instead of Earthlings. "We control the vertical. We control the horizontal."

The Twilight Zone

If The Internet actually came with a narrator, it would be Rod Serling. And if the Net had a soundtrack, it'd be the music from *The Twilight Zone*. Of course, *twilight zone* can also refer to the daylight outside your windows when you finally realize that you've been surfing for 96 consecutive hours without even getting up to go the bathroom. You may even have to remind yourself, "IP, therefore I am" as you head for the john.

Information Overload

Once you start spending time on The Internet, especially on the World Wide Web and in Gopherspace, you'll come to realize the vast amounts of information out there waiting to overwhelm you. A lot is useful, much of it is entertaining, but some of it proves that some Internet folk have way too much free time on their hands. It doesn't matter whether you're trying to do real work out there or not; you'll see that there's no way you can keep up with the glut of data that 30 million people can create. Welcome to Information Overload. Luckily, you can be sure that the surfing tools, especially Web browsers, will continue to improve over time, helping you navigate your way through the sea of information.

Appendix

How to Get RFCs

*O*ne way to get RFCs is to look at them online, using telnet, Gopher, or the World Wide Web. RFCs are available from many Anonymous FTP sites, but especially the following two sources:

- ✔ InterNIC (NIC for short) Directory and Database Services server, at ds.internic.net on The Internet
- ✔ Department of Defense NIC, at nic.ddn.mil on The Internet

You can also ask the NIC to e-mail you the RFC(s) you want, or get them via FTP.

Getting a Complete List of RFCs

You must request RFCs by number, not by topic. So, unless you have memorized all the RFCs by number (there are over 1,750 as of this writing!), your first task is finding the *rfc-index*. This is a file that lists the RFCs with both their numbers and their names.

1. Connect to the InterNIC using Anonymous FTP. Figure A-1 shows an example of connecting to ds.internic.net. (If you want to use the Department of Defense NIC, Figure A-2 shows just the start of connecting to nic.ddn.mil.) Both sites have a directory for RFC files.

2. Look in the RFC directory (/rfc at both sites) for the file named rfc-index.txt. This file lists all the RFCs in reverse chronological order by number, name, and author. In Figure A-1, you can see the /rfc directory at ds.internic.mil, but you can't see the files it holds.

3. Find the rfc-index in which you're interested. Figure A-3 illustrates a search of the directory using the * wildcard for the filename. Notice that there are actually three indexes.

4. Once you have found the RFC index you want, use the FTP get command to transfer it to your computer. (If necessary, you can reread Chapter 9 to brush up on your FTP knowledge.) ■

Figure A-1:
The
InterNIC is
an excellent
source of
RFCs.

```
$ ftp ds.internic.net
Connected to ds.internic.net.
220-            InterNIC Directory and Database Services
220-
220-Welcome to InterNIC Directory and Database Services provided by AT&T.
220-These services are partially supported through a cooperative agreement
220-with the National Science Foundation.
220-
220-Your comments and suggestions for improvement are welcome, and can be
220-mailed to admin@ds.internic.net.
220-
220 ds.internic.net FTP server ready.
Name (ds.internic.net:leiden): anonymous
331 Guest login ok, send ident as password.
Password:
230 Guest login ok, access restrictions apply.
Remote system type is UNIX.
Using binary mode to transfer files.
ftp> dir
200 PORT command successful.
150 Opening ASCII mode data connection for /bin/ls.
total 875
drwxr-xr-x   3 welcome  1         1024 Apr  8 03:54 fyi
drwxrwxr-x   4 welcome  60        3072 Apr  8 03:51 iesg
drwxrwxr-x182 welcome  60        6656 Apr  8 03:51 ietf
drwxrwxr-x   3 welcome  60       44032 Apr  8 03:52 internet-drafts
drwxr-xr-x   6 welcome  30        1024 Jul  1 1994 internic.info
drwxrwxr-x  24 welcome  60        1536 Aug 26 1994 isoc
drwxr-xr-x  81 welcome  1         2048 Jul  8 1994 policies-procedures
drwxr-xr-x  22 welcome  1         1024 Apr  8 10:00 pub
drwxr-xr-x  11 welcome  1         1024 Jun 17 1993 resource-guide
drwxr-xr-x   3 welcome  1        24576 Mar 31 04:56 rfc
drwxr-xr-x   3 welcome  ftpguest   512 Apr  8 03:54 rtr
drwxr-xr-x   3 welcome  1         1536 Mar 24 04:53 std
drwxr-xr-x   4 0        1          512 Feb  8 1993 usr
226 Transfer complete.
```

```
$ ftp nic.ddn.mil
Connected to nic.ddn.mil
220-*****Welcome to the DOD Network Information Center*****
      *****Login with username "anonymous" and password "guest"*****
      *****You may change directories to the following:*****
        ddn-news          - DDN Management Bulletins
        domain            - root zone files
        gosip             - DOD GOSIP  Registration and Information
        internet-drafts   - Internet drafts
        netinfo           - NIC information files
        rfc               - RFC repository
        scc               - DDN security bulletins
        std               - Internet protocol standards
! And more!
```

Figure A-2: The DDN (Department of Defense network) also maintains a NIC with RFCs.

```
Ftp> dir  /rfc/*index.txt
200 PORT command successful.
150 Opening ASCII mode data connection for /bin/ls.
-r--r--r--  1 welcome  ftpguest    6259 Mar 27 14:36 /rfc/fyi-index.txt
-r--r--r--  1 welcome  ftpguest  241777 Mar 28 04:59 /rfc/rfc-index.txt
-r--r--r--  1 welcome  ftpguest    7918 Mar 27 14:36 /rfc/std-index.txt
226 Transfer complete.
```

Figure A-3: Look all the way to the right of this listing. There is an RFC index for FYIs, one for RFCs, and one for STDs.

RFC name format

RFC filenames use these naming conventions, where the #### represents the RFC number without leading zeroes:

```
rfc####.txt
rfc####.ps
```

The .txt extension indicates a text file; the .ps extension indicates a Post-Script file. The PostScript version often contains figures and graphics that cannot be represented in plain text, but you need a PostScript printer or PostScript previewer software to use the file.

Thus a PostScript version of RFC 1291 is located in the file named /rfc/rfc1291.ps.

Understanding entries in the rfc-index.txt file

The entries in the RFC index list contain the following information:

RFC number

Author

Title

Date issued

Number of pages

Format: text (.txt) or PostScript (.ps)

Type: whether it's an FYI or STD

Relationship of this RFC to any others (whether this RFC is an update of an existing RFC or has made a previous RFC obsolete)

For example, the entry for RFC 1129 contains the following information:

```
1129        D. Mills, "Internet time synchronization: The Network
            Time Protocol", 10/01/1989. (Pages=29) (Format=.ps)
```

This entry tells you RFC 1129 is authored by D. Mills, and titled "Internet time synchronization: The Network Time Protocol." It was issued October 1, 1989, and contains 29 PostScript pages. It has not updated or been replaced by any other RFC. It is not an FYI or a STD. (Remember, this is an example. Things may have changed by the time you're reading this.)

Using FTP to Get an RFC

Once you have read the RFC index file and decided which RFCs you want to copy, you're ready to go. Follow the tutorial instructions again to connect to ds.internic.net or nic.ddn.mil. (RFCs are stored on many Anonymous FTP sites, so you're not limited to just these two.) Use the FTP **cd** command and get into the /rfc directory. Then use the **get** command to transfer the files you want to your computer.

```
Ftp> cd /rfc
250 CWD command successful.
Ftp> get rfc10.txt
local: rfc10.txt remote: rfc10.txt
200 PORT command successful.
150 Opening ASCII mode data connection for rfc10.txt (3348 bytes).
226 Transfer complete.
3348 bytes received in 0.186 seconds (18037 bytes/s)
Ftp> quit
221 Goodbye
```

Figure A-4: Getting into the /rfc directory and retrieving a copy of RFC 10.

In Figure A-4 we are retrieving RFC 10.

Using E-mail to Get an RFC

You can also request RFCs via e-mail. The InterNIC maintains an automated mail server that you can access by sending a message to mailserv@ds.internic.net. In the body of the message, include the following line of text:

    document-by-name rfc####

where #### is the number of the RFC.

For PostScript RFCs, specify the extension .ps, as in

    document-by-name rfc####.ps

Requests for several RFCs can be sent in a single message by specifying each document in a comma-separated list, as in

    document-by-name rfc####, rfc####

or by including multiple document-by-name commands on separate lines.

You can also request the RFC index by e-mail. Include the following in the body of your message.

    document-by-name rfc-index

Glossary

· ·

10Base2 The coaxial cable used for thinwire Ethernet. Over 10Base2 Ethernet, the maximum network transmission rate is 10 megabits of data per second.

10Base5 The thick coaxial cable used for the original thickwire Ethernet. Over 10Base5 Ethernet, the maximum network transmission rate is 10 megabits of data per second.

10BaseT Twisted-pair Ethernet cable. Over 10BaseT Ethernet, the maximum network transmission rate is 10 megabits of data per second.

ACK (Acknowledgment) The response from the recipient back to the sender that data was successfully received. TCP uses ACKs as part of its reliable transmission scheme. If an ACK is not received, data is retransmitted. *See also* NAK; retransmission.

address mask The set of bits used to mask an Internet address to create a subnetwork. *See also* subnet mask.

address resolution The translation of an Internet address into the physical (hardware) address of your network interface card. The Address Resolution Protocol (ARP) does the address resolution.

Address Resolution Protocol *See* ARP.

Anonymous FTP *See* FTP.

ANSI (American National Standards Institute) The organization that defines standards for the United States, including network standards.

Archie A program and a group of network servers that help you locate files on The Internet. Archie is strictly a file finder; after locating the file you want, you can use FTP to copy the file to your own computer.

ARP (Address Resolution Protocol) The TCP/IP protocol that translates an Internet address into the hardware address of a network interface card.

ARPA (Advanced Research Projects Agency) The United States government agency that funded the ARPANET, predecessor to the Internet. ARPA is now called DARPA, Defense Advanced Research Projects Agency.

ARPANET (Advanced Research Projects Agency Network) The U.S. government-funded network that evolved into The Internet.

article A message posted in a Usenet news newsgroup.

authority zone The part of a DNS domain for which a name server has responsibility. *Authority* is sometimes called "knowing the truth" about network name/address translation.

backbone The physical cable in a building from which network segments radiate. 10Base2 (thickwire Ethernet) and fiber optic cable are two popular backbone media.

bandwidth The range from highest to lowest frequencies transmitted on a network. Measures network capacity.

baud rate The speed rating of network transmissions. Theoretically, baud rate is equal to the number of bits transmitted per second; however, transmission overhead reduces the actual data transfer rate, and data compression increases it.

Berkeley UNIX The UNIX operating system developed by the University of California at Berkeley. It was the first version of UNIX that included TCP/IP.

binary A number system based on 2. The place columns of the number are based on powers of 2: 1, 2, 4, 8, 16, 32, 64, 128, 256, and so on. A network administrator who creates subnet masks must understand binary-to-decimal conversion (or have a calculator that understands it).

BITNET (Before Its Time Network) A widely used network that connects, for the most part, universities. BITNET does not use TCP/IP. BITNET users have access to The Internet through gateways.

BOOTP (Bootstrap Protocol) The TCP/IP protocol for remote booting of diskless computers and other network devices.

bridge A network device that connects two networks that use the same protocols; the bridge forwards packets between the connected networks, if necessary.

broadcast The transmission of packets to all hosts attached to a network.

brouter A network device that combines bridge and router functions.

browser A client program for navigating the hypermedia information on the World Wide Web. The best browsers are graphical (such as Netscape and Mosaic), but text-only browsers (such as Lynx) are also useful, especially on low-speed dial-up links.

caching server A DNS name server that stores in memory the information it receives from other servers. *See also* DNS; DNS domain.

Cello A World Wide Web browser. *See also* browser.

chat *See* IRC.

client A program that requests services from a server. The DNS resolver is an example of a client program. It requests name/address resolution services from a DNS name server. *See also* client/server; server.

client/server A style of computing that allows work to be distributed across hosts (computers). For example, a PC client can request file access from a file server. TCP/IP uses a client/server architecture and enables development of client/server applications. *See also* client; server.

collision Occurs on an Ethernet network when two hosts transmit packets at the same time. *See also* CSMA/CD.

connection A link between network processes running on different computers.

connectionless service An IP delivery service that sends each packet (including the source and destination addresses) across the network without expecting an ACK to signify that the packet was received. Connectionless delivery services may lose packets and do not guarantee that packets will be delivered in order. *See also* ACK.

CSLIP (Compressed Serial Line Internet Protocol) An optimization of SLIP. CSLIP reduces the need to transmit redundant address information. *See also* SLIP; PPP.

CSMA/CD (Carrier Sense Multiple Access/Collision Detection) A network transmission scheme by which multiple network devices can transmit across the cable simultaneously, possibly causing collisions. If a collision occurs, both devices retransmit after waiting a random amount of time. Ethernet is the most well known network type using CSMA/CD technology.

cyberspace A virtual world of computers, applications, and services. Another term for The Internet.

daemon A program that runs continually, especially on the UNIX operating system, to provide a service for a protocol or application.

DARPA (Defense Advanced Research Projects Agency) *See* ARPA.

data link layer Layer 2 in the ISO OSI Reference Model and the TCP/IP network model. This layer handles logical connections between networked computers. *See also* ISO OSI Reference Model.

DCA (Defense Communication Agency) The organization responsible for the DDN (Defense Data Network) and the Department of Defense InterNIC.

DDN (Defense Data Network) A broader term for MILNET and the United States military components of The Internet. *See also* MILNET.

DHCP (Dynamic Host Configuration Protocol) The TCP/IP protocol for allocating IP addresses dynamically when they are needed.

distributed computing Programs and/or data that function together and are spread across networked computers. Client/server computing can be a form of distributed computing if the client and server are on different computers.

DNS (Domain Name System) The name/address resolution service that uses a distributed database containing FQDNs and addresses. DNS makes it easy for people to refer to computers by name rather than by numeric address. DNS is the name/address resolution service used by The Internet. *See also* FQDN; name/address resolution.

DNS domain A group of computers using the same DNS name servers and managed within the same administrative unit.

dog's breakfast A little of this, a lot of that.

domain *See* DNS domain; NIS domain

domain name server A program that converts FQDNs into their numeric IP addresses, and vice versa. The computer that runs the program. *See also* FQDN.

Domain Name System *See* DNS.

dotted decimal notation Used to represent IP addresses. Each part of the address is a decimal number separated from the other parts by a dot (.). For example, 130.103.40.4 is an IP address in dotted decimal notation.

dumb terminal A terminal that has no processing capabilities and no graphics support, such as a VT100 terminal.

Dynamic Host Configuration Protocol *See* DHCP.

dynamic routing A way of moving data across an internet; when one path is unavailable, dynamic routing can use an alternate one. Originally designed to ensure that The Internet would be available if a military attack disabled any of the network paths.

e-mail Electronic mail; also called email and mail.

epoch The current era, starting January 1, 1900 as far as The Internet is concerned. Many network applications measure time as the number of seconds since the start of the epoch.

Ethernet A LAN technology that uses CSMA/CD delivery. Ethernet runs over many different media, ranging from thick cable (10Base5) to twisted-pair wire (10BaseT). Most Ethernet networks operate at 10 megabits per second, but Fast Ethernet, running at 100 megabits per second, is under development. Ethernet is the most common type of LAN used with TCP/IP.

Ethernet address The hardware address that identifies the Ethernet network interface card inside a computer. Also called the physical address. No two Ethernet addresses are identical.

FAQ (Frequently Asked Questions list) A FAQ is usually provided as part of each Usenet newsgroup, to introduce new users to the newsgroup and its etiquette.

FDDI (Fiber Distribution Data Interface) A token ring network technology based on fiber optic cables made of bundles of glass or plastic. Used for high-speed and/or long-distance networks. The typical network transmission rate is 100 megabits per second. *See also* optical fiber.

Fiber Distribution Data Interface *See* FDDI.

file server A computer that provides file-sharing services to client computers on the network.

file services Applications and services that allow network users to share disk space on networked computers. NFS is an example of a file service.

finger A client/server application that displays information about users on the network. System administrators may disable the finger server for security reasons. *See also* whois.

firewall A network security measure that works by allowing and preventing receipt of certain kinds of network messages.

FQDN (Fully Qualified Domain Name) The "full" name of a computer, including all subdomain and domain names, separated by dots. For example, frodo.support.lotus.com is an FQDN.

frequently asked questions list *See* FAQ.

FTP (File Transfer Protocol) A TCP/IP application, service, and protocol for copying files from one computer to another. Before the server will transfer the files, it requires the client to provide a valid username and password. Anonymous FTP is used at public network sites. It allows file transfer using a standard username, "anonymous," plus the user's e-mail address as the password.

ftpmail The process of accessing an FTP archive via e-mail, rather than via an FTP client.

FYI The television newsmagazine on the television show *Murphy Brown*. OK, not really. An FYI is an RFC that documents something just For Your Information. *See* RFC.

gated (gateway daemon) A program that must run on a computer using TCP/IP's RIP protocol. *See* RIP.

gateway A computer that connects multiple networks, and routes packets among them. Also, any computer that translates information from one format to another (*see* SMTP gateway).

good-deed doers Volunteers. To name a few: RFC authors and reviewers; the inventors of MIME; the organizations that provide Anonymous FTP sites; the creators of ftpmail and GopherMail.

Gopher A client/server system for publishing information on the Internet in a menu-oriented fashion. To access Gopherspace, you use your own Gopher client or use telnet to get to a publicly accessible system and use their Gopher. *See also* Veronica, a program to help users navigate Gopherspace.

GopherMail The process of navigating Gopherspace via e-mail, rather than via a Gopher client.

Gopherspace The worldwide collection of Gopher servers and the information they publish on The Internet.

GOSIP (Government Open Systems Interconnect Profile) The United States government procurement standard that requires the OSI network model for networked computers.

graphical user interface *See* GUI.

GUI (graphical user interface) An application or operating system appearance that usually involves windows, icons, and a mouse.

hardware address The physical address for the network interface card.

Used by the low-level hardware layers of a network. TCP/IP's ARP protocol translates IP addresses into hardware addresses.

host A computer on a TCP/IP network. Sometimes means any device on the network.

hosts file A text file that lists host names and their IP addresses on a network. For small networks, the hosts file is an alternative to DNS.

HTML (HyperText Markup Language) The language used to write pages for the World Wide Web.

HTTP (HyperText Transfer Protocol) The TCP/IP protocol for transferring World Wide Web pages across The Internet.

hypermedia A system for linking related multimedia objects, such as a text file and sound and video clips, that reside on different network sites.

hypertext A text system for linking related documents, such as a main document, an attachment, and footnotes, that reside on different network sites.

IAB (Internet Activities Board) The group of people responsible for research into the direction of The Internet and the development of TCP/IP. The IAB creates task forces to research Internet issues.

ICMP (Internet Control Message Protocol) The TCP/IP protocol used to report network errors and to determine whether a computer is available on the network. ICMP is used by the ping utility.

IESG (Internet Engineering Steering Group) Manages the IETF.

IETF (Internet Engineering Task Force)
Part of the IAB; responsible for research into Internet issues. RFCs document the IETF specifications.

IGP (Interior Gateway Protocol) A protocol used by routers and gateways to transfer routing information. RIP is a well-known IGP.

Interior Gateway Protocol *See* IGP.

internet, an A group of interconnected networks using the TCP/IP protocol suite.

Internet, The The international collection of internets that use TCP/IP to work together as one immense logical network. You really didn't have to look this up after reading the book, did you? We'll assume you just chanced on this entry.

Internet Activities Board *See* IAB.

Internet address (IP address) A 32-bit (as of this writing) unique numeric address used by a computer on a TCP/IP network. The IP address consists of two parts: a network number and a host number.

Internet Control Message Protocol *See* ICMP.

Internet Engineering Steering Group *See* IESG.

Internet Engineering Task Force *See* IETF.

internet layer Layer 3 of the TCP/IP network model.

Internet Research Task Force *See* IRTF.

InterNIC (Internet Network Information Center) The Internet administration center that registers networks as part of The Internet. RFCs are available from the InterNIC. The InterNIC is sometimes called the NIC for short, but an organization may run its own NIC for its internet. A computer's network interface card is also called a NIC. You'll have to tell from the context which NIC is which.

interoperability The capability of diverse hardware and software from different vendors to cooperate and communicate. For example, a Macintosh can share a file that's on a UNIX computer.

IP (Internet Protocol) One of the two main parts of the TCP/IP protocol suite. IP delivers TCP and UDP packets across a network.

IRC (Internet Relay Chat) A way for many people on The Internet to "chat" electronically. Unlike the talk program, which allows only two people to converse. IRC conversations are live, as compared to Usenet news, which is not.

IRTF (Internet Research Task Force)
The part of the IAB that is responsible for research and development of TCP/IP.

ISO (International Standards Organization) A group that defines international standards, including network standards. ISO defined the seven-layer network model for network protocols, called the ISO OSI Reference Model.

ISO OSI Reference Model The ISO-defined, seven-layer network model for network protocols. From the bottom up, the layers are: physical, data link, network, transport, session, presentation, and application.

Kerberos A TCP/IP security scheme, developed at MIT, for authenticating logins and passwords, and for accessing

Kerberos-ed network services in a secure fashion.

LAN (local area network) A network that spans small distances, for instance, between buildings in an office park. Ethernet is a well-known example of LAN technology.

link A general term referring to a network connection between two processes or computers.

local area network *See* LAN.

mail In this book, mail means electronic mail, or e-mail.

mail transfer agent *See* MTA.

mail user agent *See* MUA.

MAN (metropolitan area network) A large LAN or set of connected LANs, operating over metropolitan size areas at high speeds.

MILNET (Military Network) A spin-off from the ARPANET.

MIME (Multipurpose Internet Mail Extensions) Extensions to the standard SMTP e-mail message body to support attachments and other nontext data. *See also* SMTP; MTA; MUA.

MIT Massachusetts Institute of Technology.

modem (modulator/demodulator) A device for connecting to networks and other computers across telephone lines. Modems may be internal or external to the computer.

modem pool A set of modems established for shared use.

Mosaic A graphical World Wide Web browser.

MTA (mail transfer agent) The TCP/IP application that uses SMTP to move an e-mail message to another MTA until the message reaches the addressee's computer, where the message is delivered. *See also* MUA.

MUA (mail user agent) The mail program used by the end-user computer to create and read e-mail messages. The MUA passes the message to the local MTA.

NAK The response from the recipient back to the sender that data was not successfully received. A NAK says that the data almost arrived, but there was some kind of error. *See also* ACK; retransmission.

name/address resolution Translation of a computer name or FQDN (for instance, bilbo.support.lotus.com) into a numeric address (for instance, 130.103.140.12). Local hosts files or domain name servers do the name resolution.

name server *See* domain name server.

Netscape A graphical World Wide Web browser.

Network File System *See* NFS.

network number The section of the IP address that is the same for a group of computers on the same network.

network information center *See* InterNIC.

Network Information Service *See* NIS.

network interface card *See* NIC.

Network News Transfer Protocol *See* NNTP.

network operations center *See* NOC.

network throughput The amount of data that can be transferred across the network medium in a fixed time period.

newsgroup A "category" for a set of articles written by users of The Internet's Usenet news. Each Usenet newsgroup is about one general topic, and the articles are on related subtopics. Newsgroups are a way for Internet users to share information, opinions, and feelings without actually meeting.

newsreader A program for reading and responding to Usenet news articles. Examples are tin and rn. Newsreaders communicate with a news server via NNTP.

news server *See* NNTP server.

NFS (Network File System) A protocol and service that allows networked computers remote, transparent access to directories and files. The remote files appear to a user to be local.

NIC A computer's network controller board (network adapter), required for transmitting and receiving signals on a network. A computer, especially a laptop, may have an external network adapter rather than an internal one. The electrical connection to the network is done at the NIC level. NIC is also a nickname for the InterNIC. *See also* InterNIC.

NIS (Network Information Service) A service for networked computers, providing a single, shareable copy of common system and configuration files. Developed by Sun Microsystems and licensed to all UNIX vendors. Formerly called Yellow Pages. *See also* YP.

NIS domain A group of UNIX computers that share a single copy of system administration files such as the passwd file.

NNTP (Network News Transfer Protocol) The TCP/IP protocol used to transfer Usenet news articles between two NNTP servers and between a newsreader and an NNTP server.

NNTP server The computer and/or program that sends and receives Usenet news articles to and from other NNTP servers and newsreaders.

NOC (network operations center) The "nerve center" for monitoring and managing a network. For many organizations, the network administrators and SNMP management stations are located in the NOC. *See also* SNMP.

NSFnet (National Science Foundation Network) The backbone for a collection of networks started with funds from the United States National Science Foundation.

open systems Open systems provide a standards-based computing environment, possibly including but not limited to UNIX, TCP/IP, APIs, and GUIs.

Open Systems Interconnect *See* OSI.

optical fiber Plastic or glass network medium. Theoretical maximum transmission speed is the speed of light.

OSI (Open Systems Interconnect) A set of protocols specified by ISO for interconnecting networks.

OSI Reference Model *See* ISO OSI Reference Model.

packet A network message that includes data, a header, error control data, and addressing information. When data is sent, each network layer adds information to the packet before passing the packet to the next layer down. When data is received on a computer, each layer strips off the data added by the sending layer before passing the packet up one layer.

ping (Packet Internet Groper) A program that sends an ICMP echo request to a remote computer and waits for the computer to reply that it is reachable across the network. Tests the network availability of a remote host.

Point-to-Point Protocol *See* PPP.

port A number used by TCP and UDP to indicate which application is sending or receiving data. *See also* socket.

PPP (Point-to-Point Protocol) A protocol that provides serial line connectivity (that is, dial-up with a modem) between two computers, between a computer and a network, or between two networks. PPP can handle several protocols simultaneously. (Compare to SLIP, which handles only TCP/IP.) *See also* SLIP and CSLIP.

print server The software that allows a printer on one computer to be shared by computers across a network; and/or the computer to which the shared printers are attached and on which the software is running. Printers that are attached directly to the network allow sharing, too, although technically they are not called print servers.

protocol Rules and message formats for communication between computers in a network.

protocol layers The divisions of a hierarchical network model. Each layer performs a service on behalf of the layer directly above it. Each layer receives services from the layer directly below it.

protocol stack A group of protocols that work together across network layers.

ps The UNIX program for seeing what programs and daemons are running on the computer.

rcp One of the Berkeley UNIX r utilities. The rcp utility allows users to copy files between computers on their internet and The Internet. Functionally similar to FTP.

reference model *See* ISO OSI Reference Model.

remote Describes other computers, disks, directories, and files that are across a network from your computer.

Remote Procedure Call *See* RPC.

repeater A network device, operating at the physical layer, that amplifies and repeats electrical signals from one network segment to another, thereby allowing the network segment to be lengthened.

Request for Comments *See* RFC.

resolver The client that queries DNS name servers for computer name/IP address resolution on a TCP/IP network on behalf of an application such as telnet or FTP.

resources System and network components, such as memory, disk space, and CPU.

retransmission Resending a packet that was not received at the destination computer. The sending computer knows to retransmit because it receives a NAK or it does not receive an ACK from the remote computer. *See also* ACK, NAK.

RFC (Request for Comments) The documentation for The Internet, TCP/IP, and other networking standards. RFCs are maintained by the IETF and are publicly available from the InterNIC and numerous Anonymous FTP sites. Among other things, RFCs describe network and TCP/IP protocol standards, answer questions about TCP/IP and The Internet, and propose changes to TCP/IP. Some RFCs are also FYIs or STDs. *See also* FYI and STD.

RIP (Routing Information Protocol) Nope, it's not Rest In Peace. RIP is one of the TCP/IP protocols for dynamically routing information along a LAN. RIP requires routed (the route daemon) to be running.

rlogin One of the Berkeley UNIX r utilities. The rlogin utility allows users to log in to remote computers on an internet or The Internet. Functionally similar to telnet.

route The path that network data follows from the source computer to the destination computer. Each packet in a message may or may not follow the same route before arriving at the destination.

routed (route daemon) The program that is a prerequisite for RIP to route network data.

router A network device that interconnects multiple network segments and forwards packets from one network to another. The router must determine how to forward a packet based on addresses, network traffic, and cost.

Routing Information Protocol *See* RIP.

routing table A table that lists all the possible paths data can take to get from source to destination. The routing table is stored in memory on routers, gateways, and computers.

RPC (Remote Procedure Call) A programming mechanism for clients to call routines over the network. RPC was originated by Sun Microsystems and is defined by RFC 1057. RPCs are often used to create distributed applications.

rsh One of the Berkeley UNIX r utilities. The rsh utility allows users to run programs on remote computers on an internet or The Internet.

RTFM Read the Fabulous Manual.

r utilities Berkeley UNIX and TCP/IP programs including rcp, rlogin, and rsh.

Serial Line IP *See* SLIP.

server A computer program that provides services to clients; and/or the computer that runs the server program. The FTP client, for example, requests file transfer services from the FTP server. In a networked environment, the server may be on a computer different from the client.

shielded twisted-pair *See* STP.

Simple Mail Transfer Protocol *See* SMTP.

Simple Network Management Protocol *See* SNMP.

SLIP (Serial Line IP) The TCP/IP protocol that enables dial-up networking from a computer equipped with a modem. RFC 1055 describes SLIP. *See also* CSLIP and PPP.

SMTP (Simple Mail Transfer Protocol) The TCP/IP protocol for sending and receiving e-mail across a network. SMTP specifies that all messages must be text. SMTP is specified in RFC 821. *See also* MIME, MTA, and MUA.

SMTP gateway A computer program that translates e-mail messages from one format to another to interconnect two different e-mail systems, when one system uses SMTP and the other does not. May also refer to the computer that runs the SMTP gateway program.

SNA (System Network Architecture) IBM's proprietary network architecture and protocols. You need an SNA gateway to move data between The Internet and an SNA network.

SNMP (Simple Network Management Protocol) The protocol used by management stations (computers that monitor network activity and performance) to communicate with one another, and the computers (agents) they are monitoring. RFCs 1065 through 1067 describe SNMP.

socket A data structure that allows programs on an internet to communicate. A socket is an API (Application Programming Interface) used by programmers writing network applications. It works as a pipeline between the communicating programs. The socket consists of an address and a port number.

STD An RFC that documents a standard component of TCP/IP. *See also* RFC and FYI.

STP (shielded twisted-pair) Shielded twisted-pair cable. Most token ring networks use STP.

subnet A piece of an internet. The act of splitting an IP network range into pieces by means of a subnet mask. For example, an organization may subnet its class B network into 256 class C networks. *See also* subnet mask; supernet; supernet mask.

subnet mask A 32-bit number used to separate the network and host sections of an IP address. A custom subnet mask subdivides an IP network into smaller pieces. *See also* subnet; supernet; supernet mask.

supernet An internet formed by combining two subnets into one network. *See also* supernet mask; subnet; subnet mask.

supernet mask A custom subnet mask used to link together two or more IP networks into a supernet. *See also* supernet; subnet; subnet mask.

System Network Architecture *See* SNA.

talk A program that lets two users "converse" on an internet. *See also* IRC.

TCP (Transmission Control Protocol) One of the two principal components of the TCP/IP protocol suite. TCP puts data into packets and provides reliable packet delivery across a network (packets arrive in order and are not lost). TCP is at the transport layer in the network model, just above the Internet layer and the IP protocol. RFC 793 is the specification for TCP.

TCP/IP (Transmission Control Protocol/Internet Protocol) A set of network protocols that connect The Internet. This whole book is about TCP/IP. You didn't really expect to get a complete answer here in the glossary, did you?

telnet The TCP/IP protocol, service, and application for logging in to remote computers. Telnet provides VT100 terminal emulation for PCs and workstations. RFC 854 is the specification for telnet. *See also* tn3270.

terminal server A network device that connects dumb terminals to a host. Can also provide a modem pool for dial-in or dial-out use. Can act as a network interface card when used "backwards."

TFTP (Trivial File Transfer Protocol) The TCP/IP protocol used for downloading software and remote booting for diskless computers. TFTP is a subset of the FTP protocol, but does not require a valid username and password. TFTP depends on another TCP/IP protocol, UDP (User Datagram Protocol). RFC 783 is the specification for TFTP.

thickwire *See* 10Base5.

thinwire *See* 10Base2.

throughput *See* network throughput.

timeout Occurs when a timer expires, usually because data was sent but not acknowledged. When a timeout occurs, the protocol usually retransmits the data.

time to live *See* TTL.

tn3270 A version of telnet that provides IBM 3270 terminal emulation. *See also* telnet.

token A set of bits that permits a computer on a token ring network to transmit messages. Computers on a token ring wait to receive a token before transmitting on the network. The token controls the transmission of all traffic on the network.

token ring A LAN technology that runs over various network media, most often shielded twisted-pair cable. Most token ring networks operate at 16 megabits per second, but some older ones run at only 4 megabits per second.

traffic The data on the network.

Transmission Control Protocol *See* TCP.

transport layer Layer 4 in the ISO OSI Reference Model and TCP/IP network model. The TCP and UDP protocols reside at the transport layer.

Trivial File Transfer Protocol *See* TFTP.

TTL (time to live) The amount of time a network object remains valid. For example, the amount of time a DNS server can store information in the cache.

UCB (University of California at Berkeley) The site where BSD UNIX and some of the early components of TCP/IP were developed.

UDP (User Datagram Protocol) A TCP/IP protocol found at the network (internet) layer, along with the TCP protocol. UDP sends data down to the internet layer and to the IP protocol. Unlike TCP, UDP does not guarantee reliable, sequenced packet delivery. If data does not reach its destination, UDP does not retransmit as TCP does. RFC 768 is the specification for UDP.

Uniform Resource Locator *See* URL.

unshielded twisted-pair *See* UTP.

URL (Uniform Resource Locator) The standard notation for referencing information on The Internet and especially the Wide World Web; for example, http://www.lotus.com. The first part of a URL, before the colon, specifies the protocol for accessing the information. The rest of the URL, after the colon, specifies the location of the information.

Usenet news A TCP/IP service consisting of a worldwide collection of online newsgroups. Each newsgroup is an electronic conversation group about a particular topic.

User Datagram Protocol *See* UDP.

UTP (unshielded twisted-pair) Unshielded twisted-pair cable. Telephone wire and 10BaseT are examples of UTP.

UUCP (UNIX to UNIX Copy Program) Older, non-TCP/IP dial-up networking. SLIP and PPP, both TCP/IP protocols, are better choices.

Veronica A program that helps users navigate Gopherspace; stands for Very Easy Rodent Oriented Network-wide Index to Computerized Archives. It lets you know which of Gopher's many menus have information on topics you request. Veronica does for Gopher what Archie does for FTP.

VT100 The industry-standard dumb terminal (except for IBM's 3270 terminal), created by Digital Equipment Corporation. Many Internet hosts and programs (such as telnet) communicate in VT100 mode.

WAIS (Wide Area Information Services) A program for keyword searching through libraries on The Internet.

WAN (wide area network) A network spanning large geographical distances, often consisting of interconnected LANs.

whois A TCP/IP protocol and service that requests information about network sites. The whois utility is well known for its former role, finding users at Internet sites. Recently, when the volume of Internet users became too large to manage, whois information became restricted to network sites rather than individual users. *See also* finger.

wide area network *See* WAN.

WinSock (Windows Sockets) An API (application programming interface) for Microsoft Windows programs to communicate with TCP/IP. Based on the Berkeley UNIX socket specification.

World Wide Web *See* WWW.

WWW (World Wide Web) A hypermedia information system on The Internet. Also known as "the Web" or W3. *See also* browser.

XOR Stands for the binary mathematical operation eXclusive OR. The result of XORing two bits is 1 if and only if the value of both bits is 1; otherwise the result is 0.

X Window System The graphical user interface (GUI) software developed at MIT. Uses TCP as its transport protocol.

Yellow Pages *See* YP and NIS.

YP (Yellow Pages) The original name for NIS. British Telecom owns the trademark on Yellow Pages, but not the initials YP. *See also* NIS.

zone The group of computer names for which a name server has authority.

Index

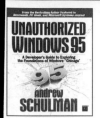

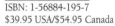

ORDER FORM

IDG BOOKS WORLDWIDE™

Order Center: **(800) 762-2974** *(8 a.m.–6 p.m., EST, weekdays)*

Quantity	ISBN	Title	Price	Total

Shipping & Handling Charges

	Description	First book	Each additional book	Total
Domestic	Normal	$4.50	$1.50	$
	Two Day Air	$8.50	$2.50	$
	Overnight	$18.00	$3.00	$
International	Surface	$8.00	$8.00	$
	Airmail	$16.00	$16.00	$
	DHL Air	$17.00	$17.00	$

*For large quantities call for shipping & handling charges
**Prices are subject to change without notice.

Ship to:

Name _____

Company _____

Address _____

City/State/Zip _____

Daytime Phone _____

Payment: ☐ Check to IDG Books Worldwide (US Funds Only)

☐ VISA ☐ MasterCard ☐ American Express

Card # _____ Expires _____

Signature _____

Subtotal _____

CA residents add
applicable sales tax _____

IN, MA, and MD
residents add
5% sales tax _____

IL residents add
6.25% sales tax _____

RI residents add
7% sales tax _____

TX residents add
8.25% sales tax _____

Shipping _____

Total _____

Please send this order form to:
IDG Books Worldwide, Inc.
7260 Shadeland Station, Suite 100
Indianapolis, IN 46256

Allow up to 3 weeks for delivery.
Thank you!